Marketing and the Consumer Movement

Marketing and the Consumer Movement

Editor: **Jeremy Mitchell**

McGRAW-HILL Book Company (UK) Limited

London · New Work · St Louis · San Francisco · Auckland · Beirut
Bogotá · Düsseldorf · Johannesburg · Lisbon · Lucerne · Madrid
Mexico · Montreal · New Delhi · Panama · Paris · San Juan · São Paulo
Singapore · Sydney · Tokyo · Toronto

Published by
McGraw-Hill Book Company (UK) Limited
MAIDENHEAD · BERKSHIRE · ENGLAND

British Library Cataloguing in Publication Data

Marketing and the consumer movement

1. Marketing—Great Britain
2. Consumer protection—Great Britain
I. Title. II. Mitchell, Jeremy
658.8   HF5415.12.G7   78-40138

ISBN 0-07-084514-X

1 2 3 4 5 W & J M 8 0 7 9 8

Printed and bound in Great Britain by W & J Mackay Limited, Chatham

Contents

Foreword
  Sir John Methven   vii
Introduction
  Jeremy Mitchell   ix
Contributors   xi

THE CONSUMER MOVEMENT

1. Some Lessons for Marketing
   Jeremy Mitchell   3

2. Consumers' Association and *Which?*
   Daphne Grose   9

3. The Legal Framework of Consumer Protection
   Bill Thomas   24

4. Consumer Protection in Local Government
   Roger Manley   50

5. Local Advice for Consumers
   Derek Prentice   61

6. Nationalized Industry Consumer Councils
   Alisdair Aird   72

THE RESPONSE OF INDUSTRY AND TRADE

7. A Marketing View of the Consumer
   Peter B. Blood   83

8. Market Research and Consumer Attitudes
   Elizabeth Nelson   88

9. Handling Consumer Complaints
   Chris Moore   97

10. The Retailer's Response to the Consumer Movement
    Rosemary McRobert   108

11. Standards and Marketing
   Gill Ashworth   120

12. Future Developments in Marketing
   Leslie Rodger   129

CODES OF PRACTICE

13. A New Initiative
   Jim Humble   143

14. What a Trade Association Can Do: The Motor Agents
   Association
   Alan M. Dix   154

15. What a Trade Association Can Do: The Association of British
   Launderers and Cleaners
   Colin Fricker   160

ADVERTISING AND THE CONSUMER

16. Advertising: What the Consumer Wants
   Maurice Healy   171

17. Advertising as Information for Consumers
   Patricia Mann   182

18. Advertising: The Legal Framework
   Richard Lawson   195

INTERNATIONAL DEVELOPMENTS

19. Consumerism: An American Response
   Esther Peterson   209

20. Representing the Consumer in Business: J C Penney—
   A U S Case Study
   David Schoenfeld   220

21. The European Perspective
   William Roberts   229

22. Glossary of Organizations Active in Consumer Affairs
   Julia Aspinall   241

Bibliography
   Susan Samuel   276

Index   291

Introduction

Jeremy Mitchell

The purpose of this book is to help people in industry and trade to achieve a better understanding of consumers' needs and how these can best be met. In particular, it is intended to tell marketing professionals—and students—something about the developments that have been and are taking place in organized consumer protection, both inside and outside Government. It also looks at possible future developments, not only in the UK, but also in the US and the EEC.

The genesis of the book was a series of six special supplements to the periodical *Marketing*, issued between October 1975 and August 1976. The series was sponsored jointly by the Office of Fair Trading and the Institute of Marketing. The response was so favourable that the best way to follow it up seemed to be to develop the ideas touched on in the special supplements and to treat them more systematically in book form.

The contributors are drawn from a wide variety of backgrounds—manufacturing industry, advertising, marketing, retailing, and trade associations, as well as the consumer movement itself. Inevitably, and rightly, there are some differences in the points of view expressed. But there is a remarkable degree of consensus about marketing's current weaknesses and the steps which might be taken to improve its role as a channel of communication—not only from producers and suppliers to consumers, but conversely.

As well as the chapters dealing with different aspects of the book's main theme, there are two contributions which marketing professionals should find useful in their day-to-day work. First, there is the Glossary of Organizations Active in Consumer Affairs (chapter 22). Many people are confused by the number and variety of organizations in this field, especially as most of them carry the word 'consumer' in the title. The Glossary is an invaluable guide to the objectives, structures, and activities of all the major organizations, and it will be particularly useful to the reader who comes across an organization for the first time and wants to find out more about it.

Second, the Bibliography is an extensive survey of literature published in the U K, the U S, and elsewhere which ranges well beyond the references cited by the authors of the contributory chapters. A relatively small proportion of what has been written about the consumer movement is in book form, so the Bibliography's coverage of leaflets, reports, magazines, and journals is especially helpful.

I have prepared and edited this book in my personal capacity, but I am grateful to the Office of Fair Trading and the National Consumer Council for allowing me the necessary time alongside my other duties. I am also grateful to the Institute of Marketing for the constant support I have received, and particularly to its Director-General, Peter Blood, for his understanding of the importance to society as a whole of marketing as a bridge between industry and consumers. However, neither the Office of Fair Trading, the National Consumer Council nor the Institute of Marketing are responsible for the views expressed by contributors. Many of the themes that are dealt with in the book were discussed with Sir John Methven when he was Director-General of Fair Trading, and I learned a great deal from his pragmatism and his willingness to identify what industry and the consumer movement have in common, rather than what divides them. Colleen Smith and Liz Blakey contributed so much to the organization and preparation of the material that I now realize that the book would never have taken shape without their help. I owe a particular debt of gratitude to Julia Aspinall both for preparing the index and for organizing the preparation of so much of the material.

CHRIS MOORE is information controller for Rank Leisure Services Ltd, and his responsibilities include the Customer Services Department. He is the author of several books, including *How to Handle Customer Complaints*.

ELIZABETH NELSON is chairman of the Taylor Nelson Group, a group of companies which carry out market and social surveys. A psychologist by training, Dr Nelson has specialized in the relationship of consumer attitudes and behaviour.

ESTHER PETERSON is special assistant on consumer affairs to the President of the US. She previously held a similar post under President Lyndon B. Johnson, and in 1970 joined Giant Food, Inc., as president of consumer programs.

DEREK PRENTICE is the Advice Centre Development Manager for Consumers' Association. He previously held managerial appointments with a multiple chain-store and a supermarket group. He is a member of Lambeth Borough Council.

WILLIAM ROBERTS is in charge of the Public Affairs Office at Consumers' Association. He read politics at Essex and Kent Universities, where he was awarded his PhD.

LESLIE RODGER is head of the Department of Business Organisation, Heriot-Watt University, Edinburgh. He previously worked in industry and commerce and has extensive experience of both consumer and industrial marketing.

SUSAN SAMUEL was formerly librarian for the Office of Fair Trading and the Monopolies and Mergers Commission and before that a copywriter at Masius Wynne Williams, senior assistant librarian at Reading University, and publications officer at the Department of Trade and Industry.

DAVID SCHOENFELD is the resident consumer advocate of J. C. Penney Company (USA). Previously, he held positions with Consumers Union and President Johnson's Committee on Consumer Interests. He is the author of *The Consumer and his Dollars*.

BILL THOMAS is a solicitor who writes, lectures, and broadcasts widely on all aspects of the law.

THE CONSUMER MOVEMENT

1. Some lessons for marketing

Jeremy Mitchell

'Marketing and the consumer *movement*? But isn't marketing all about consumers themselves—fulfilling their wants by supplying goods and services of the right quality at a reasonable price? Why can't those engaged in marketing be left to get on with this important job? Why should they be harrassed by self-appointed consumer spokesmen and by politicians who think that allying themselves with the consumer movement might swing a few votes at the margin?'

This typical gut reaction to the consumer movement is likely to win a lot of support among marketing professionals, preoccupied with matching their competitors and always conscious that a consumer cannot be persuaded—more than once, anyway—to buy a product that is poor value for money. The constraints and challenges of the market place are formidable. Selling goods and services profitably is not easy and never has been. The last thing that most marketing professionals want is a semi-public contest with the organized consumer movement in which they sense that the dice—and the media—are loaded against them.

There is so much truth in this emphasis on the value of the direct links between marketing and consumers through the market place that it is sometimes difficult to persuade marketing professionals that when they ignore the organized consumer movement, or shut their eyes and wish that it would go away, they are rejecting a source of information and ideas which might help them to do their job better. Of course, there is no substitute for the sensitivity of the market place. If a product does not match its market, something must be wrong—design, quality, price, distribution, promotion. Only the market place can provide the answer. And quite apart from the more systematic aspects of their job, marketing professionals develop a 'feel' for the products and markets they know which they often find difficult to translate into words.

To understand what the consumer movement has to offer, it is worth examining why it has developed in the way it has, and what it has achieved. The words 'consumer movement' condense a wide range of aspirations, objectives, functions, and institutions in a misleadingly simple phrase. In one sense, the roots of the consumer movement can be traced back virtually as far as the beginnings of commerce and trade, to a preoccupation with matters such as the accuracy and standardization of weights and measures and the purity of food, where the consumer's knowledge and bargaining power have always, inevitably, been weaker than the trader's. The framework of legislation and enforcement on such basic matters tends to be taken for granted in the U K and in other developed countries, but it took centuries to evolve, frequently in the teeth of bitter opposition from manufacturers and traders. Even today, this basic framework of consumer protection scarcely exists in the developing countries.

Consumer Affluence

Despite its deep roots, the organized consumer movement as it is manifest today is the product of a post-1945 society in which comparative affluence presented a significant segment of the population with problems of choice. For example, for the first time many families had enough money to buy household durables, such as refrigerators. But what were the advantages of buying a refrigerator? How long would it keep food fresh? How much would it cost to buy? To run? What about spares and servicing? Did the manufacturer's guarantee mean anything? What size was needed? Which brand was the most reliable?

The problems of choice became particularly acute for three reasons. First, a wide variety of goods and services came within the purchasing range of many families for the first time—notably, major household appliances. Second, technological developments brought the introduction of new types of products which people did not know how to choose or use. For example, the properties of wool, cotton, linen, and silk were firmly rooted in family culture and domestic arts. The knowledge had been handed down from one generation to the next. Faced with a bewildering array of synthetic fibres, the housewife had no reference point, no way of relating the new to the old.

The third reason was the dearth of information available from manufacturers, compounded by the erosion in the amount of personal advice available from retailers. The failure to understand and meet consumers' *information* needs was the major failure of marketing during the new consumer affluence of the 'fifties and 'sixties. Indeed, it is not obvious that the lesson has been learned even now.

Independent Information

The single date that can be put against the first development of the organized consumer movement in the U K is 1957, when Michael Young set up Consumers' Association (C A) and the first *Which?* test reports were published. For the first time, consumers had access to detailed information which was not controlled by manufacturers or retailers. In chapter 2,

Daphne Grose describes the origins and progress of CA, but it is worth remarking on the indirect effect that the publication of test reports had on the climate of public discussion about goods and services. This became much freer, with the press, radio, and television prepared to be less inhibited in their comments. While uncomfortable in the short run for some marketing professionals, it is obviously a healthy development that commercial activities should be in the arena of public discussion along with politics, education, the arts, sport, and a hundred other subjects.

The provision of independent test reports about goods and services was the first major step forward in the development of the organized consumer movement outside Government. This national movement was paralleled in cities and towns by the growth of local consumer groups, brought together in the National Federation of Consumer Groups, which produced reports on local shops and services. Once again, the emphasis was on information to consumers to help them take better decisions, rather than on political pressure.

Government Interest

While it would not be fair to say that there had been no Government interest in the problems of consumers, the first occasion on which Government took a coherent look at the legislative framework of consumer protection was when the Molony Committee was appointed in 1959. The Committee limited itself to goods, excluding both the nationalized industries and services such as garages, laundries and dry cleaning, and electrical repairs. It produced a substantial list of recommendations about product safety, standards and labelling, marks, seals of approval, comparative testing, civil redress, trade descriptions, and advertising and sales practices. The report was the cornerstone of a series of new laws, though there have been some legislative changes which had other origins—for example, the report of the Crowther Committee led to the Consumer Credit Act 1974.

The new framework of consumer protection legislation is described in more detail by Bill Thomas in chapter 3 and by Richard Lawson in chapter 18, but it is possible to detect three distinct strands in the changes that have taken place.

—The quality—and sometimes the quantity—of information to consumers (e.g., ensuring the accuracy of trade descriptions) has been improved.
—There has been tighter control of undesirable trading practices (e.g., unsolicited goods and services).
—The consumer's civil law rights (e.g., stopping traders from contracting out of their common law obligations) have been improved.

Role of Local Government

Before exploring in more detail how marketing might use these three strands as clues to ways in which legislation can be anticipated, it is worth

noting the remarkable change that the new structure of consumer legislation brought to local government. Of course, local government's role in
enforcing weights and measures and environmental health laws goes back
to the nineteenth century and before, as Roger Manley points out (chapter
4). But following the U K pattern of *national* consumer legislation enforced
locally, local authorities took on a wide range of new functions. Weights
and measures inspectors found that they had to concern themselves with
such matters as the accuracy of trade descriptions and the enforcement of
consumer credit law. In addition, the link between enforcing the law and
giving advice and information became apparent. As Derek Prentice
explains in chapter 5, many local authorities considered that the demand
for consumer information and advice was so pressing that they should
respond by taking on the job. At the same time, the Citizens' Advice
Bureaux found that an increasing proportion of the enquiries they dealt
with were about consumer matters.

Fair Trading

At national level, the Fair Trading Act 1973, initiated by a Conservative
Government, established the Office of Fair Trading (OFT). Apart from its
statutory powers and duties in the field of consumer protection, OFT
provided for the first time a link between consumer protection and competition policies designed to make industry and trade more efficient. This is
a link which has still not been fully explored, but which may be of great
significance for the future. It has always been one of the basic principles of
the U K consumer movement that, quite apart from the benefits to the
individual, the economy as a whole benefits from having consumers who
are well informed and who buy goods and services that best suit their
needs. How industrial structure affects consumer choice and what forms of
competition most benefit consumers are questions that remain largely
unanswered.

National Consumer Council

A further development at national level was the establishment by the
Government of the National Consumer Council (NCC) in 1975. This added
two new dimensions to the consumer movement. First, the NCC was given
the job of identifying and representing the interests of poorer consumers.
Second, the NCC's remit covers *public* services, not just the private
sector. As well as the nationalized industries, this means public services
which the consumer pays for indirectly through rates and taxes, such as
education and the social services.

The Primacy of Information

What can marketing learn from these rapid and wide-ranging developments in the consumer movement, both inside and outside Government? Above all else, the need for improvement in the quality and quantity of information available to consumers. We have already seen how the thirst for information was the mainspring for the regeneration of the consumer movement in the late 'fifties, how a great deal of consumer legislation has been concerned in one way or another with information, and how local authorities have become involved in providing consumer information and advice. But has the lesson really been learned by marketing professionals?

Of course, there have been developments on the marketing side. The Advertising Standards Authority, through the self-regulatory Code of Advertising Practice which it administers, is concerned with the truthfulness of information conveyed through advertisement. Jim Humble (chapter 13) describes how the Codes of Practice negotiated by the Office of Fair Trading include a variety of provisions about consumer information and the voluntary obligations accepted by the car trade, and by launderers and dry cleaners are explained by Alan Dix (chapter 14) and Colin Fricker (chapter 15).

In spite of these hopeful signs, it is doubtful whether many marketing professionals yet realize consumers' hunger for information about goods and services—indeed, that information is itself a commodity, a free gift that goes with every product. In the context of advertising, Maurice Healy (chapter 16) points to some of the deficiencies in what consumers are offered at present, while Patricia Mann (chapter 17) examines the suggestion of 'information standards' canvassed by the National Federation of Consumer Groups. But perhaps the most interesting examples of what might be done come from across the Atlantic. Esther Peterson (chapter 19) and David Schoenfeld (chapter 20) describe the innovative approach of two very different types of retailing organization in the U S, both of which have an assessment of information needs as the cornerstone of their consumer programmes.

Raising Standards of Trading

Looking beyond the fundamental appraisal of consumer information, how can marketing professionals improve marketing as a way of identifying and responding to consumers' needs?

Again, the legislative changes that have already taken place provide clues as to what might be done. Much legislation has been concerned with regulating undesirable trading practices. This is not just a question of dealing with rogue or ethically marginal manufacturers or traders. The commercial history of this country embodies a continual improvement in the standards of trading, but that is no reason for complacency. The O F T-approved Codes of Practice show what can be done over and beyond statutory requirements, where the trades and industries concerned have realized that setting high trading standards—and adhering to them—is a powerful marketing tool, quite apart from the benefits it brings to consumers.

Consumer Complaints

The improvement in consumers' civil law rights, combined with easier methods of redress for consumers who have a justified grievance, points the way to a much more positive attitude towards consumer complaints. Consumer complaints and the ways in which they are dealt with are not normally thought of as part of the marketing process. This may be because it has not yet been realized that a substantial flow of consumer complaints is an *inevitable* accompaniment of modern technology, production, marketing, and distribution. In chapter 9, Chris Moore examines what can be done to get the system right, but many firms do not properly realize the need to respond to complaints fully and generously—nor the value to management of the information that consumer complaints provide.

The Informed Minority

Last, but not least, marketing professionals might have much to learn from the criticisms and comments which stem from the consumer movement. In the UK, these criticisms are constructive rather than destructive and are notably untainted by ideology. Nobody—least of all the leaders of the consumer movement—claims that the consumer movement is in any direct sense representative of the broad mass of consumers. Listening to the consumer movement is not a substitute for interpreting consumers' behaviour in the market place or for the answers that market research can sometimes provide. But it does give marketing professionals the opportunity of learning from the reactions of a significant minority who are knowledgeable about the issues at stake, who are able to articulate worries and concerns which may be widely felt, and who can provide insights about the way in which the future may unfold.

2. Consumers' Association and *Which?*

Daphne Grose

In 1960, the U K Consumers' Association sent a hand-painted card to greet their U S cousins at Consumers Union who were just 25 years old. The card showed a multiplicity of pilgrim ships setting out for the four quarters of the world. On board were the consumer pilgrims. One of the ships was bound for the U K. That metaphorical ship arrived in the U K in the period after 1945. From the U S, it brought information about how in the late 'twenties a new magazine had given form to the idea that not just Government and other institutions but also private individuals had a right to the technical and other detailed information needed for making a rational choice when selecting and buying goods and services.* The 'thirties saw the establishment of a second, and in the longer term more successful, organization and magazine, Consumers Union of the U S and *Consumer Reports*. The now familiar pattern—providing information about the nature of goods, comparative information on brands based on testing, warnings of hazards, and comments on claims in advertisements—was set from the beginning. The first issue of *Consumer Reports* gave the costs of daily breakfast cereal for a family of five, which it said could vary from $0·45 to $3·85 per month between types and brands. The nutritional value of the various types was discussed. Seven inexpensive brands of stockings were compared. The ratings of the stockings were based on the results of both laboratory tests and user wear tests. Of a well known medicine C U said: 'The chief appeal of Alka-Seltzer to the unwary public is the noisy fizz that it produces and the pain-relieving effects of aspirin'. A warning was issued on the lead hazard in toys.

The American Precedent

The Consumers Union said its aims were 'to give information and assistance on all matters relating to the expenditure of earnings and the family

*See Bibliography p.277—Roberts (1966).

9

income; to initiate, to co-operate with, and to aid individual and group efforts of whatever nature and description seeking to create and maintain decent living standards for ultimate consumers'. This chapter was written against the background of the depression and poor working conditions. Times have changed. Yet CU's objectives in those early years still remain at the heart of the now worldwide consumer movement.

—First is the provision of data based on the independent comparative testing of goods and services so that buyers can make, if they so wish, a well judged choice among the competing products of the market place.
—Second is a wish to improve standards of goods and services.
—Third is the strong desire to help the poorer members of the community.

In the UK the second facet of the movement was to play a vital role in the launching of the first consumer organization. During the late 'forties and the early 'fifties several groups of people were concerned about the quality of goods, and particularly those for export. In the Board of Trade a paper was prepared which suggested that the Government should finance the testing and provision of information about goods in order to raise standards. This did not come to fruition, although the idea lingered on in the manifestos of the Co-operative and Labour parties. Further, it was the main stimulant for the creation of the British Standards Institution's comparative testing magazine *Shoppers' Guide*, which lived from 1957 to 1964 (see chapter 11), and it was a concept that found strong expression in the Memorandum of Association of Consumers' Association, which was also founded in 1957. This read: 'The principal object for which the Association is established is to improve and maintain the standard of goods or commodities sold and services rendered to the public'. This objective was not to be achieved by the imposition on trade of mandatory standards but by the power of information to influence the individuals' buying decisions and, therefore, indirectly the competitive forces in the market place.

It was a grand ambition for a small organization. It was an ambition later to be shared by local consumer groups. Writing in 1976 about their activities the National Federation of Consumer Groups (NFCG) described their aim as 'raising the standards of goods and services locally'.

Early History

Consumers' Association and its magazine *Which?* were set up in 1957. The very first issue of *Which?* was based on principles already established by Consumers Union of the US. The organization must be financially independent. The first issue was made possible by a loan from CU and a charitable trust, but from then on it was to derive its funds from the sale of its magazine to subscribers (it has never been available on bookstalls) and other forms of information. The goods it reported on were bought anonymously in shops. The tests were carried out by independent laboratories and scientists. The reports in the first issue compared the performance and safety of electric kettles and the price and eating characteristics of cake mixes. In the succeeding years the methodology of testing was to become more complex and the range of subjects much wider, but the broad principles remained the same. In subsequent years the monthly *Which?* alone could not carry all the subjects on which people wanted information and so other magazines were added as quarterly supplements: *Motoring Which?* (1962), *Money Which?* (1968), *Handyman Which?* (1971), and *Holiday Which?* (1974).

Membership

The consumer organizations are regularly accused of being middle class. The accuser may make the challenge to demonstrate that they are a small unrepresentative group that may safely be ignored, or to urge them to greater concern with the needs of the poor. It is undoubtedly true that the voluntary workers in the consumer groups are mainly managers from industry or professional people and their wives. It is also true that a higher percentage of the subscribers to *Which?* belong to the higher socio-economic classes than do people in the whole population. However, at the latest sample survey of subscribers (6507) in 1976, over half belonged to the skilled worker and clerical groups. It is the unskilled workers who are less well represented. The younger middle-aged, between 25 and 45, tend to be heavily represented. Over half of this recent sample of *Which?* subscriber households had children, and the main household sizes were four or five people. Almost a third were two-people households. In other words, the people who take *Which?* come from the solid central core of the population who buy so many of the goods and services and who are a favourite target of advertisers. At present they number about 650 000. Readership of *Which?*, as opposed to the number of subscribers, has never been certain. An early survey produced over ten readers of one copy. Present estimates are nearer five to one.

Scope

The reports appearing in *Which?* or one of the quarterly magazines are not there because of the whim of the editor. Consumers' Association is governed by an unpaid Council whose members are elected by the Ordinary Members of the Association. Anyone who has been a subscriber for three years may apply to become an Ordinary Member. The Council have the final word as to the subjects that will appear in the magazines, just as they decide all other matters of broad policy. Before making recommendations to the Council, the staff will seek the views of members. A questionnaire is sent to a sample of members. The questionnaire normally gives a very long list of subjects, and asks readers to say for each whether they would be interested in seeing a report in *Which?*. There is room for readers' own ideas too. Equally important, each month a sample of members are asked about their interest in the reports in the previous issue. Recently, subscribers have been asked which of all the reports published in recent years they have found most useful. It was pressure from the members which lead to the continuous programme of testing consumer durables so as to try to keep up with changes on the market. It was the concern of members that dictated the development of surveys to assess people's experience of the durability of goods, and to test the services provided by both private and public industry, such as electrical servicing, insurance, and the telephone service, as well as state services like the National Health Service. Above all, subscribers have made it clear that, although they like some variety in the issues of the magazine, and are interested in some 'campaigning' subjects, what they want above all else is information they can use to help themselves when selecting goods and services. Asked in the 1977 survey what the most important thing about the magazines was, they put 'best buy/buying advice' first (38 per cent) and 'independence' next (20 per cent). The members of the local groups are creators, and therefore more altruistic, but the essential thinking underlying their work is still self-help, whether they are dealing with local driving schools or public libraries or the latest traffic scheme.

Why Consumer Testing?

Eirlys Roberts in her book *Consumers** discussed the questions that a manufacturer might put. 'Why should consumer organizations do all this research? We are carrying out research on consumer goods all the time. We are experts. They are amateurs. Why don't they leave it to us?'

There is one obvious answer. Manufacturers do not give shoppers the data produced by their research. A buyer cannot tell from looking at a spin drier how much water it will extract in comparison with rival models. Less obvious, the consumer might not ask the same questions as the manufacturer researcher if given the opportunity to test the goods before buying. The buyer might ask: 'What is the lowest price at which I can buy a satisfactory product?' The manufacturer might ask: 'What is the lowest price at which I can produce a marketable product?' Deceptively similar sounding, these questions can produce very different answers because there is no necessary correlation between satisfaction and marketability. The manufacturer of a cooker, having decided on size, features, and price range for the particular model, may then decide on the substance of the metal frame and the quantity of insulation he can afford while keeping costs low enough to allow a desirable level of profit. The potential buyer, looking at a series of cookers, may first decide how many features and characteristics he would like, then whether a cooker exists with them within a price bracket he can afford, but vital facts are hidden from him.

Without comparative data facts will remain hidden. One manufacturer may have succeeded in producing for sale at a lower price a good cooker

*See Bibliography p. 277—Roberts (1966).

which also has lower running costs than the rest, but this information is not normally given in the trade literature. Another producer is pleased with the design of his cooker with five pilot lights; the buyer will be unhappy with his gas bill. The cutting back of the metal frame of the cooker and a too heavy grill pan may cause the pan to slide forward and out, if pressure is applied to the front of the cooker; the buyer is peeved.

More basically, although buyers tend to assume, and normally justifiably, that the cooking performance will be satisfactory, a mistake in design can create problems. Frequent changes in design and the constant need to pare costs sometimes mean a once-sound product develops faults. The models of a brand of refrigerator that for years have earned a reputation for good performance, are redesigned once again. The designer who has been cutting back on the insulation, in order to reduce costs, crosses a hidden boundary and the new model no longer keeps food at the recommended temperature. Commercial pressures make this so easy. There have been times when the producer's research workers have known what has happened but nobody else in the company wants to believe them. Or the company crosses its collective fingers and hopes that the decline in quality will be so small that it will not be noticed.

For all these reasons, the independent testers of a consumer organization know they have a part to play. They also believe that they are a potential ally of the designers and laboratory staff of industry who want to maintain reasonable standards. Therefore they think it is important that industry understands the way comparative testing is undertaken.

Comparative Testing

The active workers in the consumer organizations never cease to be surprised that even now some people from commerce believe that testing is carried out in some small basement by a group of amateur housewives. In fact, Consumers' Association's staff includes engineers experienced in testing products in industry, qualified social and market researchers, as well as graduates trained by the organization as experts in the designing and writing of consumer test reports.

When an investigation begins, the staff member—called a project officer—who is responsible for the programme of work leading to a comparative test report has to decide which of the characteristics of the product or service are likely to be considered of importance by the purchaser. To help the project officer, samples of members are asked by questionnaires what they consider important about a product. In the 'sixties more detailed studies of some of the consumer durables were undertaken. Questionnaires, interviews, and observational studies were used to discover how people used their appliances and the extent to which their expectations and needs were met or frustrated. Even now, after 20 years of test work, these questions are re-examined each time a new project starts.

Having decided the questions that have to be answered about a product or service, a research programme is designed to produce the information for the answers. Laboratory tests, laboratory user tests, outside user tests, surveys—all are used to produce the necessary data. Since 1970 CA has had its own laboratory where tests can be carried out in controlled ambient conditions. Most of the electro-mechanical work and laboratory user tests are carried out in this laboratory. Some other tests are still undertaken by independent laboratories, both in the UK and overseas. The car testing is centred on a separate unit. The test methods used may be taken from British or other standards, if appropriate methods exist. If not, the technical staff develop new methods. The criteria for judging a method are its ability to test effectively, reproducibly, accurately and verifiably, while simulating what will happen to the product in real use by real users. The central need is to produce data which is comparative so that products can be ranked.

CA sometimes uses British Standard or other national and international standards as a guide, but they do not, as a matter of principle or practice, start from British Standards. For example, when testing binoculars CA used a Japanese Standard because it seemed to be a better simulation of reality from the consumer's point of view. On one or two products there has been extensive consultation with the technical staff of the industries concerned—for example, washing machines, detergents, paints, and mattresses.

The survey work on which assessments of services and servicing are made is designed and organized by CA's own group of trained social and market research staff. The prices being asked in various regions and types of outlets for goods and services are checked by freelance shoppers in a maximum of 12 towns. The result is a detailed set of reports on the safety and performance of goods, reports of their reliability and durability, and reports on the quality of and consumer satisfaction with services. The magazines are also full of information about prices, including (since 1971) an annual survey of grocery prices.

The comparative testing organizations in the UK and overseas have been criticized for not paying enough attention to design and brand reputation. Design preferences are personal. Branded goods are the bread and butter of testing; unbranded goods are extremely difficult to compare in a report. Comparative test reports—particularly durability surveys—are all about what people really think of a brand.

Influence

The question is often put, whether the independent consumer movement has any influence on peoples' buying habits or on manufacturers' or retailers' trade practices. The trade must believe that the magazines have some influence on consumers since they protest if their product is left out of a test report. At least some want to discuss published reports constructively.

On average, 150 manufacturers and traders write to CA each year questioning or asking questions about a report on their products or services. Less than 10 per cent of the resulting correspondence is totally negative: the other traders may even be offering congratulations, but more often they are seeking information or wanting to discuss the findings and are prepared to do this constructively. Almost 10 per cent of the last group imply or state in their final letter that they may be taking some action based on the report findings. In some ways, the most satisfying from CA's point of view is the lengthy correspondence, to take one example, which begins with a somewhat hostile challenge, but ends with changes being made to the product and the generous statement that 'We have learnt something in the course of our discussions'.

One of the major US retailers sends Consumers Union each month a commentary on their last issue when findings duplicate their own experience and criticizing anything with which they do not agree. There is nothing comparable in the UK. Nonetheless, retailers have on the whole shown a greater interest than manufacturers. CA receives fairly regular requests for permission to circulate multiple copies of *Which?* reports to retail staff. Permission is given so long as the company is willing to give an undertaking not to use the material for promotional purposes. One of the most frequently heard complaints about retailers and their staff is lack of knowledge of their merchandise. CA is pleased therefore when the trade wants to use *Which?* as a training tool. It can provide information about goods, but it also describes both consumers' and retailers' legal rights and obligations. Only when both sides understand these is a reasonable, balanced relationship possible.

The influence of comparative test reports on the design and quality of goods and services is more uncertain. Sometimes people accuse *Which?* of not being as aggressive and unafraid as in the early days and they justify this accusation by pointing to the number of goods in a report selected as 'Good value for money', and the less frequent selection of one brand as the 'Best buy'. It is true that 'Best buys' are scarcer, but in the 'seventies there is a greater uniformity in the performance of goods. Sometimes outstanding performance has a higher price attached but among lower priced products there are often a number of a perfectly satisfactory standard. Still CA would not claim that it had done more than create the climate in which goods are expected to be fit for their purpose; it would agree that many improvements have still to be achieved.

Present Needs

In the middle 'sixties there was a prophecy that within 10 years the consumer movement would have withered away, because all goods would be of good quality. Why has the consumer movement not shrivelled, but grown? Quite apart from the question of people's need for assessments of the particular characteristics of good quality products, a market place supplied with goods and services of an adequate standard still seems remote. A consumer movement will be needed until the conditions below disappear.

—Economic and commercial decisions, nationally and in firms, are taken without regard for consumer interests.
—It is possible for a potentially good product to be spoilt because it has not been designed for durability, or ease of use, or economy in use.
—It is possible for a good product to be ruined by an almost complete lack of quality control or failure to design packaging appropriate to the particular product, so that it is damaged in distribution.
—Servicing is slow and unsatisfactory.
—Services fall short of users' expectations.
—Suppliers of goods and services fail to give their customers enough information to make a real choice.

It is because these things still happen that people join consumer organizations.

A series of *Which?* reports on one product is sometimes a history of the decline of a once good brand or the lack of change of a once good product compared with the technological advances of its competitors. Price competition may have been met by cutbacks in quality and not greater efficiency or increasing quality. CA members reported in 1976 that 60 per cent of all automatic washing machines and dishwashers developed faults during their first two and half years. The goods had not been designed for durability. *Which?* often rings a warning bell for those who will listen. For some years before the Office of Fair Trading started collecting and issuing figures for complaints which were to demonstrate consumer discontent with electrical servicing in the mid 'seventies, *Which?* had reported similar views from its members. Other recent alarm bells have been the report, based on a sample, that a quarter of furniture and of cookers are delivered with defects.

Which? regularly highlights the inadequate information provided with goods and services—for example, furniture and insurance policies.

Worst of all are safety defects in products. CA has found it necessary to establish a purple alert system. When its testers find an imminently hazardous product, immediate action can be taken. An alert is not often necessary but it should **never** happen. On three or four occasions CA has cooperated with manufacturers on a recall programme.

Level of Quality

The consumer movement started not just to prevent standards slipping to quite unacceptable levels but to raise them. This is a difficult area. When considering products already on the market, only the individual can decide whether the difference between adequate and superb performance is worth an extra £10 or an extra £150. The same person, according to temperament, might be willing to spend the additional money on sound equipment but not on a dishwasher, or the other way round. The comparative testing organization provides information to assist the decision. Sometimes such detachment is not so easy for the consumer organization. In an age of inflation and rising labour costs, service standards fall. The footwear trade is an example. Fewer and fewer retailers provide a fitting service and shoes in a range of sizes. The consumer organization can tell people what the consequences of this development is likely to be. They can press for graded codes of practice so that even in self-service shops people can do their own foot measurements and in shops with a fitting service people know they will get skilled attention. They cannot force people to demand and pay for a higher standard of service. In all this there is an acceptance of the status quo. Therefore some members of the consumer organizations have a sense of failure. They feel that, so far, consumer organizations have accepted goods and services as they are offered in the market place, and have not done enough to try to improve economic and efficient design so that products and services may more truly meet the needs of people.

In conjunction with Loughborough University, Consumers' Association in 1970 set up the Institute for Consumer Ergonomics, with the purpose of finding out what goods and services people really want or need to have. So far, the greater part of the Institute's work has been on the design of equipment for the disabled and the safety of products. They have undertaken research on working heights in kitchens. They found in a small survey that eight out of ten housewives got aches and pains when using an ironing board. They concluded the boards needed to be adjustable in height. So far, the British Standard committee has not accepted the conclusion of this report. It will be sad if consumers and industry cannot work together on this type of problem.

Safety is a characteristic that people want to take for granted. When an accident proves to them that it has been ignored then they are angry. People may argue theoretically that it is going too far to require an interlock on a spin drier, but, confronted by a child with a mangled arm, their view changes and they demand an explanation of how it could happen. This is why the work of the Institute for Consumer Ergonomics, in helping to develop the Government's surveillance scheme to collect data on the causes of accidents involving consumer goods, has been so important. The next step will be to investigate why some goods are so frequently associated with accidents and to try to establish if changes in design could reduce the hazard.

Campaigning

Safety was one of the subjects which forced the independent consumer organizations to face the fact that information alone could not change the faults in the market place, or at least not quickly enough to prevent too many people being put in personal or economic danger. In the early years they found that when they reported on products and services a second time, still the same problems recurred. They felt frustrated. They believed that people had a right to an assurance that the products they bought to use or eat would not be the direct cause of physical illness. They believed that they had a right not to be misled by advertisements, labels, price displays, or guarantees. They even believed that people had a right to full and factual information about the nature, quality, and durability of the goods they were buying. Yet their studies of the products on the market and consumer experience told them that these rights were far from fulfilment. They quickly came to see that it was going to be hard work to gain these rights.

In the very first issue of *Which?* four electric kettles were found to have poor insulation. From early in the 'sixties CA wrote to the Government, the British Standards Institution, trade associations, and manufacturers about electrical safety. Very real improvements took place, but in the end electrical safety legislation was seen to be essential.

The third issue produced a discussion of the way hire purchase rates of interest should be declared and tables setting out the range of rates available for different products. Thus began a series of studies on rates of interest, one of which was to be major evidence for the report of the Crowther Committee on consumer credit,* the Government report which preceded the Consumer Credit Act 1974.

The fourth issue of *Which?*, in the summer of 1958, reported that CA (then called Association for Consumer Research Ltd) had sent the National Federation of Dyers and Cleaners an alternative draft agreement, known as the 'Conditions of Acceptance'. The then cleaners' agreement limited liability for almost anything that might go wrong. CA drafted what they felt was a more reasonable contract. During the following years this trade was responsive† but other services were not. CA did not give up and went on campaigning. Almost 20 years later and following a Law Commission report, the Unfair Contract Terms Act 1977, which established the principle of fair and reasonable terms in service contracts, was approved by Parliament.

Also in the fourth issue was a report on cut price groceries which concluded. 'As consumers, we can welcome cut prices. We should not expect low prices and expensive services at the same shop but can be glad of the opportunity to choose which we shall have'.

Three years later, in 1961, CA conducted a survey among its members and the general public and found that the majority were against resale price maintenance. This practice was effectively abolished by the Government in 1964. This might well have happened without the survey, but it helped those who had to take the decision.

The campaigning element in CA's work thus existed from the beginning, but changes have not always come quickly or easily. The 1966 Toy (Safety) Regulations, which came two and a half years after the *Which?* report on

*See Bibliography p.281—Trade and Industry, Department of (1971).
†Described at greater length in chapter 15.

lead in constructional toys and the connection of lead and mental retardation, was one of CA's first major victories.

Consumers' Association has been joined in the campaigning and representation work by the National Federation of Consumer Groups and, often, by women's organizations, More recently, the National Consumer Council has been set up. Neither of the independent consumer organizations can devote large resources to campaigning—CA puts about three per cent into this kind of work. Most of it still arises directly out of the research undertaken for the magazines. For example, the Cleveland Consumer Group raised the question of the confusion created by some 'flash offers' (2p off what?) in 1973, and the NFCG turned it into a national campaign, with other groups collecting examples of the practice. Recently both organizations have been grasping the nettle of major issues, such as the Common Agricultural Policy and competition policy, where the individual alone can have little influence.

The Consumer Constituency

The consumer organizations are often asked about their constituency. Whom do they represent? They do not see themselves in those terms. Their aim is to create the following conditions within the market place.

—A consensus opinion that the individual buyer has a right to the information which will enable him to make a rational choice, if he so wishes.
—A framework of fair trading practices that would enable the individual to help himself.

They have the following goals.

—The civil law and the legal system should permit the individual who believes himself to have suffered damage to seek redress.
—The criminal law should be effective so as to make it difficult for the rogues to operate.

The means of achieving these objectives can sometimes be obvious. For example, people should be given information about price in the simplest form possible. Other information that people might find useful often calls for research to discover how it will be understood and used. CA has undertaken, for example, survey work on food labelling—including the listing of food additives—and on product liability. Intellectually, the proposition that producers should accept some responsibility for the safety and quality of their goods seemed sound to CA. In an economy where most goods are prepacked and the retailer has only limited control over their condition, the present legal position, that places on him all the obligations to the buyer, seemed to CA less than fair or sensible. Nevertheless, CA conducted a survey of members and the public to discover their views on who was and should be responsible. Only when this survey supported their view did CA finally decide its policy and conclude that producers should share responsibility with retailers for their products. They continue to campaign for this.

The consumer movement started because of the exposed position of the individual consumer. The 1962 Molony Report on consumer protection has often been quoted.* It is worth repeating.

> The business of making and selling is highly organised, often in large units, and calls to its aid at every step complex and highly expert skills. The business of buying is conducted by the smallest unit, the individual consumer relying on the guidance of experience, if he possesses it and, if not, on instinctive but not always rational thought processes.

Undoubtedly there has been some shift in the balance since those days. No longer can the consumer's legal rights in relation to goods be removed. There is better information about measures. Food is more fully labelled, as are textiles. Some footwear and furniture are beginning to carry information about their properties, but there is still much to be achieved. However, in the larger decisions which determine how the market place will operate, consumers in general are even more helpless than an individual consumer without mechanical knowledge when buying a motor car. Import controls are imposed to protect agriculture and trade. Mergers are permitted to take place for reasons unrelated to the consumer interest. The public services have to react to Government policy rather than consumer demand. The consumer is far from being sovereign. The consumer organizations are still needed to provide information and to fight for the consumer interest.

The Deprived Consumers

Some groups of consumers are even less sovereign than most. These groups include those not trained to collect and assess information, who find choosing difficult, and the physically disabled, whose special needs are not catered for in a mass market. In 1965 CA decided to attempt to spread information and advice to a wider public than the readership of *Which?*. To reach this public, CA explored the possibilities of a tabloid type magazine, but research suggested that there were sections of the population who were sceptical of all printed information and that, for them, face-to-face question-and-answer sessions were the solution. So CA pioneered high street Consumer Advice Centres, whose development is described in more detail in chapter 5. CA also undertakes assignments on a fee basis for television companies and newspapers who wish to run consumer information features.

*See Bibliography p.277—Trade, Board of (1962).

Local Consumer Groups

Which? can report on goods and services on a national basis, but it cannot say which shops in Plymouth or Glasgow provide a good choice of products or which local garages or builders provide a good service. At some future time such information might be collected locally, stored centrally or regionally on a computer, and then disseminated as needed by individuals; for the present this is a dream. So it was natural that the national provision of consumer information should inspire the development of local organizations established to undertake localized research. In the early 'sixties members of Consumers' Association were asking if there was anything they could do on a voluntary basis. So in October 1961 a conference was held in Aylesbury to which members came from all over the country. They decided to encourage people's enthusiasm and interest in consumer matters in the areas in which they lived and to form local groups of consumers. Ten days later the Oxford Consumer Group was formed. During the next 18 months another 32 groups were established, over an area from Glasgow and Tyneside to Bristol and Brighton. Membership was not limited to CA members; the groups were independent; and their work was entirely voluntary. In March 1963 the groups decided that they could give each other support and so a National Federation of Consumer Groups (NFCG) was created to maintain communication between the different groups, to provide services for them, and to represent their joint views at national level. Since they depend on volunteers, some groups inevitably come and then go. A number of the original groups still exist, including Oxford and Brighton. At the end of 1976 there were 52 federated groups and 9 in the process of formation. Their income is mainly derived from members' subscriptions. Many produce a magazine or newsletter.

The local consumer groups try to reach wider audiences than just their members. The weekly programme run by Brighton, Hove and District Consumer Group on BBC Radio Brighton broadcasts information, answers listeners' questions, and invites local traders to give their viewpoint. The disabled and other minority groups present very different problems. The Southend Consumer Group produced a *Guide for the Disabled* (1973). The information was collected by a hundred volunteers who investigated every aspect of accessibility to premises in the area that a disabled person might want to use.

International Work

The UK consumer organizations have close links with both the worldwide IOCU and the Bureau Européen des Unions de Consommateurs. Both organizations provide a forum for the exchange of information and a recognized channel for consumer representations, to the UN agencies and the European Economic Commission, respectively. The European testing organizations have combined informally in the European Testing Group.

As a result, *Which?* reports sometimes now begin with a statement such as: 'We have tested 21 stereo tuners, in collaboration with the Belgian and Dutch organizations.' This is possible because a European market is developing and, of the brands and models available in any one country, a substantial number will normally be on sale in several others. Care has to be taken to ensure that models are identical, and not produced in different factories to slightly varying specifications. Since the final reports are comparative and answer questions appropriate to particular populations, the reports will not be identical. Such collaboration is nevertheless fruitful, since it enables costs of testing to be shared. Further, consumer organizations in certain countries are developing their own particular expertise which they share with the others. Thus, slowly and tentatively, the consumer organizations are trying to keep abreast of international marketing.

Attitudes to Consumerism

The consumer organizations have made progress but they are far from being equal social partners with employer and employee organizations. Yet marketing men have been known to argue that the comparative testing of goods and the philosophy of the consumer movement have undermined the morale of industry and even made commerce a dirty word. Certainly, the Public Interest Research Centre was established by people who were inspired by the work of the Nader organization in the U S and who believed that democracy is debased by lack of accountability in Government and in any other major centre of power, including the large corporations. Few of us as individuals enjoy having to account for our decisions and actions, but most of us have to do so. Institutions also must be accountable in a free society. Basically it is a matter of openness rather than secrecy. Openness should not be seen as a threat. If it debases and demoralizes then something is very wrong.

Some marketing people—fortunately not all—argue that, if consumers are happy to buy goods irrationally, why try to change this. If the housewife is happy with a 'meat' product that contains a large quantity of novel protein, does she need to know what it actually contains? If motorists are happy to buy a pound's worth of petrol then why do they have to be given the price per gallon? If some people can be made to feel better by the placebo effect of a 'medicine', why should not extravagant claims be made?

The rapid growth of the consumer information producers has demonstrated that many people are not prepared to accept such a mindless role. Suppose, however, that people had not responded to the technologically advanced society and its massive choice of goods and services with a demand for information. What would have happened? The freedom to choose among competitors, and to take one's custom elsewhere when not satisfied, is supposed to ensure a market responsive to consumer needs and demands. Without informed choice, competition between products may be based on entirely superficial characteristics and the essential functions may be sacrificed. Unless choice can be based on the real qualities of a product, in the end the buyer is likely to become disillusioned. By this time we might be facing demands for far more drastic action.

In 1971, a Swedish Royal Commission reached a most controversial conclusion about the market place. They decided that consumer demand, however well provided with information, is in itself inadequate. The consumer's aspirations may be 'too modest'. The information available to him may be too difficult to assimilate and use. The consumer's free choice is an ineffective means of influencing what is produced—standards have to be imposed. The UK consumer organizations to date have refused to subscribe to such a pessimistic view. They believe that information is the way to ensure freedom for both consumer and trader. The marketing men will demonstrate by their actions whether consumer organizations are right or wrong about this. If they are wrong, other, stronger, views will eventually prevail.

3. The legal framework of consumer protection

Bill Thomas

There are two legal codes: *civil* and *criminal*. The former regulates dealings between parties to a contract and provides remedies in the event of a breach of duty; but it is for the aggrieved person to seek compensation by resorting to the law—no one will do it for him. The criminal law enables the state to attempt to protect the public and, through various agencies, to punish traders who cheat and lie. In the fields of food and drugs and agriculture it imposes standards of hygiene and content; and there are laws about weights and measures and trade descriptions. This definition is over-simple, but the differences should become apparent. Normally the two codes do not overlap. An infringement of the criminal law may result in a trader being prosecuted but the same default may well not give a customer any rights under the civil law. There have been attempts lately to alter this by legislation creating overlapping definitions.

There is another distinction which must be grasped, especially by traders relating to ordinary everyday shopping transactions. This is the difference between *sales of goods* and *supplies of services*. A sale of goods takes place when some commodity is sold for money—the essence of the transaction being the transfer of a tangible article (or one which is about to be made). Thus purchases in shops or other retail outlets are sales of goods, provided something is handed over—whether it is food, furniture, clothing, or a motor vehicle. The size is immaterial—the same legal principles cover the sale of a book of matches or a battleship. Practically all other 'consumer' contracts are about supplies of services. Using a dry cleaner, leaving shoes for repair, having a watch mended or a car serviced, employing a solicitor or doctor, a plumber or a builder—all these are supplies of services. The list is long and other examples will be given later. The importance of the distinction is that the law about the sale of goods is reasonably certain. It is codified and gives the shopper considerable protection. Although the law on the supply of services is intelligible to lawyers, it is still being developed and there can be disagreements about its interpretation; and the trader can impose terms on his customer. It is not codified and can be difficult for the layman to recognize. It should also be noted at the outset that there are important distinctions in the law and legal systems between England and Wales, and Scotland. Some of these are examined towards the end of this chapter (see page 47).

Sales of Goods

These are the commonest types of consumer transaction and the principles are easy to state. Consumer protection is frequently seen by traders as an attack on them which imposes restrictions and additional work and liability. Much of this fear is needless because the law simply tries to regulate fair dealing. It is true that until 1973 a contract could be loaded against the consumer, but only in a minority of cases (albeit for larger items of expenditure) was this done. The trader had and has considerable freedom himself. He chooses what he sells, the price, and his customer. Obligations under the contract, when it is made, work both ways; the customer has to do things as well as the trader. There are imperfections, but recent changes in the law seek to remove them.

First of all, there is no obligation upon a trader to sell anything to anyone. He does not have to allow people into his premises, or even open them. There are many rules about when he should close and about Sunday trading; but only pubs and other licensed premises have to *open*. The display of goods in a window or in a shop does not mean that they are for sale. Any labelling or information must be accurate—or the trader may infringe the criminal law—but a customer has no right to buy 'the one in the window' or any other article. Display is called an 'invitation to treat'—literally asking the public to come and haggle.

Offer and acceptance

The basic elements for the formation of a valid contract for the sale of goods are an offer by one party to buy or sell goods for money which is unconditionally accepted by the other. In a consumer context, practically every offer comes from the shopper. It is then open to the trader to accept the offer, reject it, or make a counter-offer. Until that decision is made—and, indeed, afterwards if he refuses the offer—the trader has complete freedom whether or not to do business with the customer.

The offer may be made in writing, by word of mouth, or by conduct. As far as the sale of goods is concerned, only contracts of guarantee or those under the Hire Purchase Acts have to be in writing. Many commercial contracts are made in writing, with both the offer and the acceptance being contained in correspondence or by using printed standard forms of contract. In consumer contracts, standard forms are less common, the most notable example being for motor vehicles. Many traders will prepare an 'order' or an 'invoice', which may have some terms and conditions printed on the back. If the document is completed with the knowledge of the consumer, it may well be the contract. But if it is sent later, or with the goods, then it may be no more than evidence of what was orally agreed—and in such a case it would not be possible for any printed terms to be incorporated. There is no reason why a prudent trader should not make his consumer contracts in writing and protect himself by making provisions about delivery dates, time and method of payment, and, for example, that goods should remain his until they have been paid for. He cannot now exclude his liability for what he sells, and it is desirable that the 'small print' should be clearly legible.

It is essential in any contract that the terms and conditions be drawn to the consumer's attention *before* the contract is made. If they are not then they do not form part of the contract, and the trader will not be able to rely on them.

Offers are most frequently made by word of mouth. 'Will you sell me that?'; 'I would like to buy the one on the right.' If the trader says 'yes', then immediately there comes into existence a binding contract. If the article turns out to have been wrongly priced or sold to someone else then the trader is in difficulty. In the former case the loss will fall on him; in the latter he is in breach of contract. In most cases of confusion or mistake a satisfactory compromise is worked out; the problem of who said what may only have to be resolved by a court when the parties are at loggerheads. That is why it is so important to grasp the legal rules about making a contract. It is much better for a salesman to ask a customer to wait while he checks price or availability before he commits his firm to a contract and all its consequences. The urge to make a sale or earn a commission can be fatal.

Offers by conduct are also commonplace. A weekend walk around a supermarket ends in a trolley full of goods being exchanged for large sums of money without a word being spoken. The consumer *offers* to buy each item by handing it to a checkout operator who then *accepts* the offer by pressing keys on a cash register. Each item is separately sold. In the same way a contract is made when the appropriate number of pence is handed to a newsagent, tobacconist, or salesman when self-selection is normal.

Once an offer is made, it is for the trader to decide what to do. Any unconditional acceptance means that a contract is made then and there. But if the trader makes any qualification, by revising the price or specification, he is not accepting but putting a counter-offer to the customer—who then has the same right to accept or reject. And a refusal of the offer means, of course, that there is no legal relationship.

The Sale of Goods Act 1893, as amended by the Supply of Goods (Implied Terms) Act 1973, lays down what the law is when goods are sold. Although some parts of it are not open to argument, other sections merely provide a guideline or remedy in cases where the parties fail to cover a circumstance themselves. The 1893 Act was intended as a commercial code to regulate dealings between traders, and, contrary to popular belief, the implied terms and other benefits in the Act existed before it was passed and were merely put into writing by the Act. The Act has worked extremely well in practice and there are very few court decisions about its meaning; those that have been reported have invariably been between commercial interests. It is sometimes difficult for consumers and traders—and even their legal advisers—to appreciate that legal cases involving ships and freight, generators or cigarette slot machines have just as much relevance to buying tins of peas or curtain lining.

Unless money is involved the deal is an exchange, not a sale of goods. How and when the price is to be paid is a matter for agreement. It can be paid when the contract is made, or when the goods are delivered or at any other time; it can be paid in cash, by cheque or credit card or by using credit. If credit is involved the nature of the transaction may be different. Payment by instalments often means hire purchase, conditional sale or credit sale, all of which are already covered by special legislation. In the case of hire purchase and conditional sale there is no contract between the seller and the consumer. Where other types of credit are concerned (which will be regulated by the Consumer Credit Act 1974 when it is fully in force) there is a contract of sale between the trader and the consumer financed by a third party—the creditor. What the price for the goods should be is primarily for the parties to decide. If it is not agreed, the Act says that the buyer must pay a reasonable price. So if goods are ordered at an agreed price but are supplied at a later date when the price has risen, the loss falls on the trader. If the contract provides for the price current at the date of delivery, then that is what the consumer has to pay. The reasonable price the consumer has to pay in the absence of agreement depends on the circumstances of each case.

Deposits

There is considerable misunderstanding about deposits. If a consumer pays a deposit and asks a trader to keep an article on one side for a few days until he returns to decide whether to buy it, the 'deposit' is a payment for an option to buy at the later date. If he comes in as agreed, the money paid is usually allowed for in the price. But if the customer fails to appear within any stipulated time, the trader can keep the money. If a trader requires the payment of some money as a condition of making a contract, that payment *is* a deposit. If the consumer fails to complete his side of the deal or is in breach of contract he will forfeit the deposit and the trader may be entitled to other compensation as well. But if, when the contract is made, the consumer pays some money towards the price on the understanding that he will pay the rest on delivery, that payment is *not* a deposit but a 'part-payment'. If the consumer breaks the contract he will not automatically forfeit his part-payment and may be able to recover it in full if he can show that the trader has suffered no actual loss. The test of a deposit is whether the trader would have entered the contract without some money being paid.

If he would, it is a part-payment; if he would not, it is a deposit.

At law, a trader is entitled to be paid the agreed price in the correct amount of cash; he is not obliged to give change or to accept a cheque. If he does allow payment to be made by cheque, he may be well advised to insist on the presentation of a cheque card and to ensure that he complies with the conditions on which the issuing bank will honour the cheque. The trader is allowed to charge one price for cash and another if credit is taken. (Under the Consumer Credit Act 1974 all goods must be available for cash if they are offered for sale on credit terms.)

Time

The time for performance of the contract is, again, something to be agreed between the parties. If no time is stipulated, the goods must be supplied within a reasonable time. The customer can make time *of the essence*—that is, a condition upon which the contract will stand or fall—by giving the trader notice that he should fulfil his obligations by a stated date. If the trader fails to do so, the customer may repudiate the contract and claim compensation. If he wants goods by a particular date—a wedding dress just before a wedding, or furniture in time for moving into a new house—then he should require a delivery time to be included. Equally, a trader may protect himself against being let down by suppliers by indicating that time shall not be of the essence, that no date for delivery can be stipulated—and go further and say that time shall start to run against the customer when the trader gives him notice that the goods are ready. If the customer fails to take delivery and pay for the goods in the period allowed then the trader can repudiate the contract.

Ownership

It may be very important to know *when* the property in goods—that is the ownership—is transferred. Normally, when existing goods are sold in a shop the property passes then and there, at the moment the contract is made and before any money changes hands. The trader may well have the right to retain *possession* of what have now become the customer's goods until he is paid, but the general rule is that risk passes with ownership so that if the goods are lost or damaged without any negligence on the trader's part, it will be the customer who loses. If the shopper who has passed through the supermarket check-out discovers he has no money, the goods are still his; the shop may hold them until he pays and must take reasonable care to ensure that the goods are not stolen or re-sold. The onus on the trader is not as great as it seems. He does not have to put the goods in a locked place or stand guard over them—he has merely to take reasonable steps to safeguard and return them to their owner in due course.

If, on the other hand, the trader has to do something to the goods to put them in a deliverable state—like assemble parts or put finishing touches to them—the property does not pass until that work has been done, and the consumer has been given notice. Where goods are sold on 'sale or return' or on approval, the property passes when the consumer accepts the goods, or signifies his approval, or retains them beyond the agreed period—or, if there is no agreed period, for a reasonable time. Complications can arise when what is being bought does not yet exist—furniture, for example, or a motor car. The property does not pass until the goods are appropriated to the contract. Appropriation takes place when the trader delivers the goods to the customer *or* to a carrier to take them to the customer. The trader may arrange with the manufacturer to deliver direct to the customer; if the carrier loses or damages the goods then, if by arranging this carriage the trader has appropriated the goods to the contract, the risk will be with the customer, who may be quite unaware that he now owns the goods. Traders and manufacturers may each believe the other is responsible, but if the contract is silent then the customer may be the ultimate loser.

If the trader is authorized or required to send the goods to the customer, delivery to a carrier is treated as delivery *to* the customer. But the trader must make a reasonable contract of carriage, having regard to the nature of the goods and the circumstances of the case. Failure to make such a contract allows the customer to decline to accept or pay for the goods if they are damaged or lost; or he can accept and claim compensation from the trader. So to send expensive equipment or machinery by a carrier who has a compensation limit of £10 would probably be regarded by the court as an unreasonable contract of carriage.

Implied terms

Turning to the contract itself, there are implied or written into it a number of *conditions*. A condition in legal jargon is a fundamental term of a contract, one that goes to the very basis of the agreement—and any breach of condition gives the injured party a right to reject the goods and cancel the contract. These implied terms are contained in the Sale of Goods Act and cannot, in a contract between a trader and consumer, be excluded or limited in any way.

First, there is an implied condition that the trader has the right to sell the goods. A breach of this enables the customer to recover the price he has paid, because the contract wholly fails.

Second, there are conditions that the goods will correspond with any description which may have been applied to them and that the bulk of any goods sold by sample will correspond with the sample. The latter condition exists even where the customer selects the goods himself. These terms apply to any contract, not merely those by traders. Any private seller may be met with a claim by his buyer if what he 'sold' turns out not to have been his or if it failed to meet the description applied to it. So, if a car or lawn-mower advertised as being 'in first class condition' or 'nearly new' is not so in fact, a private buyer will be able to claim the return of the price from another private seller.

There are two other important conditions—ones which perhaps go to the heart of consumer protection. Where a trader sells goods 'in the course of a business' there is an implied condition that the goods are of 'merchantable quality', except for defects specifically drawn to the consumer's attention *before* the contract is made or for defects which an examination ought to reveal *if* the buyer examined them, again *before* the contract is made. Selling in the course of a business means any business. So if a retail furnisher sells a secondhand car to a private buyer, the consumer will have the same rights in respect of the vehicle as if he had bought it from a garage. Merchantable quality is a woolly term; goods meet it if they are as fit for the purpose for which they were bought as is reasonable to expect, having regard to any description applied to them, the price (if relevant), and all other relevant circumstances. For mechanical or electrical goods, this really means that they should work, that a buyer should be able to take them home, plug them in, and switch on, and find that they do what he wants them to.

The second important condition is this. Where a trader sells goods in the course of a business, and the consumer makes known expressly or impliedly any particular purpose for which the goods are being bought, there is an implied condition that they are reasonably fit for that purpose. So a cooker must cook; glue must stick. The only exception is where the circumstances show that the buyer did not rely on the trader's skill or judgement, which means the trader must have sold against his experience to a consumer who insists on making an inappropriate purchase.

The significance of these two last conditions for the consumer is twofold. First, if the goods do not comply with them, he can reject them, cancel the contract, and recover the money he paid. Second, in a consumer sale, the trader cannot avoid his responsibility under the Act. A consumer sale is one where goods of a type ordinarily bought for private use are sold to a person who does not buy them, or hold himself out as buying them in the course of a business. So, to determine whether the full panoply of protection applies to a given situation, one must find out what the goods were and how the buyer presented himself. A private individual who buys a computer or cash register, for example, may be outside the limit, because these goods are not ordinarily bought for private use. A person who buys a carpet but pays from a trade bank account may also be outside protection because he holds himself out—however unwittingly—as buying in the course of a business.

In all other contracts for the sale of goods—between traders and their distributors or manufacturers—exclusion clauses avoiding or restricting the seller's liability are permitted, but they are subject to a test of reasonableness. The court will take into account the bargaining strengths of each side, any inducement to agree to the term which the buyer may have received, whether the buyer knew of the term and its extent—having regard to custom in the trade—and whether the goods were specially made for the buyer.

Although the property in goods has frequently passed to the consumer at the point of sale, if, when he gets them home, the buyer discovers that they do not comply with the implied conditions, he may reject *his* goods—thereby transferring the property back to the trader—and cancel the contract. But he must do so quickly, and must not have *accepted* them. Acceptance takes place when the buyer tells the seller that he has done so, or if he keeps them for a reasonable time and does not reject them—or when the goods have been delivered to him and he does anything which is inconsistent with the ownership of the seller. So a consumer can plug in and use a machine to see if it works. If it does not, or if it fails, then he can reject the goods. But if an appliance has been installed and used for several weeks is that not wholly inconsistent with the ownership of the seller? Can one say that if the goods break down after some weeks, they still belong to the trader? An appeal court decision in 1977 held that it was too late to reject the goods in question after six months (even though, in that case, the car concerned had been off the road for five of them). So the longer the consumer delays the better placed a trader is for contesting and defeating a claim by a consumer for the return of the price.

What does this mean in practice? Once a contract has been made, the goods delivered and accepted and in use, the consumer cannot claim his money back if an inherent defect develops. But the consumer does have another remedy. In addition to conditions, the law classifies as *warranties* lesser terms in a contract which are not fundamental to it and which are collateral to its main purpose. There are a number of implied warranties set out in the Sale of Goods Act—e.g., that the buyer will have uninterrupted use and possession of the goods, and that they are free from any debt or credit agreement not made known to the buyer at the time the contract is made. A breach of warranty gives rise to a claim for compensation only. A consumer may elect to treat a breach of condition as a breach of warranty (in the case, for example, where it is too late to reject them). The remedy for breach of warranty is the 'estimated loss directly and naturally resulting in the ordinary course of events from the breach'. So the consumer can claim the cost of repairing defective goods or, if the defect results in a total loss, claim the difference between what he paid and what the goods in their defective condition are worth, which may well be the same as the price. Many of the matters discussed so far can be provided for in a simply worded written contract; all that such a document cannot do is take away from a consumer his right to be supplied with goods meeting their description, of merchantable quality, and fit for their purpose.

Once a contract has been made, both sides have obligations. Most of the trader's have been described; but a trader also has rights. First, to retain possession (but not ownership) until he is paid. This right is lost if he parts with possession even to a carrier, unless the trader reserves the right to dispose of the goods. A seller can always provide in his contract that he will retain the right to dispose of goods if he is not paid. This means that ownership does not change hands until that condition is met. A trader can re-sell goods which are perishable or if he gives the buyer notice of his intention to re-sell and the buyer fails to pay within a reasonable time. A trader has the right to sue for the price if the buyer wrongfully fails to pay for the goods. And where the consumer fails to accept and pay for the goods, there is a right to sue for damages for non-acceptance. This right to sue should be exercised with some care. Some people, of course, set out to acquire goods without paying for them. But there are also cases where a consumer does not pay because the goods are defective and there has been a breach of condition or of warranty. Any claim by a trader may well be met by a defence and counterclaim by the consumer; it would be wise to determine, where possible, why the bill has not been paid rather than treat every non-payer as a defaulting debtor. Incidentally, once goods have been rejected by a consumer he is under no obligation to return them unless the contract specifically so provides.

Complementing these rights are obligations upon the consumer. He must accept and pay for the goods, which, as far as most traders are concerned, is the most important aspect of their business. He is at risk for loss of profit if the trader cannot easily dispose of the goods following his breach of contract, but if there is a ready market the trader will still be entitled to nominal damages because of the consumer's breach.

If the trader breaks the contract, the consumer can sue for the price of the goods, if the breach is a breach of condition. Or he can make a claim for damages for breach of warranty. In either case, the consumer is entitled to claim any out-of-pocket expenses (e.g., fares, and loss of wages, where appropriate), and if he has to buy the goods at a higher price the difference may also be claimed as part of his damages. Any person who has sustained loss as a result of a breach of contract is under an obligation to mitigate his loss. He must take reasonable steps to reduce his claim or at least not allow it to become inflated by doing nothing. In rare cases a court can make an order for the specific performance of a contract—that is, direct the seller to sell a specific, identifiable, item of goods.

Returns and credit notes

There are other circumstances which arise after a contract has been completed. The consumer may wish to return goods and ask for an exchange or a credit note. If there is nothing wrong with the goods, there is no obligation upon the trader to have anything to do with such a request. Any action he takes will be a matter of goodwill only, not a legal duty. A credit note will remain in force for whatever period is shown on it. But any conditions to which it is subject should be made plain when it is offered.

The only remedy for breach of contract is a claim for money. It is therefore an attempt to defeat the spirit of the law to offer a credit note to a consumer who has a good claim for defective goods. And it can be argued that, even if the consumer accepts it, he is still entitled to change his mind and ask for money. Finally, a consumer cannot demand a replacement, even if the goods are defective; he can only seek money. But if a replacement is offered and both parties agree, then that is quite in order.

Injuries caused by defective goods

If a person is injured or property damaged by goods, what is the legal situation? Much will depend upon the status of the victim. All that has been said so far emphasizes the importance of a contract and its consequences. It is because of the contract that a consumer has a claim against a trader. If the goods are merely defective, the consumer has no claim at all against the manufacturer—because there is no contractual relationship between them. He can only turn to the trader. If the goods cause injuries, the consumer who bought them may have a right of action against the trader in contract (because the goods are unfit for their purpose); he may have a claim against the manufacturer *if* he can show that the latter was negligent. That is to say, the claimant has to prove that there was fault. This can be difficult or impossible to prove. How can a person with limited resources prove that a lemonade bottle was filled carelessly, or that the manufacturer of a colour television set failed to take sufficient care to ensure that the set would not catch fire? He also has to prove that the defect which caused the injury was present when the product was still in the hands of the manufacturer. Take the case of a new motor car which crashes because of a brake failure. Was it the car maker's fault? Or the fault of the manufacturers of the braking system? Or that of the synthetic components within the hydraulic system itself? Or was it anyone's fault at all? So long as the consumer is the *buyer*, he can claim against the seller. But when the injured victim did not buy the goods himself, his only claim possible is in negligence against the manufacturer—and he will face the problems just described.

Product liability

That the person primarily responsible for designing, making, advertising, and recommending the price of goods has no obligation to the ultimate user if he is injured has caused much disquiet. A body of opinion has developed in the last few years that this avoidance of responsibility is contrary to the public interest. A new label, *product liability*, has been coined to describe the obligation which a producer ought to meet. And the debate has been widened by the recent publication of three documents which have had an important influence on the way in which the principle will develop. The member States of the Council of Europe have issued a Convention on Product Liability. This is called the Strasbourg Convention, and if the U K signed it there would follow legislation to make manufacturers responsible, and liable to pay compensation, for death or personal injury caused by defects in their products. The victim would not have to prove any fault or negligence on the part of the manufacturer. If other countries signed but the U K did not, British manufacturers would be at a disadvantage. One problem could be that the Convention prohibits the adoption of another scheme which might be more favourable to victims. There is a Royal Commission investigating compensation for personal injuries which could make recommendations which might be even better for victims. Some pressure groups have urged the introduction in the U K of a State-run compensation scheme for all accident victims, whether the injury is sustained in the home, on the road, or at work (on the lines of the system already working in New Zealand). Should the Royal Commission make that sort of finding, there could be political difficulties in aligning the two schemes.

The Council of the European Communities have issued a draft Directive about liability for defective products. While there are similarities with the Convention, the E E C propose a strict liability on producers generally—not merely on those who put goods into circulation in the course of a business—which could include a person who makes jam for a fête, for example. The draft Directive also precludes payment of compensation to victims for 'pain and suffering', which is quite contrary to the principles for the assessment of damages for personal injuries in the courts. There is also a global limit for the compensation to be paid for all injuries caused by identical articles having the same defect. This could mean that the first claimant could 'scoop the pool', and subsequent claimants go empty-handed. The E E C also propose that producers should be strictly liable for some kinds of property damage (except to the article itself) if it was a consumer product bought privately. There are limits for such claims. But this extension of the principle to property rather than to personal injury goes much further than the Strasbourg Convention, which is limited to death or injury.

The Law Commissions for England and Wales and for Scotland have also issued their report on liability for defective products* in which they make recommendations and also comment on the Strasbourg Convention and the E E C draft Directive. Their main point is that producers who put their products in circulation in the course of a business should be strictly liable for injuries caused by defects in their products. A *producer* is a person who makes things—not an agent or distributor. 'Own-brand' sellers, or others who sell goods which do not identify the producer, would also be liable as producers. A product would be defective if at the time it was put into circulation it did not meet a reasonable standard of safety. This standard would be determined having regard to instructions and warnings sent with the product and the use to which it would be reasonable to put it. The Law Commissions recommend that existing legal remedies for negligence be retained. A victim claiming under the product liability principle would have to show that he was injured, that the injury was attributable to a defect in a product, and that the person from whom he claimed was the producer.

*See Bibliography p.280—Law Commission and Scottish Law Commission (1977).

Apart from disproving the first two points, a person sued would have a defence if he could show that the product was not defective when he put it into circulation.

The English Law Commission is in favour of the principles in the Strasbourg Convention, which they see as a substantial improvement to the law in England and Wales. The Scottish Law Commission is not in favour of accession to the Convention. But both Commissions are opposed to the principles set out in the E E C draft Directive, which they consider (even if amended) would be detrimental to the development and reform of the law in the U K for defective products.

What has been said about product liability should place it in some sort of perspective. It is not nearly such a far-reaching matter as is sometimes thought. It does not allow the consumer to make any claim against the manufacturer for goods that are defective *unless that defect causes injury*. It will help victims who did not themselves buy the goods and who would not have a claim in the absence of negligence. How it develops depends on the reaction in Europe to comments on the E E C draft Directive, the report of the Royal Commission, and the attitude of whatever Government is in power at the time.

Other obligations

From time to time customers are injured in shops when they or their children slip or fall. A trader has an obligation to ensure that people who come into his shop are safe. He must ensure that floors and passages are kept clear and clean, and he must look out for and wipe up spillages quickly.

Customers break things in shops; are they liable? Unless there is a sign asking people not to touch the goods, they are only liable if the trader can prove that they were negligent (the need to prove fault, again). The law does not hold parents responsible for the negligent acts of their children. A child will be subject to a lower standard of knowledge of the consequences of his acts than an adult. And a customer cannot be made to pay for breakages because the goods are not his until he has made a contract with the seller.

Guarantees

These come in different forms. Many traders offer them, and many manufacturers send them with the goods they make. How valuable they are depends on what they say and what, if any, legal effect they have. As has been indicated, a trader has obligations about the quality and fitness of what he sells that he cannot avoid. So some guarantees offered are no more than the law demands. But the legal obligations relate to defects present at the time of the contract. A trader who says that he will repair free of parts and labour charges for a year or more any article he sells will be going much further than the basic legal requirements and will be offering something of real value. Some retailers go further still: Marks and Spencer's say that they will refund money on any goods returned to them even if the customer has only changed her mind or picked the wrong size. And, of course, they meet their obligations under the Sale of Goods Act as well. Some traders offer guarantees which require the consumer to pay for either parts or labour charges, or both. Where these are an attempt—deliberate or otherwise—to reduce the legal rights of the consumer, the document is made illegal by an Order made under the Fair Trading Act 1973.

Manufacturers' guarantees vary from being useful additions to the consumer's rights against the trader under the Sale of Goods Act to pieces of paper with writing on which are of no value at all. As there is no contract with the manufacturer, the 'guarantee' cannot be enforced. It is in the discretion of the company giving it whether or not to meet what it offers. Many guarantees appear to offer to repair goods or replace parts 'free' within a limited period, and then immediately list the limitations and terms (for example, that the customer has to pay the cost of carriage and labour charges) and seek to remove some of the conditions implied by law. It may say that all decisions about repairs are to be made by the company, that any interference with the goods invalidates the guarantee, and it may exclude all liability for negligence. Some control has been attempted by an Order under the Fair Trading Act which bans any clause in a guarantee which seeks to avoid or limit the consumer's rights under the Sale of Goods Act 1893; and this is being extended to delivery notes and other documents, and to containers and packaging. The Unfair Contract Terms Act 1977 makes void any term in a guarantee issued to a consumer which excludes or limits liability for loss or damage caused by goods proving defective as a result of negligence in the manufacture or distribution. Other objectionable terms in guarantees limit their effect to parts in a machine supplied by the company issuing the guarantee; require a registration card to be sent within a very short period of purchase; and contain vague suggestions about expenses which may be claimed from the consumer. The best advice to the consumer is to read the guarantee before buying goods so that its terms can be compared with others. But as guarantee cards are frequently packed deep inside the container, that may well be impracticable.

Supplies of Services

All that has been said so far deals with the sale of goods. But many contracts are made for other things which are not sales of goods, although goods may form part of the deal. These contracts are classified loosely as supplies of services. Some examples of the supply of services have already been given. The installation of double glazing or central heating and having an extension built onto a house are all supplies of services with goods added. Because the contract will be for the whole job—labour and parts included—it is not possible for the consumer to have the protection of the Sale of Goods Act for the goods aspect of the deal. It was, until the Unfair

Contract Terms Act 1977, possible for a trader to contract out of *any* obligation he had under the Common Law by inserting exclusion clauses in the contract. Now these clauses will not have any effect in a consumer contract where they seek to exclude or restrict liability for description, quality, or fitness.

A contract for the supply of services is made in the same way as any other: an offer by one party is accepted by the other. 'Will you do some plumbing for me?'; 'Will you mend my watch for me?'; 'Will you move my furniture to my new house?' If the answer is 'Yes', then there is a contract. Many service contracts are in writing and a number are in printed forms of standard contract which the consumer will in practice probably be unable to alter. Indeed, he (or she) may not know that they exist, but if he has signed a contract which contains terms and there is sufficient indication on the front of the form that they are set out on the back, then he will be presumed to have read, understood, and accepted them. It is now no longer possible for a trader to avoid his liability for death or injury. To try to avoid responsibility for negligence or for breach of contract, to claim to be allowed to perform the contract quite differently ('If we cannot take you to Spain as you wanted, we can take you to Iceland'), or not to do it at all, will mean that the offending clause will be subject to a test of reasonableness by the courts.

A contract for the supply of services contains terms implied—not under the Sale of Goods Act, because it is not a contract for the sale of goods—but under the Common Law. A tradesman must exercise the sort of skill of a reasonably competent member of his calling; the same principle applies to lawyers and doctors and dentists. If he does not belong to a trade as such—where a neighbour, perhaps, may repair or service a car—he must exercise such skill as he holds himself out as possessing. The goods and materials which a tradesman uses must be of good quality and reasonably fit for the purpose for which they are supplied.

Many traders try to rely on exclusion clauses, whether in the contract or by notices stuck up in their premises. The Unfair Contract Terms Act 1977 covers many of these already; but there is an added safeguard for the consumer (or indeed anyone against whom an exclusion clause is set up). The law says that such a clause will be construed against the interest of the person who seeks to rely on it; and if there is more than one interpretation, the court will accept that which is least favourable to the person relying on it. In South Africa, for example, a judge held that a sign in a car park saying 'Cars parked at Owner's risk' meant 'at the risk of the owner of the car park'—and not, as the car park owner urged, the owner of the car! The notice must be carefully worded to ensure, from the trader's point of view, that it covers what he is trying to avoid. 'No responsibility for damage' would cover neither negligence nor injury, so a person whose goods were damaged due to the negligence of the trader or his staff, or who sustained injuries, would be able to claim compensation. The trader would not be able to rely on the notice to protect himself.

Bailment

When goods are left with a tradesman for repair or for work to be done, the arrangement is what the law calls a *bailment*. This occurs when one person takes possession (but *not* ownership) of someone else's goods. So it is a bailment to lend a ladder or hire a car, to pawn a ring or to have goods sent by a carrier. Apart from the obligation on a person who is to do work to exercise the appropriate amount of skill, there is also a duty to take reasonable care of the goods themselves. If payment is being made for the bailment (10p to leave a coat in a cloakroom, or a storage charge to a furniture remover) more care will be needed than if the bailment is free (leaving the trolley full of goods in the supermarket, or agreeing to look after a neighbour's dog while he is on holiday). This duty to take reasonable care has limits: the trader is under an obligation to take reasonable care and if he proves that he did so and still the goods were damaged, the loss falls on the owner of the goods—not on the trader.

The onus is on the trader to show that there was no negligence on his part. A case in 1977 showed this clearly. A lady sent a carpet worth £900 to be cleaned. There was a term in the contract limiting the cleaners' liability to £40. The carpet was never seen again, but the cleaners were unable to say what had happened except that it had been lost; they couldn't say if it had been stolen, or wrongly delivered, or what enquiries had been made. The Appeal Court held that this showed that they had been negligent—and so they could not rely on the limiting term and had to pay the owner £900.

Exclusion clauses

Reference has already been made to the Unfair Contract Terms Act 1977. This affects liability under contracts other than those for sales of goods. It bans altogether any clause in a contract which seeks to avoid liability for death or injury to anyone; it bans any consumer guarantee clause excluding liability for defects causing damage arising from negligence in the manufacture or distribution; it repeats the bans in the Sale of Goods Act (so that all the law on exclusion clauses will be in the same place); and it bans clauses in consumer contracts for the supply of services which exclude liability for the description, quality or fitness of goods where possession or ownership changes hands. All other exclusion clauses relating to loss or damage from negligence, arising in contract, under consumer indemnity contracts, and those relating to the right to transfer goods are subject to a test of reasonableness. This test in England and Wales is whether the term would have been fair and reasonable having regard to the circumstances which were, or ought reasonably to have been, known to or in the contemplation of the parties at the time the contract was made.

The Act also deals with the burden of proof in cases where questions arise about the validity of a clause. It is for those who claim that a contract term does meet the test of reasonableness to show that it does. For example, a coin-operated launderette owner may by a notice disclaim liability for damage to clothes washed in his machines. It will be for him to justify this notice. If he satisfies a court that no one is there, that the general public have free access, and that anyone who is so minded can interfere with the machines and thus cause damage to clothing—and that in any event the customer is only paying a small sum for the use of the machine—it may very well be that the notice will be upheld. Second, it is for a person who contends that a party does not deal as a consumer to show that he does not.

Service contracts may exist between a consumer and a manufacturer when arrangements are made for the maintenance of goods. These are usually for one year at a time and so can be terminated by either side on notice of the appropriate length. They can also be varied—most often by the supplier wanting to raise the price for the service provided. In such cases, of course, the consumer has the backing of the law of contract with the manufacturer and so may be able to claim damages from him direct in the event of any breach of contract giving rise to loss or damage. Many such contracts do contain clauses which are objectionable to consumers but which they cannot do anything about because the supplier adopts a 'take it or leave it' attitude.

Estimates and quotations

Traders and consumers are often confused by these. An estimate is what it says it is—an approximate judgement of what the price for a service will be. The final bill may be more or less than the estimate (it invariably seems to be more). The consumer must pay the bill provided it is reasonably near the estimate—a margin of ten per cent either way would probably be regarded as appropriate by a court. If it was a lot more, then it almost certainly would not be reasonable and the trader would have to stand the loss. A quotation is different—it is a positive statement of the price at which a service *will* be provided. So if a builder gives a quotation to do a job at, say, £75, and it is accepted, the consumer will be bound to pay that price, even though the work is completed in a short time. Where Value Added Tax is involved, the trader ought to specify at the outset, in either the estimate or quotation, that the tax is to be added (or that it is inclusive, if that is the case). If no prior mention is made of the tax, a consumer can refuse to pay it.

Credit

The obligations of each party when goods or services are supplied on credit depend on the type of credit provided. Hire purchase and conditional sale agreements can only be for goods. The distinction in reality is minimal. In the former, the consumer negotiates with the retailer who sells the goods to a finance institution (or maybe provides its own credit), which then hires them to the consumer, who will have an option to purchase the goods at the end of the term. In the latter, the goods are to be sold to the consumer who will pay by instalments, the property in them remaining with the retailer until the payments have been completed. A credit-sale agreement may be made for goods. Here the property passes on the completion of the contract so that, in the event of anything going wrong with the goods, the consumer does have a claim as *buyer*, because they belong to him. In each of the three cases there exist statutory provisions about the form and content of the agreement to be made, the legibility of documents which the consumer has to sign and be given copies of, and the rights and obligations of each party. These are contained in the Hire Purchase Act 1965 and in regulations and orders from time to time made by the Government, which tend to treat this form of credit as a way of regulating the economy.

Because of the restrictions which these forms of credit impose—both as to form and obligation (the creditor or hirer of goods having duties to ensure that they are of merchantable quality, fit for their purpose, and meet any description that may have been applied to them)—other forms of credit have been developed. Personal loans, second mortgages, cheque trading, and budget accounts have grown over the years.

These have largely been outside all forms of control by government with the result that lenders have been able to state their terms and conditions without any sort of scrutiny by anyone on behalf of the borrower. This led to serious abuses particularly where people were induced to sign loan agreements in their homes (often in order to get rid of a persuasive salesman) only to find that they were held to long-term credit arrangements for goods which either didn't appear or, if they did, were shoddy. Sometimes, they found that the firm which had sold the goods had gone out of business leaving them with defective goods and a millstone of debt.

This unfortunate state of affairs was recognized by the Government of the day which set up a Committee (known as the Crowther Committee, after its Chairman) to investigate the law and practice of the provision of credit and to recommend improvements and alterations. This Committee, which started work in 1968, reported in 1971* but it was not until 1973 that a White Paper was issued closely followed by the first Consumer Credit Bill. After a change of Government, the present Consumer Credit Act received the Royal Assent in July 1974.

Licensing

This far-reaching and detailed Act imposed upon the Director General of Fair Trading the responsibility of enforcement of its main provisions. The first of these was the principle that everyone who was concerned with the provision of credit—whether as banker, finance house, retailer with arrangements with a lender, broker, debt-collector, or advisor should be licensed. This is proving to be a mammoth task with the prospect that the

---

*See Bibliography p.281—Trade and Industry, Department of Consumer Credit: Report of the Committee (1971).

number of licence applications will run into six figures. The Act required the Director to be satisfied that each applicant for a licence be a 'fit person'—which was as widely defined as one could conceive. The Director shall have regard to any circumstances which appear to him to be relevant, in particular to any evidence tending to show that the applicant or any of his employees, agents, or associates (past or present) have committed any offence of fraud, dishonesty or violence; have contravened anything under the Act or other credit-regulating Act; discriminated on grounds of sex, colour, race or in connection with any business or engaged in any business practices which appear to the Director to be deceitful, oppressive, or otherwise unfair or improper (whether unlawful or not). To trade without a licence is a criminal offence—the Act creating 34 new crimes. There will be detailed regulations about the advertising of credit, and all credit agreements will have to be in forms which comply with the Act. All credit agreements signed away from trade premises will be subject to a 'cooling off' period which will be in effect for 14 days.

Legal remedies

The Consumer Credit Act gives a new remedy to someone who claims for misrepresentation or breach of contract. He may claim against the creditor if the goods or services fail to come up to expectation. This will be of considerable value where a supplier goes out of business. Such claims have a lower limit of £30 and a maximum of £10 000. Within those limits, claims may be made. This applies to goods bought by the use of a credit-card, although, by an odd anomaly still the subject of dispute, the protection may only apply to benefit holders of cards issued on or after 1 July 1977. Added protection is given to consumers, who must be given a written 'default notice' if the creditor claims that they are in breach of the agreement. No action can be taken until this has been done and any attempt to do so means that the agreement will not be enforceable.

Repayment

The Consumer Credit Act imposes a duty on a creditor to allow a borrower who wants to repay a loan ahead of time. In addition, a rebate for early settlement should be provided. Subject to regulations, the rebate will be calculated on the basis of the so-called 'rule of 78', with possible modifications in favour of the creditor. A new protection is given in the case of an *extortionate credit bargain*, which includes *any* agreement whenever it was made. The Act defines as extortionate a credit bargain under which the borrower has to pay sums which are 'grossly exorbitant', or which otherwise grossly contravene ordinary principles of fair dealing. The scope of these words will give courts—and lawyers—ample room for lengthy argument.

Hiring

An important and sometimes overlooked feature of the Consumer Credit Act is that it applies to hire business as well as to credit. This means that all hire firms will have to be licensed if they make agreements with consumers which are not hire purchase contracts, which are capable of lasting for more than three months, and where the total amount of money payable does not exceed £5000. A hirer will be allowed to terminate a hire agreement after 18 months (although certain trade hirings are excluded). A borrower who has paid off a loan will be able to require the creditor or lender to give him a statement saying whether or not (and if not, why not) the debt *is* paid.

Enforcement of the Act at local level will be by local authority Trading Standards Departments, who will supply the Director-General of Fair Trading with information about the working of the Act. They will have to notify him of any intention to prosecute any of the 34 offences. It is worth noting that among its miscellaneous provisions the Act prohibits sending circulars about credit to minors, bans the mass mailing of credit cards, and puts an end to the doorstep selling of cash loans. Credit reference agencies (which receive and store information about the creditworthiness of members of the public) will have to be licensed and their files will, for the first time, be open to public inspection. Any person may ask a trader to supply him with the name and address of any agency which has been consulted. Upon payment of a fee of 25p, the consumer will be able to ask the agency for a copy of the file on him and, if he disagrees with any entry, ask for a correction to be made. If the agency refuses, the consumer can ask the Director-General to mediate.

The principle of 'truth in lending' is embodied in the Act by requiring disclosure of the true annual rate of interest, so that people who wish to borrow money will be in a position to make a true comparison of the actual cost to them of various types of credit before making a choice.

The Act has taken far longer to bring into force than originally expected. There is some complication because the Department of Prices and Consumer Protection is responsible for the drafting and introduction of the regulations and orders, while the Office of Fair Trading has the task of implementing them. The Office has collected a considerable amount of information about all aspects of the Act which is available to the public without payment. Anyone who is likely to be affected by the Act should turn to this.

Small Claims

An increase in consumers' use and awareness of the County Courts as a way of resolving disputes with traders has followed the introduction of a 'small claims' arbitration scheme for claims not exceeding £100. This scheme is intended to enable people to have small cases resolved quickly and cheaply. The use of lawyers is discouraged by rules which prevent a loser being ordered to pay lawyers' fees for the winner—unless he has brought the action upon himself or has acted unreasonably. Some 12 000 cases were referred to arbitration in 1976 (although this should, perhaps, be contrasted with the 1½ million summonses issued in the County Courts in the same period).

There are deficiencies in the County Court system. For example, courts vary in the latitude they give to laymen bringing or defending cases themselves; the set of rules is potentially stultifying; expert witnesses—who may often be essential to enable a litigant to prove his case beyond reasonable doubt—are expensive; and, where the sum involved exceeds £200, there is a risk of becoming involved in appeals, with the attendant expense and worry. On the other hand, the County Court is available to most people reasonably easily; the initial cost is low—a fee of 10 per cent of the claim is payable, up to a maximum of £19; and the defendant cannot refuse to take part. If he ignores the summons the claimant can proceed to a judgement in default and then arrange for the court to try to enforce it.

The Office of Fair Trading has been instrumental in persuading a number of trade associations to introduce Codes of Practice which are intended to regulate the way in which their members do business with the public. These are described in more detail in chapters 13, 14 and 15. Seven of the Codes contain an arbitration scheme which can be invoked if conciliation by the trade association concerned fails. This is intended to be a low-cost and quick way of settling disputes. I have some doubt as to whether these schemes are working as well as was intended. Two drawbacks to this form of independent arbitration are that it only applies to traders who belong to the appropriate association (and the consumer may well not know this before doing business with the trader), and that if the trader (or the consumer, if he loses and has to pay money to the trader) does not recognize the award, court proceedings have to be taken to enforce it. So one might just as well have gone to court in the first place. Whatever else may be said in favour of arbitration, there is a view that it causes confusion by proliferating methods of dispute solving.

There are two private arbitration schemes available to the public in London and Manchester. These are cheap, because they are subsidized by grants, and reasonably effective. They suffer from the drawback that no one can be forced to go to the arbitration—about a third of people against whom claims are made in the London court do not accept its jurisdiction and the claimant has to resort to other courts.

Criminal Law

All the sanctions and procedures which have been talked about so far have been those provided by the *civil* law (except for the criminal aspect of the Consumer Credit Act 1974). For individual consumers' grievances, the criminal law is less relevant, although it may be critically important for manufacturers and retailers to observe its provisions. The enforcement is normally by agencies of the State or by local authorities (but a citizen can take action himself if no one else will do so for him), and the penalty is a fine or imprisonment. The courts now have the power to order money to be paid as compensation in clear cases of financial loss, but this sort of order is less common than a fine. Action to enforce the criminal law arises when there is a breach of the rules laid down in the many Acts designed to regulate trade and protect the public. The main purpose of most is to require conformity to standards of health, of content, and of measurement. The widest set of rules relates to agriculture and food hygiene. The Ministry of Agriculture, Fisheries, and Food controls milk and dairy products and superintends the regulations affecting farming and import of livestock. The Food and Drugs Act 1955 covers the production, handling, preparation, and sale of food, and is the fount of many regulations about the cleanliness of kitchens and shops. Enforcement is by the Environmental Health Departments of local authorities. Much work is done by this agency in advising and obtaining an improvement in standards without prosecution, which only takes place in a minority of cases, where an offence is so serious that an example ought to be made.

Weights and measures

The use of weights and measures is controlled to ensure that scales are accurate, that the customer does not receive short weight, and, increasingly, that information is given about the quantity and make-up of packages. The objects, simply, are uniformity and accuracy—to ensure, for example, that a litre of petrol bought in Cornwall or in the Hebrides really *is* a litre. The scales and weights have to be inspected and marked, although there are some notable exceptions, like milk-measuring instruments. Many foodstuffs and other goods have to be sold by weight, by measurement, or by number, and many pre-packed food articles must be marked with a weight or measure—or must be sold by number in a manner which conforms to the legislation. The main Act is the Weights and Measures Act 1963, which is enforced by Trading Standards Departments of local authorities.

Quality and composition

Standards of quality and composition are regulated by a number of Acts covering precious metals, at one extreme, to seeds and fertilizers at the other. For motor vehicles and motor cycles there are regulations about construction and use, which are currently being increased by Directives from the EEC. The Consumer Protection Act 1961 is an enabling Act which allows regulations to be made about the design, composition, and construction of goods in order to give protection from the risk of death or injury. Only a handful or regulations have been made, covering oil heaters, nightdress fabric, carrycot stands, paint on toys, electric cable colour-coding, electrical fittings, and blankets. These require goods falling within their scope to be manufactured to British Standards. A breach of the regulations is a criminal offence—and it is a breach to sell, or have in stock, or store any such goods, and retailers, distributors, and manufacturers are all liable. Enforcement is by local authority Trading Standards Departments.

The Consumer Protection Act also gives, unusually, a civil remedy. Anyone who is injured by goods which are sold in breach of the Act can sue in the civil courts the trader who sold it; this is an extra form of redress, since there would be a claim against the seller in contract under the Sale of Goods Act. As the Consumer Protection Act was passed before the reform of the Sale of Goods Act in 1973, and so at a time when retailers could avoid their liability, that is probably the reason for this oddity. It is not repeated in other legislation. Now, if the seller was prosecuted, the court could award compensation to the victim, although it would not do so if there was difficulty over assessing the amount. The Government has said it wants to introduce new legislation about product safety, but so far no Parliamentary time has been found for this.

Trade descriptions

The Trade Descriptions Act 1968 makes it an offence to sell or supply any goods to which a false trade description is applied. This means any indication of the size, quantity, composition, or any other physical characteristics—the date of manufacture and the history of the goods. The Act covers statements by word of mouth as well as written descriptions. It also makes it an offence to give a false indication of the price at which goods are sold. There are some qualifications for traders who want to mark down from previous prices. Any quotation of a previous price is assumed to mean that the goods were offered at the higher price for at least 28 days continuously during the last six months. The onus is on the prosecutor to show that this has not been done—and this is extremely difficult to prove. A Review of the working of the Act was carried out in 1976 by a committee under the first Director General of Fair Trading and this report recommended the reversal of the burden of proof so that it would be for the trader to show that he *had* complied with this rule, but no action has yet been taken by Government on this or other recommendations in the Review.*

The Act also makes it an offence to make a false statement about services which a trader will provide—provided that the trader knew that it was false or made the statement recklessly. The Review of the Act found that this part of the Act was unsatisfactory and recommended that it should be a new offence to supply services, accommodation, or facilities which do not correspond to any description which was applied to them. A defence to action under the Act is that the offence arose by mistake, or on reliance on information supplied by someone else and that the trader took all reasonable precautions to avoid breaking the law. In one case a company avoided prosecution by showing that the mistake was made by its manager. Enforcement officers are understandably reluctant to take employees to

*See Bibliography p.280—Office of Fair Trading. Review of the Trade Descriptions Act 1968 (1976).

court, especially when they suspect that the man is putting into practice the policy of the company. The Review recommended that this defence should only be available if the trader can show that the method of trading which led to the offence does not involve a high risk that offences will be committed by staff errors.

The enforcement of the Trade Descriptions Act is in the hands of local authority Trading Standards Departments. There have been a large number of successful prosecutions under the Act which suggests that, increasingly, the public are aware of the protection it affords and know to whom to turn for help.

Fair trading

The Fair Trading Act 1973 widened the scope of consumer protection. This measure created the job of the Director-General of Fair Trading and involved setting up the Office of Fair Trading. OFT's main task in the consumer protection field is to keep under review trade practices which may adversely affect the economic interests of consumers in the U K and to receive and collate information and evidence about such practices.

The Director-General may refer to a statutory body set up under the Act, the Consumer Protection Advisory Committee (CPAC), the question whether a particular trade practice adversely affects consumers' economic interests. If he considers that these interests are adversely affected in any one of a number of ways that are specified in the Act (for example, if consumers are misled about their rights or obligations), he may include in the reference to the CPAC proposals for statutory control of the trade practice by an Order made under the Act.

The CPAC consists of up to 15 members with knowledge or experience of the supply of goods and services to consumers, the enforcement of consumer protection legislation, and consumer representation generally. After the Director-General has referred a trade practice to them, CPAC then have three months—which may be extended by the Secretary of State—in which to consider it and to make recommendations to the Secretary of State. The CPAC may agree with the Director-General's proposals or indicate what modifications they would find acceptable. The Secretary of State may then introduce an Order by statutory instrument which has to be approved by both Houses of Parliament. Such an Order makes the trade practice a criminal offence.

There have been four references to the CPAC, three of which resulted in Orders being made. One Order concerned information to be given by mail-order advertisers, and this Order was considerably weaker than the measure which OFT proposed in the reference to the CPAC. Another Order makes it an offence to display a sign or notice which has the effect of applying terms to a contract which are void under the Sale of Goods Act—in other words, where traders continue to try to avoid their liability under the Act for the quality and fitness of goods. The third Order controls traders' insertion of small advertisements disguised as private advertisements eliminating a very widespread hidden abuse. An Order is expected. The fourth reference was about the practice of quoting prices which were exclusive of Value Added Tax, or which makes no reference to the tax at all. OFT proposed that advertising goods and services with a VAT exclusive price should be an offence unless it was accompanied by an equally prominent inclusive price; traders should be able to quote a tax inclusive price with an indication of the price less tax; and recommended prices should not be advertised to consumers without the tax being shown.

The Director-General also has power to take action against traders under Part III of the Act. If a trader persists in a course of action which is detrimental to the interests of consumers—interests which are economic or in respect of health, safety, or other matters—and which is unfair, the Director-General can seek a written assurance from the trader that he will cease. Unfair conduct includes breaking criminal statutes to the detriment of consumers or failing to comply with obligations under the civil law. If a trader will not give an assurance—or having given one, breaks it—the Director-General may take proceedings in the courts. If the court is satisfied, it can make an order against the trader and breach of an order may be contempt of court, punishable as such by imprisonment or a fine. Over 100 such assurances have been given.

One function of the Director-General which has been used to considerable effect is his power to arrange for the publication of information and advice to consumers. OFT has issued leaflets, posters, and booklets and has promoted information sheets and meetings with local newspapers so as to provide guidance for individual consumers, especially about their rights and obligations.

It is the duty of the Director-General, as has already been described, to enforce and give publicity to the Consumer Credit Act 1974 and he is responsible for its licensing role. He also has important functions in respect of monopolies, mergers, and restrictive practices, but these lie outside the scope of this book.

Although the Fair Trading Act 1973 does not in itself create any criminal offences or set up any new civil remedies, it is a measure which enables unfair trading, once identified, to be dealt with quickly. The dissemination of advice and information, and the emphasis by successive Directors-General that they are not 'on the side' of the consumer but there to strike a balance, have done much to improve the general level of consumer satisfaction and awareness—and to bring home to traders their obligations as well as their rights.

Scotland

Scotland is, for practical purposes, a separate country, with a different legal system. It is a foolhardy English lawyer who claims to speak authoritatively about Scots law. What follows is an outline summary of some of the major differences.*

The Sale of Goods Act 1893 applies to Scotland, and the basic principles of formation of a contract there are similar. But in Scotland there is no truck with conditions and warranties. If a seller fails to supply goods or to perform any of his obligations, the Scots buyer has a general right to reject the goods and recover his money—unless the defect is very minor. If the buyer decides to retain the goods and have them repaired then he may claim the cost of the repair. The major difficulty which faces the Scots consumer is that there is no small claims procedure easily available. The Sheriff Court has a new form of process, the *Summary Cause*, for claims of up to £500, where consumers can issue the proceedings themselves without—as is almost always the case—employing a solicitor. If the other side does nothing, once he has received the summons, or if he admits the claim and offers to pay by instalments, the consumer will be able to apply for a decree without having to appear in court and present his case. If the defender wants to defend, or if the consumer does not accept the offered instalments, then a day will be fixed for a hearing. A consumer can do all the steps himself; although he can be represented by a non-lawyer at intermediate stages, he cannot at a full hearing. There he must either do it himself or employ a lawyer. There is no arbitration procedure available in Scotland under the court system. The Unfair Contract Terms Act 1977 applies to Scotland.

The credit systems available to consumers are similar to those in England, and the Consumer Credit Act 1974 applies to Scotland. There are separate Hire Purchase Acts and Food and Drugs Acts, but the Consumer Protection Act 1961 and the Trade Descriptions Act 1968 both apply in the same way. Where there is a marked difference between procedure in Scotland and in England is over prosecution. Criminal proceedings are initiated by a state prosecutor—the Procurator Fiscal. Any local authority enforcement officer has to prepare his case and then submit it to the Procurator Fiscal, who then decides whether or not to take action. (In England criminal proceedings under the Weights and Measures, Food and Drugs, Trade Descriptions, and Consumer Protection Acts—as well as any others enforceable by local government—are initiated by the local authorities themselves: in some authorities, it is the enforcement officers who attend the hearing and present the case without any lawyers being involved.) The general level of enforcement of offences under the Trade Descriptions Act 1968 and Weights and Measures Act 1963 is considerably lower than in England and Wales.

In Scotland, there is not at present any means by which criminal courts dealing with a convicted person can make any order for compensation to the victim. In Scotland civil remedies of compensation or damages are only available in the civil courts. A committee under Lord Dunpark is inves-

*For more expansive treatment, see Bibliography p.281—Clarke (1976), Martin (1977), and Scottish Law Commission (1977).

tigating the case for altering the law in Scotland, and some consumer pressure has developed for Scotland to be brought into line with the rest of the U K in this respect.

Conclusion

There has grown up in recent years the use of the expression 'consumer law'. This is merely a shorthand term to indicate all the many different aspects of the general law—whether contained in Acts or made by judges—which affect shoppers and traders. But many people seem to believe that one can simply find a book on consumer law and immediately solve their problem. Life does not work like that—would that it did! The application of basic principles of law to everyday transactions is a comparatively new concept—although it is something which ought to be readily understood by any lawyer. It will take time before it becomes generally accepted and before these new laws have been assimilated. Any lawyer will say that there is far too much legislation of all kinds; one item which might in the long run be of considerable benefit to the community would be one Act containing all facets of consumer law so that, on the civil side at least, a person—consumer or trader—would know precisely where he stood about all aspects of his relationship across the counter. However, this remains something of an ideal—there is little prospect of it coming about in the near future.

4. Consumer protection in local government

Roger Manley

The consumer movement is often thought of as a modern phenomenon, dating back 20 years or so. While this may be true so far as the development of independent consumer organizations is concerned, the roots of consumer *protection*—and of the involvement of local authorities in enforcing consumer protection statutes—can be traced back to the Middle Ages, and beyond. The most basic of all consumer protection needs are the standardization of weights and measures and control of the accuracy of instruments used for weighing and measuring goods sold to consumers.

Broadening Scope

Until relatively recently, this aspect of the work of local authorities was carried out under the Weights and Measures Act 1878 (with some subsequent amendments). It was not until 1963 that a new and comprehensive Weights and Measures Act was introduced, following some 11 years after the recommendations of the Hodgson Committee. The early 'sixties also saw a broadening of the consumer protection work on weights and measures. In 1959, the Government appointed a Committee on Consumer Protection, the Molony Committee, with widely drawn terms of reference. The Molony Committee's work was the cornerstone of a spate of Government action to extend the scope of consumer protection, including the establishment of the Consumer Council, which did excellent work until its abolition in 1970, and the passage of legislation on product safety (Consumer Protection Act 1961), hire purchase and—eventually—misleading descriptions (Trade Descriptions Act 1968).

In accordance with the UK pattern of central Government legislation enforced by local authorities, local authority Weights and Measures Departments grew and changed character to take on their added responsibilities. Their name became increasingly anachronistic and they are now known as Trading Standards or Consumer Protection Departments.

Environmental Health

Parallel with these developments, there were significant changes in the other main area in which local authorities are concerned with protecting the consumer—that of health and hygiene. Historically, one of the main stimuli to this aspect of consumer protection was the need to protect consumers from adulterated food and drink. More recently, great emphasis has been put on food labelling, to ensure that consumers are given information about what they are buying. The key statute in this field is the Food and Drugs Act 1955. This represented a major consolidation as well as an extension of the existing law, and allowed for future flexibility by providing for the introduction of regulations about the production, composition, labelling, and sale of food. At the end of 1977 the Government announced its intention of undertaking a major review of the legislation on food and drugs.

Other local authority duties in the field of health and hygiene cover the fitness of food for human consumption and the hygiene of food premises, as well as atmospheric and water pollution and waste disposal. The officers with these enforcement duties have held various titles over the years, but the widely known title of public health inspector, established in 1956, has recently given way to environmental health officer.

Reorganization

Both the trading standards and the environmental health duties of local authorities represent only a relatively small part of much broader functions which embrace education, planning, housing, social services, and much else besides. In the context of the debate about the restructuring of local government which took place in the late 'sixties and early 'seventies, there was much discussion about the level at which consumer protection functions should be pitched. The general pattern of the reorganization, embodied in the Local Government Act 1972, was that there would be two tiers of local authorities. The top tier would consist of county councils, or their equivalent, including conurbations based on the major cities, while the second tier of district councils would replace the existing urban and rural districts.

Eventually it was decided that environmental health functions should be a function of the second tier authorities, while other consumer protection functions should be placed with the top tier. This decision was not entirely in accord with the pattern adopted for the reform of local government in London some years previously, when *all* consumer protection functions were allocated to the London Boroughs, with the Greater London Council having little involvement.

The London reorganization allowed boroughs to combine for specific purposes, and a number of 'consortia' were set up. Some soon fell by the wayside, but others still continue. Variations were also possible in other parts of England and Wales when reorganization was implemented in April

1974 (one year later in Scotland), as counties were permitted to grant their consumer protection powers to district councils. This was done in only a handful of places. Some of the agreements have since been relinquished, but others persist. In one remarkable instance it is possible to observe the situation of a county council granting 'agency' to a district council, which promptly retains the county's department of consumer protection to carry out duties on its behalf. Despite some specific difficulties and anachronisms, the pattern of local government responsibility has nontheless improved.

The current picture of local government responsibility for consumer protection looks like this:

County Council (including Metropolitan County Councils and Scottish Regions)
Weights and measures
Food and drugs
Trade descriptions
Consumer safety
Fair trading
Consumer credit

District Council (including Metropolitan District Councils)
Environmental health
Shop opening hours

London Boroughs
All functions

If the definition of consumer protection duties outlined above seems to be tied closely to statutory duties, it should be added that there are many other functions performed by county councils which are not mandatory, or which may be seen as consumer protection by one authority but not by another. An outstanding example is consumer advice.

Advice

The development of consumer advice services is described in chapter 5, but it is important to realize that the present need for and form of advice as an optional service provided by local authorities is closely linked to the expansion of the statutory duties. For many years before the first separate and identifiable consumer advice service was set up, local authority Weights and Measures Departments had been receiving enquiries and complaints from the public and traders about various trading malpractices. The unique knowledge and experience of weights and measures enforcement officers made them capable of providing advice even when an enquiry was seen to involve scarcely or not at all their statutory power. In this way, advice was given on an *ad hoc* basis long before a formal service was provided. In some local authorities a particularly active or forward looking officer encouraged his authority to permit him to become the 'champion' of consumers. In other places little or no service was given outside the statutory duties of the authority.

As the duties of local authorities developed in the 'sixties so there was a move away from the traditional dominance of weights and measures and food and drugs enforcement. The former Weights and Measures Departments of local authorities began to emerge under new titles, such as Consumer Protection Department or Trading Standards Department. Enforcement of criminal law became linked with advice to consumers about civil remedies. Officers who had been somewhat remote in their concern for the protection of the community as a whole became closely associated with the resolution of individual disputes.

In some local authorities it was thought to be improper that an officer enforcing the criminal law in the trading commmunity could, in the next instant, be seeking redress for a consumer and even assisting in a civil action. Where authorities expressed concern about this it became normal for them to split advice and enforcement, even dividing them physically. However, in most cases it could be seen that the advice service was dependent on the expertise of the existing enforcement officers. In some instances advice was seen as an inferior service which merely filtered out the enquiries which might be of no concern to the enforcement of the law, which was the 'proper job' of the local authority.

The error of such an approach was clearly indicated by the professional body which represented enforcement officers, the Institute of Weights and Measures Administration. Nailing its colours firmly to the mast of a comprehensive service, the Institute changed its name to that of the Institute of Trading Standards Administration (ITSA), and set about urging both its members and the Local Authority Associations and Government that the only viable consumer protection service was a firm alliance of advice and enforcement in a single local authority department. This advice met considerable support from many consumer organizations, including Consumers' Association and the National Association of Citizens' Advice Bureaux. To a great extent the advice was heeded, and much of the present local authority policy in consumer protection is attributable to the efforts of the ITSA of that time.

Typical Functions

The system of local authority democracy in the UK, coupled with a high degree of local autonomy, makes it an ambitious undertaking to describe a 'typical' authority role. In addition, the vast differences in geographical size, population, and degrees of urbanization and industrialization all have a significant effect on the form of local consumer protection services, but an approximate picture may be as follows.

The County Council

The local authority formally constituted as the weights and measures and food and drugs authority is the County Council. It will normally place its responsibilities for consumer protection functions on a committee of the Council consisting of elected councillors. Often, this committee will have other functions. It may be called the General Purposes Committee, or it may be more specific and be constituted as the Public Protection Committee. The Committee will usually be responsible for functions of more than one Department of the Council, probably the Fire Department and the Trading Standards or Consumer Protection Department. Normally the Committee will decide all matters relevant to its business, with the full County Council merely ratifying its decisions.

The Committee will be advised by the Council's legal officer and by the chief officer of the relevant department. In its turn the Committee will place responsibilities for licensing, prosecution, staff control, and budgetary control on the chief officer, who is required to act within the Committee's agreed policy, on which he has previously advised. Therefore it is ultimately upon the chief officer that the greatest power rests for influencing the authority's activity in protecting the consumer. The chief officer of the County Council's Department is subject to the control of his Committee and the full Council but exercises considerable discretion within his delegated powers.

The District Council

The District Council performs its duties in a very similar manner to the County Council, with one significant difference. In many Districts the chief environmental health officer has no delegated power to institute legal proceedings and must discuss each intended case with his Committee before starting. In some places he may only be required to report the more doubtful breaches for consideration. My own view is that such a practice is outmoded and may result in undue delay and even prejudicial publicity where such decisions are taken in public.

Control of the Local Authority

The law of the land applies to local authorities and their officers in exactly the same way as it does to all citizens. Enforcement officers may not exceed their powers nor may they show partiality. In most cases enforcement officers who are in receipt of privileged information or who witness confidential trade processes may not pass on information. A good example of the control of officers is to be found in Section 28 of the Trade Descriptions Act 1968, which prohibits the use of any information other than for the purpose of that Act. This prevents an officer from giving evidence in a civil court if his knowledge had been gained by exercising his statutory powers.

In addition, all local authorities are subject to investigations by a commissioner for local government (or ombudsman), who may, on complaint, require explanations from an authority for its conduct.

The ultimate sanction against the performance of a local authority is expressed by the local electorate at the ballot box. However, it is probably unrealistic to anticipate that consumer protection is a determining factor in elections, although it often features prominently in electioneering. Changes in the political colour of local authorities have, in the past, had little effect on the zeal of any authority in the performance of its consumer protection duties. However, the local elections of May 1977, which saw a major swing in control of local authorities to the Conservatives, did have a marked effect on the consumer advice service given in certain areas. In some instances the advice service was reduced and in others it was withdrawn.

Objectives

The basic objective of a local authority consumer protection service (sometimes obscured by that very name) is the promotion of a fair trading environment. The authority should be concerned for the well-being of the whole community, of which the consuming public is just one part. It is therefore essential that an authority should seek to apply the law uniformly, without taking sides in any conflict between consumers and traders. However, such a basic approach is an over-simplification of the situation, for although the protection of the law must be equally available to all, it is obvious that some have greater needs than others. For example, a coal merchant receiving bulk supplies of fuel has greater knowledge and resources to protect his interests in an inter-trade dispute than the ultimate retail customer. Therefore there is a tendency for the enforcement of laws designed to regulate trade to be seen as action on behalf of consumers. If examined more rationally, however, it can be appreciated that the uniform enforcement of law is directly in the interest of honest traders, as the tendency is for the law to make continued trade difficult for the disreputable trader who indulges in practices which cannot be overcome by fair competition.

Enforcement

Consumer protection in the U K is firmly based within the ambit of criminal law. Many criticisms have been made against local authorities for their frequent use of criminal sanctions, and yet the number of prosecutions made by local authorities is only a small proportion of the offences detected or of the complaints received. Although statistics on consumer protection prosecutions are difficult to categorize because of the wide and varying description of 'consumer protection', it is worth examining data on complaints and prosecutions to see how frequently (or infrequently) local authorities have recourse to prosecution.

The Office of Fair Trading (OFT) receives returns on consumer complaints and convictions from local authorities and Citizens' Advice Bureaux (CABx) and other sources. The latest available full year figures, for 1976, are shown below in Table 4.1.

Consumer complaints	Number made in 1976
To CABx	52 269
To local authorities	
Trading standards/consumer protection	472 066
Environmental health	59 342
Others	10 057
Total for year	593 734

Table 4.1   Consumer complaints for 1976 **(Source: *Office of Fair Trading*)**.

Against this figure of complaints in 1976 may be set the convictions for offences against the criminal statutes enforced by local authorities (Table 4.2).

Criminal convictions	Numbers for 1976
Under trading standards/consumer protection	
legislation	6 286
Under environmental health legislation	6 648
Total for year	12 934

Table 4.2   Convictions for offences under criminal statutes enforced by local authorities **(Source: *Institute of Trading Standards Administration and Environmental Health Officers Association*)**.

Examination of these figures clearly indicates that the recourse which is had to criminal courts is very small indeed compared with complaints made by the public. Although it is possible to use the data given for such a broad generalization, it must be pointed out that a high percentage of consumer complaints relate to matters of civil law. In addition, the convictions obtained by local authorities are not directly linked to the incidence of consumer complaints, as enforcement officers detect infringements directly without any consumer involvement. It is probable that well under one quarter of infringements detected by enforcement officers arise from consumer complaints.

It has been suggested that a suitable alternative should be found to the criminal sanctions which are normally applicable to the trader who breaches consumer law in the U K. Such suggestions arise for a number of reasons, but the one most often quoted is the feeling that a trader who accidently gives short weight or measure or who misdescribes goods in the best of faith should not be classed as a criminal. The logic of this is hard to grasp for it is abundantly clear that short measure is directly akin to theft and that misdescription is similarly placed.

When it is argued by consumer representatives that criminal law is inappropriate, the real reason may be that, with few exceptions, criminal sanctions imposed on a convicted party do not afford redress to an aggrieved consumer. It is entirely wrong to suggest that criminal law is inappropriate—first, because the high standard of detection and investigation required of the prosecution is directly in the interest of the accused; second, because in the criminal courts the onus of proof rests firmly on the prosecution; and third, because every criminal statute clearly sets out the defences to a prosecution and the limitations on the prosecution. As the vast majority of criminal proceedings take place before a bench of lay magistrates, trivial prosecutions or matters of a purely technical nature are greeted with penalties which reflect the seriousness with which they are likely to be considered by the ordinary consumer.

Local authority enforcement officers do not adopt a partisan role or believe that all consumers are good and all traders bad. Nor do they prosecute in all cases of infringements which are detected. Rather, they apply considerable discretion to the offences encountered, preferring to reserve prosecution as a final deterrent for the careless, the reckless, and the rogue. Because of the highly technical nature of some of the law—for example, the law about food labelling—it is necessary to use the courts to interpret the law. However, once again, litigation is a last resort, only employed when a dispute arises between an enforcement authority and a trader which cannot be resolved by negotiation or compromise.

Perhaps the most important reason for retaining the role of criminal law is that the criminal consumer statutes are concerned with the well-being of the whole community rather than with finding redress for individual complainants. So a criminal prosecution usually tends to be an unbiased attempt to cause a wrongdoer to mend his ways.

Many enforcement authorities prefer to avoid litigation whenever possible because the process is so demanding on resources for both prosecutor and defendant. Protracted negotiations often take place between a trader and the local authority when it is alleged than an infringement is detected which has a wide significance. The following example of such negotiations illustrates the disinclination of local authorities to prosecute.

New products

In the mid 'seventies, a new process was introduced in the manufacture of meat products. Bits of meat were comminuted, their fibres realigned, and the resultant paste-like meat (with possible minor additions) was extruded and formed into suitable shapes. Some of the manufactured product was used in addition to untreated meat in pies and similar meat products, and some was sold as breaded 'steakettes' or in pat form. Different manufacturers used different names for their products. Some used such words as 'chopped and shaped' or 'reformed meat', while others coined new names. Enforcement authorities considered that the food labelling law required a clear indication that this meat had been treated in such a way as to make it different from 'ordinary' meat. Most manufacturers employing the process also recognized that they should use some form òf description that made it clear to the public that this was a different product.

When enforcement officers took exception to some of the descriptions being used for these foods, the majority of manufacturers cooperated with the officers in discussing the problem. Lengthy negotiations took place with a trade association which had recommended to its members a formula of words designed to comply with the law and to satisfy the food technologist, the marketing department, and the enforcement authority. At least one manufacturer who was unwilling to negotiate or even consider objections to his labels was prosecuted and convicted, but in general, new technology was introduced, a new product marketed, and all sides were satisfied without litigation.

This pattern of enforcement is largely followed today. Whenever possible an authority seeks to counsel and advise rather than to prosecute. However, local authorities are redoubtable in their enforcement of the law, having no hesitation in prosecuting when there is no alternative or when the facts clearly indicate that it is necessary. Government agencies, nationalized industries, international companies, and major firms receive the same consideration and attention as does the smallest local trader. Once engaged in court, local authorities seldom quit the fray, being prepared to pursue infringements to the highest court in the land if necessary.

Although it is a fact that prosecution policy varies from one authority to another, there is little evidence that the minor variations which exist cause any injustice to the trading community or to the public. Indeed, it may be argued that the ability to determine policy locally, permits the enforcement of the law with a desirable degree of flexibility which takes into account the trading patterns and resources of the local community.

It would be entirely incorrect to emphasize the prosecution activities of local authorities in a way that suggests that their major objective is to secure convictions. In such a complex area of law it is obvious that the threat of detection and punishment is a considerable deterrent to crime. Additionally, for a trader, the adverse publicity attracted by a conviction in the local courts may be a disproportionate penalty.

Collaboration with traders

In contrast to the controlling function of local enforcement is the educative or preventative role practised by the majority of local authorities today.

Most local authority enforcement officers have increasingly adopted a positive enforcement role whereby traders are advised and counselled how to comply with the law, remedy deficiencies, and avoid litigation. Such a role is distinct from the more negative approach of 'detect and prosecute', presenting rather a preventative and collaborative method of operation.

Collaboration takes place in many forms and is best illustrated by the local authority whose officers are well known by the development staff of all local manufacturers, so that a company consults the enforcement officer at an early stage seeking comments on the labelling and description of a new product. Subsequently, the officer is invited to comment on marketing techniques and promotional material and, when production is fully operating, a regular inspection of the product is welcomed.

However, collaboration may, with advantage, take place at a more general level—as in the continuing relationship between various trade associations and local officers or, more appropriately, with the professional body, the Institute of Trading Standards Administration (I T S A). Representatives of trade associations, representatives of I T S A, and senior civil servants from Government departments meet regularly to discuss and advise on different aspects of consumer protection. For example, such consultations have benefited the progress of metrication and are currently taking place in the context of possible new weights and measures legislation. Similarly, there is considerable collaboration under the auspices of the British Standards Institution, where enforcement officers sit with industry representatives on many technical committees drafting standards whose purpose and scope is described more fully in chapter 11. Enforcement officers also sit on the Food Standards Committee, which advises the Minister of Agriculture, Fisheries and Food on food law.

It is often argued that the opinion of a local enforcement officer is of little merit and that national manufacturers are able to avail themselves of far superior legal and technical advice. However, the very development of collaboration between officers and a large number of individual companies and trade associations must indicate that some value has accrued from past consultations. It is probable that this value lies in the wide experience of local officers, their immediate contact with the consuming (and sometimes complaining) public, and their ready appreciation of the interpretation of law most frequently adopted by the lower courts. The specialist expertise of enforcement officers in weights and measures is also of considerable help to manufacturers and traders as a source of advice on the accuracy of their equipment.

Results

The collaboration that has been described may not be marked by any individual activity that demonstrates outstanding results; rather, it is a process of gentle influences and the avoidance of mistakes or offences that might otherwise occur. However, the considerable recent development of codes of fair trading practice, described in chapters 13, 14 and 15, may be attributed to the continuing advice given by enforcement officers to traders that they should demonstrate clearly to their customers that they want to trade fairly. Also, the relatively low incidence of labelling offences in modern food production is due in no small measure to the involvement of local enforcement officers.

Perhaps the most significant result of enforcement on manufacturing and marketing policies arises from the effect of enforcement of trade description law. The knowledge that false descriptions will rapidly be detected and an appreciation of the need to trade fairly have helped to produce an admirably high degree of honesty in trading in the U K. It is significant that in the much criticized field of advertising not one conviction has been obtained against a television commercial since the passing of the Trade Descriptions Act 1968.

By contrast, the failure to cope with some of the abuses of promotional activities connected with price and price discounts is not attributable to the enforcement agencies. It is the result of the inadequacies of the law in dealing with changing price structures and practices. There continue to be many minor prosecutions over false price reductions but most of these arise from retail management rather than from marketing practices as such.

Little evidence exists to indicate that a producer's statutory obligation to label or pack products honestly has interfered with the legitimate objectives of marketing. Even in such areas as food labelling, where there exist explicit requirements to present certain information in certain ways (including size of print and contrast with background), the law has seldom forced major changes in package design, although it has ensured that consumers get the information they need.

It would be correct to see local enforcement of consumer protection legislation as one of the many checks and balances which exist in modern society. It has rather more to do with an equitable trading climate than with consumer protection and is, therefore, better described as fair trading control.

5. Local advice for consumers

Derek Prentice

Are consumers *really* short of advice? People have been seeking advice from family, friends, and neighbours ever since the beginning of a market economy based on money—and even back into the days of barter. Advice based on personal experience is by no means the only source. Shopkeepers have always been prepared to advise their customers about the goods they sell. And with the spread of branded goods throughout the economy, manufacturers are increasingly involved in giving information to consumers—for example, in the form of advertising, product labelling, and point-of-sale literature. More recently, consumer organizations like Consumers' Association (through its magazine *Which?*) provide testing and other information about a wide range of goods and services.

Isn't all this enough? Aren't consumers in danger of being overloaded with information? Without in any way decrying the value of all these sources of information to the consumer, they all have their limitations. In particular, the consumer has found it difficult to obtain expert advice which is tailored to his own particular situation or problem. If my washing machine starts disgorging dirty washing, instead of clean whites, three days after I have bought it, my family, friends, and neighbours may well not know how I should go about getting it put right. The shopkeeper may blame me and claim that I have not followed the manufacturer's instructions. The manufacturer's instructions and the *Which?* test report may not help. Where do I go for advice?

Another limitation of the established sources of consumer advice is that they are more accessible to—and more easily used by—relatively well-off people than poorer consumers. Buying goods to eat and use in the home consumes, for most of us, the largest percentage of our disposable income. The well heeled, well informed, and articulate sections of society normally surround themselves with the widest range of goods and chattels. In doing so they have the greatest opportunity to seek advice on the what and whereby from their friends and acquaintances and from other sources. When things go wrong, they are in a better position to put things right and have the self-confidence to speak up for themselves.

However, most people are not so well placed—and particularly not those who suffer the effects of social, educational and economic deprivation. These members of the community have much lower levels of disposable income and the largest percentage of their income is normally spent on rent and food, leaving less for household goods and clothing. Their opportunities to seek advice are limited, and professional contacts tend to be rare. It is important that they should receive positive help in getting good value for their money and in getting professional advice when they run into problems. Until recently, the reverse was true. While information and advice were available, it was often at a cost prohibitive for most people, or tucked away in libraries not frequented by those in need. Indeed, when the information was available it was often in a form that required a fair degree of literacy to understand it.

Need for Local Advice

It is this situation that more than anything else underpins the philosophy of the developing consumer advice services. The objective is to make freely available to everyone information and advice that will assist consumers to buy on the basis of sound information and help them to sort out any problems. In the increasingly complicated and rapidly changing shopping situation of today, there are few consumers who feel able consistently to obtain value for money, and fewer still with the knowledge and confidence to tackle their shopping complaints unaided. Making the most of the family budget is fraught with difficulties and, as the Government has acknowledged, especially in connection with food prices, consumers have never been in greater need of information and help to shop economically. Buying technically complex products which place a heavy burden on the family income is still more difficult without the information to judge value for money. Any time something goes wrong, more often than not consumers find they need the help of an impartial adviser if their complaints are to be resolved quickly and fairly. The best source of help may be a local advice centre.

If consumers are to be helped effectively at local level, certain needs should, ideally, be satisfied.

—They need to be able to obtain impartial pre-purchase information and advice about specific goods and services, about methods of buying (for instance, the different types of credit), and about their legal rights concerning faulty goods, guarantees. etc.
—They need access to simple but effective help in dealing with those complaints that seem to be intractable; this help should cover all categories of consumer complaints, not just those which involve a breach of criminal law by the trader.
—They need to be able to voice their opinions and explain their problems and needs as consumers to a body at local level which will take notice and

action where necessary—for example, collating opinions and evidence and passing them through the appropriate channels to such bodies as the Department of Prices and Consumer Protection and the Office of Fair Trading.

—They need to receive consumer education in the most general sense— that is, to have their rights explained to them and to be shown how to be informed and careful shoppers.

—They need protection from illegal trading practices by effective local enforcement of national legislation.

How are such needs met? Three different kinds of institution are involved—Citizens' Advice Bureaux, local authority Trading Standards (or Consumer Protection) Departments, and Consumer Advice Centres. All have rather different structures and functions.

Citizens' Advice Bureaux

The Citizens' Advice Bureaux were first developed in 1938, and were designed to deal with the multiplicity of problems the community would face in the event of a wartime emergency. Funds which originally came from central Government were used to develop an extensive system of some 1000 bureaux during the war years. In 1945, a Government circular encouraged local authorities to provide funds for the Citizens' Advice Bureaux in their areas, and the Local Government Act 1948 gave councils specific powers to finance bureaux. A large number of local authorities continued their financial support for bureaux but some did not. The result was that by 1950 the number of bureaux had fallen to less than 500. During the next decade the survival of the bureaux depended heavily on the devotion of the C A B workers.

The turning point as far as consumer advice is concerned came in 1963 when, in response to the Molony report on Consumer Protection, to which the National Association of Citizens' Advice Bureaux (N A C A Bx) gave evidence, the then Board of Trade provided a significant grant. This grant has continued ever since and is now the responsibility of the Department of Prices and Consumer Protection. Further growth has been possible since December 1973 when Sir Geoffrey Howe, Minister of Trade and Consumer Affairs at that time, announced a development grant of £1·43 million to be spread over five years.

This grant, with increases for inflation, now totals £2·5 million. Also, individual bureaux get support from local authorities and other local sources. One consequence of this has been that the number of bureaux increased from 473 in December 1963 to 710 in March 1977, and during this period the number of enquiries handled rose from 1·28 million in 1966 to over 2·7 million for the year 1975-6. While the bureaux provide a general advice service, not confined to consumer enquiries, an analysis for the year 1965-6 reveals that over half their total enquiries fell into three main categories: family and personal; housing, property, and land; and consumer, trade, and business.

The major advantage of the bureaux is their widespread (though not comprehensive) national coverage. Their disadvantages in the field of consumer affairs are as follows: lack of adequate finance often means that the service is operated in relatively inaccessible offices away from the public eye; they generally only deal with post-shopping matters, such as consumer complaints; and, being manned mainly by volunteers, they cannot match the professionalism of highly trained, full-time consumer advisers. However, one cannot under-estimate the substantial contribution the Citizens' Advice Bureaux have made in assisting consumers to obtain a fair deal, and as the link between individual bureaux and local authority Trading Standards Departments strengthen, some of the disadvantages will lessen considerably.

Trading Standards Departments

The functions of Trading Standards Departments are described fully in chapter 4. In this context it is worth saying that, virtually without exception, they are involved in giving help and advice to consumers with complaints and problems, although inevitably their statutory enforcement functions tend to take precedence.

Consumer Advice Centres

During the late 'sixties, Consumers' Assocation (CA) began studying methods of bringing consumer advice to a much wider public than the then predominantly middle-class readership of *Which?*. In 1969, CA opened the UK's first Consumer Advice Centre (CAC) at Kentish Town, in North London. This CAC, which was to run for two years and deal with over 40 000 enquiries, had as its predominant features the fact that it was situated in shop premises in the main shopping street and that it gave impartial pre-purchase advice and information free to all comers. This CAC was in many ways an experimental project, but above all it proved to be the spark for one of the most rapid developments ever seen in local government in the UK. By 1971, a wealth of data and experience had been assimilated from this highly successful experiment. During its two years not only had it proved its worth but it had enabled CA to build up the information systems and training requirements that any future centres would need. Following this success, CA in 1971 launched a campaign to persuade local authorities to establish similar CACs. Central to this campaign were the facts that CA had proved the need for such centres and that for maximum usage they had to be situated in prime high street sites. The CACs needed to be operated like a shop, in an informal atmosphere, and to provide general consumer information, pre-shopping counselling, and help with post-shopping complaints. It was this overall approach which for the first time in the UK offered to those in need a complete and professional consumer advice service. Prior to this, advice on complaints, but not pre-shopping advice, was available from some of the local authority Trading Standards Departments and, of course, from CABx.

From CA's first approaches to local authorities in 1971, it took just one year to see the first local authority CAC opened. This was in the London Borough of Greenwich and within a short time the London Boroughs of Havering, Lambeth, Hillingdon, Haringey, Wandsworth, Merton, and Camden (who took over the original CA centre in Kentish Town), plus the Scottish town of East Kilbride, followed suit. Originally, CA had envisaged CACs being operated by the Trading Standards (or Consumer Protection) Departments of local authorities. However, of the initial crop of CACs only one came under such a department's direct control (though the pattern is very different now). Indeed, in the case of the London Borough of Havering, the local authority asked CA to staff and operate the CAC for them. This proved to be an invaluable opportunity for CA to develop the service further, together with Havering Council, and the CAC became a focus for the new expanding service and a showpiece for other interested local authorities. From its opening in September 1972 to the reorganization of local authorities in May 1974, Havering was to prove an outstanding success, both in its own right and as a model for other local authorities to copy.

Support for the development of CACs was given added impetus when, in November 1973, the then Conservative Government's Minister for Trade and Consumer Affairs, Sir Geoffrey Howe, held a series of meetings with local authorities and other interested parties in London, Cardiff, and Edinburgh to discuss and encourage the expansion of local advice centres.

Local authority reorganization in 1974 (England and Wales) and in 1975 (Scotland) was, however, to prove the turning point. This was particularly true in the new large Metropolitan authorities. Of all the services for which they were responsible, only one, Trading Standards (Consumer Protection), brought them into direct contact with the public. Local politicians were not slow to realize this. The number of CACs in the UK grew from a handful in 1972, to 75 in 1975, 110 in December 1976 and around 125 in May 1977, though it should be pointed out that a number of local authorities, especially those with dispersed and predominantly rural populations, decided not to set up CACs.

The services offered by CACs vary enormously from area to area, depending on policies laid down by the controlling local authorities.

Those CACs providing the widest range of services for the consumer tend to be those run by local authorities who operate their services on the basis of the original concept of a CAC, as conceived by Consumers' Association in 1968-9. They therefore have Consumer Advice Centres in the best high street sites; their centres are run predominantly in a shop with professional displays and an awareness by the staff that they, like any retail concern, have to maximize their customer flow. It is from this positive approach that consumers benefit, for from this style of operation comes the widest range of services offered—and a greater probability that disadvantaged consumers will be reached.

Irrespective of the expansion of advice and information provided by CACs, three foundation services remain paramount: general information on consumer matters, pre-shopping advice, and a post-shopping service.

General consumer information

The role of a general consumer information service is to answer the vast array of questions on which the consumer—or local trader—seeks information. At its simplest, this can be informing the consumer where the nearest branch of a particular shop is or where brand X can be purchased locally, but of course the questions can also deal with problems requiring much more fact-finding and explanation. The range of information provided is enormous and the centre should be able to cope with a wide range of problems—from how to remove red wine from a carpet to informing a consumer of his or her rights in law. Traders have sought advice on the latest EEC Directives affecting business, or how they should word a particular advertisement they wish to place. It is the proud claim of most CACs that no one is ever sent away without an answer to his or her problem.

Pre-shopping advice

This is one of the major services still misguidedly underestimated by a significant number of local authorities. Its function is to help purchasers to obtain the best possible value when buying major domestic consumer durables. If a prospective purchaser comes to a CAC seeking advice, say on a washing machine, the staff will not just turn to the latest *Which?* report. The aim is to provide a far more personal service than any magazine could ever hope to do. In pre-shopping advice the consumer is able to have an individual discussion with a trained adviser. This discussion can take up to an hour during which the consumer and the adviser will identify the needs and requirements of the former; the adviser will be pointing out what the product can or cannot do, and what the advantages and disadvantages of particular features are. The purpose of this process is to help the consumer to choose a product that will meet his or her specific requirements. After their discussion, the adviser will refer to an information store on all the nationally available washing machines (or any other of 20 different domestic consumer durables). With this the adviser can take the requirements of the consumer and match them to the brands which are suitable. Normally, this means that the consumer leaves the centre with a choice of, say, four or five products, all of which are geared to his particular requirements.

So successful has this service been that in some areas shopkeepers actively encourage prospective buyers to use the service before making a purchase. Choosing products from an informed standpoint—and buying a product knowing exactly what it will or will not do—helps everyone. It helps the consumer obtain the best value for his or her money, and helps the shopkeeper because the purchaser has chosen from information supplied in a totally unbiased and factual manner. This is important—many complaints arise not because the product is inherently faulty but because the consumer has false hopes of its performance.

The provision of positive help to consumers in dealing with post-shopping complaints is a vital function of any consumer advice service. CACs are not there to be on the side of the consumer, right or wrong but—and this is particularly important in relation to complaints—to see that fair and equitable trading takes place and to deal with matters in an objective and unbiased manner.

Post-shopping complaints

These fall into two categories: those of a criminal nature (for example, offences against the Trade Descriptions Act 1968) and those of a civil nature (for example, complaints falling within the Sale of Goods Act 1893). The distinction between the criminal and civil law is dealt with more fully in chapter 3. In this context, enforcement of the criminal law is in the hands of local authority Trading Standards (Consumer Protection) or Environmental Health Departments, to which such complaints as are made to CACs are referred. Indeed, the investigation of such complaints was the responsibility of local authorities long before the advent of CACs. However, since their introduction the number of complaints of a criminal nature has risen considerably. This service and the methods used are common to all centres in the UK. The same cannot be said for dealing with complaints of a civil nature—there is a large disparity between local authorities in the degree of assistance given. Whereas in the case of criminal offences the local authority has the power to prosecute, in civil cases the consumer himself or herself must take action through the courts. When consumers being their civil complaints to CACs, most CACs advise them of their legal rights. Likewise, most CACs insist that consumers first give the seller the opportunity to make redress. If the two parties can still not agree, then an adviser telephones or personally visits the seller in order to find out the seller's side of the story. The adviser also informs the seller of his rights and responsibilities in law and makes whatever suggestions seem appropriate in each case. If the adviser then still considers that the consumer has a case and the seller is not prepared to meet his responsibilities then the CAC advises the consumer on how to take action against the seller through the courts. The majority of CACs do not go any further than this. However, an increasing number of CACs actually help consumers with their court cases, advising on the completion of the various forms and, if required, actually accompanying the consumer to court.

Price information

While these three basic services are the foundation of any C A C, they are only that—a foundation. The more successful C A Cs have built up a wide range of other services to help the consumer. Probably the most common of these is local price information. The C A C at Havering was the first centre to participate in such surveys, the purpose of which is to tell consumers the price of about 30 items normally found in the weekly shopping basket. The surveys contain information gathered from at least five supermarkets and from a number of fruit and vegetable shops as well as butchers. Some C A Cs simply display the results in their centre windows, while others offer the additional service of distributing the information in leaflet form. Since 1976, such surveys have been financed by the Department of Prices and Consumer Protection.

Consumer education

It can be said that a prime function of a C A C is to educate its clients. One of the most successful methods of achieving this is by way of display-based projects. The object of such projects is yet again to help consumers to obtain the best value for money. An example of this might be compiling a display of kitchen towels and showing the unit price of each product. Outstanding successes in this area are projects showing the contents of Christmas crackers and Easter eggs, since these are classic examples of products where consumers are generally unable to see what they are getting for their money before buying. A similar method is applied to tasting sessions. Here, C A Cs take such products as coffee and soft drinks and invite consumers to see if they can taste the difference between various brands. The object behind these sessions is simple—if you cannot taste the difference between the dearest and the cheapest, why buy the dearest? C A Cs provide a whole range of services analogous to these examples, but for the future perhaps the most important role they are developing is consumer education in schools. Classes are encouraged to come to the C A Cs not only to see the work carried out, but to use the centres' facilities for their projects.

Involvement with manufacturers

The involvement of manufacturers and retailers in the development of C A Cs has been fundamental to their success. It was foreseen in the original concept of centres that a significant part of their success would depend upon them having a shop environment. This, of course, involved displays of various products on which the C A C would be advising. As such products will always have to be current models, CACs have come to rely heavily upon the goodwill of manufacturers to lend them examples of their products. The support of manufacturers, particularly in lending equipment, has been enormous. In addition, manufacturers now regularly send to CACs information on their latest product ranges, and the staff find manufacturers very helpful, not only in lending products but in assisting them with information and advice on complex technical matters. A number of larger companies have produced consumer education material, much of which is displayed in CACs, and one large trade organization now regularly holds seminars especially for consumer advisers.

It was always envisaged that the exchange of information would be a two-way process. The staff of CACs come into contact with a large number of consumers and so have a wealth of up-to-date information on the response of consumers to the latest products. Regrettably, few companies have yet taken advantage of this.

Liaison with retailers

The involvement with and the relationship to CACs of retailers has in the past been a delicate issue. On the one hand, CAC staff want to maintain good relationships with their neighbours in the high street, but, of course, many of the complaints they will be dealing with and trying to resolve will be coming from these same shops. Initially most retailers view the opening of a CAC with some understandable misgivings. It is seen by them as yet another 'shop-bashing' exercise but, given time, the vast majority come to accept that the service is there to help achieve fair trading in the community in an unbiased and impartial manner—and that means helping the trader as well as the consumer.

Nothing gives advisers more satisfaction than helping traders when they bring their problems to the CAC, and the relationship between the local trader and the longer-established CACs tends to be excellent. Perhaps the biggest laurel given to CACs by traders is when they send their customers to the CAC for pre-shopping advice, or where the advice centre is asked by the trader to arbitrate in a dispute with a consumer. Both these are not infrequent occurrences. This indicates the mutual trust which has evolved between CACs and traders.

Future Developments

The number of CACs has grown rapidly in the last six years, but what does the future hold? In 1976, the Government gave local authorities £1·4m to establish a further 49 CACs and in 1977-8 the Department of Prices and Consumer Protection gave a further £3·0m to meet the running cost of the 120 CACs in operation throughout the UK. Government support at this kind of level is continuing in 1978-9. However, financial and political changes in local authorities have led some authorities to question the extent to which they should be involved in such an activity. One local authority, West Midlands, has closed all its nine C A Cs. One can anticipate that the overall pace of expansion may well slow down, with expansion in one area offset by contraction in another, but the existence of a network of C A Cs, however patchy it may look on the map, is not really in question.

This geographical patchiness—not just of C A Cs, but of all advice services for the citizen—was one of the preoccupations of the 1977 reports on advice services produced by the National Consumer Council (N C C) and Scottish Consumer Council (S C C).* The kind of consumer advice that is the C A Cs' prime function, and the consumer complaints function that constitutes a significant minority of the work of the Citizens' Advice Bureaux, represent only part of the citizen's needs for advice at the local level. Family problems, housing, finance, employment, social security, education—the range of subject matter is almost limitless. The N C C report, while recognizing that there is a strong case for a 'mixed economy of advice centres' comprising both statutory and voluntary bodies, pointed out the need for a fundamental assessment of the direction in which advice services should go. It pointed out that the lack of close collaboration between all the agencies involved was wasteful and confusing to the public, that the services were unevenly distributed and that there was no clear indication that areas of greatest deprivation were getting the services they needed.

At the time of writing, the Government had not announced its reaction to these and other points made in the N C C and S C C reports. There are two problems of outstanding importance which need to be resolved. First, how to provide an integrated system of advice for citizens which draws on the best characteristics of generalist (e.g., C A Bx) and specialist (e.g., C A C) advice services. Second, how to reconcile the need for a geographically comprehensive advice system with the differing autonomy of both local authorities and voluntary organizations.

So far as the C A Cs themselves are concerned, one of the most worrying aspects of their development has been that too many are purely complaint shops, rather than comprehensive C A Cs. This may often be the direct result of a chief trading standards officer's own philosophy towards this facet of the service. Trained primarily in the enforcement of legislation, they sometimes fail to grasp the concept of a comprehensive approach that includes pre-shopping advice, consumer education, and a wide variety of information dissemination as part of a C A C's work. The result of such a policy can be seen in the fact that these complaint shops see each year far fewer clients than those true C A Cs. If C A Cs in the future are to play their full role in helping consumers then this narrow approach must change to a broader and more enlightened one.

We have so far only seen the beginnings of the role that C A Cs can play in the community. The scope for C A Cs' activities is as wide as vision and

*See Bibliography, p.282—NCC: The Fourth Right of Citizenship (1977), and SCC: Let the People Know (1977).

70

resources will allow. As technology becomes more complex and its results affect the consumer in his home and in the market place, the C A C must constantly develop and adapt its service in order to help the consumer to be protected against the worst abuses of a technological society. We would do well to remember the words of George Herbert: 'The buyer needs a hundred eyes, the seller not one'.

6. Nationalized industry consumer councils

Alisdair Aird

Nationalized industries are largely insulated from normal consumer pressures. On the one hand, they tend to be monopolies—or, if they are not, to be structured and provided for in such a way that they can behave as if they were monopolies. On the other hand, they can look to the State for protection and in particular for financial support, and this shields them from the commercial need to strike a good market bargain with their customers in the way that private sector firms must if they are to survive. Given this background, it is perhaps surprising that the great public corporations have put as much effort as they have both into market research and into marketing and product improvement. What role in this has been played by an institution which at present has no parallel in private industry, and which to some extent might be a substitute for consumer-based market forces—the consumer council?

Origins

The fuel industries, railways, and post office all have statutory councils or committees which differ in title, purpose and composition, but all of which—broadly speaking—are charged with putting the consumer case to their industry, both about the industry's general operations and about individual complaints from consumers. These bodies are known widely as 'nationalized industry consumer councils' or NICCs, although some are actually called user councils, or consultative councils or committees. Most of the NICCs were originally cobbled together rather hastily as part of the post-war nationalization legislation (they had not been a thought-out part of the planned programme), and in the patchwork of diverse influences and intentions behind their birth lie many clues to the way they have worked since then. (The recent more purpose-built exception is the Post Office Users' National Council (POUNC), though the Post Office itself has been run as a State concern since the seventeenth century).

The initial impulse behind the NICCs was a political one. The Conservative opposition argued that it was dangerous for the State to grant a monopoly to an industry—in this first case, coal—and then to leave the right to fix prices entirely to that monopoly; and there were backbench doubts within the Labour Party itself about the extent to which this new monopoly could be relied on to work altruistically in the interests of the nation and of its customers. The Domestic Coal Consumers' Council (DCCC), the first of the NICCs, was devised as a piece of window-dressing to stem criticisms on these lines. But its powers for independent action were in practice severely truncated by its being made virtually a part of the Ministry of Fuel and Power, with coal producers and merchants sitting on it alongside the consumers themselves. And the Minister of the day, Emanuel Shinwell, confessed that it was the *appearance* of usefulness in the new NICC which mattered, even if the Council actually proved abortive.

So the DCCC was designed to pay lip-service to the idea that consumers should be given some say in the workings of the coal industry—to be a palliative to consumer-oriented opinion, rather than a vehicle for its successful expression. If it was to have a practical value, that value was to be in providing a forum for representatives of the industry, the trade, and consumers to talk to each other.

The other NICCs of the late 'forties followed much the same lines. Their organization was regional rather than national. In the case of gas and electricity, this was because the industries were to be organized regionally, although they have since become more national than regional; in the case of transport, because complaints were thought likely to be more local than national (there was to be a national committee to consider the more central issues). It is worth noting that, at the time they were set up, it was not envisaged that the NICCs would deal with consumer complaints.

The intention that the NICCs were to be rather less than independent was again made clear: they were to be paid for by their industries. The Transport Ministry actually spelled out that its NICCs were not to be independent consumer watchdogs, but were to be part of the Transport Commission's own machinery.

Composition

One special factor leading to the establishment of the gas and electricity NICCs was to have an almost preponderant influence over their character—indeed, it has controlled their composition right up to the present day, although the reason for it is now virtually lost in history. The new industries were not so much nationalized private firms as nationalized local authority undertakings, so throughout the local structure of both major political parties there were quite a lot of noses out of joint. To soothe things, it was laid down that at least half the members of the NICCs were to be drawn from local authorities.

So, some 30 years ago, there were the NICCs: some 850 people of standing, most of them local councillors, brought together into a total of 37 committees, meeting once a quarter or so, usually talking things over with senior managers from the relevant industry; the small staffs paid for either by the industry or the sponsoring Ministry; getting their information primarily from the industries; having the right to consider individual complaints, but not the power to enforce any decisions they might take about those complaints. In addition, the gas and electricity NICCs spawned a network of over 100 local committees, with a similar pattern of membership.

The members of the regional and national NICCs were appointed by the Ministers charged with overseeing the affairs of the relevant industry—for example, the Minister of Fuel and Power for the gas, electricity, and coal NICCs. The chairmen were paid and, in the case of gas and electricity, sat on their industry's management boards, emphasizing the way in which these NICCs were to be as much a part of their industry's own structure as the transport NICCs' sponsoring Ministry said they were intended to be. In 1972 the Gas Act abolished regional gas boards—and thus its NICC chairmen lost their Board seats. And today the Department of Prices and Consumer Protection sponsors the NICCs.

Handling Complaints

Since they started, the most notable development in the gas and electricity NICCs has been the way that their complaints work has snowballed until it now dominates their character as well as occupying most of the time of their staff. The great increase came in the 'sixties: for example, the number of complaints handled by the South Eastern Electricity Consultative Council rose from 81 in 1961-2 to 920 in 1969-70, and this tenfold increase over the decade was quite typical. So, although they were not intended primarily as a form of complaints machinery and in their earliest years dealt with perhaps only two or three dozen each a year, that is what they have become.

How well do the NICCs fill this role which they have taken on themselves? First, it should be emphasized that the NICCs are supposed to consider a complaint only if the person involved has previously been in touch with the industry about it—and, presumably, not been satisfied by the industry's response. Taking this into account, the NICCs deal relatively successfully with complaints: on the evidence of independent surveys (by the Consumer Council in 1968,* Consumers' Association in 1974, and the National Consumer Council in 1976†) they satisfy most people, leaving only one in five not at all satisfied.

However, there are quite a number of hidden lessons, both for the NICCs themselves and for managers of any business concerned with

*See Bibliography p.282—Consumer Council (1968).
†See Bibliography p.283—National Consumer Council (1976).

customer satisfaction, which emerge from a more detailed analysis of their complaints work.

Communication

Any process designed to deal with individual complaints must have as its first task provision of communications channels so comprehensive that anyone, whatever their problem, can get it dealt with sympathetically. There are obvious difficulties here, in finding the right balance between the two extremes: on the one hand, the faceless monolith utterly impregnable to complaint or query; on the other, the organization so studded with complaints desks and arbitrators as to frighten off any potential customer by making them think that all this must mean complaint is an inevitable consequence of doing business with them.

At first sight, the NICCs seem a promising approach: independent but with close ties to the nationalized industries, offices in every region, and (at least in the case of gas and electricity) literally hundreds of local representatives to give local coverage. Moreover, their independence, combined with the way in which they are supposed to deal only with complaints or problems which have been left unsatisfied by the customer's dealings with the industry itself, gives another important advantage. It emphasizes the way that a firm can draw a line between the general run of problems (including what most customers might well think of as 'complaints') which it would expect to deal with routinely as a part of its normal business and as an acceptable and necessary component of any but the very simplest relationship with customers; and, on the other hand, the—hopefully very much rarer—real complaint which marks a breakdown of the firm's relationship with a customer.

The gas industry is beginning to use this distinction rather well in practice: it has recently introduced centralized regional telephone service/reception centres where staff deal both with routine service requests and with problems or complaints, without the defensive reaction of seeing complaints as attacks. That this is paying dividends was demonstrated by the National Consumer Council's 1976 survey referred to above. The National Consumer Council found that people with serious problems—that is to say, when they had to make more than one approach to the industry—were more likely to get at least some action than, say, people with electricity problems; people were far less likely than with electricity to give up altogether because they thought it would be pointless or futile to seek a solution; moreover, people who had fed their complaints into this telephone reception system were more likely than others to report a satisfactory solution.

Despite popular mythology (the 'Bernard Levin's mother' syndrome), the gas industry seems to be scoring to some extent over electricity by being readier to treat problems and complaints not as criticisms which must be denied but as questions which need a satisfactory answer. But if there is a difference between gas and electricity in this respect, how much greater is the difference between both and public transport. There, the National Consumer Council's survey showed that although over one in three users reported a serious complaint in the last year, virtually none of these people had done anything about it—usually because they thought it would be futile, and that no-one would take any notice. It would be easier to dismiss such a general reputation for being impervious to complaint and dissatisfaction as something irrelevant to commercial success if the public transport undertakings had not been losing customers altogether on such a massive scale.

Impact on Policy

Solving individual complaints is a less important side of customer relations than improving performance to avoid complaints. Many of the strongest reasons why the NICCs have had only limited success in persuading their industries to meet the needs of their consumers more efficiently are unique to nationalized industries. Most obviously, some of the most critical decisions—about investment plans, for example—have been so heavily modified by Government intervention that industry efficiency and customer satisfaction hardly get a look-in. And the NICCs have never been given the sanctions they need to make them an effective substitute for market price-demand and competition mechanisms as a restraining factor in wage bargaining and price setting—a factor which the nationalized industries have largely been able to ignore.

Limitations

Beyond these points, the National Consumer Council in its report on the NICCs, in common with earlier assessors (most notably the 'old' Consumer Council and the House of Commons Select Committee on Nationalised Industries), found that the NICCs had been limited in influencing their industries by factors which might be expected to operate in private industry as much as in nationalized. On the one hand, their power is that of persuasion, and they cannot be expected to persuade unless they use their information and research to the full (which they have sometimes not done either by default or by reason of the inadequate time given them by their industries in which to consider some proposal). On the other hand, however persuasive any independent observer or critic—at most, a non-executive director, which in effect is what the electricity NICC chairmen have been within the industry itself—that persuasion is unlikely to shake a strongly held management position. And finally, the NICCs' position has often been weakened by unduly restrictive terms of reference: the transport NICCs, for example, are currently allowed to consider only a restricted range of questions concerning rail, and virtually no bus ones (recent Government proposals would widen their scope).

The converse of this is that successful NICC policy moves have necessarily been backed by a conjunction of favourable circumstances, conditions which might well be seized successfully by any firm.

Post Office watchdog

The most telling analyses of management proposals have often been those carried out by the Post Office Users' National Council (POUNC). Its statutory terms of reference are unusually open-ended, so it has felt it can question every aspect of Post Office business. In doing this it has put a lot of effort into *ad hoc* research, sometimes employing consultants for the purpose, and (as the National Consumer Council has commented) its reports are in substance reminiscent of those of the National Board of Prices and Incomes. So they have carried weight, usually with the outside world (giving POUNC the important strength of widespread consumer sympathy, which the other NICCs have not always had), and often with the Post Office itself—to its own advantage as well as to that of its customers. What might be termed the style of POUNC—very much the personal style of its late chairman, Lord Peddie—serves as a fruitful example in this field. Its work gives a taste of the impression that would be given by the endeavour of a single-minded executive director whose business had given him the specific task of questioning every major policy decision against the yardstick: 'Will this maximize the value which customers get from our service?'; and given him whatever specialized staff resources he called for in doing this; a supporting committee including the firm's biggest customers; and the duty of looking into unresolved individual complaints and seeking satisfaction for them through the department concerned. Moreover, this 'customer director' would also be expected to develop higher customer performance targets for the entire business, setting continually higher standards of service rather than seeking merely to do less for higher prices.

But that general picture is something for the future, certainly so far as the UK is concerned (two American precedents are described in chapters 19 and 20). What of the more practical immediate details?

Complaints records

An important resource to all the NICCs, except that for coal, has been their record of complaints. This resource has not always been used efficiently: for example, regional NICCs may each have been following up, in regional isolation, complaints of national prevalence; too often, the target has been solution of the complaint itself, rather than agreement with the industry to provide automatic solution for such problems in future. Complaints records and their analysis have tended to be too sketchy and unsystematic (the same problems 'filed' under different headings in different regions, for example). But the gas NICCs now use a more or less consistent recording and analysis procedure which lets them—particularly through their national body—speak authoritatively about complaints trends both to the British Gas Corporation and even to individual gas appliance manufacturers. This pinpoints what might be called 'consumer pressure points', which it is so obviously in everyone's interest to eliminate.

Future development

There is a great deal of support, from the industries and the NICCs alike for the idea that industry and consumer both benefit from pre-operational exposure of industry plans to friendly but unequivocal representatives of the consumer point of view. To work effectively, this sort of influence demands that such exposure must be full and frank, and preferably should include policy options. The consumer representatives, for their part, should be fully armed with research-backed knowledge of consumer attitudes, experience, and needs. Ideally, in terms of any round-table discussion, they should also be a fair match for representatives of the industry. These three requirements have not all been met invariably for all the NICCs—though there is no reason why they should not be, either for the NICCs themselves or for any 'consumer director' which a private firm chose to appoint with the same objective of improving customer service.

What the NICCs are

The NICCs are statutory bodies appointed mainly by the Secretary of State for Prices and Consumer Protection and funded through that Department. Their duty is to represent consumer interests to the nationalized industries. All except the Domestic Coal Consumers' Council handle several thousand individual complaints each year.

Gas. Twelve regional Gas Consumers' Councils, about two dozen members and seven staff each (often appointed from within industry). Chairmen (paid) and up to 19 others on London-based National Gas Consumers' Council (NGCC) with stronger staff; NGCC is the official statutory link both with British Gas Corporation and with DPCP. Also, some 75 local committee members in each region, making up four to eight District Committees.

Electricity. Twelve regional Electricity Consultative Councils, about two dozen members and five staff each (often appointed from within industry). Chairmen paid, as part-time Electricity Board members. 'National' council, covering England and Wales, set up in 1977. Also District Committees, similar to gas.

Coal. Domestic Coal Consumers' Council (DCCC), London-based: includes merchants and suppliers as well as consumers. Unpaid chairman, small staff. Complaints instead dealt with by trade's own Approved Coal Merchants Scheme; DCCC members join its panels. Alone among NICCs in that National Coal Board has no statutory duty to inform or consult it.

Post Office. Post Office Users' National Council (POUNC); 33 members, 16 staff—as with coal, seconded civil servants. London-based. Also Scottish, Welsh, and Northern Irish Post Office Users' Councils, closely linked to POUNC but with separate right of access to Minister. And some 200 Post Office Advisory Committees not formally linked to POUNC: usually local initiatives by Post Office or business.

Transport. Eleven Transport Users Consultative Committees (unlike gas and electricity, no direct alignment with British Rail's regional management). Some 20 members; very small staff (seconded from British Rail) often shared between two TUCCs. Largely confined to rail questions, not allowed to consider fares, charges, or proposed service cuts. TUCC chairmen (paid) and up to seven others on London-based Central Transport Consultative Committee (CTCC), the formal link with Minister. TUCCs have additional formal role of carrying out hearings on proposed rail closures. A 1978 Government White Paper (The Nationalized Industries: Cmnd. 7131) proposes that some of the present restrictions on the CTCC's work should be lifted, to give it more general concern with surface public transport.

THE RESPONSE OF INDUSTRY AND TRADE

7. A marketing view of the consumer

Peter B. Blood

Hospitality has been cynically described as an attempt to make people feel at home when you wish to hell they were . . . . I can't help thinking that some marketing executives display the same ambivalence towards their customers. They know they're there all right but they often wish they weren't!

Of course, this situation represents a rare extreme and most marketing people do an excellent, skilled job under increasingly difficult business conditions. But it would be foolish to suggest that all is well, and if there are customer dissatisfactions it becomes, by definition, a clear marketing responsibility to put these right. My authority for saying this springs from two sources: first, the Institute of Marketing's own definition which states that 'marketing is the management function responsible for identifying, anticipating and satisfying customer requirements profitably'; second, the words of that highly-respected management guru, Peter Drucker, who said that 'consumerism is the shame of the marketing concept'. Since consumerism represents the organized expression of consumer dissatisfaction, both the failure and the responsibility of marketing become very evident.

Different Kinds of Marketing Failure

The reasons for this failure are not hard to find and are summarized below (I would not claim that the list is exhaustive).

—Conceptual failure. Unless an entire company, from the chairman downwards, is prepared to accept the marketing approach and, consequently, to give the satisfaction of its customers the highest corporate priority, it is virtually impossible for staff further down the line to implement a successful marketing programme. I myself have too often heard the plaint from junior marketing executives that, although they want to get it right, the boss simply doesn't understand or want to know.

83

—Organizational failure. As a result of the failing just mentioned, there are too many companies that do not possess the organizational structure to deal with consumer affairs or consumer problems. Even where such a structure does exist, the staff employed are frequently too junior for the responsibility involved and, additionally, have not received sufficient training and motivation.

—The 'semantic cover-up'. This is a situation which has occurred too often in British industry. The semantic cover-up occurs when a perfectly capable sales manager is suddenly told that from tomorrow onwards, he will be called 'marketing manager'. His duties remain as before, he is given no additional training, but the company sees this as, in the first place, a kind of inexpensive promotion, and second, a form of equally inexpensive obeisance to what they see as a fashionable management technique. At its best, the semantic cover-up represents muddled thinking and the belief that marketing management is really no more than a slightly elitist form of sales management. At its worst, it represents a rather shabby form of intellectual dishonesty.

—Education and training failure. Even where the semantic cover-up technique has not been used, too many marketing people are promoted, or appointed, to positions for which they are not professionally qualified. Good, broad experience is, of course, essential, but sophisticated modern marketing now demands a reasonable and established threshold of theoretical knowledge. Anything less than a balance of these two requirements means that the company's marketing, and consequently its customers, may suffer.

—Remoteness. Especially in consumer goods marketing, the company may be hundreds, even thousands, of miles from its customers. Psychologically, they might almost be on the moon. Market research does, of course, close this gap, but its methods tend to be rigid and formal. Retailer contacts, often inhibited by competitive pressures, are too likely to take the form of unconstructive criticism and prejudice.

Marketing and the Point-of-Sale

While these are important factors affecting a company's relationship with its customers, I believe the most important one of all is the degree of attention paid by a company to the *point-of-sale*—the shop, store, or supermarket where the goods are made available to and, hopefully, transferred to the customer. I doubt if many consumers realize quite how much human effort goes into the process of bringing a product before them—including product, market, and customer research, technical development, tooling, production, investment finance, distribution channels, advertising, packaging, and sales. You could say, in truth, that the entire resources of the company are deployed in order to bring the product to the customer. That effort could be represented by an inverted cone, the apex of the cone representing the point at which the product is seen by, or offered to, the customer (see Fig. 7.1). So is it not strange, and wrong, that so much genuine effort should be so often— too often—set at naught by the inefficiency, lack of knowledge and lack of interest of so many shop assistants? I believe that this sets up a kind of reverse cone—the cone of dissatisfaction— spreading out to a wide circle of potential customers—so that one might depict it as a diabolo (see Fig. 7.2). It is at the junction of the apexes that the problem occurs. Some well known stores have, of course, discerned this problem and have first-rate programmes of training and motivation. But much more needs to be done so that the cone of dissatisfaction becomes, in fact, a cone of satisfaction. A frequent source of irritation, for example, is the complete absence of information, leaflets, or descriptive literature on high priced consumer durables such

Fig. 7.1

Fig. 7.2

as hi-fi equipment, cameras, washing machines, freezers, refrigerators, heaters, etc. The lack of appropriate information is, in my view, a considerable disincentive to purchase. Marketing is about big and little things. We have all concentrated, inevitably and correctly, on trying to get the big things right. My point is that we have sadly neglected some of the 'little' things and it is these, above all, which are causing customer irritation and frustration.

My marketing colleagues may well be thinking, at this stage, that I have been too critical of them and insufficiently sensitive to the problems they have to face and resolve. So let us now turn to some of the feelings and fears which marketers have when considering their customers in particular and 'consumers' in general. They would certainly draw a very firm distinction between the two categories.

I have not the slightest doubt that the majority of British companies fully realize the importance of customer goodwill and take reasonable steps to ensure that their products and services are providing satisfaction. More and more directors and senior executives are marketing-oriented and have received specific training in marketing. The large companies, in particular but not exclusively, have admirable market research and complaints-handling facilities. My chief observation here is that too many companies are looking at their customers through the wrong end of a telescope and that, in consequence, there is both a structural and a psychological remoteness between themselves and their customers. I shall suggest an answer to this later.

The Consumer Lobby

A very different situation exists when one considers the attitude of industry to what might be called the consumer lobby. The early criticisms of the

Consumers' Association, the publishers of *Which?*, have now waned, but there is still a feeling that the impartiality of the product testing is limited by the test equipment available and the somewhat specialized reactions of the field testers. While the presence and policies of John Methven gave the Office of Fair Trading a head start in terms of commercial confidence, the same cannot be said for the National Consumer Council nor of the many consumer pressure groups that have sprung up in recent years. Here there is a feeling, among industrialists, of political pressures at work which may or may not be in the best interests of consumers and which certainly will be destructive to industry and commerce, upon which the whole future prosperity of this country depends. Again, a sense of apprehension exists in regard to what new legislation and other controls are being planned in Brussels. Many industrialists believe that the effect of excessive and restrictive consumer legislation will be to increase the costs of manufacture and distribution of consumer goods and that such legislation will also seriously inhibit the development of new products. This applies particularly in the pharmaceutical field, where the cost of proving a new drug is likely to become so high that a manufacturer may decide against its introduction. It will clearly become necessary, therefore, to strike a balance between reasonable customer safety on the one hand and the deprivation of patients on the other. I am utterly convinced that, unlike certain intractable problems with which we are faced in Britain today, the fundamental, practical problems of improving customer relations and of countering the root causes of consumerism can be overcome without undue difficulty. It is essentially a marketing problem, and therefore a marketing responsibility. For this reason, I believe that initiatives must be taken by representative bodies such as the Institute of Marketing and, of course, by companies themselves. The theme must be to build communications bridges, whereby the problems and difficulties on both sides can be ventilated and, as far as possible, resolved. Consumer organizations must be made to feel that their contributions can be of real assistance to companies but, equally, that some of their demands may be either undesirable or impossible for very clearly defined and quantified reasons. I am very pleased to report that, following an initiative taken by the Institute of Marketing, regular and constructive informal meetings now take place between the Institute, the Office of Fair Trading (which provides the chairman), and two of the leading consumer organizations, Consumers' Association and the National Federation of Consumer Groups. I hope that this successful arrangement will broaden and deepen as the months go by.

Building Bridges

Consumer affairs conferences, such as that organized during March 1977 by Forbes Publications in association with the OFT, IM, CBI, the Retail Trading-Standards Association, and the US Embassy, are also most useful, and the presence on that occasion of two US specialists, Mrs Esther

Peterson of Giant Food Inc. and Mrs Satenig St. Marie of J. C. Penney Co. Inc., produced two of the most constructive sessions on consumer affairs that many British marketing executives had ever heard. Mrs Peterson's contribution is set out in chapter 19. This leads me to the next level of bridge building: shortening the actual and psychological distance between the company and its customers. Market research alone cannot do this. The technique of recruiting a leading consumer affairs specialist to design and implement a 'consumer programme' for the company is nothing less than brilliant entrepreneurial marketing and, like all good ideas, has been rapidly copied in the US. There are some important considerations in making such an appointment if it is to be of real benefit to a company's customers and not merely a cosmetic treatment.

—The person must have a credible background of consumer affairs activities.
—The appointment must be at board level and the person must be intellectually 'comfortable' at that level.
—The responsibility must essentially be first to the customers, then second to the company.
—Reasonable independence of action must be guaranteed.

I find this one of the most interesting and constructive developments affecting consumer affairs in recent times and it represents the building of a most important communications bridge between manufacturer and customer.

But, however useful and constructive the meetings, the conferences, the consumer affairs appointments, and other bridge-building activities may be, we cannot escape the fact that the starting point for action must be the marketing director or the managing director. It is he or she who must realize that good customer relations are good business and that every angry or frustrated customer sets up a radiating cone of dissatisfaction resulting in far more than merely one lost order. We cannot and must not shirk our responsibility in this vital marketing task. I conclude by quoting what I said in the first issue of the recent *Marketing and the Consumer* series, jointly sponsored by the Institute of Marketing and the Office of Fair Trading, and published as a supplement to *Marketing*:

A truly great step forward will have been taken when companies stop merely paying lip-service to the marketing concept and finally accept its inescapable basic message: it is that the first, vital purpose of any business is to secure and keep customers. Once this thinking permeates every level of the company, from the Chief Executive to the shop floor, we can look forward to a new era in which the interrelationship between the customer and the supplier is based on mutual confidence and trust.

8. Market research and consumer attitudes

Elizabeth Nelson

Social forces are increasingly measured by market research techniques, and consumerism as a social force has been investigated in some detail over the last decade in the U S* and over the last six years in the U K.

We have found in the U K that the general public's view of consumerism is often very different from the 'official' view of consumerism. Market research can help in describing what is most concerning people in their role as consumers, and how rapidly that concern is likely to be exhibited in consumer behaviour.

The Nature of Consumerism

Early in 1972 qualitative research was carried out among representative samples of the U K population.† The hypothesis was formulated that consumerism is neither a simple nor a single phenomenon but that it is constituted from a multitude of different attitudes. Alienation from business and industry and a feeling that the consumer's point of view is neglected both play a part. But from a popular point of view consumerism does not mean hostility to capitalism or misplaced middle-class idealism. It comprehends the anxiety many people feel, in all walks of life, that the size and organization of both private and public enterprise militate against their individual self-interest. Although there may in this anxiety be an element of over-dependence on legislation and some misunderstanding of the importance of profit to the economy, popular consumerism is not necessarily *against* anything; nor is it confined to those with a party political affiliation.

The *Monitor* surveys of social trends in the U K have identified three aspects of consumer concern which are briefly outlined below.

---

*See Bibliography p.285—Barksdale (1972), Buskirk (1970), Gaedeke (1970), Kotler (1972), and Wight (1972).
†See Bibliography p.285—Nelson (1973).

—A feeling—even a fear—that big business, whether private enterprise or nationalized, will, left to its own devices, degrade the quality of the products and services it supplies. This factor is named *consumer scepticism*.

—An anxiety that exaggeration and sensationalism in the media, in advertising, and in sales promotion will over-persuade people to buy goods and services they do not need or which are inappropriate to their needs. This factor is named *anti-hypocrisy*.

—A suspicion that both complex marketing activity (e.g., new forms of packaging, a greater artificiality in packaged foods) and Government action or inaction (e.g., on motor traffic, aircraft noise, and pollution) are gradually despoiling the natural environment beyond hope of recovery. This factor is named *concern about the environment*.

The important thing about these three factors is that they are independent of each other. Those who are concerned about one factor are not necessarily concerned about either of the other two. People who are sceptical about the quality of goods and services are not necessarily concerned about pollution to the environment or being manipulated by media or advertising.

There has been little change in the proportions of the population registering disquiet, as Table 8.1 shows.

	1973 (%)	1976 (%)
Percentage of adults who are:		
Very sceptical about business	39	41
Very opposed to manipulation	59	60
Very concerned about the environment	29	28

Table 8.1 **(Source: *Monitor* 1973-76).**

Base = 1973—representative sample of 1250 adults aged 16-65.
1976—representative sample of 1500 adults aged 16-65.

Who Are the Consumerists?

The third trend, concern about the environment, is the only one which could at all be described as distinctively middle class, and it has been getting less so over the last four years.

	Upper-middle (%)	Middle middle (%)	Skilled working class (%)	Unskilled, semi-skilled and unemployed (%)	All (%)
All in age group 15-65	14	24	40	23	100
Consumer scepticism	13	22	44	21	100
Anti-hypocrisy	15	26	39	20	100
Concerned about environment	17	26	42	15	100

Table 8.2   Social class profile of consumerist trends, October 1976. (**Source: Monitor 1976**).

Consumer scepticism in 1973 was highly associated with the skilled working class, but Table 8.2 shows it to be equally distributed among all social classes.

A relatively high proportion of those who are most concerned about media and advertising are over 45. It is these older people who are most conscious of the increased complexity over the last 20 years of sales promotion methods and perhaps the growing persuasiveness of advertising. Those who have grown up with commercial television, retail price competition, and more sophisticated sales promotions are more inclined to accept the hard sell as part of the environment.

In these ways, therefore, it is the older and more established members of the community who are likely to press for more consumer safeguards. Younger people are likely to be more self-confident, although just as sceptical as their elders in the face of sales pressure (see Table 8.3).

	15-24 (%)	25-34 (%)	35-44 (%)	45-54 (%)	55-65 (%)	All (%)
All in age group	22	21	19	19	19	100
Consumer scepticism	22	22	21	18	17	100
Anti-hypocrisy	16	21	19	19	25	100
Concerned about environment	18	21	20	19	23	100

Table 8.3   Age profile of consumerist trends. (**Source: Monitor 1976**).

Consumerist Attitudes and Consumer Behaviour

Those people with the greatest degree of concern in our society are the 'activists' and these activists can be easily identified in any further investigations by establishing certain basic information at the beginning of the interview. For example, do they appear to be disturbed by the quality of products, or to be afraid of being manipulated by advertising or media; or do they suspect that pollution is ruining the natural environment?

Activists tend to carry through their attitudes into behaviour. Those who are most sceptical of British business and fear that the quality of products and services is deteriorating prefer to buy retailers' own-label brands.

There is a strong connection between being concerned about the quality of goods and services and preferring to buy own-label, as Table 8.4 shows.

	All (%)	Consumer sceptics (%)
'Packaged products sold under a store's own name are as good as any of the nationally advertised brands.'		
Strongly agree	20	32
Agree	52	58
Neither agree nor disagree	14	6
Disagree	13	4
Strongly disagree	1	—
	100	100

Table 8.4   Attitudes to own-label goods. (**Source: *Monitor* 1976**).

During the period of rapid inflation, many people became extremely sceptical about the fairness of big business (public and private). They discounted the rise in import costs, wage deals, and the fact that business needs profits in order to invest. Housewives became particularly resistant to price increases. In an economic climate of this kind, it becomes more difficult for manufacturers of some types of products—washing-up liquids and some canned foods, for instance—to persuade women that the 'guarantee of quality' offered by manufacturers' brands can justify higher prices. This has led in turn to an increasing approval of own-label brands which, whatever the objective truth of the matter, are seen as offering a fairer deal than many branded items. As many as 7 out of 10 consumers strongly agree that packaged products under a store's own name can be virtually as good as well known, advertised brands. Housewives are prepared to trade off a possible small variation in quality against a price difference. Very often consumers have more faith in an own-label product than they do in the recommendations of consumer organizations.

Those who are most concerned about being manipulated by media and advertising react by demanding more safeguards over the content of advertising and sales promotions—in particular, free gifts, competitions, and stores' advertising of cut prices.

Concern about the environment is particularly closely related to concern about packaging and certain pollutants (see Table 8.5).

	1973 (%)	1976 (%)
Which of these, if any, are damaging to the environment?		
Factory waste in rivers	88	86
Road traffic noise	40	32
Sewerage in the sea	73	70
Petrol exhaust fumes	74	63
Pesticides in the soil	50	46
Factory smoke	59	50
Oil slicks at sea	72	64
Rubbish and litter dumping	79	71
Cigarette smoking	29	33
Ads in countryside	15	16
Aircraft fumes and noise	49	36
Over-packaging	35	40

Table 8.5   Attitudes towards damage to the environment. The figures add to more than 100% because many respondents mentioned more than one item. (**Source: *Monitor* 1973-76**).

Concern about packaging is something held in common by consumer sceptics, 'anti-hypocrites', and environmentalists.

The Power of Ordinary Consumers

Government and industry can no longer assume that they know what consumers want, whether they are consumer activists or ordinary members of the public. Businesses must maintain direct personal contact with their final customers wherever possible and communicate directly with them. If exceptionally high price increases become necessary then these should be explained, and the premium price for branded goods should be justified. Consumers in the U K have yet to test their power as U S housewives did—when beef prices escalated there, millions refused to buy.

It is also necessary for manufacturers to know when sales promotions are seen as relevant and when they are not. Hostility to free gifts as the basis of sales promotions disappears if the promotion is seen as 'relevant'. Testing promotions nowadays is often a check on whether the housewife views the promotion as adding value to the specific article she is buying. For example, a duster 'given' with furniture polish might be preferred to a tea towel.

There is a widespread public demand for open (as against coded) date stamping and, although this is often inconvenient to both manufacturers and retailers, there is a growing realization that housewives are increasingly coming to look for a 'consume by' date on all perishables.

Fear of additives or chemicals in prepared goods may be based partly on ignorance—for instance, a lack of realization that food content and permitted maxima of certain flavourings are already well regulated. The high scientific integrity and degree of concern for the consumer shown by the Food Standards Committee is seldom appreciated by consumers. Nevertheless, the growing interest in 'natural' foods, which would by now have gained much more momentum but for high prices, shows that a large proportion of housewives are genuinely disturbed by articles which appear from time to time mentioning the banning of colourings which have been permitted in this country while outlawed by the E E C or the U S agencies. A growing number of articles in the press discuss such issues as cholesterol levels, or the dangers of a high carbohydrate content in the diet during early life. Specific issues come to light, such as the danger of the high salt content in some baby milks, and there is a growing discussion of the dangers of sugar.

There is merit in considering printing more nutritional information on packages, such as the calorific value or the type of fat employed in preparing the product. In general, manufacturers must be ahead of public opinion in showing essential information comprehensively and comprehensibly on packaging.

Table 8.6 shows people's attitudes on certain consumer issues. Many consumers mistrust the integrity of business, and this leads them to lend a high degree of support to a national consumer body such as the National Consumer Council (N C C). A large proportion believe that there should be more control over the content of advertisements.

They believe there should be further control of the declaration of true interest rates by hire purchase and finance companies. There is some degree of support for Government control over the activities of multi-national companies.

	Agree (%)	Disagree (%)	Don't know (%)	Margin in favour (%)
'There should be more control over what can be said in advertisements.'	65	15	20	50
'We really need the National Consumer Council to prevent big business from taking advantage of the consumer.'	72	8	20	64
'It makes me very angry when hire purchase companies do not make it clear what interest rates they are charging.'	80	19	1	61
'Multi-national companies like I B M, Ford, Esso need to be closely controlled by the U K Government.'	39	27	34	12

Table 8.6 **(Source: *Monitor* 1976).**

Increasingly, companies now consider how they can face the pressures to which they are subject and turn them into advantage for consumers and for themselves. They are increasingly interested in knowing how better to handle complaints, in giving information on product usage, and in liaising with consumer pressure groups.

Limitations of Market Research

Market research can be an effective link between consumers and industry and between consumers and Government. I have concentrated on the contributions that market research can make to the investigation of consumerism, but there are problems in using market research techniques. First, market research very often measures attitudes, and it is known that people tend to give responses which are thought to please the interviewer rather than be completely honest. Second, attitudes are often not related to subsequent behaviour. We cannot be content with defining 'attitudes' as responses to a market research attitude question. For example, looking back to the list of pollutants in Table 8.5, it might be possible to alter the percentages by a change of emphasis.

Attitudes are not necessarily related to actual behaviour. We have seen that there is a high proportion of people who are in favour of the N CC when asked a direct question and yet the spontaneous awareness of the existence of consumer organizations, as Table 8.7 shows, is very low. Furthermore, the proportion seeking help from a consumer body, as Table 8.8 shows, is very low.

	Men (%)	Women (%)
(Base = 877 young men and 936 young women.) *'What organizations or groups can you think of who represent the interests of consumers?'*		
% *who mentioned:*		
Consumers' Association/Council	31	23
Which? magazine	20	14
Dept. of Weights and Measures	16	13
Citizens' Advice Bureau	10	9
Dept. of Health/Health Inspector	3	2
Government Price Commission	2	2
Local action groups	1	1
Motoring associations	2	0
Nat./Local Press/TV	5	2
Other organizations	24	14
None	27	36
Don't know/not stated	9	15

Table 8.7 Awareness of consumer organizations. The figures add to more than 100% because many respondents mentioned more than one item. (**Source:** *Living in Britain*, J. **Walter Thompson 1973).**

	Those who bought an unsatisfactory product (%)	Those who had difficulties about repairs or replacements (%)
	(Base = 570 housewives)	(Base = 351 housewives)
Housewives who had had this difficulty		
% *who had:*		
Complained to the shop	60	67
Talked to the family	56	58
Made a point of not buying again	38	26
Talked to a friend	36	44
Complained to the manufacturer	28	34
Complained to the local authority	2	4
Complained to a consumer body	1	1
Complained to MP/newspaper	1	1
None of these	9	6

Table 8.8   Method of complaint or action taken by dissatisfied housewives (**Source:** *Housewives' Attitudes to Marketing,* **1974, J. Walter Thompson**).

A third problem in using market research to measure consumerism relating to the design of actual questions asked of members of the public is discussed in a recent paper published by the Advertising Association.* Corlett compares the results of a survey on the public's attitudes to advertising carried out by the EEC in nine EEC countries during October/November 1975 with surveys carried out in the US and the UK.

Corlett makes a number of important points about the misleading interpretation of research results. The first is that members of the public are prepared to give a fairly high level of assent to the general propositions critical of advertising which are offered to them. 'It cannot simply be taken as direct evidence that government action which attempted to remove the source of the criticism would receive widespread popular approval'.

The wording of similarly worded questions produced different answers. For example, the EEC survey used the statement 'advertising often misleads consumers'. The AA survey used two apparently similar questions 'the ads you see are often misleading' and 'I am frequently misled by the ads I see'. It can be seen from the results below that in the first two columns, where neither of the questions have a specific personal reference, the results are very similar. But a comparison of the last two columns illustrates the difference made by using a personal reference. Whereas 67 per cent feel that *people* are frequently misled, that figure falls to 28 per cent who think *they themselves* are misled. By implication, people are much more ready to attribute misleading effects of advertising to other people than to themselves.

*See Bibliography p.285—Corlett (1977).

	*EEC Survey 'Advertising often misleads consumers' (%)	†AA Survey 'The ads you see are often misleading' (%)	†AA Survey 'I am frequently misled by the ads I see' (%)
Agree entirely	33 ⎤	29 ⎤	12 ⎤
	⎬ 78	⎬ 67	⎬ 28
Agree on the whole	45 ⎦	38 ⎦	16 ⎦
Disagree on the whole	13 ⎤	20 ⎤	30 ⎤
	⎬ 16	⎬ 28	⎬ 68
Disagree entirely	3 ⎦	8 ⎦	38 ⎦
Don't know/no reply	6	5	5

*EEC 1975 survey, 1438 adults.
†AA 1975 survey, 1067 adults.

Table 8.9   Comparison of different questions about advertising as 'misleading'

Corlett concludes that one must be extremely careful about the interpretation of results which relate to public issues; and in the case of measuring attitudes to advertising we are more concerned to find out how the *respondent himself* perceives the effect of advertising on *his* own behaviour.

Market researchers must measure the right attitudes if they wish to predict consumer behaviour. Furthermore, market research should—as far as possible—be structured by the consumer. It is no good asking questions which are designed to appease either consumer organizations or manufacturers: qualitative research among consumer activists which allows them to talk about their concerns is essential. If used intelligently, market research can be predictive. It can suggest what the consumer of the future is likely to want in terms of new products and benefits.

9. Handling consumer complaints

Chris Moore

Perhaps one of the most disturbing side effects of the growth of the consumer movement has been the escalation of the 'Us and Them' philosophy—the belief among many businessmen that consumerism is in some mysterious way part of a political plot to paint damaging pictures of the free enterprise system, and, among consumers, the belief that 'Big Business' exists solely to exploit the masses for the personal gain of the bosses.

In fairness to consumer organizations, they have seldom set out to spread a gospel decrying the motivation of business concerns, preferring to see themselves as ginger groups encouraging companies and corporations to step up their efforts to provide higher standards in the goods and services they purvey. And, similarly, the best of the international corporations have grown up on the principle that the customer is and always has been right.

However, although there may not be a direct clash between corporations and consumer groups as such, the growth of consumerism might be said to have acted as a catalyst in a growing warfare between company and customer. The introduction of consumer legislation, while frequently closing monstrous loopholes, has also had the less desirable effect of hardening commercial attitudes towards what is sometimes regarded as unwarranted outside interference.

In effect, there has been a massive switch from the legal approach which prevailed for so long, that of *Caveat Emptor*—let the buyer beware—to the new attitude which might be described as *Caveat Venditor*—let the seller beware.

Business Fears

Business in general is totally confused about the rise of consumerism and the increasingly hostile attitudes encountered among individual consumers. Many businessmen feel there is some dark plot being acted out against them—possibly started by the active consumer bodies, then taken up by the media, and finally by the individual purchaser.

To some extent the businessman has cause for complaint. The media, for instance, might be said to have devoted a disproportionate amount of space and air time to consumer complaints in recent years. Unfortunately, such complaints are seldom handled by people with any business knowledge or any better motives than the search for a good story—like the battling old age pensioner who appears, on the facts as presented, to have been swindled by some vast, uncaring multi-national company.

In effect, the media have been doing the consumer a considerable disservice. By setting themselves up as complaints investigators, they could be said to be actively encouraging the customer to take complaints to them instead of to the company concerned—and ultimately fostering the notion among the public that this is the correct route to travel. If the media really wanted to bring about a better service for the public it should, in my opinion, be encouraging companies to introduce or improve their own complaint handling services.

From such a background has grown the 'Us and Them' attitude. One newspaper even has a consumer column trading under that heading. It is all very unfortunate, because there is really no basis for such a philosophy. Companies, large and small, are made up of people. It is groups of people who formulate company policies—and, frequently, one man or woman acting entirely upon his or her initiative who determines the face of the company as far as the lone consumer is concerned. When a shop assistant is rude to a customer it is, after all, highly unlikely that this is in line with company policy. Yet the chances are that the customer will form an instant opinion that the company does not know how to treat its customers.

The Individual Consumer

The main reason for far too many companies not having an effective complaint handling system is quite simple—because of the pressures of modern business life they have just not got around to the matter of the individual and his particular grumbles. It is a problem of many businesses coping with economic and environmental pressures that the only route to success lies in sheer growth. In the constant survival-of-the-largest battles which are being fought out daily in the world's boardrooms, the consumer is in grave danger of becoming little more than a statistic. When one of the meaningless statistics has the temerity to ring company headquarters and ask to speak to the chairman it is, perhaps, no wonder that a person geared to thinking of a customer as a purchasing unit, member of a socio-economic group within a given income bracket, is not educated to deal suddenly with the rantings of Mrs Adams from Rochdale whose washing machine has developed a nasty hiccup.

Even companies which profess to be sensitive towards the individual, often do not take the trouble to install a proper complaint handling system.

Too often a complaint from a customer is handled by the executive on whose desk it happens to land. Inevitably this leads to many unsatisfactory results—for, while one executive may take the proper course of action and resolve the matter speedily and effectively, another may, through indifference or inability, leave the customer thoroughly disgruntled. Big business is, as I say, only people.

One has to ask if such companies, despite their protestations that they regard the customer as all important, would allow the same casual approach towards say, accounting, market research, or personnel. Of course not. There would be departments to handle such matters, staffed by fully qualified people with sufficient resources to ensure they were able to achieve maximum efficiency. Why, then, should the customer be allowed to receive such casual treatment?

Customer Relations Department

There is only one proper fashion in which consumer complaints should be handled. That is through the establishment of a department which has as its sole function the handling of all correspondence from the company's customers. Obviously, the size of the department will depend on the size of a company and the scale of its operations: it might consist of one person, or a properly constituted group working to agreed systems.

I know there will be many company chairmen or chief executives who will disagree immediately—usually because they profess to like handling all complaints personally. I have heard a number of captains of industry proudly proclaim this philosophy. Unfortunately it is one which has to be treated with some suspicion.

A chairman of a large public company may well sign all replies to complaints but he is not likely to be in a position to investigate every one personally. It is difficult to imagine, for instance, the chairman of a retail company with outlets throughout Britain setting off to Scunthorpe to interview a salesgirl—or, come to that, even picking up the telephone and grilling the shop manager. He may do it once in a while but in most cases the complaint will be handled by the nearest executive, whose secretary will draft the appropriate letter for the chairman to sign.

It is not unknown for consumerists to condemn the handling of complaints by a specialist with a title such as 'customer relations officer'. Some regard it as insulting if replies to complaints are given by anyone other than the chief executive. Conversely, the same people are often tempted to point out with some sarcasm that although a letter carried the signature of the chief executive it was, almost certainly, not written by him.

This could well be true, but does anyone seriously expect the leading executive of a large company to have the time to devote to individual complaints—except, perhaps, in very rare cases—any more than he would personally supervise the accounts department or the personnel division? If he did claim to be in such a position, his shareholders might themselves have cause for complaint.

Qualifications of a customer relations officer

What is involved in setting up a Customer Relations Department?

The first requirement is the customer relations officer himself or herself. It is an appointment which needs to be made with great care, not only because of the straightforward administrative requirement of establishing systems and running an office but, even more important, because of the need to convince other important executives throughout the company of the vital role his department has to play.

Unlike the appointment of, say, a chief accountant or a personnel officer, there are no obvious qualifications to be satisfied, no degrees or diplomas to be produced. However, it goes without saying that it is helpful if the person appointed has a good knowledge of the company and its product or service. In an engineering company, for instance, there is no need for the customer relations officer to be a fully qualified engineer—but, equally, he ought to know the difference between a wing-nut and a widget.

The basic qualifications, apart from a thorough knowledge of how the company structure works, are an enquiring mind, a completely unbiased approach towards the consumer, and the ability to communicate, both inside and outside the company. A good command of the English language and an outline knowledge of consumer law are also essential.

Perhaps the ideal person for the post is one of the company's rising young executives who would be appointed for, say, two years, accepting the role as a rung on the executive ladder. Thus, someone who has already received a grounding in the company's operations, perhaps having served in several departments, would have the opportunity to perform a highly useful service while seeing how the work of those and other departments relates to the consumer.

One of the strongest reasons for favouring this approach is that it means that in the long run a number of executives who have risen to higher positions in the company will have spent time in direct contact with the consumer and, it is hoped, will continue to relate their experience to their future roles. It is a frequent criticism of company structures that, in an age of ever increasing specialization, far too many higher executives have never had this direct link with the consumer.

Reporting line

Ideally, the customer relations officer will report directly to the chief executive. This may not be in strict accordance with the company's family tree, but it is vitally important for a number of reasons.

First, it gives the customer relations officer direct access to the ultimate decision maker. Second, it gives the chief executive a direct involvement in the work of the customer relations officer and his department and, therefore, an indirect link with the customer. Third, it should give the customer relations officer the status he requires if he is going to carry out his task efficiently—for in many cases he is going to find that certain of his colleagues give him far more trouble than any consumer.

Many departmental heads, for instance, refuse to believe that those under their control could possibly contribute in any way to a customer grievance. Others just don't care, maintaining that anyone who complains must be a crank or a troublemaker. Their inclination may be to ignore complaints completely—but not if the customer relations officer comes directly within the chief executive's orbit.

Having taken the decision to appoint a customer relations officer and set up a department for handling correspondence from the consumer, several vital steps have to be taken to ensure the system is properly established.

First of all, the relevant employees have to be told of the appointment. There may be a case for using the house journal, if one exists. Trade union officials must be informed. In all cases it must be emphasized that the customer relations officer is not going to be a spy on company staff, any more than he is going to indulge in sending bland platitudes to customers. He is there as a protector of both the company and the customer, to ensure that both obtain the best from each other. From the company point of view, the object is to obtain a satisfied customer, even after he has had cause for complaint. For the consumer, the customer relations officer is there to ensure that he receives satisfaction, an apology where it is due, a refund or credit note where goods or services have been sub-standard, and, ultimately, a consumer who will continue to use the company's products.

Routing

It is necessary to take certain follow-up action to ensure that all complaints arriving at the company's factories or offices reach the right destination. There is little point in having a Customer Relations Department if letters continue to be passed from the mail room to the nearest available desk.

The first step might be to advise customers on how to make a complaint should it be necessary. The name and address of the Customer Relations Department might be printed on material supplied to consumers or, in the case of certain specialized businesses like restaurants, included on menus or on bills, All staff in company outlets should be made aware of the correct department and address, especially mail room staff and switchboard operators. In the latter case, special arrangements should be made to cover periods outside normal buiness hours.

Similarly, receptionists should be fully briefed in case of personal callers to the company's office. It is by no means unknown for a disgruntled consumer to walk into the head office of a multi-national company, demanding to see someone in authority because he wishes to make a complaint. It will not help to smoothe his ruffled feathers if he is kept waiting for half an hour while a harrassed receptionist tries to find out what to do with him.

Having taken steps to route complaints to the right destination, we come to the question of how they should be handled. A great deal will depend, of course, on the nature of the company's business and the volume of correspondence being handled. However, there are certain procedures which must be followed if any system is to work properly.

Complaints procedures

First of all, it is essential for a date-stamp to be used, indicating exactly when a complaint reaches the office. With great respect to the Post Office, where complaints are not exactly unknown, letters can be delayed mysteriously. If an irate consumer sends a follow-up letter demanding to know why his original missive has not been acknowledged, it will be helpful to know just when it arrived.

Second, the complaint should be logged so that the Customer Relations Department can keep an eye on its progress. A simple log sheet can be drawn up—giving details of the consumer, his complaint, action taken, etc.

Next comes the question of assessment. Once the complaint has been read, the customer relations officer has to decide whether it is one which will take some time to resolve or whether an instant reply can be given. It may be a complaint identical to one received a few days previously, in which case there may be no need for any investigation. A reply can be dictated and despatched almost by return, for all the relevant facts will be to hand. If, however, it seems that a lengthy investigation is called for, then the first step to be taken is to send a letter of acknowledgment. This can be a simple letter advising the consumer that the complaint has been received and that a full report has been called for. A further letter will be sent as soon as all the facts are available. Should, for any reason, the investigation take even longer than anticipated, a second 'holding' letter should be sent to the consumer.

Investigation

Having acknowledged the letter, the investigation begins. Again, the structure of the company determines how the customer relations officer sets about his task. He may be able to work mainly over the telephone or, in the case of a single-site factory, by visiting departmental heads. It may be necessary for him to copy the consumer's letter and forward it to an executive so that it can be studied in detail.

Similarly, the manner in which various executives report back to the customer relations officer is dependent on company size and structure. Some may favour the introduction of a report form but in general this is not satisfactory, as most complaints require individual attention and cannot be dealt with on a formal question-and-answer basis.

When the customer relations officer has all the facts at his disposal, he comes to what is perhaps the most important part of his duties. the assessment of whether the complaint is justified or unjustified. On this decision rests any further action he may take.

Of course, before reaching this decision he has to be completely satisfied that the reports he has been given contain a correct version of the facts. It is not, unfortunately, unknown for a departmental head to go to any lengths to avoid suggestions that those under his control have slipped up in any way. In such cases, the facts presented to the customer relations officer may be distorted or glossed over. It is here that it is vital for the customer relations officer to be completely impartial and, above all, sufficiently aware of a company's methods and make-up to decide whether or not he is satisfied in his own mind. After all, he is the man who is going to pen the letter to the consumer, and presenting a false view based on incorrect information may land him in deep water should the irate customer come back with incontrovertible evidence.

If the customer relations officer is quite satisfied that the complaint is not justified, the customer must be given the company's version of the facts and told, in straightforward terms, that the company does not consider itself at fault in any way. It will be helpful if he can be given as much background as possible concerning the investigation which has been made.

Follow-up

If the complaint is considered justified, and the company is seen to be at fault, then the customer relations officer finds himself with further important decisions to make. There are, of course, degrees of failure, ranging from sheer negligence to a quite unforeseeable accident.

While in most, if not all, cases an apology will be called for, a decision must be made as to whether this alone will be sufficient. The customer relations officer, having weighed all the factors, must choose between limiting his reply to an apology or going much further. It may be a case for a refund, a replacement, or a credit note—or even, in a case where simple correspondence is not enough, a personal visit to the customer.

All this, of course, is simplifying matters—possibly making it appear that the customer relations officer, apart from making a few basic decisions, has a very simple role in life. Nothing could be further from the truth. The customer relations officer has to be something of a detective, something of a diplomat.

He must also have the right conditions to work in. This will not happen unless the company has taken one fundamental decision—that the consumer is vitally important to the company and, as such, merits every consideration when he enters into correspondence with the body which has sold him goods or services. After all, the purchasing department of a large company expects its members to be treated as persons of some importance by its suppliers. Are not the members of the purchasing department spending large sums of money with them? If this is the case, why shouldn't the humble individual consumer—who may, in his own eyes, spend large sums on buying from the company—also be allowed to enjoy a certain sense of importance.

Information Feedback

If the company does take the decision to handle complaints properly, it may find itself in the happy position of receiving a bonus in the shape of an information feedback which may, in the long term, save the company money, avoid law suits, and help to build up an even better relationship with the consumer.

The efficient customer relations officer does not only solve problems for the consumer. By using information gleaned from the complaints received, he also discovers many instances where action can be taken to ensure that such complaints are not received in the future. And, bearing in mind that for every consumer who actually complains there are likely to be dozens, if not hundreds, more who register their disapproval in the most telling fashion of all—by taking their custom elsewhere—this could easily assist in maintaining the company's profits—or, on occasion, improving them.

Management, like any other body of people, is fallible. Sometimes managers make mistakes of their own. Sometimes they fail to spot those made by other people. In either case, the result could lose them custom or even take them into the law courts.

The case of the underweight cheese

Take, for example, the case of the underweight cheese. This may sound like the title of a Perry Mason thriller, but it was, in fact, a perfectly true story which could have had serious repercussions. It was solved by a particularly diligent customer relations officer, whom we shall call Mr Smith.

A visitor to a self-service café—one of the large chain—purchased a roll and butter, together with a portion of pre-packed cheese. He paid his bill at the cash point and walked away, thinking that his snack was rather expensive. Then he realized that it was the slice of cheese—a very small slice—which represented the major part of his outlay.

Very aggrieved at what he considered the outrageous price of this humble piece of cheese, he decided to complain, taking the offending item away with him. When Mr Smith received the written complaint, it seemed straightforward enough. The purchaser considered the price excessively high but, unfortunately, that is not an uncommon occurrence these days.

Mr Smith carried out his normal checks. He raised the matter with the manager of the café, who confirmed the price as quite correct according to the company's standard menus. There seemed no other course of action but to send the customer a politely worded letter to the effect that the price was in order.

Mr Smith, however, hesitated before sending his letter. Something was not quite right. The company's cafés had sold thousands of these cheese slices. There had never been a complaint before—or had there?

Carefully he sifted through his files of past complaints, using his cross-reference system to find any grumbles about prices. There were several—for as mentioned above, the price-sensitive public has its say on this subject at regular intervals. Although the slice of cheese had never been the subject of a specific complaint in the past, it had been mentioned, among other items, several times. Furthermore, it was raised only by visitors to one particular company outlet, although identical price lists were maintained throughout the nationwide chain. Needless to say, that outlet was the one at the centre of the most recent complaint.

Mr Smith sent for a copy of the company's purchase manual and a sample of the cheese sold to the customer. Immediately the plot grew thicker. The café in question was selling an item less than one third of the weight of those sold in the rest of the company's outlets.

Next he sent for a copy of the café's order forms, together with copies of the supplier's delivery notes. At last the problem was solved. While the café manager had been ordering the correct item, the supplier had been delivering a similar, but much smaller, slice of cheese which was normally sold at a lower price.

This mistake, totally unintentional on the supplier's part, had been allowed to pass unobserved for some months. As a result of Mr Smith's dogged detective work—prompted largely by his uneasy feeling brought about by years of handling consumer complaints—the company was able to put the matter right immediately. In the process, a regular annoyance to customers was terminated, and the consumer who had raised the matter accepted the facts and withdrew his threat to take the matter to the authorities.

It is important to note that Mr Smith chose to explain the findings of his investigation in full to the consumer. He was entitled to know, having raised the matter, and he was, in fact, delighted to find that, because he had taken the trouble to send in his complaint, a fault had been rectified.

There was a fault, of course, by one of the company's employees. The manager of the café had slipped up in not checking his orders against his delivery notes. But, as mentioned already, people are fallible. The chances are that he has not slipped up in that area again. A lesson learned the hard way—in this case through the intervention of another department—is a lesson not likely to be forgotten.

All this may seem to represent an enormous amount of time and trouble over a tiny item. That, however, is what the proper handling of customer complaints is all about. If a company cannot look after the smallest parts of its operation, and the smallest complaint, what chance can it be said to have in the larger scheme of things?

This example, however trivial a piece of cheese may seem to the manufacturer of, say, high cost electrical appliances, is only a demonstration of how the consumer, via the customer relations officer, can assist the company. On a more general level, consumers and their opinions can have a wide influence on company policy.

A particularly high level of complaints about one particular company outlet or product can highlight a major flaw, such as bad management or faulty design. This demonstrates the need for not only a centralized system for handling complaints but, even more important, the need to have the right man in the job. Even with a host of complaints on the same subject, if they are handled by a large number of executives scattered around the company, their sheer volume may pass unnoticed. If a slack customer relations officer reacts by sending all the complainants an identical reply, merely seeing this duplication as a chance to save himself the effort of several investigations, the company will have gained little—and so will the consumer.

It is remarkable that many companies operate suggestion schemes for employees, often giving generous rewards to successful participants, yet baulk at any effort to take heed of suggestions from the consumer. The attitude in many boardrooms is that the consumer, who has nothing to do with the business, cannot possibly have anything to offer men who spend their entire lives in a particular field. Yet any housewife can point to design weaknesses in her range of domestic appliances—weaknesses which reveal themselves only after months of regular use around the home and not after hours of testing in a laboratory. It is surely no coincidence that Marks and Spencer, which has built up a reputation for giving the consumer what he or she wants, encourages even its most senior executives to spend hours on the customers' side of the counter, listening to views, seeing how purchasers decide what lines to buy, and generally putting themselves in the place of the consumer at large.

Direct Access to the Consumer

It is an indisputable fact that the higher most executives go up the corporate ladder, the more remote they become from the customers they set out to serve. They travel to and from their offices in chauffeur-driven cars, eat in directors' dining rooms or in the best restaurants, travel in secluded comfort in trains and planes, and generally avoid the stresses and strains of everyday living.

This is not a condemnation. The pressures of modern business life give them sufficient worries to send many to a comparatively early grave. The point, however, is that in too many cases they see the world from a viewpoint seldom shared by their consumers.

The larger the company, the more this becomes a problem. All the more need, therefore, for the chief executive and his board to have a direct pipeline to the consumer and his views, his grievances, and his suggestions. 'Ah', many a company chairman will say. 'We have market research. We know all about our customers. We have it all down in black and white'.

In black and white, yes. But it is the light and shade which really matters. That comes not from page after page of neat statistics but, more often, from badly worded, misspelled letters. The consumer is not a statistic but a person. Sometimes he gets mad at the company. Sometimes he is justified in doing so. Sometimes he is mistaken in his anger. Always, however, he deserves to be heard and to be answered.

It is all rather like the film star who was regularly pilloried in the popular press. 'What do you feel about all these terrible articles they keep writing about you?' he was asked. The film star merely shrugged. 'It's when they have nothing at all to say about me that I will have to worry', he replied.

When the complaints stop altogether, it will be time for the company to worry. For a company is only people—and people are, as we have seen, not infallible. As the volume of business increases, so will the complaints. The trick is, of course, to take heed of them and correct the faults all the time. It is when the complaints stop coming that the writing is on the wall. For, almost certainly, it will mean the business is dying. The consumers will have made the ultimate protest. They will have gone elsewhere.

10. The retailer's response to the consumer movement

Rosemary McRobert

'Don't believe a word I say. All my descriptions of these things are false and the Trade Descriptions boys will tell you that they "do" me every week.' With a disclaimer like that, a salesman at a one-day sale succeeded in getting his customers to clamour to buy his cheap rubbish. The wonder is that the retail trade in the U K is the honest business it mainly is. Most traders do not need the spur of the law to advertise, promote, and sell goods and services to the public honestly and without being misleading. They want people—their customers—to be able to make a fair assessment of the quality and value for money of goods on offer.

Long before there were consumer organizations, the leading department stores were pioneers in setting high standards of retail practice. In 1935 they formed the Retail Trading-Standards Association (R T S A) to demonstrate that honest traders, who are the majority, share with the public a dislike of the deceptive and unfair trading practices which may be used by a tiresome minority of manufacturers and retailers. They found no lack of support for their objectives among members, standards-making organizations, and other trade associations. They worked out agreed standards of retail practice which laid down fair trading rules for advertising, the presentation or descriptions of goods, and selling methods. These standards of good practice have always had an over-riding rule: they must give effect to what is regarded as the public's understanding of the terms defined. The trade did not hide behind 'trade terms' understood between traders. R T S A's voluntary standards of retail practice do embody the best trade practice and they are used, knowingly or unknowingly, far beyond the membership of the Association by retailers in their dealings with the public. They demonstrate that, in everyday shopping, the conscience, business efficiency, and acumen of the individual supplier do more for the individual shopper and for shoppers in general than any law.

Most shopping is, after all, a troublefree transaction that no-one thinks about twice. Sometimes suppliers have found it convenient to write their own rules for doing business with their customers and they get away with it for a time, upsetting the balance of the market place in the process. Then, not surprisingly, the community steps in with laws to redress the balance. Laws are enacted to enforce on all retailers the standards of conduct which the majority of traders observe in any case—law or no law.

Retailers have not needed a spur provided by consumer organizations to describe goods honestly, or to use selling methods that do not blur the edges of choice so that the buyer is misled into thinking he is getting something he is not. It is not the policy of the majority of retailers to give short weight, or to misdescribe goods, or to use exclusion clauses to avoid their legal obligations. Because some retailers have traded unfairly, legislation to redress the balance has in the main been supported by honest traders. Quite apart from the protection it gives to consumers, it is also in the interest of fair trading that honest traders should be protected from dishonest traders.

What, then, is the special response that retailers need to give to satisfy the consumer movement? Why should retailers resist consumer movement requests for more and better information at the point-of-sale, or any of their other requests? Resistance, if resistance there is, comes for two main reasons. First, many retailers honestly think that they know better than consumer organizations what their customers want; second, in hard business terms, the priorities of consumer organizations may often not turn out to be the priorities of the majority of their customers. Consequently response to consumerism may come low on the list of management priorities in many retail outlets.

Importance of Choice

The distributive trade has to live with the fact that consumer organizations generally underestimate the importance of having as many strong and flourishing trading systems as possible to provide the necessary options for everyone concerned—manufacturer, retailer, and customer. The 'choice' that is implicit in the marketing concept of 'market segments' catering for defined needs is sometimes dismissed as 'confusing choice' by consumerists. Or even as 'unnecessary choice'. This is particularly true of those consumerists who adhere to the historicist approach to economics, the rational 'best buy', with its underlying implication that no 'right-thinking' person would go for anything else.

Examination of consumer organizations' criticism of retailers (which, incidentally, accounts for only a fraction of their criticism of suppliers in general) shows that the trigger word of their disagreement is 'marketing'. They see this as a concept which forces people to buy things they don't want or don't know enough about. In fact, consumer organizations have a lot to learn about human behaviour and to understand about the distributive trade in the UK before they grasp the elementary difficulty, but not impossibility, of reconciling their yearning for the high degree of product knowledge and service that characterize the best specialist retailers dealing in products that are not basic essentials with the price structure of chain or discount stores dealing in a comparatively limited range of high volume, low price, basic need products.

The marketing concept is summed up by the cliché that the answer to 'what business are we in?' should come from a customer or consumer perspective rather than one determined by the technological base of an organization. Successful retailers are in marketing, not just in selling. With their knowledge of their customers, their purchasing power, their bargaining position, shouldn't they insist that manufacturers' products and product information should match consumer organization requests? Wouldn't that be good business? The answer is that nobody really knows.

Differentiated Markets

The key influences on market requirements are, in spite of Galbraithian theories, customers' needs. I must underline the word *customers*. A retailer caters for *his* customers. He often thinks of consumers as the other fellow's customers.

The changes in retail distribution in the last 25 years in the U K, the forms of distribution characterized by relationship to customers' needs, and the role of the distributive trade are not studied, and even less understood, by the consumer movement. Since they form a background to any assessment of the need for a more positive retailer response to the consumer movement, perhaps it would be sensible to outline—briefly and over-simplistically—what the market looks like to retailers.

The U K market is highly differentiated in terms of market requirements, and the economics of retailing are peculiarly fragile. Market requirements are very little influenced by the social standing of customers, more by their income and education. The forms of distribution primarily depend on whether the goods on offer are *basic needs*—without 'value added' components, for example, food and 'value added' convenience foods—*optional needs,* or *luxury needs*. A key influence on the marketing structures which cater for these needs is completely unknown to most consumers. It is the *rate of stockturn* related to the capital employed. This influences the range of goods stocked, the degree of service, the equipping of premises, the staffing, the price, and the amount of 'mark-up' (and the amount of mark-down in sales events and special promotions).

Basic needs

Consumers' basic needs are increasingly provided for by chain stores, multiples, and discount stores. They will stock perhaps 8000 product lines. These are items which people often buy, there may be a limited choice of brands, the price range of the goods is quite well known, the rate of stockturn is high, the cost of the goods themselves accounts for a high percentage of the price, and the cost in percentage of sales and the mark-up are low. There is little or no service or product knowledge at the point of sale.

Centralized, and possibly remote, management is preoccupied with defining the market segment, planning the structures, arithmetical and otherwise, of the form of distribution to use, and installing the financial and stock control disciplines which are the key factors in this type of operation. The economics themselves dictate the decisions about the amount of service to be provided. The overriding need to get it all right and capture as large a share of the market for basic essentials as possible leaves comparatively little time for the issues that consumerists regard as important. Retailers in this type of operation argue, not altogether unconvincingly, that a requirement, let alone legislation, to add extra customer services will be reflected in extra costs, which can only come from profits or customers. As it is quite possible that some stores operating in this basic needs group will operate on gross margins of say 20 per cent and will take a 2 per cent profit on their high turnover, they may have a point. Customers, they argue, as opposed to consumerists, might prefer to have the lowest possible prices.

Optional and luxury needs

It is harder to sustain this argument with the form of distribution which caters for the 'optional needs' of consumers. Here the store—a department store, for example—may be handling 40 000 items, be satisfied with a stockturn at half the rate of the basic needs stores, work on a gross margin of say 35 per cent, with the cost of the goods accounting for a lower proportion of the price than in the basic goods category, and allowing for more service and other components. The specialist trading in 'luxury needs' may only achieve a stock turn a third as rapid as the basic needs store, with the cost of goods accounting for as little as half the price, and a gross margin of 50 per cent to provide for more services.

The distributive trade in the U K does not, in general, have to stand in a white sheet about its record. Does it, however, devote enough senior management time to the criticisms which consumer organizations voice and to the curiously paradoxical consumer expectations for high levels of customer service with the lowest price? Retailers can have three attitudes to their failure to give customers what they want—they can ride them out and hope that they will not happen to so many customers that they lose their profit or customer goodwill. They can install first-aid complaints systems that deal with problems as they arise and use a kind of slush fund to ensure a placated customer. Or they can install systems that minimize complaints and problems in the first place by their buying policies, quality control, and point-of-sale information. Retailers have the power and the ability to try things out in the market place. It may be a philosophical and emotional wrench for the leaders of the retail trade to listen to the voice of the consumer as articulated by consumer organizations. Why should they, some argue, when the voice they have to live by is the sound of their tills ringing? Retailers do have their knowledge of their customers, their purchasing power, and their bargaining position to call on to influence standards in the market place. After all, retailers are responsible under law for the merchantable quality, fitness for purpose, the description, and the marketing and pricing of the goods they sell. Why should they be put on the spot with their customers by their suppliers? Equally, retailers are in a very good position to demonstrate that it is not axiomatic that Government or consumer organizations know what is best for their customers.

Demands of the Consumer Movement

What, when all is said and done, are consumer organizations asking retailers to do?

The doctrines of the consumer movement are pretty clearly established by now. They embrace the right to information, to safety of products, to goods of merchantable quality, to adequate after-sales service, and to redress or compensation if required. If retailers are ready to take customers' money, as they surely are, what stops them adding the best practices of the 'best buys' in retailers to their marketing mix? The most cogent reason is probably that this kind of response requires a degree of commitment in top management to the issues posed by consumerism. The reality of the market place is that these issues do not have the same priority as other management problems. The criticism of retailers that features in the consumer catalogue often arises from the behaviour of firms that do not have strong, family ownership and where corporate strategies for long-term development are over-centralized and remote from markets, and people, and products.

Information

Consumer organizations consist of well educated, literate, articulate people, who set great store by the printed word and by information. They themselves are prepared to work at being discriminating. They use information if it is provided and they want to be able to assess the authority of that information. They recognize that it may be impracticable to convey information on a face-to-face basis. The complexity of products on the market and the economic pressures to make retailing less labour-intensive see to that. That is why they press for more point-of-sale labelling. They want information based on standard methods of test which are published and which can grade performance in terms that will mean something to customers. To help consumers to make comparisons more easily, they want information to be presented in a standard format. Although virtually all everyday goods are sold with a clear and unambiguous indication of prices in shops and stores the length and breadth of the country, consumer organizations would support legislation to require retailers to indicate prices, with a criminal penalty for failure to comply. They think all perishable foods should carry a clear indication of the date by which it should be consumed. They incline towards minimum quality standards for products and are unambiguously in favour of legislation for the safety of products. They recognize that much of this is the responsibility of the manufacturers, but since their contract is with the retailer, they expect him to be on their side. They want more and better information about using products. They would like clearer point-of-sale information on the lifetime cost of a product—how much energy it uses, for example; how much servicing it will need. Less emphasis on the purchase price. Less glamorous packaging. Less glamour, perhaps. Maybe less fashion. As I said, they don't know a lot about human behaviour, but that is no reason to avoid discussing the issues with them. Although doctrines are difficult to dislodge, and a great deal of the consumer movement is dotty, the fact is that they are susceptible to reason, and evidence, and to demonstration of the practical implications of their requests. They are not often given the courtesy of an intelligent response from retailers.

Any retailer worth his salt can get his colleagues, perhaps in a trade association, to join him in practical research and tests in the market place. He can try an informative labelling scheme on say, his own-brand products, test it on the market with real customers, adapt it if necessary to encourage the British Standards Institution or the Office of Fair Trading to develop a code of practice.

Care-labelling

An example of how the trade can take a lead in providing consumer information is the success over a period of some 12 years of the British Home Launderers' Consultative Council (HLCC). This *ad hoc* group of leading textile producers, detergent and domestic appliance manufacturers, and multiple and department stores formed itself into an organization to codify care-labelling of textiles. It did this without the threat of legislation. It did not do it simply for consumer information, but also as enlightened self-interest to try to reduce the number of complaints about textile products from incorrect laundering of clothes. The Council suffered in its earliest days from a powerful combination of its own and consumer organizations' *hubris*; HLCC didn't think consumer organizations represented its customers and consumer organizations didn't think a group of traders should decide on the information its customers should have, but the market power of its members ensured that the scheme got off the ground. Care labels with both symbols and words do appear on millions of garments. There is no real reason why consumers should not know about the scheme because in addition to seeing labels on garments, a guide to the code appears on millions of packs of detergents. Surveys have shown public awareness to be relatively small. The code was adopted as part of the

113

British Standard Code for Care Labelling and the majority of consumer organizations in the U K endorse it. Retailers have been comparatively slow to explain the code to their customers but in 1977 all the leading high street retailers agreed to provide point-of-sale material. Still, it is probably true to say that no very great resources were made available to the H L C C by trade.

Standards of Retail Practice

The Retail Trading-Standards Association Standards of Retail Practice codify rules for the advertising, presentation, or descriptions of goods, and for selling methods. They are based on the following underlying principle.

> An announcement or practice is inaccurate or misleading if, intentionally or otherwise, it may lead members of the public reasonably to believe that merchandise in general, or any specific article, is more desirable than is actually the case, whether by reason of lower price, higher quality, greater suitability for a purpose, or in any other way.

Since the Standards are not exhaustive, the spirit of this principle must be observed, even in cases which are not specifically mentioned in the Standards. The Standards do not simply lay down ground rules for the conduct of fair trading as between one trader and another. They are a demonstration of the trade's determination to keep faith with its customers. It is important to honest traders that a whole trade is not brought into disrepute by the activities of a few.

Price Reductions

An example of the way in which R T S A members took a lead in keeping faith with customers was the introduction of a voluntary formula to use for advertising sale price reductions. When the Trade Descriptions Act 1968 became law, this formula with very little alteration conformed with the legal requirement of Section 11 of the Trade Descriptions Act, which deals with price reductions. We reprint it here as an example of the way in which the needs of the trade to mark down goods at sale time can perfectly well be reconciled with customers' expectations and with honesty and with fair trading.

Marking down your own goods

When your goods have been offered at the higher prices for a continuous period of at least 28 days within the preceding six months, let this be your normal sale ticket.

Description
Originally 70p
Reduced to 49p

You may add if appropriate such a factual phrase as 'Half Price' or 'Saving £2'.
R T S A advises that if the goods have *not* been offered for at least 28 days during
the preceding six months suitable qualifications to this effect must be made on the
sale ticket and, of course, in advertisements—e.g., for January sales some such
statement as 'Early December Price 70p'.

When further reductions take place during a sale it is permissible to delete the
previous reduced price or prices and to describe the last price as 'Further
Reduction'. If this reduction is in fact to be the last, then the expression 'Final
Reduction' may be used. But the pre-sale price should always appear.

```
Description
Originally 70p
49p
Final Reduction 39p
```

The piece of advice about disclaiming prices if they had not been charged
during the 28 days in the specific form we proposed has proved too much
for many retailers, who have preferred to use a general disclaimer notice to
the effect that goods had not been offered for at least 28 days during the
preceding six months, which is hardly what the promoters of the Trade
Descriptions Act intended.

Comparisons with prices elsewhere

If you have bought in goods which you have not yourself sold at a higher price,
but which have been sold by your competitors at a higher price, you may use the
expression 'Special Offer' on the ticket in respect of these goods followed by the
words 'Price elsewhere'.

```
Description
Special Offer
Price elsewhere 70p
Our Price 49p
```

R T S A's general code requires claims for price reductions from competitors' prices to be capable of substantiation if required.

Comparisons with recommended prices

Beware—recommended prices often tend to be phony prices. Before you compare your own price with one recommended by the manufacturer, please assure
yourself that the recommended price is one that is not only recommended by the
manufacturer but is one that is charged in representative sections of the retail
trade in your area. If it is recommended by the manufacturer, say so. If it is an
imported product and the price is suggested by the agent it is permissible to say
'recommended price'. But the price must be one recommended by the manufacturer or producer if this type of reduction is claimed. If you are satisfied that it
is the recommended retail price in your area you should use the ticket illustrated
here.

```
Description
Manufacturer's Recommended Price 70p
Our price 49p
```

Special purchases and clearance lines

Any buyer worth his or her salt is on the lookout for special purchases and clearance lines from manufacturers which can be sold at bargain prices at the sales. For these there is often no comparative price within the requirements of the Trade Descriptions Act and they should be offered for what they are—bargains—in the particular terms which you use.

```
Description
Special Purchase
Only 49p
```

Seconds, imperfect and sub-standard

There is no question of straight comparison between perfect goods and those which are imperfect. All sale goods which are imperfect must be so marked. The nearest comparison you can make is with perfect stock in your store. In this case the perfect goods should be a regular line. This should be a matter of principle, since imperfect goods are not 'goods of the same description' as perfect goods within the Trade Descriptions Act.

```
Description
Seconds 40p
When Perfect 55p
```

Marketing Men and Consumerism

The core of the relationship between marketing men and consumerists is that consumerists believe that goods and services offered by traders for sale to the public must live up to the descriptions which the traders apply to them. The public must be given what they believe they are paying for. Cynical consumerists think that it is the marketing concept that is primarily responsible for the attitude of 'you get what you pay for' and that, provided products are attractive to look at, cheap, and available, they can be foisted on an unsuspecting public.

The public is much more robust than professional consumers sometimes care to admit. Nevertheless, the responsiveness of retailers to the consumer movement will, fairly or unfairly, be judged not on their trading figures or profitability, nor even on how successfully they serve their customers, but on how they *seem* to embrace the doctrines of consumerism. I hope I have shown, by some very simple examples, that it is possible to receive the blessing of the consumer movement, the respect of competitors, and still survive in business—because the stores that founded the R T S A in 1935 are still names to reckon with in the high street. And in the intervening years they have been joined by many non-food multiples and chain stores—very few of which feature in the list of consumer complaints so assiduously compiled for the Office of Fair Trading by advice and enforcement authorities.

The consumer movement expects retailers to know about published standards for goods. They assume that retail buyers insist on evidence that the goods that they are supplied with are made to appropriate specifications for merchantability and for performance standards such as washability, shrink-resistance, and wear durability. Many retailers do lay down the specifications for their own-brand products and monitor them. They have large and sophisticated quality control departments and work with manufacturers to develop goods with basic technical qualities. They expect retailers to reassure themselves about the safety of the products they sell. There are retailers who have a reputation for their policy about making room for well designed products; there are others who cater quite joyfully for tatty products in doubtful taste. There are specialist retailers with such a powerful stake in the market that if they don't sell a product, the market for that product may hardly be worth bothering about. Then you get the pyjama cord syndrome—the fact that one leading retailer only sells pyjamas with elasticated waist-bands. So there is no point in anyone making pyjamas with cords for the rest of the market, because it is not big enough. So anyone who wants pyjamas with cords will have to go to a very specialist retailer whose stockturn in pyjamas with cords is so slow that he has to charge the earth for them.

Consumer organizations, whose suggestions are based on testing and research, might like to remember from time to time that science laboratory tests may be reported at 95 to 98 per cent confidence levels. The poor devils who are responsible for planning in retail marketing, and the line marketing managers with their immediate task-oriented operational targets, have human behaviour to contend with. They are very lucky if they can achieve a confidence level of 60 per cent. Think of that next time you see a rack of 'unrepeatable bargains' in summer clothes at the end of a wet summer.

Fourteen Rules for Retailers

Rule 1

Don't dislike customers. This may not always be easy since customers are often unreasonable, sometimes rude and occasionally dishonest.

Rule 2

Accept gratefully that customers are parting with their money; money they too have worked hard to earn. For that reason alone they deserve consideration and a fair deal from you.

Rule 3

Recognize without reservation, and insist that your staff recognize, that under law you are responsible for the merchantable quality and fitness for purpose of the goods you sell, and for the descriptions, marking, and pricing of the goods.

Rule 4

Be familiar with the law on trade descriptions, labelling, credit transactions, not with the idea of observing of it to the minimum extent possible, but recognizing that one of its purposes is to help traders to compete fairly against other fair traders and against traders who would, if the law allowed, trade less scrupulously.

Rule 5

Similarly, be familiar with and observe voluntary codes of practice and definitions, such as those produced by the Retail Trading-Standards Association and the British Standards Institution, and with the voluntary Code of Advertising Practice, supervised by the Advertising Standards Authority.

Rule 6

Don't hesitate to stand up to your suppliers if they send you defective goods, fall down on delivery dates, and put you on the spot with your customers, and if they do not supply goods with adequate information about care or use.

Rule 7

Know your stock and what it will do and do your best to ensure that your staff do likewise.

Rule 8

Although, legally, 'time' may not always be an element in your contract with your customers, make sure that they are kept informed about delivery dates that have not been met.

Rule 9

Take staff training seriously. It is an investment for your marketing skills and your customers' goodwill.

Rule 10

Remember that a complaint well handled is one of the best ways of winning loyal customers. So have an organized complaints procedure which recognizes your statutory obligations and clearly explains your policy towards customers who are not satisfied for one reason or another. Don't let your counter hands feel that you are leaving them unprotected against customers.

If complaints are not handled on the spot by managers, make sure there is quick and easy access to a named trouble shooter in a position to make a decision.

118

Rule 11

Get to know your local trading standards department, Citizens' Advice Bureaux, consumer groups, and consumer advice centres, so that you can educate them in the facts of retailing life and ensure that their criticism, if it comes, is constructive and informed.

Rule 12

If you deal in consumer durables give special care to the efficiency of your after-sales and servicing arrangements, including a system which lets your customers know before they are committed what they can expect to pay and what is happening when there are delays.

Rule 13

Don't put temptation in the way of customers and staff by displaying goods carelessly and without proper supervision.

Rule 14

Don't confuse your customers by allowing manufacturers' staff to sell goods in your store unless they are clearly identified as owing allegiance to one manufacturer.

11. Standards and marketing

Gill Ashworth

Marketing people don't like 'standards'. Whether interpreted to mean the attainment of uniformity, the description of an 'average quality' or, even worse, of minimum quality, those concerned with marketing tend to regard standards as at best a matter for the factory floor and the test laboratory, but having little to do with the tough commercial business of buying and selling.

The fact is, however, that the economics of marketing—getting the desired product with the necessary level of performance as speedily as possible from the manufacturer to the purchaser at lowest cost—has dictated the development of national standards in Britain in this century.

An iron merchant first aired the marketing headaches stemming from the lack of industrial standardization in a letter to *The Times* of 1895:

> We have too much individualism in this country, where collective action would be economically advantageous. As a result, architects and engineers specify such unnecessary diverse types of sectional material for given work that anything like economical and continuous manufacture becomes impossible . . . . no two professional men are agreed upon the size and weight of girder to employ for given work and the British manufacturer is everlastingly changing his rolls or appliances, at greatly increased cost, to meet the irregular unscientific requirements of professional architects and engineers.

His commentary had as its backcloth both the upsurge of manufacturing activity of the industrial revolution, and the great railway boom of the middle eighteen-hundreds. This vast and simultaneous growth in the number of production points and of markets brought major problems: the diversity of sizes and qualities of similar products; the matching of components and semi-finished products from different works; the absence of consistent quality and means of securing it. By 1901, the engineering profession had taken steps to set its house in order, and an Engineering Standards Committee, forerunner of the British Standards Institution (BSI), was appointed by the Institution of Civil Engineers to standardize types of iron and steel sections.

By the First World War this still embryonic standards activity had made notable impact: the Board of Trade, the Admiralty, and Lloyds Register of Shipping had adopted British Standards; and it was estimated that all the materials used for the construction of railway rolling stock for India were to standard. In 1917 the Minister of Munitions, Winston Churchill, observed that 'the detailed standardization of aircraft materials among the allied powers now fighting the Germans is based on principles so obvious that they really do not at this time of day require even to be emphasized'.

The 'obvious principles' of standardization were later set out in BSI's Royal Charter of 1929: ' .... to simplify production and distribution, and to eliminate the national waste of time and materials involved in the production of an unnecessary variety of patterns and sizes of articles for one and the same purpose'.

Today, half a century later, we have travelled through several generations of standards philosophy. Standards work is no longer confined to the basic organization of national productive capacity, important though that is. Standards are concerned with responding to the expectations of an articulate consumer society. In a number of areas they are part of the fabric of our technical law. Increasingly, they are directed, in collaboration with other countries, and notably in Europe, to easing the complexities of international trade. They provide a means for the transfer of technology between the developed and developing worlds. The trend of these years has been to bring the business of standardization more obviously into the market place and to the attention of those whose business is marketing.

The simple vehicle for achieving these varied objectives is no more than a technical document, but one with significant features. As defined by the UN Economic Commission for Europe, it is

> a technical specification or other document available to the public, drawn up with the cooperation and consensus or general approval of all interests affected by it, based on the consolidated results of science, technology and experience, aimed at the promotion of optimum community benefits and approved by a body recognized on the national, regional or international level.

Within the terms of this definition, British Standards are public documents, produced through the voluntary participation of all the interests concerned in the work. They reflect the 'state of the art' at the time of publication for a particular product or process, and they are published in the public interest by a body of recognized status and authority. In technical and commercial exchanges, in the laboratory, in exporting, and in the drafting of technical regulations it is these features which give British Standards their distinctive place.

Post-war Developments

BSI's work did not have significant impact in the field of consumer products until after the Second World War. During the war, at the Board of

Trade's request, BSI had developed the specifications needed for the 'Utility' schemes which controlled the quality of clothing, shoes, household textiles, furniture, and bedding. When the schemes were abandoned in 1951, it was in favour of voluntary quality assurances worked out between the industries themselves and BSI.

With the UK beginning to move from war-time austerity to post-war boom, the needs of the consumer were attracting public comment and Government attention. A report of 1951 to the President of the Board of Trade on BSI's work and constitution noted that the representation of the domestic consumer in the preparation of standards now demanded serious attention. That same year BSI set up the Women's Advisory Committee (WAC), bringing together the most influential women's organizations in the country and representing the views of 1¹/₂ million women. Its purpose was to bring practical experience to bear on any aspect of BSI's work affecting the ordinary consumer and to achieve, through BSI committees, a real collaboration between manufacturer, retailer, and shopper. Four years later, in 1955, BSI moved further into the field, establishing a Consumer Advisory Council which had strong WAC representation on it but took in a far wider range of interests—retailers, wholesalers, leading consumer figures, journalists, with only manufacturing interests debarred. It acquired public presence, inviting consumer views on products and services, providing an information service, collecting data on defective products, enrolling individuals who wanted regular advice on shopping problems as 'Associates', and, in 1957, embarking on a magazine, *Shopper's Guide*, which pioneered comparative reports on different kinds of consumer products. Within weeks Consumers' Association had produced a formidable rival in *Which?* which was ultimately—seven years later—to win the day, while the recommendation of the 1962 Molony Report on Consumer Protection that a national consumer council should be established led to the natural disbandment of BSI's Consumer Advisory Council shortly afterwards.

In retrospect this period was one of remarkable fertility for BSI: in less than a decade it had changed from a solely industry-oriented organization to one actively involved, indeed leading, the early development of the modern consumer protection movement.

What came from that imaginative venture? First, a firm belief within BSI that the needs of manufacturers and consumers did not have to be in combat, despite the evident disparity in power, organization and influence between the monoliths of production and the individual citizen. Constructive dialogue could produce effective agreement to the benefit of both. Second, these years stimulated a steady development of British Standards for consumer products, and of associated certification schemes primarily based on the 'Kitemark', which provides third party assurance of compliance with British Standards, through Schemes of Supervision and Control operated by BSI based on continuous quality surveillance. In addition, use of the BSI Safety Mark is now licensed for standards solely concerned with safety. BSI is involved in the work of a number of other certification bodies, from which the BSI Test House and Inspectorate now earn over 50 per cent of their revenue. A 1975 survey of manufacturers holding Kitemark licences showed that the total value of annual Kitemark production was then £800m. Some 11 per cent were exported products, 18 per cent went to Government bodies, and 71 per cent to other UK buyers. The cost of the Kitemark facility was extremely small, £7·20 in every £10 000 of production value or 0·072 per cent. Almost all the licensees highlighted the value of the schemes of supervision and control, including regular visits by BSI inspectors, to their own production quality control and marketing operations.

Safety and Performance

Substantially, the consumer standards programme has concentrated in the post-war period on safety allied to some extent with performance aspects of standardization: defining the characteristics, setting the levels of performance, establishing the test methods by which unreasonable hazard might be eliminated and a consistent production quality attained. The range of work has included, for example, gas and electrical household appliances; oil burners; furniture and bedding; nursery goods—cots, baby buggies, toys, dummies; children's car seats and harness; personal safety equipment—lifejackets, motorcyclists' helmets, car seat belts; and so on. The development of such standards has in a major number of cases served to eliminate unsafe and dangerous products from the market place: those with decade-long memories may recall demonstrations of how non-standard lifejackets could drown the wearer; of seat belts which could not hold a teddy bear in place in a 30 mph crash, let alone an adult; of oil heaters which were a flaming death trap in the draught of a hall door.

Third, the inclusion of standards such as these within the framework of law has been an important feature since the Consumer Protection Act reached the statute book in 1961. Regulations under the Act now make reference to a number of these standards for the technical specification with which all marketed products must comply; and there have been recent welcome indications that the Secretary of State for Prices and Consumer Protection plans to extend this use of reference to standards in developing his powers in the consumer safety field. More generally, agreements to use British Standards do not have to be registered as restrictive trade practices under the Fair Trading Act, 1973. In being so recognized as serving the public interest, national standards provide the criteria for 'the state of the art' at a particular time, to which a manufacturer may turn in defending a claim that he failed to take necessary precautions. The duty of care exercised in the production of standards gives them a particular value to users bound by a similar duty of care to the public. In this respect their provisions for safety—that is, the judgement they embody as to the acceptable level of risk—attract especially careful consideration in BSI committees. The significance, and adequacy, of standards for reference purposes will acquire increased importance if the law relating to liability for defective products comes to be modified along the lines of the draft E E C Directive (see the passage on product liability in chapter 3).

Unused Standards

Lastly, it is worth noting that the initiatives of the 'fifties, and the consolidation of relationships with consumers since then, have established B S I as a world leader among standards organizations in this respect. No other country has for so long, or with such firmness, maintained the principle that if standards for consumer products are being developed, consumers must be in the committee room round the table with all the other relevant interests, taking part in that vigorous dialogue which should produce a marketable agreement. I say 'should' because not every standard is automatically adopted, when available, by all the public and private bodies which could use it. Apart from the minority of standards called up in legislation, all 7000 British Standards are voluntary agreements, and some do better than others when it comes to implementation. B S I's reaction to the patchy implementation of standards has hitherto been one partly of ignorance, partly of resignation. Ignorance, because it is in fact extraordinarily difficult to discover which standards are used, and how much they are used, in the whole complex process of designing, producing, and marketing a product, from drawing board to drawing room. The ignorance is compounded in the retail trade if the manufacturer does not mark his product as complying with a B S—even though it does—and the wholesaler, retailer, and consumer thus remain quite unaware of certain fundamental characteristics of the product. Resignation, because the production side of the standards business has been overwhelmed in the postwar period with national and international assignments and there has been little resource available to analyse, in systematic fashion, what happens to standards once they are out of the committee room.

This situation, partly born of necessity, is now undergoing rapid change, for a number of obvious reasons. Standards work is expensive: the annual B S I budget for standards production (derived from subscriptions, Government grant-in-aid, and sales revenues) is now approaching £6 million, and it is estimated that the 20 000 voluntary committee members who collaborate in standards work donate, in effect, at least twice as much again in time and expenses. It is important that this £18 million, and a great deal of effort and talent, should not be wasted. Moreover a good standard makes, and goes on making, an immediate contribution to greater economy and efficiency in manufacture, and thus to ultimate community benefit. Every unused standard, therefore, wastes money twice over. Again, the country cannot afford it. And like every other organization with a product to market, B S I must test the response of the market if its products are to be precisely tuned to customer needs. All of this points to B S I having a different emphasis in the next few years as it tries to discover more about the use of standards, and to readjust its programme accordingly.

Even in the absence of firm data, we can nevertheless make some guesses as to why some standards lie idle on the shelves. The most obvious explanation may be that they should never have been produced at all. Is it really necessary, for instance, to have a national standard for paper napkins, as was recently suggested? Or aluminium saucepans? Or school pencils? Fortunately we have already begun, with the help of our Standards Committees, to grapple with the very difficult problems of choice and priorities which beset any standards organization covering the whole range of economic activity with finite resources. The steady refinement of the resource allocation process should mean that future work programmes contain only those projects where the cost benefit, in community terms, is substantial.

It is often suggested, too, that BSI committees work too slowly. Certainly in the consumer product field, more 'high fashion' than any other manufacturing sector, the present average production time for a BS of three years is a dangerous bar to successful implementation. The 1977 report on standards by Sir Frederick Warner to the National Economic Development Council recommended a total production period of one year following receipt of an initial draft, a time scale which should be attainable for a number of national projects given the collaboration of the committee membership. And it is already BSI's commitment to work for a total production time of two rather than three years.

In theory, the production process underpinning every British Standard gives it a presumption of acceptability in the market place. By the time a standard is published it has the support of the wide range of representative interests involved in its preparation; and it has already been exposed in draft form to public comment. In practice, however, there are some weak links in this chain. On the manufacturing side—and this is particularly so in industries serving the retail trade—a standard may be agreed while the manufacturer nevertheless continues to rely, in practice, on his brand name, advertising and the speed of his response to trends in fashion, design, and taste. In short, standards may be seen only as a not very important part of the packaging rather than as a fundamental guide to the design, production, quality control, testing, and marketing of the product. When standards are developed for regulatory purposes, the concentration of the committee on these realities is much more in evidence, and the result is, most often, a far better standard.

One of the obvious dilemmas in the standardization of consumer products—and in part it explains the ambivalent approach of industry—is that the consumer view is itself difficult to identify and to represent effectively. The consumer movement, notably under the long leadership of Consumers' Association, is well organized, articulate, and influential; but its resources are over stretched and cannot cover all the representative tasks expected of it. Moreover it reflects the views of a relatively small consumer electorate which may or may not be typical of consumers as a whole. In standards work, this poses problems when it comes to setting levels of performance and safety, to securing the optimum equation between product cost and consumer benefit, and to persuading industrial representatives that these solutions are really what consumers want. In recent months BSI has been working through its Consumer Standards Advisory Committee to extend the pool of consumer representatives on which it can draw for committee work, to strengthen the training facilities and technical briefing offered to them, and to explore the use of larger regional meetings of consumer interests to sound out standards proposals and drafts before completion. These measures should help to produce more constructive discussion and consultation in the future.

When all these points have been made, however, there remains an element of truth in the assertion that manufacturers and retailers of consumer products and services are still reluctant to engage too closely with the questioning consumer, eager for information, and armed with some knowledge and opinion. It is important that this reluctance is replaced by a positive approach to collaboration and a genuine endeavour on both sides to face the needs and requirements both of the consumer market and of the industries supplying it. Standards activity is one such channel for positive alliance. The formative work of the Office of Fair Trading (OFT) in developing self-regulatory codes of practice with relevant industries is another significant influence in the right direction (see chapters 13, 14, and 15).

The Educational Approach

The relevance of these approaches is underlined by recent trends in education at both primary and secondary levels. Here BSI and OFT have collaborated in marketing teaching kits which have enjoyed considerable success in consumer education and home economics courses, although it is a matter for regret that OFT have now withdrawn from this work.

It is significant that the preliminary programme of the EEC for consumer information and protection lays considerable stress on the promotion of consumer education in schools, and studies of existing activities in EEC countries are already in hand. The education of the consumers of tomorrow—to make economic choices effectively, to assess the truth and relevance of advertising, to understand technical information on products and their maintenance, to handle purchasing in what is now a vast variety of shopping outlets (not all equipped with expert staff), perhaps above all to understand some of the implications of the choices made for the environment and natural resources on which we depend—this is a programme of considerable excitement and opportunity.

The consumer movement in the UK is here to stay. It is vigorous, independent, well led, knitted into the political as well as the economic fabric of our society. The trend of consumer education will be to consolidate its strengths and bring a greater understanding of the business of choice to a wider cross-section of the public. Consequences for both standards work and marketing activity must flow from this.

As to standards, their 'obvious principles' are, after three-quarters of a century, firmly embedded in production, in technical law (an area which will be reinforced by the E EC Directives programme for technical harmonization of product specifications), and in wider aspects of economic activity. They are, however, less vigorously supported in consumer marketing, although it is in this field that those concerned—manufacturers, retailers, and the public at large—stand in most need of clear and unambiguous signposts towards economic performance and acceptable safety levels amid the plethora of choice. Not so long ago, at a B SI consumer conference, a leading British manufacturer stated his view of consumer requirements:

> A practical consumer knows what his own requirements are and goes to whatever trouble may be appropriate to ensure that those requirements are as nearly fulfilled as is reasonably possible at a reasonable cost.

This is no longer, in today's circumstances, a helpful approach to the market place—it does not go far enough.

Consumer Requirements

What are the requirements of the practical consumer? In brief, that the product should be fit for the job; that it shouldn't collapse, explode, or poison the user, wear out with extreme rapidity, be unsafe or otherwise unreasonably hazardous—and that it should be marketed at an economic price, in relation to its performance. The practical consumer then begins to hit some rocks. The largest rock is the general absence of simple, clear information about the product. As often as not, the consumer is expected to judge on appearances. But in a retail market of unprecedented technical complexity, can he judge visually whether wiring is safe, paints poisonous, pushchairs stable, or toys death traps? How much advice can he expect from the overworked shop assistant in these days of rapid turnover and supermarket shopping?

A positive and constructive use of national standards, supported where appropriate by certification schemes, is one way forward through this impasse. It would capitalize on a well established basis of public understanding. It would harness and bring commitment to the already costly efforts of the community, through B SI, to achieve orderly and practicable answers to issues of growing technical complexity. Most important, it would produce better standards from B SI, more sensitively tuned to the needs of the market place, to both customer and supplier. B SI's work for the consumer in the post-war period has shown that a dialogue between manufacturers and consumers can produce beneficial and lasting results for the community. Those benefits can be extended over a far wider field, with gains in economic and social terms, if the national interests involved work together to achieve the possibility of *meaningful* choice which is indispensable to a free market economy.

12. Future developments in marketing

Leslie Rodger

Marketing Principles and Practice

Nearly all definitions of marketing stress three main elements. The first is the importance of identifying and satisfying customer needs; the second is the integration of effort on a company-wide basis towards this end; the third is the importance of doing so profitably. It is not seen as part of a business organization's purpose to satisfy customers' needs at *any* cost. To survive and grow, a business organization must earn a satisfactory planned rate of profit if it is to continue to serve its customers on a reliable, long-term basis, and if it is to fulfil its obligations to its employees, shareholders, suppliers, the local community, and society at large.

The marketing perspective views the purpose of business as being the creation of value—the anticipation, identification, creation, and delivery of optimum customer values—at a worthwhile profit. It sees this purpose as something that encompasses, consolidates, and integrates the whole business and permeates all areas of the enterprise.*

The marketing concept, as expressed through the firm's choice of markets (i.e., customers), its choice of products and services to sell to those markets, and its choice of specific marketing policies and methods, is the concern of everyone in the firm from the shop floor to the boardroom, from the chief executive to the telephone exchange operator and the person sitting at the reception desk in the front office. Everyone in the firm is involved to some degree in creating value for the customer or in minimizing the delivered cost of the product or service. The marketing concept aims at encouraging everyone to consider his or her individual tasks and responsibilities in the light of the customer and at making everyone aware of the impact of his or her decisions and actions on the customer. It seeks to eliminate the false distinction between those in the firm who serve the customer and those who think that they do not or that it does not concern

*See Bibliography p.283—Drucker (1969b).

them. We should not delude ourselves. The marketing concept as just described and viewed as a philosophy or set of principles that guide business actions has, as yet, made a very limited impact on management in either the private or public sector.

Marketing under fire

Since the late 'sixties, marketing practices have come in for increasing criticism from the news media and representative consumer organizations as well as from academics and from Government bodies such as the Office of Fair Trading (OFT). The contrast between principles and practice has led many people to question the validity of the marketing concept.

The marketing concept, it has been claimed, 'is more honoured in the breach than the observance'.* The mounting tide of criticism levelled at marketing and marketers, which has found its most articulate and militant expression in the developing consumer movement, has focused on the following apparent shortcomings:†

—Marketers, through their misapplication of the tools of persuasion and manipulation such as advertising, sales promotion, packaging and pricing, are frequently guilty of deceiving the consumer whose interests the marketing concept purports to advance.

—Marketers are under pressure to maximize their firms' profits at the expense of the consumer by lowering quality, raising unit prices, or reducing services. Although top management may profess belief in the marketing concept, the line marketing executives, who are judged and rewarded on sales performance, may not practise it faithfully.

—Marketing places too much emphasis on material goals at the expense of non-material and social goals and it conspires with modern technology to develop innovations which people do not really need and which waste resources. If eight out of every ten new consumer products fail to become commercially viable, marketers' judgements must be pretty abysmal.

—Marketing has been insensitive and slow to respond to consumers' real needs and expectations. Consumerism, which has been described as 'the shame of the total marketing concept'‡ reflects the latter's moral and intellectual bankruptcy and its inability to define for itself a socially responsible role.

—There is, at best, only limited protection against the deliberate exploiter, the business firm that will consciously compromise product quality or safety, or that will use misleading promotion and unscrupulous pricing methods and credit practices in order to boost profits.

*See Bibliography p.284—Levitt (1970).
†See Bibliography p.284—Rodger (1973).
‡See Bibliography p.283—Drucker (1969b).

130

Weaknesses in philosophy and practice

It has already been noted that the marketing concept has three main elements—customer orientation, integration of effort, and profit direction.

Marketing was intended to put the customer at the very centre of the firm's planning activities. Knowledge of the customer, through researching and analysing his needs and behaviour, was to be the basis of the firm's marketing decisions and actions. In practice, it has neither prevented this knowledge and understanding of the customer from being used against him whenever this was felt to be in the firm's self-interest nor precluded the artificial and wasteful stimulation of customers' desires. In other words, the pursuit of short-run profit has not led automatically to the maximization of consumer satisfaction. It *may* do so, but it is by no means axiomatic. Marketing has done little to allay the basic human emotions of suspicion and scepticism based on fear of being cheated, persuaded against one's will, manipulated, and exploited.

Marketing was also intended to secure the integration of effort aimed at using the firm's full resources to the best advantage—research and development, design engineering, production, finance, selling and promotion, distribution, and after-sales service. In practice, even as an organizational and managerial concept, marketing has failed to live up to its promises. Organizational changes introduced as part of the new marketing orientation 'have spawned much interdepartmental conflict and concern'.*

Finally, the marketing approach was intended to minimize business risks and improve profitability, in both the short and the long term, through the use of systematic market research, the acquisition and analysis of market data relevant to decision-making, better market and sales forecasting, and improved product planning and selection.

In practice, average profitability in manufacturing industry, as represented by the return on capital invested before interest and tax (at replacement cost and after allowing for stock appreciation), has fallen by two-thirds over the past 20 years and consumers continue to reject the great majority of new products offered by manufacturers.

In sum, these three propositions—customer orientation, integration of effort, and profit direction—do not add up to a marketing philosophy. Customer orientation and integration of effort have merely been operational means to an end—the generation of profit.

In other words, the marketing concept as widely interpreted and currently practised, carries no firm commitment that a company is dedicated to the consumers' welfare or that it exists to serve their real long-range interests.

Making the Marketing Concept Work

If the marketing concept is to be made to really work then, at the

*See Bibliography p.284—Kotler (1966).

philosophical level, company managers and employees must demonstrate an active and positive concern for and a real commitment to the legitimate aspirations of consumers, and they must organize their firms' activities effectively to meet consumers' needs at the day-to-day operational level. Business management's response to the challenge posed by the consumer movement lies in the active and positive presentation of its concern for consumers' rights and aspirations. And, therefore, the way in which it expresses that concern must be studied in the interests of credibility. There should be no need to emphasize that if business fluffs this opportunity, it is unlikely to be given another chance to put its own house in order.

If the purpose of marketing is to respond to the legitimate needs and aspirations of consumers then the consumer movement should be seen not as a threat, but as an opportunity for marketing. Many marketers, particularly at the selling end of the business, have been guilty of getting things the wrong way round, by viewing the consumer merely as a means of generating short-run profit, without regard to long-term interests. Whereas, it should be clear to those company managements that have given the matter any serious thought, that their own and their consumers' long-term interests are best served by adopting consumer-regarding policies that provide satisfactory solutions to consumers' problems.

Marketing's commitment to the consumer

The marketing concept *is* capable of providing a channel of commitment to the consumer in proportion to the degree that it enhances the quality of consumers' judgements and maintains fair, competitive market conditions that allow consumers to choose freely between alternatives. Profit is the reward earned for correctly judging how best to meet consumers' needs and expectations, consistent with the above conditions. This has two implications.

—Any signals, whether actively sought by marketers through market research or gratuitously proffered by responsible and representative consumer organizations concerning consumer needs, expectations, or complaints, should be studied and acted upon as appropriate.
—The maintenance of fair, competitive market conditions and the safeguarding of basic consumer rights—to safety, to fair and respectful treatment, to be heard, and to have access to remedies for just complaints—cannot be left solely to the self-regulatory codes of practice of businessmen themselves.

As the first Director-General of OFT, Sir John Methven, said, 'If you get an informed consumer then the amount that you have to regulate by statute becomes so much less and that certainly is an objective.' This view is supported by Gordon Borrie, the present Director-General of OFT, who comes down firmly on the side of self-regulation as a first resort in business–consumer relations and advocates legislation only when the voluntary approach is seen to fail.

Some measure of Government preventive intervention, by legislative or other means, is unavoidable in order to maintain fair trading and competition, to prevent or control monopolies (both state and private) which limit consumer choice, and to safeguard consumers' rights. But the legal protection of the consumer should be kept to a minimum and enacted only as a last resort. Long-term consumer education, self-regulatory codes of practice, adverse publicity for those who transgress such codes, combined with a determined effort to ensure that consumers understand their rights under existing law, are likely to prove more successful in providing real consumer protection. For the quality of consumers' judgements in the market place will not be enhanced by removing from consumers the necessity to make their own decisions, or by imposing on the market conditions which limit the freedom of consumers' choice or the means of developing their powers of judgement. Indeed, if we go back to the seminal 1956 Report of the Molony Committee on Consumer Protection, we find support for this view in the following infrequently quoted passage:

> The measures we recommend in aid of the consumer do not aim to relieve him of the duty to look after himself. No system of protection can avert all the consequences of folly or eliminate every possibility of hardship. We have not tried to achieve this and we are sure it is neither possible nor desirable to do so. The law cannot guard against every wile or adjust every trifling injustice. The consumer's first safeguard must always be an alert and questioning attitude.

The progressive transfer to the state of individual responsibility for exercising judgement and making decisions is an ominous trend, inimical to the consumers' own long-range interests, and ought to be stoutly resisted.

So much for the philosophy. What of the practice?

The predominant mode of implementing the marketing concept has been to establish marketing as a specialized activity carried out by a separate department. Marketers have made use of a variety of diagnostic, analytical, and planning techniques in relation to consumer markets and then applied a battery of selling and promotional weapons in these markets. In retrospect, this has been a divisive rather than a unifying and consolidating development.

Instead of getting everyone in the firm to understand, accept, and identify with the marketing concept—an essential pre-condition for its successful implementation—the setting up of a separate marketing department and the creation of a separate marketing plan within the firm has been seen as a means whereby a group of executives have sought to impose on all other departments in the business something different from that which is ordinarily done. It has been seen as a grafting-on operation rather than as a fundamental reorientation of the total system.

Internalizing the marketing concept

The marketing concept needs to be internalized so that it is absorbed into the very ethos and fabric of the firm. The process of internalizing or institutionalizing the marketing concept has been well described by Professor Theodore Levitt of the Harvard Business School. Marketing thinking and planning must be fully integrated with the total business thinking and planning of the firm. The total business plan is the vehicle which harnesses, controls, and directs the firm's whole resources, human and material, in order to achieve its defined goals. It alone involves and commits all departments and functions of the firm.

Putting the marketing orientation into the business plan ' . . . has the particular virtue of not presuming to create something separate like a marketing plan and to this extent it reduces some of the resistance in the organisation that you may get'.* Since everyone, ordinarily, accepts the necessity of some sort of business plan on an annual basis, a more widespread acceptance and adoption of the marketing concept is more likely to come about by making it part of the thinking and planning that is already being carried on. Everyone, from the chief executive downwards, is, in this way, introduced to the marketing concept by a questioning process which focuses on the needs and expectations of customers and provides a perspective for decision-making at all levels of the firm.

This process of internalization is most important if the marketing concept is to be made to work properly in practice. It should not be seen as a subtle and devious way of advancing the interests and power of a particular department or function within the firm. The marketing reorientation of a firm requires a profound and broadly based attitude change, and the normal built-in processes of thinking and planning have proved to be the best channels to effect such a change.

There are three essential elements in this basic attitude change.†

—First, an active and positive commitment is needed to make the consumer the focus of all marketing decisions through service that delivers genuine consumer values and through the provision of factual information that improves the quality of consumers' judgements. There are a number of ways in which firms can demonstrate a real concern for the consumer in both these respects.

—Firms can supply more and better product information to the buyer— nutritional information, product use and care instructions, content information, safety and health warnings, unit pricing, and open dating.

—Firms can set better criteria of acceptability for promotion in relation to the selection and presentation of facts in advertisements, the substantiation of product/service performance and ingredient claims, the level of verbal extravagance, and public taste and sensibilities.

*See Bibliography p.284—Levitt (1972).
†See Bibliography p.284—Rodger (1976).

134

—Firms can have particular regard for the advertising and promotion of products in certain sensitive areas, such as drugs and medicines, tobacco, alcoholic drink, children's toys, and baby products.
—They can apply strict safeguards in respect of the employment of children in advertising, the use of advertising and other promotional appeals directed at children, the promotion of lotteries, competitions, special price offers, coupons and premiums, and the use of misleading packaging.
—They can provide better after-sales service, easily accessible complaint procedures, and efficient redress for consumer grievances.
—They can accept responsibility for the effects of the use of their products and services and for auditing how their products affect people and the environment.
—They can ensure that service contracts, notices, and guarantee provisions are clear and easily understood, and free of exceptions and exclusion clauses which purport to take away consumers' rights.
—Second, there can be greater emphasis on company integration based on a more positive and direct approach, on an industry-wide basis if necessary, towards optimizing consumer values and achieving an acceptable balance of company and social objectives and responsibilities.
—Third, concern for the environment and for consumer wellbeing should not be looked upon as constraints but rather as new opportunities for creating satisfactions. The reward for doing so efficiently is a reasonable profit. But the community will demand that it be 'socially responsible' profit that does not exploit the consumer, damage the environment, or incur unacceptable human and social costs.

Anything less than a genuine concern for the consumer and a total commitment by top management and line marketing management to the principles of the marketing concept as previously outlined is not only bound to fail; it will surely hasten the detailed surveillance and control of business practices by legislation.

Past Imperfect, Future Conditional

The past imperfections and present inadequacies of the marketing concept have been laid bare. Little has been said about the imperfections of the market mechanism as a means whereby consumers' needs can be properly expressed and efficiently met. It has been argued that despite its operational shortcomings, the marketing concept has validity as a business philosophy and is capable of providing a channel of commitment to the consumers' short- and long-run interests.

The future credibility of this view will depend upon the degree to which business succeeds in developing more sensitive and well tuned marketing responses to consumers' existing and emerging requirements and expectations. The spirit in which business tackles this task will matter more than the letter.

The marketing response

Marketers who monitor, anticipate, and work with the activities of a growing and self-confident consumer movement are likely to derive significant competitive advantage over erstwhile rivals who merely sit back and adopt a more passive role.

Apart from a growing commitment by managements to a more open dialogue with consumers, there will have to be a deliberate planned effort to institutionalize their concern for the consumer in a number of practical ways that go beyond the minimum that the law demands.

Consumer complaints

First, there will need to be considerably more attention paid by manufacturers and service organizations to the efficient handling of consumer complaints. Still too few companies provide easy access in cases of dissatisfaction. The Confederation of British Industry has highlighted the main criticisms of the present handling of complaints by consumers. Firms are frequently defensive in their dealings with consumers, offer only vague assurances, delay or fail to reply or to commit themselves to do anything positive to redress a particular complaint. This unconstructive approach is most glaring in a monopoly situation and it is partly the reason why the National Consumer Council (NCC) has devoted such a large proportion of its resources to studying the nationalized industries and public and social services and has recommended sweeping changes in existing arrangements for consumer representation.

Many firms have yet to accept that it is in their interests to ensure that the proper machinery is set up to deal effectively and expeditiously with consumer complaints, at the right management level. Few firms have as yet considered the merit of having a 'hot line' for consumers, with readily accepted reversed charges. Consumer complaints departments will have to become more systematic in their analysis of complaints as a source of information for managers to act upon in relation to the design, quality, distribution, safety, and reliability in use of their products. These ideas are dealt with at greater length in chapter 9.

Codes of practice

Second, there will have to be much greater progress made in devising self-regulatory codes of practice for each industry and profession that really work, the principles and practices of which are examined in chapters 13, 14, and 15.

Clearly, the main advantages of such codes of practice are the raising of standards for consumers, the reduction in consumer scepticism about the preparedness of firms to tackle sources of dissatisfaction, and the avoidance of legislation that would be difficult, slow, and costly to administer and enforce. However, it must be said that if firms are to establish real credibility in the eyes of consumers, and if these codes of conduct are not to be dismissed as cosmetic, window-dressing exercises, then business must be seen to be monitoring its own performance seriously, providing watch-dogs with teeth that really bite, and not flinching from the public exposure of, and the application of sanctions to, those of its members who break the rules.

Conflicts in marketing management

Third, business managements, steeped as they are in their own case law and with a tendency to apply old organizational solutions to new problems, must come to realize that the appointment to boards of companies of full-time marketing directors and the education of employees at all levels in the organization as to the meaning and rationale of the marketing concept will not, in themselves, be enough to ensure that the right things happen. Especially, marketing management must accept that it cannot be both judge and prosecutor in its own case. Marketing executives, in the final analysis, are required to prosecute the firm's business policies and are responsible for producing results. They are subject to the conflicting pressures of making a profit for the firm, meeting the immediate requirements of customers and, one hopes, having regard for consumers' long-run interests.

Institutionalizing the consumer affairs function

Fourth, concern for the consumer may best be brought about by institutionalizing the consumer affairs function within the particular industry and within the individual business enterprise. It will have specific responsibility for representing the consumer—his needs, expectations, and frustrations—at the highest policy-making level.

In the US a growing number of firms are developing policies which are designed to take heed of the signals, suggestions, and criticisms coming from the consumer movement. Among leading companies which have introduced consumer-oriented policies are Giant Food (a supermarket chain), Whirlpool and Zenith Radio Corporation (electrical goods), American Motors and Ford Motor Company (cars), J. C. Penney and Montgomery Ward (department stores), Proctor and Gamble (soaps, detergents, health and beauty-care products), Corning Glass (heat resistant glass products), New York Life Assurance, and Coca-Cola (soft drinks). Consumer policies, naturally, vary from firm to firm, and the detailed experience of Giant Food is described in chapter 19, but all have three things in common. First, the policies are designed to improve profitability as well as being a positive response to pressures from the consumer movement. Second, consumer affairs (or consumer relations) is regarded as an executive function with responsibility for it being assigned at a high, sometimes board, level. Third, an important part of the function is the provision of consumer education programmes covering publications, buying guides, teaching modules, and visual aids.

According to a report of a survey carried out by the U S National Industrial Conference Board on consumer affairs departments within U S firms, about three-quarters of those studied had been set up since 1970. Just over 60 per cent operate as self-contained units reporting to general management, rather than as part of the marketing function. Among the major responsibilities most commonly listed are complaints handling, communications with consumers about the firm's products, liaising with consumer groups, and acting as a kind of internal consumer ombudsman. The primary function of the company consumer affairs adviser is to represent the consumers' interests to management rather than to act as the company's ambassador to consumers.

Based on American experience, a possible model for U K firms is for the consumer and environmental viewpoints to be represented by a senior executive, possibly at director level, and attached to the office of the chairman or chief executive. He or she will be independent of operating management or any other staff group. It will be his job to act as the firm's antennae and to monitor, report on, and make recommendations to the board on movements in consumer, social, and environmental opinion impinging on the firm's offerings, policies, and operations. In this role he will be a listener, not a lobbyist with consumer groups, politicians or Government departments. He will not be the keeper of the corporate conscience—this is a collective responsibility of all board members. But it will be his task to ensure that other board members are kept informed about the implications of the firm's marketing policies and actions as they affect consumers and the external environment generally. He may have a small personal staff but will have authority to call on the firm's own or external market research facilities and on legal advisers to carry out enquiries on his behalf or to provide advice. He will have regular consultations with representative consumer bodies and relevant Government agencies concerned with consumer and environmental affairs. His title should reflect the nature of the firm's markets and the scope of the job. 'Director of consumer affairs' might be appropriate for a consumer goods manufacturer or service organization; 'director of customer relations' may be more suitable for a manufacturer of industrial products. Much more important than the title, however, is what lies behind it—what scope and what specific responsibilities its holder has, what authority he carries, and at what level he reports within the firm.

Whatever the title, the consumer affairs or customer relations function must be concerned, in one direction, to learn how the firm is influenced by and can be made more sensitive and responsive to changes in the demands of the consumer environment and, in the other direction, to learn how the consumer environment is influenced by, interprets, and responds to the various actions by the firm.

It may be argued that a senior director with overall responsibility for consumer and environmental affairs may be fine for a big multi-million pound firm but that smaller firms cannot afford to employ a full-time executive in this capacity. For reasons already stated, it will be obvious that it is not a part-time job for another (possibly underemployed) functional executive. There is scope here for an industry-wide resource to be made available to small firms, through trade associations or professional bodies.

Consumer consultative councils, another form of institutionalizing the concern for customers of nationalized industries and public services, have proved to be relatively ineffective according to the National Consumer Council. The Government is seriously at fault here for not practising (in areas where it can exercise control) what it purports to preach to others— that is, providing consumers with an effective voice, listening intently to what they have to say, and taking active steps to redress their grievances. New modes of consumer representation will have to be found—e.g., having consumer/user repesentatives on the boards of nationalized corporations. This aspect is examined in more detail in chapter 6.

In the longer term, it is conceivable that there could be an amalgamation of consumer representation at an official level alongside the Confederation of British Industry (CBI) representing industrial concerns, the British Institute of Management (BIM) representing professional management and the Trades Union Congress (TUC) representing the labour movement. The consumers' point of view must be represented at the time that policy is being determined and not after the key decisions have been taken.

Certainly there is scope in the shorter term for appointing non-executive consumer directors to the boards of, say, the 200 largest private companies and of the nationalized corporations, and to the top administrative councils of the National Health Service and other social services.

The EEC perspective

Fifth and last, the burgeoning consumer protection regulations likely to flow from the EEC Commission in Brussels, and more particularly from the strengthened Environment and Consumer Protection Service, present an urgent and growing need to have the views of British marketing and business strongly represented in the councils of Europe. This will require much greater coordination and cooperation between the different marketing bodies—the Institute of Marketing, the Marketing Society, the Market Research Society, the Industrial Marketing Research Association, the Advertising Association, the Incorporated Society of British Advertisers, and the Institute of Practitioners in Advertising. Within the EEC, the law is very often the first rather than the last resort. A member country that prefers to opt for self-regulation may find itself carried along by the legislative tide against its better judgement unless it organizes itself to resist such encroachments. As history testifies, one must not confuse morality with legality, domestically or internationally.

The anticipated developments in marketing and consumer representation which have been briefly touched on in this chapter have probably never been more critical for British business nor the demands that will be made upon our business leaders more challenging.

CODES OF PRACTICE

13. A new initiative

Jim Humble

During the past five years, the Office of Fair Trading (OFT) has been involved in negotiations leading to the publication of twelve codes of practice in six major industries—namely, the package holidays, electrical servicing, automobile, footwear, drycleaning, and furniture industries. Also, at the time of writing, codes for mail-order photographic equipment and funerals are under consideration. Each code is self-regulating and consists of a comprehensive statement of the best trading practices of the industry, together with a system for settling disputes and complaints.

Self-regulatory codes of practice were not, of course, invented by the OFT. In the 'sixties the food and advertising industries both took important voluntary measures to regulate abuses. The food industry introduced codes about the fill, composition, and labelling of canned fruit and vegetables, and the advertising industry, through the Advertising Standards Authority, drew up detailed rules for advertising and sales promotion practices.

At that time, there were a number of other industry and trade association codes which were rather less effective. Some consisted merely of generalized statements of goodwill and good intention which were difficult to interpret, monitor, or control. Others included provisions which tended to restrict competition and inhibit innovation by maintaining market shares or guaranteeing minimum prices. Agreements of this type tended to fall foul of restrictive practices legislation.

The Beginning

In 1973, after the Fair Trading Act was passed by Parliament, OFT was established—a new agency with powers to explore the connection between consumer protection and competition problems and propose effective remedies. One of the Director-General of Fair Trading's many duties was, in the words of Section 124 of the Fair Trading Act, to 'encourage trade associations to prepare and disseminate to their members, codes of practice for guidance in safeguarding and promoting the interests of consumers'.

These 'consumer protection codes' had to steer clear of restrictive practices legislation and—unlike codes with a statutory base, such as the Highway Code and those prescribed by the Health and Safety Commission—they could not be *imposed* by the Director-General. The codes were the property of the sponsor trade association and the Director-General's role was one of encouragement. Let me now describe how, in the early days of OFT, we approached this task of encouragement and how our thinking evolved at that time.

A number of difficulties were immediately obvious. An industry could refuse to prepare a code of practice. Benefits agreed in a code would be available only from the members of the trade association. Some traders, even for good and proper reasons, might not wish to belong, while others—the dishonest fringe responsible for a disproportionate number of problems and most in need of a code of conduct—were unlikely to subscribe to the jurisdiction of a trade body. How would a consumer be able to discriminate between members and non-members of a trade association? It was obvious that some trade associations were weak and ineffectual and that, even if they were able to draw up a code they would be unable to enforce any sanctions on members who ignored it. Other industries had a multiplicity of trade associations representing different sectors or different points of view. These might produce quite different codes, and any gains in standards might be offset by an increase in consumer bewilderment and confusion. On the other hand, attempts to form a common front were likely to result in the lowest common denominator.

To set against these drawbacks, codes of practice developed by trade associations appeared to offer some distinct advantages. The principles and norms should be sensible and practical, representing, at best, the highest standards of the industry. Provisions voluntarily agreed on this basis were likely to be adhered to far more enthusiastically than imposed controls. Certainly, business was less likely to spend time and ingenuity trying to get round the letter or the spirit of an agreed set of standards.

If codes failed, OFT had other powers. Legislation could be proposed to prohibit trading practices which were shown to be against the economic interests of consumers. Assurances could be sought from traders who persisted in a course of conduct detrimental or unfair to consumers. Refusal to give such assurances or failure to observe these provisions could be dealt with in the County Court or Restrictive Practices Court.

_Codes had other benefits. The responsibility for enforcement would fall on the trade association, helping to relieve the burden on the overstretched local authority trading standards officers. This would allow them to concentrate their resources on areas of trade where no such voluntary protection existed and ensure that the costs to society as a whole were kept to a minimum. At the same time, encouraging a code could sometimes be much more satisfactory than promoting legislation to curb and control business. Changing the law is slow, time consuming, and expensive. General laws can rarely fit the circumstances of every industry, and attempts to legislate for some of the minor irritants of trading behaviour—such as slow service and a defensive attitude to complaints—might be draconian, if not downright impossible. A trade association code should be able to deal with this type of behavioural problem quickly and flexibly, with solutions tailormade to the customs and practice of the industry concerned.

Aims and Objectives

This, then, was the theory. In 1974, OFT began to clarify its aims and objectives and it was clear that, if the scarce resources of the Office were to be put to best use, priority should be given to the development of industry codes for trades where there was evidence of widespread consumer dissatisfaction and complaint. An essential pre-condition was a strong and viable trade association with the will to cooperate in the improvement of standards.

There was no shortage of willing candidates. Consumers protection in the preceeding decade had undergone a metamorphosis, with new legislation, a rapid expansion of local authority consumer protection and advice services, a Minister of Consumer Affairs, and a Director-General of Fair Trading. The media adopted a keen crusading interest and many traders, shell-shocked, felt worried that the undoubted failings of a small minority of their colleagues reflected badly on the reputation of their particular industry.

Many businessmen and women began to appreciate that a code of practice might be used to put their house in order and that, if the changes were of substance and of benefit to the consumer, the members of the trade association would also reap benefits—certainly, in terms of public relations.

In 1974, OFT embarked on a series of detailed consultations with consumer organizations and their expert advisers. Consumer complaints were analysed and it became obvious that a number of industries had a particularly high ratio of problems, with complaints falling into four major categories.

—Breakdown of equipment and a general dissatisfaction over the quality of goods and servicing.
—An obstructive, evasive, or defensive manner adopted by the small number of traders who were the subject of dispute or complaint.
—Lack of information about the composition, care and maintenance, durability, performance, and price of goods and services—all of these being information which would help consumers to make a careful and informed purchase.
—The persistence of a number of unfair trading practices, such as the use of small print exclusions of liability, dubious bargain offers, and the misuse of customer deposits.

We soon saw that many of the problems might be tackled in codes of practice but some obviously could not. For example, in the short term, little

145

could be done about the problem of shoddy goods by using a code as a means to raise directly the standard of products such as motor cars, washing machines, shoes, or suites of furniture. Indeed, a consumer has been legally entitled to receive goods 'fit for their purpose' since 1893 and this right continues to exist without the need for an express provision in a code of practice. However, it seemed to us that something could be done about the handling of complaints, the provision of clearer information, and the abandonment of unfair trading practices. This, then, was our early 'codes philosophy'. The following paragraphs set out important features of codes which were encouraged by the Office of Fair Trading and show how they were embodied in codes which have already been published.

Dealing with Complaints

The central core of all OFT-sponsored codes is a clear and simple system of handling consumer complaints. I have already mentioned that consumer advisers had told us of the shortcomings and defensive attitudes of many traders. To overcome these, we have evolved a simple four-stage system designed to resolve disputes quickly and sensibly and minimize the cost of complaints to everyone concerned.

Stage One. The consumer is referred to the supplier or seller. The supplier or seller should have an established policy, known to all members of staff, designed to ensure that immediate and effective action is taken to achieve a fair and just settlement.

Stage Two. If no settlement is reached, the consumer or trader may seek independent help and guidance from the local Trading Standards Department, Citizens' Advice Bureau or Consumer Advice Centre. A proportion of disputes is inevitably due to conflicts of personality. Disputes of this kind can often be quickly resolved through the mediation of a third party at local level.

Stage Three. Conciliation should, if necessary, be provided by the trade association. The secretariat of a trade association has direct access to its members and may be able to resolve difficult issues by persuading them to take a broad view about the reputation of the industry. The trade association may also be prepared to incur the cost of testing, when necessary.

Stage Four. A small number of complaints will need further attention. At this stage, OFT advocates an independent, legally binding solution. This could be either a simple form of 'documents only' arbitration conducted by the Institute of Arbitrators or the small claims procedure in the County Court (in Scotland, the new Summary Cause procedure in the Sheriff Court).

It is impossible to be certain about the *total* volume of consumer complaints, but some idea of the magnitude relating to each stage of the procedure may be gained from the figures below. Studies undertaken by OFT indicate that on average four per cent of consumer complaints are referred to our advice service. On this basis it is estimated that in

146

1975-76 there were approximately 1 000 000 consumers dissatisfied with their motor cars. Of these, 44 438 complained to consumer advisors. Only 5215 were referred to the Motor Agents Association for conciliation and 182 were settled by arbitration. In the case of electrical appliance servicing, out of an estimated 150 000 consumer complaints, 6429 were referred to local consumer advisers, 829 to the trade association at the conciliation stage, and only one case to independent arbitration.

Consumer Information

A complaints procedure operates only *after* problems have arisen and so, if a code is to be effective, it must be drafted or designed in a manner which will help to prevent subsequent disputes. Many of these disputes seem to arise because a consumer has unreasonable expectations about his purchase. Sometimes it is the consumer's fault because he has not read or followed the operating instructions but there are many cases which can be traced directly to the lack of information or inadequate information provided by the manufacturer or retailer.

A code may be used to make trade definitions more meaningful to consumers and set out minimum requirements for the provision of product information in a way that can be understood by the purchaser.

A number of provisions taken from codes already published will serve as examples. In the service industries, a great deal of irritation arises over the size of a final account for repairs or servicing or over the minimum cost of a service engineer's 'call out' charge. Of course, no-one likes to pay high bills, particularly during periods of high inflation, but problems of this type can and have been minimized by firms adopting a policy of advising the cost of work before servicing commences, either by means of quotations or by detailed estimates. Further, responsible firms always take care to obtain authorization immediately it appears likely that any estimate will be exceeded.

Still on the subject of charges, the price of goods or services should *always* be clearly displayed and should include the cost of Value Added Tax. Receipts and invoices detailing the separate cost of parts and labour should be provided. All the codes contain provisions of this nature and the charges have not been found to create undue difficulty for suppliers and service engineers.

Consumers sometimes have unreasonable expectations about the life or durability of a product. Durability depends to some extent upon care and usage but a manufacturer can and should give guidance by indicating the minimum periods for which spare parts will be available. This has been done most effectively in the code prepared by the Association of Manufacturers of Domestic Electrical Appliances (AMDEA). In the case of complex products some problems can be avoided if greater care is taken over the presentation of instructions on installation and use and the drafting of warranties in unambiguous terms. Information should be given about all 'field' servicing appointments, and OFT is particularly keen to encourage appointment systems. The provision of this type of information applies to a wide range of industries. Examples taken from existing codes include requirements for clear information about a customer's liability if he cancels a package holiday; the main materials in the soles and uppers of shoes; labelling information about the care of upholstered furniture; the fuel consumption of new motor cars; and an undertaking to pass on details about the previous history and service record whenever a member of the Motor Agents Association sells a used vehicle.

Unfair trading practices

Codes can be very effective in regulating practices which, though legal, are deemed by consumer organizations to be unfair. For example, until 1973 suppliers of goods could limit their liability by the use of guarantees which substituted less demanding terms on the supplier than would otherwise have been implied by the Sale of Goods Act 1893. The Supply of Goods (Implied Terms) Act 1973 made such terms void. However, before Parliament passed the Unfair Contract Terms Act 1977, the law allowed traders providing *services* much greater latitude—for example, to disclaim responsibility for their own negligence. Responsible traders were quick to point out that they tended not to enforce this type of exclusion but OFT urged with some success that 'small print' exclusions of liability should be banned on a self-regulatory basis. This was readily accepted by all the trade associations with whom we discussed the problem—notably, the travel agents, dry cleaners and launderers, and those responsible for the servicing of electrical appliances and motor cars.

Another trading practice which causes concern is the use of fictitious or exaggerated bargain price offers. Claims are sometimes made that goods have a much higher 'value' or 'worth' than is really the case; that discounts are *'up to'* a certain amount, or that similar goods can be found at much higher prices 'elsewhere'. These claims may be ambiguous, misleading, or unverifiable, but they do not constitute an offence under trade description legislation. The electrical dealers, shoe retailers, and garages have banned this type of misdescription on a self-regulatory basis.

There are, of course, many other examples of practices which could, and might in the future, be dealt with by legislation. But the Parliamentary timetable is crowded and one might tend to think it a misuse of scarce resources to propose general legislation when abuses are prevalent in only one sector of the market place. Broad spectrum legislation can have unexpected and undesirable consequences and it would seem far better to test the controls, voluntarily, on an industry-by-industry basis. Existing codes already ban some practices, including 'switch-selling' by some electrical dealers; the overbooking of holiday hotels; mail-order traders operating a business using customers' deposits as working capital; over-optimistic promises of early delivery by furniture dealers; and the use of standard mileage disclaimers in the used car trade. The fact that problems of this type can be dealt with in the context of a code of practice is a weighty benefit for the customer—and a way of avoiding more legislation for the trader to remember.

Enforcement

The essential kernel of self-regulatory codes of practice is that they are of little value unless they are obeyed. This is not to say that OFT expects a dramatic overnight transformation remedying all known abuses among trade association members. Even the existence of legal sanctions and the imposition of heavy financial penalties cannot achieve this utopia. Rather, we expect a steady improvement in behavioural and trading standards over a period of time. The period will vary from industry to industry and from code to code with the ever present danger of a 'Catch 22' situation—namely, immediate, 100 per cent observance of a code probably means the standard was set too low and the code is open to criticism as a worthless recitation of existing practices. However, if the provisions are demanding, set at the standard of the best (or better than the best), there will inevitably be failures and the code is open to criticism as being ineffective.

The responsibility for the enforcement of the code and for advising and training members clearly falls upon the trade association, but there is then a problem about the type of sanctions which can reasonably be imposed on members who occasionally or even persistently break the code provisions. Only a small minority of members are likely to be involved, but when it comes to sanctions and enforcement the reputation of the industry might well depend upon its treatment of these few members.

A trade association depends, for its existence, on the subscriptions of members, but if these self-same members are perceived to behave irresponsibly then any public kudos achieved by the publication of a code will be quickly dissipated. It is important to have an effective sanction. In the case of the Association of British Travel Agents (ABTA), breaches of the code may be dealt with by financial penalties and even expulsion from membership, which, because of the nature of the agreements between travel agents and tour operators, is likely to result in substantial loss of business. Other codes refer to expulsion with adverse publicity or invite recalcitrant members to explain their behaviour before the trade association council. These may be considered to be light penalties but, although the disapproval of a peer group is ill-defined in comparison with legal sanctions, its power as a regulator of personal and company behaviour should not be underestimated.

Monitoring

The OFT brings reported breaches of a code of practice to the notice of the relevant trade association and also helps to inform consumers about a code's potential benefit. However, after the initial launch of the code, OFT's primary efforts are directed towards a detailed and careful monitoring programme. The monitoring programme on each code is substantial. In each industry the complaints received by trading standards officers, Citizens' Advice Bureaux, and Consumer Advice Centres are examined on a systematic basis. The complaints against members and non-members are analysed and relayed to the trade association for possible revision of the code. On this basis the problems of last minute surcharges imposed on holidaymakers and the overbooking of continental hotels were dealt with by an amendment to the code of the Association of British Travel Agents.

In supporting any code of practice, OFT requires trade associations to analyse complaints received and monitor the performance of their own members. The details of these studies help to highlight failures. They are published in trade association annual reports and are sent to OFT on a regular basis.

Additionally OFT undertakes its own research by sending questionnaires to consumers and it has commissioned market research agencies to carry out detailed surveys of current trading practices and adherence to the provisions of a code. The National Federation of Consumer Groups has also helped to monitor the effectiveness of codes. In due course the findings of these monitoring studies will be published, but at this early stage in the programme there have been a few encouraging signs and some disappointments.

First, it does seem that trade associations are putting substantial effort and resources into training and advising their members. For example, the Motor Agents Association (MAA) make observance of their code an essential condition of membership. Articles about the MAA Code appear regularly in the Association's magazine having a circulation of 27 000 copies. Six regional centres have been opened to deal with complaints about cars directly from the public and it is rare for an officer of the MAA to make a speech at a seminar, or to take part in a radio or television programme, without a reference to the code requirements. The MAA's efforts are described fully in chapter 14.

Second, the volume of consumer complaints about traders who subscribe to a code appears gradually to be diminishing. In the case of AMDEA members, the change was quite dramatic. In 1974 a study of complaints about electrical servicing revealed that 75 per cent of complaints concerned members of the Association. Two years later, after the introduction of the code, a similar study revealed that members' share of complaints had fallen to 27 per cent.

Third, we seem to be witnessing a general improvement in standards, with a widening performance gap between the members and non-members of a trade association.

On the debit side, there is widespread ignorance among the general public about the existence of codes. Sometimes companies and their employees are slow to adopt the necessary code provisions. There has been a failure by some of the leading electrical manufacturers to meet the three-day target for a first servicing visit laid down in the A M D E A Code. Many used-car dealers continue to adopt unacceptable forms of odometer disclaimer, and unfair 'small print' conditions continue to appear in the literature of a few drycleaners and travel agents. However, these failings do seem to relate to a minority and our experience has been that the great majority of companies are prepared to change their practices once deficiencies are brought to their attention.

Earlier I pointed out that codes could do little to deal directly with the problem of shoddy goods and poor service. This is not always strictly true. Some codes do require goods to be produced in accordance with British Standards. Codes can also require that manufacturers submit pre-production samples of a new product for independent testing and analysis to ensure that areas of weakness are properly remedied. This has been done with most beneficial results in the case of shoes. Most important, every code demands that the monitoring system is associated with a feedback of complaints to manufacturers and service agents. Many problems have continued in the past simply because the manufacturer had insufficient information about the manner in which his product performed in the market place. This policy of monitoring and feedback will, perhaps more than any other factor, help to encourage a reduction in the rates of failure.

Limitations

It is becoming clear that codes can work only if firms take their obligations seriously, change their management information systems, and introduce new staff-training programmes. Even so, there are clear limitations. I have already pointed out the difficulty of prescribing an *improvement* in the quality of goods or the standard of workmanship in servicing and have no doubt that, whatever the state of law or self-regulation, engineers and mechanics will continue to make mistakes in servicing complex goods like motor cars and washing machines. The codes might help a little and produce pressure for improvement by the acknowledgement of errors through the operation of the complaints system.

Codes of practice cannot be expected to induce a trader to change a practice which, in the prevailing market conditions, is substantially to his competitive advantage. A case in point is the practice of inflating recommended retail prices, a policy which appears to be being adopted by a number of well-known manufacturers. It is important to recognize that certain problems are not susceptible to treatment by voluntary means and these should be tackled by other measures, such as legislation.

A third point is that codes are restricted in their application, applying solely to the members of the trade association. This will always be a critical weakness but one which can be somewhat mitigated if trade associations seek to extend their membership to include all responsible firms within the industry. The Vehicle Builders' and Repairers' Association, with an existing membership of 1800 repairers, received 500 new membership applications within three months of the code being published. It also helps if members display a logo, sign, or symbol signifying their clear adoption of a code of practice. This allows 'informed' consumers to discriminate in their favour and helps to increase their share of the market.

Codes or Legislation?

It should be recognized that OFT's policy on codes is still experimental. The early signs are encouraging, but unless codes bring substantial benefits to consumers there is likely to be increasing pressure for them to be put in a legislative framework.

Various options might be canvassed. For example, the adoption of the letter and spirit of a code could be deemed to be a licensing requirement, the necessary pre-requisite to the right to trade or carry on business. Alternatively, persistent breaches of an approved code might be considered a course of conduct detrimental to the interests of consumers, within the provisions of Part III of the Fair Trading Act 1973. This would enable OFT to seek an assurance of good behaviour from the trader concerned.

The codes might have added status if they had statutory backing, perhaps by being used as a reference mark for action in civil or criminal cases. Individual code provisions may foreshadow criminal provisions in certain cases. This has already happened in the case of VAT-exclusive prices, the display of void notices in shops, and the Unfair Contract Terms Act 1977.

However, before introducing legal sanctions into the area of voluntary agreement and self-regulation, the Government would wish to satisfy itself that the existing policy had failed to promote better standards and that legislative support was necessary. Indeed, it often seems that each breach of a code adds to the chorus of voices proposing this type of solution.

Quite apart from the cost of drafting and enforcing new legislation, unnecessary costs might be imposed on large numbers of traders who, although they observed the highest standards, would be faced with re-organizing their business to avoid the possibility of criminal conviction.

Trade associations would be understandably reluctant to draw up codes in specific terms if this could increase the chances that members might fall foul of legislation. Statutory codes would be more difficult to amend, trade associations less willing to enforce them, and the very real benefits gained by consumers when traders observe the spirit as well as the letter of a code might be lost.

Conclusions

Self-regulatory codes are still new, but already there are signs that they are helping to promote the interests of consumers. Consumers who discriminate in favour of trade association members who adhere to a code of practice help to enlarge the core of honest, fair, and responsible traders.

152

Improvements in standards will not be achieved overnight (worthwhile improvements seldom are), and they will not be achieved on a universal basis. But if traders adopt the provisions of a code seriously, in a determined manner, it should lead to an overall, but positive, improvement in general standards of trading. In this respect the enforcement of the code and a regular system of monitoring are crucial.

Higher standards are of limited value if consumers remain unaware of their existence. Once companies become convinced they can abide by the higher standards of a code they should do much more to promote its existence, for example, by taking every opportunity to incorporate the code symbol or logo in their advertising and marketing programme. It is not good enough for the whole burden of publicity to be left to the trade association.

I have stressed several times that codes of practice are still in the experimental stage. After some five years of personal involvement in their evolution, I hope and believe they will succeed. I therefore ask the critics of codes—those in industry and those in the consumer movement—to pause and to ponder whether they ought not to be encouraging and supporting these initiatives rather than belittling them. If the enthusiasm which is being put into promoting codes of practice, and of which the following two chapters provide abundant evidence, is decried to the extent that the trade associations and firms concerned lose heart, then consumers will undoubtedly be worse off.

14. What a trade association can do: The Motor Agents Association

Alan M. Dix

A trade association by its very nature is an organization which looks after the interests of companies or individuals engaged in a given industry or trade. Some might even say it is a pressure group. In the case of the Motor Agents Association, our income consists in the main of membership subscriptions. Given those facts, it takes a certain amount of enlightened self-interest and knowledge of marketing and all that it entails before any trade association decides voluntarily to sign a code of practice.

The Motor Agents Association made that decision when, in December 1975, we signed the Motor Industry Code of Practice after prolonged consultation with the Office of Fair Trading. Other signatories to the Code were the Scottish Motor Trade Association, with whom we are closely allied, and, on behalf of the car manufacturers and importers, the Society of Motor Manufacturers and Traders.

Motor Industry Code

What is it? Why did we do it? What are our obligations? And what do we expect to gain from it in the future?

The Code sets out to govern the conduct of manufacturers, importers, and retailers on the one hand, and consumers on the other, in relation to the supply of new and used cars, petrol, parts, and accessories. It also embodies standards of car servicing and repair, and it is fair to state that the principles outlined have, in fact, been observed by the majority of the industry for very many years. The principles embodied in the Code are not intended to interpret, qualify, or supplement the law of the land, and are not intended to be applied to non-consumer sales.

The Motor Agents Association regard it as a duty laid on their members that they will accept the Code in its entirety. The Code was drawn up and signed in the realization that proper guidelines for the relationship between car retailers and their customers over a period of time would bring their own rewards, not the least of which would be to improve the retail motor industry's image.

As an Association, we take the view that it is not our function either to defend the indefensible or to whitewash the wilfully negligent or dishonest actions of a member. That, in any event, would not improve the image.

We believe that any large number of people associated in common tasks, such as is the case with our members, get approximately the reputation they deserve and if that reputation leaves something to be desired then the cure is not assisted by some sort of cosmetic action. It is only when the root causes of complaints and dissatisfaction have been identified and eliminated that we may expect a cure—following which, the reputation takes care of itself.

The second reason why we approached the drawing up of the Code in a very serious and determined manner was because buying a car, and its subsequent maintenance and repair, are frequently rather emotive subjects so far as the consumer is concerned. It is only right and proper that the rights and obligations of both parties should be agreed upon and printed for the widest possible distribution and knowledge—although the obligations on the consumer tend to be moral rather than legal. It is with great deliberation that I just stated 'the rights and obligations of both parties', because it is a fact that a properly drawn up code of practice is not intended to be, and must never be, a means whereby the consumer may more easily abuse the retailer or vice versa.

Third, we felt that *vis à vis* the growing consumerist movement, most of which is both fair and honest, we wanted it to be seen that we were a realistically consumer and marketing orientated trade, as marketing by definition is 'doing all that which makes the consumer want to buy your product'.

Fourth, we felt then, as we still do, that it is always better to do the right thing voluntarily than to have it rammed down one's throat by legislation; there is some doubt in our minds whether the country can, in fact, afford any more legislation than it has already, especially as much of it, regrettably, is punitive, useless, expensive, unnecessary, and frequently based upon envy.

Overcoming Doubts

It would have been unusual, of course, if at the time when our Code was adopted, it had found absolutely universal favour and acceptance with all our (and the Scottish Motor Trade Association's) 17 000 members. Some saw the Code as abject surrender to the offensive of the consumer movement.

There were, in fact, a few who decided to ignore the Code or, equally negatively, decided only to pay lip service to it: while their management would sing its praises, their staff—who were really the ones most likely to breach it—were never told about it, and therefore were not in a position to adhere to it even if they wanted to.

The decision was made, therefore, to place continuing emphasis on the subject of the Code through all means available to the Association other than advertising (which, unfortunately, was not within our financial resources).

Nevertheless, since its inception, the Code has been mentioned in detail whenever officers or staff of the Motor Agents Association have been interviewed on radio or television. It has also been the subject of both leader and feature articles in our own monthly industry magazine which, apart from its distribution to our members, goes regularly to finance houses, banks, members of the Government, the Civil Service, and others. It is a standing instruction in the Association that, whenever officers or staff address any audience—and this happens many, many times a year—mention of the Code in some detail must take place, and facts about it must feature prominently in such newsletters as go to the membership from time to time, including the Association's Annual Report.

To emphasize the seriousness with which we view the Code, adherence to it, by official resolution by the Management Committee and National Councils, has been made a condition of new membership and of continuing an existing membership, and the Association's annual membership renewal reminder has been reprinted to make this point.

It will be seen, I hope, that we are not treating the Code lightly—we want it to succeed, and take our obligations seriously; so seriously that any attack upon the Code from any source is answered personally by me, as chief executive of the Association.

Does that mean that the Code has enemies? Yes, it means that, particularly among local authority trading standards officers, there are some who believe the Codes—not only our Code, but any Code—are a waste of time because they 'do not have teeth' and should be replaced by legislation. Fortunately, a change in attitude of certain senior trading standards officers has taken place in recent times because the Association has been able to prove that, whenever they complain to us about non-adherence, we take immediate action to support their case. Such action by us is obviously never going to win us any popularity contests with offending members. In fact, we might even lose a few. Unfortunate as that may be, we shall have a better, stronger Association as a result. Being optimistic by nature, I dare say that those who leave in anger may well regret their decision and return to the fold at a later date. If not—so be it.

Identifying Members

In order for the Association to comply with Section 8.1 of the Code, which states:

> As subscribers to the Code of Practice, retailers should ensure that the symbols of their appropriate association(s) are clearly displayed for the information of consumers as indicating adherence to the Industry Code of Practice

we took the opportunity to update our rather old-fashioned logo by having a new one designed. This has now been embodied in a new identification programme which, in due course, will appear on the premises of all our members. This will enable the public to identify from a distance motor traders who are under an obligation to adhere to the Code from those who, because they are not our members, are under no such obligation. These signs are sold to our members at cost, plus an advertising surcharge which, at the appropriate moment, will be used to conduct an advertising campaign aimed at informing the consumer of the advantages of the Code.

Consumer Complaints

The most obvious advantage of the Code is that it provides for the proper handling of complaints from a consumer, with conciliation by the Association and, if necessary, independent arbitration. It is on this point, I suspect, that our critics believe us to be the least efficient. In their opinion, an association cannot side with a consumer against one of its own members— and even if it could, so they say, it is not in a position to punish anyone as seriously as the law might if the Code were replaced by legislation.

Frankly, they are misinformed. A consumer who has a complaint about the quality of services or goods connected with his motor car should, in the first place, refer it to the dealer concerned. Should he receive no satisfaction by discussing it with the service receptionist or service manager, he should see the proprietor or managing director. I have never, in over 30 years in the industry, met a proprietor or managing director who is not willing to see that justice is done. In fact, among the larger distributors and dealers it is not unusual these days for them to have an executive specially appointed to deal with complaints.

In those cases where the above-mentioned procedure fails to satisfy the consumer, the consumer has a right to refer his complaint in writing to the Motor Agents Association or, in Scotland, the Scottish Motor Trade Association, if the dealer concerned is a member of either one of those two Associations.

The Association concerned will use its best endeavours to try to resolve the complaint, and if it fails to reach a satisfactory conclusion then its member must agree to go to arbitration, except in those cases where the trade association is of the opinion that it would be unreasonable for the member to do so. In other words, the final decision on whether or not a case goes to arbitration is almost inevitably that of the consumer. Arbitration has many advantages. First, it is quick; second, it is inexpensive; third, the award of the arbitrator is enforceable in the courts by any party; and, fourth, it is totally independent as it is carried out through the Institute of

Arbitrators. There can therefore be no question of the arbitrator having a vested interest in the final decision.

Enforcement

It is of interest in this connection that the signatories to our Code—the Motor Agents Association, Scottish Motor Trade Association, and Society of Motor Manufacturers and Traders—are under an obligation to keep statistics of complaints received, indicating how they were resolved, and these facts must be published in the Associations' Annual Reports each year.

Before the introduction of the Code, of those cases in which a court judgment was made against a member of the retail motor industry, only 6·5 per cent of them related to members of the Association. This reflects well upon the Association, whose members sell and service in excess of 90 per cent of all cars sold at retail in the U K and almost as much of the petroleum products sold at retail.

That the Code has had a substantial influence is borne out by the fact that one year after the Code had been introduced, the above-quoted percentage dropped by 2·2 per cent to 4·3 per cent, which is evidence that those who are against Codes in general, and certainly ours in particular, are not viewing the situation either fairly or dispassionately.

The argument put forward by the opponents of Codes is that the worst that can happen to a member who has engaged in a breach of the Code is for the Association concerned to have him in front of its Disciplinary Committee, where usually he gets a warning or, at worst, is expelled from the Association.

From the Association's point of view, we defend this procedure as being totally adequate for many reasons.

—We are not a police force, nor do we wish to become one.
—The Code is as yet so new that it requires more time before total adherence to it can be expected.
—Many of the breaches of the Code are in themselves breaches of the law, and a sufficiently good enforcement system exists for dealing with that.
—The inconvenience, expense, and embarrassment caused to a member who has to face a Disciplinary Committee has proved, in the main, to be sufficient warning for the member not to breach the Code again.
—To expel a member for a first or perhaps even second offence serves very little purpose. An expelled member is no longer under an obligation to adhere to the Code and, perhaps worse still, no longer under the influence of the Association in any matter, since we have no means of communicating with dealers who are not in membership.

Last, I believe that, given the required patience and the necessary length of time, the day will come when the public will seek out members of the

158

Association because of their good past performance, rather than dealing with those people who either do not wish to belong to the Association or are unable to do so because they do not come up to our standards.

Not the least of the obligations on the Association is to bring the Code up to date as occasion demands. As I write, a Working Party of the Association, in conjunction with the other two Associations concerned and the OFT, is negotiating for the inclusion of several important changes which will strengthen the Code.

The Consumer's Role

As well as the motor trade, the consumer also has a part to play, because it is only by cooperating fully with those who make, sell, and service cars that the consumer can get the maximum benefit from his purchase—in particular, by maintaining his car in accordance with the manufacturer's instructions and by giving as much information as possible to anyone servicing it.

The consumer should not hand his car in for repair unless he has signed a workshop order form and unless he has received an estimate for the work to be performed. If it appears later that the estimate will be exceeded by a significant amount then the consumer should be notified by the dealer and asked for permission to continue with the work. Provision of a quotation should be treated with care and it should be realized by both parties that the acceptance of a quotation constitutes the basis of a contract.

Disseminating the Code

What are the difficulties in making a code of practice work? Our as yet relatively short experience has shown that, where more than one Association is involved, agreement should be obtained beforehand on the following very important points: the printing of the Code, and its distribution.

In our case, the Motor Agents Association have assumed the responsibility for printing the Code but at this time the manufacturers and importers have dragged their heels over our request that the Code should be distributed by them, at their cost, in each new vehicle sold. Were they to agree, this would automatically mean that approximately 1·3 million new consumers would know of the Code each year and as it is likely that the Code would remain in the car together with the service manual and owner's instruction manual when it was traded in for a new one, it would be a relatively short time before the effects would be felt throughout the used car trade. It is to be hoped that this problem will be resolved soon because it is the only major problem which we have encountered.

All other minor problems are gradually sorting themselves out and we notice with satisfaction the increasing acceptance by the membership, not only of the need to do a professional job, but of the need to be seen to be doing it—and to be held accountable when these standards are not achieved.

159

15. What a trade association can do: The Association of British Launderers and Cleaners

Colin Fricker

In the early 'sixties, faced with a serious decline in its share of rising consumer purchasing power, the laundry industry, through its trade association, commissioned various surveys to find out why this decline had occurred.

The reasons which were eventually given for this decline were partly physical and partly psychological. Among the physical reasons were the following:

—Ownership and use of washing machines had increased.
—Self-service launderettes had become more numerous.
—Drip-dry and non-iron clothes had grown in popularity.
—Other goods and services had become dearer.

These physical, and objective, reasons had to be accepted as facts; but the psychological factors were, it was hoped, more susceptible to adjustment, based as they were on the public's image of the industry and therefore being essentially subjective. There were two main psychological factors:

—The (usually female) customer felt that using laundries would in some way deprive her of the opportunity of demonstrating to her family her own skills as housewife and mother.
—The customer was afraid that, if anything went wrong, the laundry or drycleaner would be 'difficult'.

The first of these two factors could be dealt with by a marketing strategy aimed at emphasizing the professionalism of the service provided by laundries, particularly in the standard of finish. This is very much the case in drycleaning, for which the ABLC has been the trade association since 1968. The customer had to be convinced that she was obtaining a service which she could not reasonably be expected to provide herself, mainly because it was patently superior to that which she could achieve with her own resources. This strategy resulted in the virtual elimination of the basic 'bagwash' type of service, and in concentration on the higher grade services and on drycleaning.

The second factor was perhaps more difficult to overcome because it involved a complete reassessment of customer relations policy. Although only a very small fraction of the millions of laundry and drycleaning transactions taking place each year gives rise to any cause for dissatisfaction on the part of the customer, it is these few cases, inevitably, that receive adverse publicity in the media and which tend to colour the general attitude of the public towards the industry.

Small Print Conditions

Why did customers have this fear that the laundry or drycleaner might be uncooperative and ungenerous if anything went wrong? There seems little doubt that the main reason was the lengthy set of terms and conditions of acceptance used by quite a number of companies; indeed, the trade association had itself prepared and issued a model set of such terms and conditions for use by its member companies. This 'small print' appeared in laundry books, tickets, receipts, and on notices in shop premises.

Many of these conditions were little more than what we now regard as advice to customers. One such condition, for example, emphasized the need to attach a completed label to each bundle; another drew attention to the disinfection requirements of the Public Health Act. Others set out the procedures to be adopted in the event of a complaint, such as a requirement that a complaint must be registered within X days. Unfortunately, from the customer's viewpoint, non-compliance with these procedural conditions was stated to be fatal to any claim.

Perhaps the most significant group of conditions consisted of those which excluded or restricted legal liability for loss or damage, sometimes by denying responsibility altogether for certain items, such as curtains, furnishings, etc., which were therefore accepted on an 'owner's risk' basis; sometimes by limiting the amount of compensation payable in the event of negligence to an arbitrary sum unrelated to the value of the item concerned.

Most of these terms and conditions could be justified on historical and accounting grounds. For example, because the price charged for laundering or drycleaning did not, and still does not, vary according to the value or quality of the item concerned, it had been thought reasonable to incorporate a condition to restrict the amount of compensation payable in the event of negligent loss or damage to 20 times the price for laundering (10 times the drycleaning price). This was based on figures calculated for insurance purposes, which showed that the insurable value of all items on the premises at any one time was roughly equivalent to 20 (or 10) times the relevant turnover. The so called '20 times' condition gained considerable publicity, perhaps more for its existence than for its observance by companies, who invoked it only rarely.

The 'owner's risk' condition was used for a few items the quality or inherent nature of which are so unpredictable that some cause of dissatisfaction on the part of the customer is a distinct possibility, however carefully and expertly the laundering or drycleaning process might be carried out. Curtains are sometimes in such a soiled state that removal of the dirt may result in a measure of fabric breakdown for which the customer, unaware of the extent of the soiling, which will have occurred only gradually over a period, blames the laundry or drycleaner.

A third group of conditions referred to loss or damage outside the laundry's or drycleaner's control and not due to any negligence on their part. These included restrictions about faulty manufacture, misuse by the customer, or normal but perhaps unrecognized wear and tear. Such causes of damage are inherent defects in the items which come to the laundry or drycleaner, and the latter could not be legally responsible at common law for damage attributable to them in the absence of negligence. Unfortunately, these conditions were worded in a way which suggested that the laundry or drycleaner was trying to avoid responsibility.

These, then, were the type of 'small print' conditions which, however justifiable they might have seemed at the time, were undoubtedly a major factor in creating an unsatisfactory image for the industry. It was clear that a new marketing strategy, aimed at emphasizing the professionalism of the service provided and improving the overall image of the industry was necessary.

Marketing involves an attitude of mind which accepts that an industry exists to serve the consuming public and that the satisfaction of customer needs is the first consideration. Ultimately the last word lies with the user; she can withdraw her patronage at any time and take her custom elsewhere. She may change to another laundry or drycleaner; buy or make more use of a washing machine; switch to self-service washing or drycleaning in launderettes; decide to purchase more easy-care fabrics which can be washed at home—all these alternatives, and perhaps more, are open to her.

What alternatives are open to the laundry or drycleaner? Either he must continue to lose dissatisfied customers and fail to replace them with new customers or he must take positive steps to retain existing customers and gain new ones. Obviously, only the second alternative is practicable, because the former would lead to bankruptcy or liquidation.

Minimum Standards

It was accepted within the industry, once the results of the market and economic surveys had been digested, that the 'small print' terms and conditions, and the attitudes towards customers that the use of such conditions seemed to indicate, would have to be reconsidered. The Association (or Institute, as it was then) took the lead in this reappraisal.

In 1968, after much deliberation and discussion within the industry, and the preparation of earlier versions, the Association approved a final set of Minimum Standards of Service for Domestic Laundry and Drycleaning Work and recommended their voluntary adoption by members. Widespread acceptance of the need for such a minimum level of service would, it was felt, do much to improve the industry's public image by both eliminating potential causes of customer dissatisfaction and enabling the maximum public relations capital to be made by the Association in its dealing with the media.

The major breakthrough for which the Minimum Standards were responsible was the acceptance (by those members who adopted them) of the principle that full compensation should be paid in the event of loss or damage due to negligence or, except where the customer had her own insurance, fire or burglary.

Although a considerable number of members did formally adopt them, it is fair to say that some did not; in several cases this was because the level of service already provided by members was higher than the minimum recommended—for example, where the A B L C Good Laundering Guarantee, prepared a few years earlier, was being used.

Code of Practice

While the Minimum Standards were kept under review to ensure their continuing validity in the light of new legislation and changing economic conditions, no further action was taken by the A B L C for three or four years, to give time for the underlying principles to be properly assimilated. But in the early 'seventies, dissatisfied with the extent to which the industry's image had so far been improved, and conscious of the strong growth of consumerism within the country, the A B L C began considering the possibility of a code of practice which would incorporate the best features of the Minimum Standards and go still further.

At about this time the Government of the day reacted to the public's demand for more regulation of consumer transactions by introducing what became the Fair Trading Act 1973. This Act imposed a duty on the newly appointed Director-General of Fair Trading to encourage the adoption of codes of practice by consumer industries.

The A B L C very soon contacted the Office of Fair Trading (O F T) to explain the steps already taken to improve the industry's relationship with its customers and to see whether a code of practice on the lines of the Minimum Standards would be consistent with O F T's interpretation of the type of arrangement industries should come to.

The Association, whose member companies are divided into 20 Regional Sections, each of which meets several times a year to discuss matters affecting them, immediately started an extensive dialogue within the industry as to the possibility of adopting a far-reaching code of practice. This exercise took some time but it was considered to be essential to take members along in spirit at this formative stage. A code of practice, if it is to have any effect, has to be believed in by those expected to comply with it, because it is a product of a self-regulating process. The desire to comply must be paramount.

On the other side of the coin, an effective code of practice is one with which it is quite possible to comply, rather than one setting excessively high ideals. The difficulty is to pitch the code's requirements at just the right level to satisfy aspirations and objectives *and* be reasonably attainable.

By the end of 1974 the Association had been given the authority by its members to go ahead and prepare a code of practice, which would consist of a series of undertakings together with an explanatory booklet. The booklet would amplify the undertakings and explain the principles underlying them. It would therefore have two main roles, declaratory and explanatory.

After much discussion within the A B L C and consultation with O F T, a final wording was agreed and formally approved by the Association's ruling Council. With the imprimatur of O F T, the Code was launched in April 1976.

The Code's Undertakings

The Code of Practice Statement consists of an opening declaration that member companies undertake not to restrict their liability under the general law. This effectively prohibits the use of terms and conditions limiting or restricting common law liability. Thus in one simple statement the industry had voluntarily given up what was at the time a perfectly legal commercial activity and one carried on by many other service industries. How had this position been reached? By accepting that the common law, which, of course, includes the law of contract, is a perfectly reasonable framework within which legal relationships with customers can be determined, without the need for any interference by means of exclusion clauses. After all, common law does *not* impose absolute liability in every circumstance on the part of the trader, nor does it require that every unsubstantiated claim by the consumer should automatically be accepted as determining rights and obligations in any particular transaction. It therefore provides as much protection for the trader as it is reasonable to expect him to have.

A further consequence of the abandonment of small print conditions is the elimination of arguments as to whether a notice containing the conditions in question was drawn to the customer's attention when the transaction was being made.

After the opening declaration, there are eight specific undertakings with which A B L C members will, so far as is reasonably practicable, comply.

1. Handle all clothes, linens, furnishings and other items accepted by us for processing with proper and due care and attention.

These words help to emphasize the personal service aspect of what the member offers.

2. Investigate any complaint promptly and, if requested, re-process free of charge any article which is unsatisfactory due to fault on our part.

This undertaking commits the members to a proper and efficient system for receiving and for promptly acknowledging and investigating customer complaints and for acting in response to justified complaints. All customer complaints should be treated with respect and should receive an adequate and considered response. This is clear recognition of the fact that the satisfaction of the customer is paramount. The reference to an adequate and considered response is particularly significant because a complaint which may be only of a minor nature can be made to appear much worse by lack of effective communication.

The offer to reprocess free of charge, if the customer wishes this, is obviously in the interests of both parties; often the laundry or drycleaner will be able to improve the appearance of an item to the customer's requirements by reapplying the process.

3. Pay fair compensation for loss or damage due to negligence on our part.

These simple words reflect the principle of full compensation which was the main feature of the earlier set of Minimum Standards. It is in the part of the booklet dealing with this undertaking that the explanatory role of the Code is most marked.

The Molony Committee on Consumer Protection said in its report in 1962 that it saw the need to promote and coordinate efforts to guide the consumer in the business of sound buying and that many of the consumer's troubles arise from his uninformed approach to the business of buying. Obviously the need for consumer education remains no less important than it was then and the booklet goes some way towards satisfying this need by setting out in layman's language what is meant by liability at common law, negligence, fair compensation, etc. Elsewhere in the booklet can be found similar explanatory comment on the Trade Descriptions Act 1968.

These explanations are of no less value to member companies, as they are a standing reminder to them, and to their customers, that the common law protects the trader to a reasonable extent. In particular, the booklet draws attention to the causes of damage for which the laundry or drycleaner is *not* responsible at law. (Compare this with the old form of

condition which implied that the A B L C member would have been responsible had it not been for the condition.)

4. Train our staff to be competent, courteous and helpful at all times.
5. Keep our shops, vans, containers and premises clean and tidy.

These two undertakings reflect A B L C members' determination to ensure
that the image of the industry is maintained and to reinforce the idea of
personal service which the first undertaking, and indeed the Code as a
whole, seeks to emphasize.

6. Maintain the highest possible standard of quality and service consistent with the
   price charged.
7. Display in shop premises a list of prices for standard articles.

As a means of avoiding subsequent misunderstandings, A B L C members
wish to eliminate, before the work is undertaken, any uncertainties about
price and the type of service that will be provided. They therefore undertake to ensure that all their advertising is clear and unambiguous, particularly so far as special offers or discounts are concerned; they also
undertake to display a price list covering principal items and types of
service and to enter the appropriate price on receipts issued from shop
premises.

8. Have all orders ready or delivered at the time stated, unless prevented by
   exceptional circumstances.

Other paragraphs in the Code deal with hours of business and uncol-
lected goods and are partly declaratory and partly explanatory.

Complaints Conciliation

Even if the Code ended there it would still have done much to improve the
industry's image. But there is one extra feature which is perhaps the most
important of all—the provision of a conciliation service by the A B L C to
help resolve those disputes between members and customers which for one
reason or another cannot be resolved by the parties concerned.

It must be emphasized that this is not an arbitration service—the Association does not make an award, but uses its good offices to try to bring the
dispute to a conclusion satisfactory to both parties. If complicated technical considerations are involved, the A B L C Customer Advisory Service,
which operates this part of the Code, may arrange for an independent
laboratory test at its own expense. If such a test is not considered necessary, perhaps because a similar case has been the subject of a test before,
the customer may still have a laboratory test, but at her own expense. The
test fee is returned to the customer in whole or in part if the findings of the
test support her. In the Code's first year of operation, such tests were

considered necessary in only 15 cases (out of 671). Four tests were carried out at the customer's request and expense; in one of these cases the test fee was returned.

The Association has long had a Customer Advisory Service but it has now been recognized in the Code as fulfilling the vital function of ensuring that customers do not, through lack of communication or some other reason, feel that they have been left high and dry and still dissatisfied.

It is this service to the public which enables the Association to claim with justification that customers using members' services can be sure of a fair deal.

Monitoring

Careful monitoring of members' compliance with the Code is provided for and a summary of the results of the Customer Advisory Service's conciliation work is published in the ABLC's annual report. The effectiveness of the Code is therefore open to public scrutiny.

Perhaps because of the manner in which the principles of the Code were so thoroughly discussed—and accepted—during its formative stage, there was ready agreement by members that adherence to the Code should be a firm condition of membership of the Association.

There has not been any case of a member refusing to pay what the ABLC felt was fair compensation. The Code booklet provides that a continued breach of any provision will be raised with the member concerned, and the Association's constitution provides for expulsion from membership in appropriate cases.

More than three-quarters of laundries and drycleaners in England, Wales, and Scotland are ABLC members. They display membership symbols and Code of Practice Statements in their shop premises to make it clear to the public that by patronizing them the customer will come under the protection of the code of practice and, of course, have access to the services of the Association. Members are encouraged to trade to even higher standards if this is their policy, and provision is made in the Code booklet to accommodate this.

Achievement

What has the Code achieved? Undoubtedly it has given the industry, or at least the majority of it which is in ABLC membership, a much more human and sympathetic image and has gone a long way towards eliminating the anxieties which the market surveys of the past suggested the customer might have. It is reasonable to assume that it has in this way contributed to the continued profitability of member companies.

By the time the Code became effective, many members had already been using the underlying principles as the broad basis for their terms of trading and customer relations policies for some time. But the significance of the

Code is that it covers all aspects of trading policies for all members and is there in writing for all to see. It will establish the custom and practice for the domestic laundry and drycleaning sector of the industry. It also goes beyond the strict legal requirements of the Unfair Contract Terms Act 1977, which allows restrictive conditions if they satisfy a test of reasonableness.

The Code has created a feeling of 'togetherness' among the A B L C membership, which benefits as a whole from the considerable interest and publicity it continues to provoke. All in all, everybody has benefited, and that is surely adequate justification for this example of the self-regulatory approach.

ADVERTISING AND THE CONSUMER

16. Advertising: what the consumer wants

Maurice Healy

I must, I think, start with a personal word. I have, in the years I worked on *Which?*, been involved in or responsible for most of the reports in the magazine dealing with advertising. So I have probably been involved in the writing of more rude things about individual ads than anybody outside the advertising industry. Professional partisans of advertising can be deeply suspicious of criticism from outside the industry and ascribe it to prejudice and hostility. There are people who feel a basic personal distaste for advertising. I am not one of them. For me, advertising is a tool; like any other tool, it is neither good nor bad in itself. What matters is the way in which it is used and the uses to which it is put.

What Consumers Expect

What do consumers want from advertising? That must be conditioned by what they have learned to expect from it. What do they expect from it? Not a great deal of help, I would say.

These sweeping generalizations set the context for the points that I want to develop in this chapter: that consumers are largely indifferent to advertising in general; that individuals' experience of individual advertisements may be important—both economically and in terms of their attitude to advertising; that, broadly, consumers accept the existence of advertising, albeit with a great deal of cynicism; and that its perceived value to consumers may be little to do with its avowed purpose—to persuade people to buy the products it is advertising. It is useful, too, to look at the kinds of complaints that consumers make about advertising and to discuss what needs to be done to make things better.

What sort of advertising are we discussing? Obviously, first, *commercial advertising*—that is the advertising of goods and services to consumers, with the intent to persuade them to buy. An important sub-category is *direct-response* advertising— that is, advertising to which consumers

171

respond by making a purchase direct from the advertiser. This is important for two reasons: first, because the advertisement acts as the shop window for the advertiser, the spur to immediate action is more direct than with other commercial advertising; second, because it has traditionally been an area of consumer concern and complaint.

But, as well as commercial advertising, it is worth considering *classified ads* in newspapers—again for two reasons. Classified ads are often advertisements to consumers by consumers, so perhaps they can tell us something about what consumers see themselves as wanting from ads. And they have in recent years been expanding rapidly, which suggests that they work.

What Consumers Want

Singularly little work seems to have been done to find out what consumers in general want from advertising in general. Perhaps this is not very surprising—the relationship between consumers and the advertisements that they are presented with tends to be a highly particular one. The point of advertising is to persuade consumers to buy a defined product or service; each individual consumer will want from the ad the precise information which is critical for his decision.

One published piece of research is contained in the report on advertising prepared by the Bureau Européen des Unions de Consommateurs (BEUC).* This covers group discussions held with two middle-class groups and one working-class group. When asked what they wanted from advertising, the two things specifically mentioned were that all advertisements should clearly display price information and that mail-order catalogues should offer better descriptions of the products in them. And the people in the groups also wanted better and clearer information on special offers and the terms of direct-response advertising for book clubs and similar subscriptions.

So this would support a view that what consumers want from advertising is *information*. This may seem a somewhat tortuous way to arrive at a conclusion so commonsensical that one might take it as an axiom. But consumers' reasons for buying products and their reactions to advertising are often so far from being the kind of rational behaviour that people who work in consumer organizations might like them to be that it is better not to make any assumptions without evidence.

Of course, information is what consumers *ought* to want from advertisements, since the usefulness of an advertisement to a consumer is to help him or her to make a decision to buy. This information may be simply that the product exists; it may be visual information about what the product looks like—it is not too fanciful to look ahead to the days when technology will allow ads to give information about what a product sounds, smells, or

*See Bibliography p.290—BEUC, *A study of advertising* (1974b).

feels like; it may be information about the qualities the product has to offer the user. How much a consumer wants the information depends entirely on his own individual needs—for instance, for someone who is buying a refrigerator which has to fit into a particular space in a kitchen, an advertisement which doesn't give dimensions is virtually useless.

It is this limitation which throws into relief the major limitation on the usefulness of advertising to consumers. As a source of information it is partial. It is partial in the sense that it is incomplete: ads do not—I am tempted to say cannot—give all the information that a consumer needs to make an accurate decision. It is also partial in the sense that it is biased—its concern is to present only the information which shows the product it is selling in the best possible light. (It is interesting to see that this has produced a trend in cigarette advertising which gives no information at all about the product, except a pack picture.) Now it is hardly an original thought that advertising is a less-than-perfect source of information—an ad which claimed it was not would not be accepted by the Advertising Standards Authority Ltd. What is important is that consumers—let us call them people from now on—recognize the functional limitations of advertising as an information source. And this recognition profoundly colours their view of its importance. In the group discussions held for the B E U C report, it was thought that it would be bizarre to compel advertisers to give information about a product's limitations: 'You can't expect anyone to tell you what it won't do, it's ridiculous.' Equally, the recognition of advertising's partiality produces strong defensive feelings towards it: 'If you fall for an advertisement that's your lookout ...'. 'More fool me for believing in it.'

These feelings about the limitations of advertising's usefulness occur elsewhere too. Table 16.1 shows some data from the Advertising Association's latest review* of public attitudes towards advertising:

	TV ads (%)	Newspaper ads (%)	Women's magazine ads (%)
Advertisments are			
Useful to you personally	23	43	41
Informative about the products	60	67	63
Helpful in choosing purchases	43	54	50

Table 16.1   Agreement with statements about advertising

To put these figures in a negative way, about a third of the people surveyed did not find advertisements in these media informative about the products; about a half did not find them helpful in choosing purchases; over half did not find them useful personally—in the case of T V, three-quarters found no personal use for the ads.

*See Bibliography p.288—Advertising Association, *Public Attitudes to Advertising* (1976).

Since people clearly have a mental slot into which they put advertising—partial information, of partial usefulness—and since they seem to accept this, it is perhaps not surprising that they do not regard advertising as a subject of enormous importance. Certainly the Advertising Association's survey suggests that they do not. The survey asked which of a list of subjects people talked about most, which they held strong opinions about, and which they felt needed major change. Advertising came bottom of all three. Now, one cannot take the Advertising Association survey too seriously: whoever classified the list of subjects advertising was compared to had a somewhat overblown idea of the importance of advertising: you hardly need a survey to tell you that people find advertising a less important subject than bringing up children, education, family life, the Government, religion, trade unions and politicians. Anyone who works in consumer affairs carries with them the humbling realization that consumer issues other than inflation and prices engage people only occasionally and usually temporarily. The Advertising Association might have got a different view of the relative importance of advertising if they had asked people their view of it as compared with other consumer protection issues. But there can clearly be no argument that people regard advertising as unimportant as far as they are concerned in comparison with concerns that might be thought of as of national interest.

If we had not already thought of the reasons why this might be so, this would clearly be an amazing conclusion. Here we have a multi-million-pound industry whose products, the ads, pervade our lives—on TV, increasingly on radio, in newspapers and magazines, on poster sites, on and in buses, trains, and stations. But people do not talk about it and do not care about it. It is clear that this indifference has to result from people making a positive, perhaps unconscious, effort not to notice ads and, therefore, not to think about advertising. And this in turn must follow from an attitude to advertising which regards its messages as of limited usefulness.

So I suggest that what people expect from advertising is a result of the very way advertising functions now—as a highly partial advocate. And this expectation has conditioned them to expect that ads will often *not* give them the information that they would find helpful in making a purchase.

Could ads be more useful to the people who want to get information from them? Let us look at some classified ads—surely the most compressed form of sales information ever devised. Here is a selection from a local paper:

BICYCLE, gent's, 26 in, three-speed, dynohub lights; £12   435 6806

Carpet handbags with wooden handles, £4   267 3432

Sink, stainless steel, double bowl, right hand single drainer with taps; £8   340 3434

MGB GT 1971 K, bronze-yellow, radio, overdrive, wire wheels, 51,000 miles, taxed, MOT; £1,150   455 3839

All these ads follow a common form: a brief description of what is on offer, with details of any particular features, a price, and a way of getting in touch. All the information that a potential purchaser needs to know whether the advertisement is worth following up. And we have already seen that price is a piece of information that consumers say they want in ads. In fact, of course, many commercial display ads and broadcast ads do not give any price information. As an example, I counted the commercial ads in one *Sunday Times Colour Supplement*. This is what I found:

No price information	23
Imprecise information (e.g., 'twice the price of some other beers')	3
Precise information	16

There were six direct-response ads—that is, ones inviting people to make a commitment by filling in an order coupon then and there. Of these, four gave precise price information and two imprecise—they were both book club offers, where you had to commit yourself to take, say, four books in a year at prices '25 per cent to 30 per cent below publishers' prices'. If we take out the direct-response ads, we find that only one-third of the display advertisements contained precise price information.

Obviously, the price is a basic piece of information for the consumer who wants to make a rational decision about a product. The precise function of the consumer in a free market economy is to decide how much of his resources he wants to spend in order to gain a particular benefit. (Of course, we often do not behave in this sensible way, but that is no reason to abandon the principle.) Advertising which does not tell the consumer what allocation of his resources he is going to have to make to get the benefit the ad promises is by definition unhelpful. Direct-response advertising recognizes this, since it has, as it were, to close the deal on the spot.

It can be no accident that such a large proportion of display ads do not give price information. It suggests that an intrinsic part of the process of persuading people to be interested in the product, which is what display advertising is about, consists of concealing from people what they are actually going to have to pay for it. I found a particularly bizarre example of this in a colour supplement ad for a German steam iron, in which the copy was largely about how expensive the iron was, because it was so well-made and so on, without ever actually mentioning the price. Now there are difficulties about quoting prices in ads—in times of inflation, they change quickly and, in the absence of resale price maintenance, the price in the shops can vary widely. However, advertisers get over these problems, when they do want to quote prices, so the difficulties are far from insuperable.

It seems, then, that advertising's functional need to persuade takes precedence over any need to give helpful information to consumers. A large proportion of consumers are aware of this. Their awareness colours their expectations of advertising: in particular, it creates in them a defensive attitude which tries to screen out the many messages they receive daily from ads. As a result, they tend not to think very much about advertising at all, unless they bump against an individual ad which affects them personally.

What Consumers Value

At this stage, it is worth looking again at the Advertising Association's survey of attitudes. Here are the figures for responses to two other favourable statements about advertising.

Advertisements are	TV ads (%)	Newspaper ads (%)	Women's magazine ads (%)
Entertaining	65	22	34
Interesting	53	51	55

Table 16.2   Agreement with statements about advertising

You can see that the numbers of people who value what might be thought of as the side-effects of advertising (its entertainment and interest values) are roughly of the same order as those who value its functional effects (usefulness, information about products, help in choosing purchases).

This is hardly surprising: a wealth of creativity goes into commercial advertising. It is now a cliché to state that more time, trouble, and talent often go into the creation of ads than into the creation of the information medium they grace. The Theatre of Persuasion is an integral part of many people's TV watching. There is no need to labour this point: no-one, I think, would question the enormous visual variety that advertising brings into our lives or the fact that it is very often brilliant. People do place value on this. Many of us turn advertising messages into part of the environment of our homes—I certainly have. We do this not because we value the message, but because we value the expression of it.

Specific Complaints

So far I have been discussing how far there is any correspondence between advertising and consumer needs in general terms. But it is the individual consumer's experience of individual advertisements which will most potently colour his vision of advertising.

The most valuable source of information about complaints is the bulletin regularly published by the Advertising Standards Authority, giving details of the complaints it has had about advertisments and describing, briefly, what its judgment on those complaints is and what action has been taken.

The Advertising Standards Authority is the self-regulatory body which polices ads within all media except broadcasting and direct mail and its work is described more fully in chapter 18. It administers the British Code of Advertising Practice which lays down general criteria for all advertising—for instance: 'Consumers should not be led to overestimate the value of goods whether by exaggeration or through unrealistic comparisons with other goods or other prices.'

It also lays down specific guidelines for the advertising of some products, where there has been difficulty in the past or where advertising is particularly sensitive. For instance: 'Antiseptic gargles should not be presented as cough treatments'. 'Advertisements for products or courses of treatment purporting to increase the height are not acceptable'.

The ASA invites complaints about advertisements which are considered misleading or which appear to break the British Code of Advertising Practice in some other way (the Code has provisions about taste and decency, for instance). In March 1977 the ASA dealt with 158 cases, of which 57 were complaints about mail-order advertisements which did not relate to the claims in the advertising (some were about non-delivery of goods, for instance).

It would be difficult to categorize all these complaints, but it is possible to see some trends.

First, there are complaints which result from mistakes or carelessness in the production of ads. Here are some instances:

—Picture in a hotel brochure a different place from the one captioned.
—Picture of some garden gates, wrongly priced.
—Picture in an ad for a housing development of a house which was not on the development and was not for sale.
—'100 grams of white bread (28 oz. loaf)' which should have read '100 grams of white bread taken from a 28 oz. loaf'.
—Claim that a book contained 'up to date facts and figures of the 20 countries of the Middle East' when there were more than 20 countries in the Middle East.

However cross mistakes like these make the individual people who are affected by them, realistically we have to accept that mistakes are bound to creep into ads from time to time. It would seem far more appropriate to direct attention towards seeing that people who are caused economic loss or personal distress by human error of this type get some appropriate recompense rather than to having a mechanism for chastising the advertiser (though it is obviously useful to see that mistakes are not repeated). In fact, advertisers are sometimes reported as offering to fulfil the original terms of the ad or to compensate the complainant for any loss. But there appears to be no methodical system for doing so. Where a mistake in an advertisement constitutes a breach of the Trade Descriptions Act 1968, it would be possible for the person affected to seek to persuade a trading standards

177

officer to prosecute and then to seek compensation, but this seems an extraordinarily roundabout way of dealing with what will often be relatively trivial sums of money in compensation.

The next sort of complaint results when people's experience of some product or service differs from what they had gathered from the advertisement:

—A man who had read an airline's claim in the leaflet 'You can . . . pay on board the plane' had to buy a ticket before he boarded. In the event this case turned upon whether or not he wished to deposit his baggage at the forward baggage acceptance desk or take it with him to the departure gate. (Interestingly, the A S A did not uphold the complaint, although this particular complication does not seem to have been explained in the leaflet.)
—Various complaints were made about the performance of a computer dating service, which in the event did not live up to its promises of providing suitable partners. The A S A upheld the complaints and advised media about them. Advertising for the service ceased.
—Someone who had bought an electronic watch and had to have it serviced complained about a subsequent ad which claimed 'needs no conventional "servicing" '. It turned out that what he had had was not conventional servicing.

With this sort of complaint, what is at stake is the actual performance of the firm concerned. And if a complaint is justified, then the person affected really needs compensation. Sometimes people are clearly seeking the only avenue they can find to express their dissatisfaction with the product or service. But these complaints can at least perform a useful service for other consumers, if, as in the case of the computer dating service, the media carrying the ads can be warned that the performance in practice of the firm concerned may be dubious.

Then people make complaints simply because they distrust or have found what they think is a mistake in an ad. They may well have suffered no loss or have no particular experience of the product concerned. Some examples:

—A complaint that a testimonial for a car's reliability could not be true (broadly speaking, it was).
—A complaint about a British Rail ad, which dealt with the stresses of car driving compared with those involved in travelling by train.
—Complaints about electricity industry advertising for off-peak storage heating.
—Complaints that the film *King Kong* was claimed to be original, when it was not. (More people complained about this than about any other single item in that month.)

This is probably what most people think that complaints about advertisements are all about. Nobody is really hurt directly—in fact the only damage that is done by unbelievable or over-enthusiastic ads is to the general credibility of advertising. A mechanism for compensating consumers is clearly inappropriate. What is needed is a strong mechanism for checking and stopping ads which offend in this way.

This thought brings me to the last major point I wish to make about advertising.

The Right to 'Puff'

In this country—indeed generally—the right of an advertiser to make enthusiastic claims about his product is taken to include the right to make fantastic claims for it.

The relevant sections of the British Code of Advertising Practice say:

> It is seldom possible to substantiate general claims by an advertiser that his product is of superlative quality (best, finest) in a way which is universally acceptable. Such claims, however, are permissible under this Code, provided that their inclusion in an advertisement does not create a false impression concerning any quality possessed by the product which is capable of assessment in the light of generally accepted standards of judgement.

> Obvious hyperbole, which is intended to attract attention or amuse, is permissible provided that it is not likely to be taken as a positive claim to superior or superlative status.

There are two examples of the way that this attitude towards advertising influences judgements about individual ads in the ASA's March 1977 report:

—Someone complained that a car's claim to be 'the only compact car with style, space, and strength' was wrong because four other cars met the same criteria.
—Someone complained about a London Transport leaflet which said 'London Transport run the capital's extensive bus and underground network—cheap (the fares are among the world's lowest) and convenient...'

In the first case, the ASA rejected the complaint, because they felt that 'the claim was acceptable puff and was unlikely to create a false impression about the product'. What this implies is that the ASA consider that a claim to exclusivity or a superlative in an advertising claim about subjective qualities like 'style' is meaningless. More important, it implies also that the ASA recognize that people reading the ad would also consider the claim meaningless. I have no reason to believe that the ASA are wrong. In the case of the second complaint, it transpired that the comparison with world fares had been tenable when the leaflet was first produced, but was now, the ASA said, open to question. The ASA accepted a redraft of the leaflet which read 'London Transport run the capital's extensive bus and underground networks—cheap and convenient'. What this implies is that the ASA consider a claim to 'cheapness' in the abstract tenable, when the only relevant data about relative price levels shows the claim is open to question. Again this implies that the ASA believe that people reading the ad leaflet will take an 'unqualified' claim to be 'cheap' as meaningless. Again I have no reason to believe them wrong.

None of this is any criticism of the Advertising Standards Authority. They are merely interpreting, probably correctly, existing attitudes towards claims in advertisements. But the existence of these attitudes is, I believe, precisely what makes consumers' view of the usefulness of advertising so prejudiced. There can hardly be two pieces of information more useful to consumers than that a product embodies a unique combination of useful qualities or that it is cheap. But if we see this information in an advertisement, we regard it as meaningless.

I believe that the greatest single step that advertisers could take towards overcoming the cynicism about advertising that Governments, businessmen, the advertising industry and consumer organizations all bemoan would be to abandon the principle of the 'puff'. This would not mean that advertisers could not be enthusiastic about their product or service; it would just mean that they would have to be right in their enthusiasm. It would not stop ads being funny, dramatic or beautiful—it would just mean that the jokes, the drama and the beauty would have to be true too. Most important of all, it would mean that when consumers looked at ads they could take the information at face value. Accurate information is useful information. If all the millions of pounds spent on commercial advertising were spent on giving useful information, accepted as such by consumers, we should all be a great deal better off.

Possible Ways Forward

The argument about how far advertising should be controlled by legislation and how far by voluntary self-discipline will doubtless continue for as long as there is advertising. There is no doubt that both are needed and this is not the place to argue what the precise balance should be.

But people working in advertising and consumers have a common interest in seeing that advertising gives better information to consumers and that, if it does so, consumers recognize the usefulness of the information they are giving. Here are three ways that people's cynicism about advertising might be overcome.

First, there should be much better and simpler mechanisms for compensating people who suffer loss because of misleading advertisments. If someone buys from a firm which offers free delivery, only to find out that the offer was qualified in a way that excludes him without this being made clear, he ought to get adequate compensation. This would have immediate beneficial effects: it would help persuade consumers that the information in ads was serious, since they could get money if it was wrong; it would also help to improve the standard of ads because advertisers would take more care to prevent mistakes and misconstruction.

Second, advertisers should be required to present evidence for disputed claims publicly. However extensive the research carried out by advertisers and however honourable the consideration of it by a body like the Advertising Standards Authority, it is absolutely clear that evidence will not command public acceptance unless it is publicly demonstrated. The claim is public; its justification should be too.

Third, advertisers should abandon the puff. There can be no consistency in attitudes which simultaneously seek greater acceptance and credibility for advertising claims and allow them to be, literally, meaningless.

17. Advertising as information for consumers

Patricia Mann

The consumer movement and the advertising industry have often been presented as opposite sides of not so much a fence as a brick wall. In fact, there is a great deal of common ground between the two camps and it would clearly be profitable to build on this.

One of the divisive factors has been the whole concept of 'information'. The informative role of advertisements is generally accepted as useful and necessary but perceptions of what constitutes information differ. Many consumer activists appear to believe that information is in some way absolute: that a fact is a fact which is capable of only one interpretation and which holds good in all circumstances. It is also commonly held that information and persuasion can be separated. (It might be interesting to speculate whether 'WARNING by H.M. Government: SMOKING CAN DAMAGE YOUR HEALTH' is regarded as informative or persuasive.)

In practice, the kinds of facts which hold good in all circumstances are very limited and most communications—commercial or otherwise—are translated into 'information' by consumers. The traditional communication chain of Sender-Medium-Message-Receiver has been invalidated by the recognition that what is put into an advertisement—its information content—may be, and very often is, quite different from what the reader or viewer takes out of it. Today's advertisers recognize that the chain has five elements: Sender-Medium-Receiver-Stimulus-Response.

Stimulus and Response

The consumer is active, not passive. He or she does not absorb information, but responds to stimuli and draws a conclusion which may be diametrically opposed to the written or spoken message. Jeremy Bullmore (Chairman, J. Walter Thompson) has used the example of a comedian:

> I very much doubt if any comedian, at least more than once, would get up on the
> stage and begin by saying: 'Ladies and Gentlemen. The first thing I think you

should know about me is that I am funny.' The comedian is a far more skilful communicator than that. He knows that if the audience is to think he's funny, he has to make them laugh. So he tells a joke, the audience laughs and it's their *response* that he's funny. It's their contribution, not the comedian's.

How people respond is conditioned by a variety of factors: their relationship with the sender; the medium or environment; their own preconceptions and attitudes; and their experience, whether personal or second-hand. To this must also be added the distortion of those who mis-hear or misread, ignore what they do not wish to know, 'adjust' information to fit their preconceptions or expectations, or simply indulge in wishful thinking.

It is worth looking briefly at some of the many factors affecting consumers' acceptance of information and contributing to the ways in which an advertisement's content is perceived.

Advertiser's announcement

Every advertisement must be clearly identifiable as such, carrying a specific heading if necessary. Consciously or unconsciously, most consumers mentally preface its message by 'The advertiser says . . .'. It is not expected to present a balanced and unbiased case both for and against a product or service, any more than a defending barrister is expected to paint his client's character in black as well as white. Nevertheless, it is important to ensure that over-selection does not present a misleadingly favourable case.

Source

The signature of the advertisement—who is telling the story and paying for the space or air-time—also matters. It is not simply a question of commercial reputation, although clearly this can be very important. The consumer may question why a particular message is placed by a particular body, and the motive he or she attributes to the advertiser can affect whether the content is accepted, rejected, or modified. Many people—with justification—regard Consumers' Association, the publishers of *Which?*, as an extremely reliable source of unbiased fact. One reader, however, complained that an advertisement reporting that '75% of one make of television set failed' was misleading, in that it referred only to 75 per cent of the sample tested and not to 75 per cent of *all* sets of this make. The complaint may have been an attempt to be clever; but it more probably came from a genuine expectation that *Which?*'s reputation and authority would ensure that the full facts were spelt out.

A name may add to consumer's information when a particular brand has perceived values over and above its physical and functional properties. This is evidenced by blind versus named product tests:

	Blind (%)	Named (%)
Percentage preferring overall		
Brand K	37	49
Brank L	63	51
(excludes 'don't knows')		

Table 17.1   Blind v. named product test: household product

Quite clearly there is something in Brand K as a brand which raises its value to that of Brand L. It cannot be a physical or functional thing— since that would presumably have arisen in the blind test. Brand K clearly has more added, non-functional values than Brand L.*

Beliefs, attitudes and forcing a fit

People's preconceptions, expectations, and prejudices of a particular product field or area often shape their response. Fact, figure, and argument about, say, seat belts serve only to harden the entrenched anti-seat-belt views of the tiny minority prejudiced against them. Advertisements reassuring existing users of a product, by contrast, often confirm their view.

When new information contradicts currently held beliefs, there is a conflict to be resolved. 'Cognitive intrusion' theory holds that consumers actively seek out information that confirms their viewpoint or decision and actively avoid information that would challenge it. This is particularly true after a major purchase—a house, a freezer, a car—when changing the decision would be extremely expensive. New car owners read advertisements about their own car avidly, to confirm their wisdom in choosing it. Many buying decisions, particularly in product fields with a wide choice and fairly low cost, may be taken emotionally and information sought afterwards to justify and rationalize those decisions.

Practical experience

If a message is in line with what people have experienced, whether themselves or at second hand, it is more likely to receive a positive response. The use of appropriate testimonials can provide 'borrowed experience'. So, indeed, can a familiar brand name help the acceptance of a new product from the same stable. A claim (i.e. 'information') that goes beyond people's experience and beliefs is likely to be rejected or met with incredulity. Conversely, any nuances intended to moderate claims may be ignored by those who are enthusiastic supporters of the product.

Environment

Where an advertisement appears can influence its message in several ways. A simple photograph of a glass of Heineken with the headline 'Refreshes the parts other beers cannot reach' took on a new meaning in the pages of *Playboy*. Woolworth's soles and heels for do-it-yourself shoe repairs may

*See Bibliography p.288—King (1973).

184

have met with rather mixed reactions when advertised in *The Times*. On the other hand, consumers looking for information about a particular product field—such as cameras or garden supplies—may expect to find a range of such products advertised in the specialist press and in certain circumstances the absence of an advertisement in such a publication may make the product seem somehow less 'serious'.

Presentation

Tone of voice, style, and appeal are also required to be appropriate. Reactions to style and format tend to be stronger than reactions to image. Criticisms of the 'irritating' or 'insult to the intelligence' variety may arise from irrelevance or from lack of understanding of how the product is perceived. Information is more readily acceptable when its presenter or presentation is appropriate and appealing. Price cutting and sleazy promotion may devalue a product in its users' eyes, as intelligent use of humour may underline the advantages of a product which does not take itself too seriously.

Behaviour

Information is likely to be distorted or ignored if it conflicts with the potential users' behaviour patterns. Automatic washing machines once suggested that the housewife could go to bed and find the wash ready to hang out at breakfast time. The idea was unacceptable because it was so dramatically at variance with her current practice. It was far more effective to explain how the machine operated while she was doing other familiar jobs around the house.

The same piece of information may result in quite different behaviour from different people. A simple sign saying 'WET PAINT' may be accepted as a helpful warning by those who avoid the paint, and as a challenge by those who feel obliged to verify its truth by touching it.

Conditioning responses to advertisement content

The processing of information is why advertisements are directed towards specific target groups sharing common attitudes and behaviour, and why they are designed to provide the stimuli to produce the desired response from that specific group. In theory, it is very simple. In practice, the media available do not reach such very precise target groups and therefore a great many advertisements are seen by people outside the target group. Inevitably, they respond differently. At best, they will recognize that the advertisement is not speaking to them, and ignore it. At worst, their misconceptions or lack of experience could lead them to misinterpret the content and receive *mis*information.

This is perhaps aggravated by some advertisement pre-testing, on two counts. First, considerable pains are taken to select research respondents from within the target group. This is reasonable and responsible in terms of getting the best value for advertising money but it gives no indication of the possible effect on those outside the target group. Second, there is often a preoccupation with whether the advertisement communicates what the advertiser wishes to say. It may be that a proportion of advertisers are not sufficiently concerned with finding out what people want or need to know. It is not a wilful concealment of facts on their part but rather ignorance of the role the particular advertisement plays in contributing to the sum of knowledge upon which buying decisions in the product field are based. A detailed study of information needs and the role of advertisements in supplying them might be expensive, but it could pay for itself by increasing the value and effectiveness of advertising campaigns.

Consumer Information Needs

Clearly, the information upon which buying decisions are based varies from product field to product field, and within them from brand to brand, or supplier to supplier. It might, however, be a useful starting point to consider the Consumer Information Standards being proposed by the National Federation of Consumer Groups (NFCG).

The NFCG feel that consumers 'still have a severe lack of valid comparative information about the goods they plan to buy'. Their proposals, if implemented, would require standard basic information in given product categories, expressed in terms that are relevant and understandable to the consumer and would initially concentrate on infrequent and costly purchases. The reason for proposing Consumer Information Standards is the concern that 'the knowledge available to consumers is largely at the discretion of manufacturers and retailers and is severely deficient in several important areas'. Performance, durability, and running costs are given as examples of areas where accurate consumer information is hard to obtain.

The proposals include evaluating how the importance of introducing a Consumer Information Standard might be assessed. To arrive at an overall evaluation, it is suggested that the product is rated separately against each of the following factors and a judgement then made (so that a high rating on one factor would compensate for low ratings on others):

Criterion	Low importance of CIS examples	High importance of CIS examples
Cost of article	Cheap (felt-tip pens)	Expensive (car)
Repetitiveness of purchase	Frequent (photo film)	Rare (mattress)
Variation of quality	Little (lemonade)	Wide (furniture)
Current availability of data	Ample (cars' performance)	Little (cars' reliability)
Type of consumer	'Hobbyist or the rich'	General public, the poor especially
Qualities' obscurity to the consumer	Apparent (size, colour)	Not apparent (reliability, durability)

186

From this starting point, other criteria might be added. The novelty of the product might have an important bearing, as consumers could not consult others about their experience or opinions. The role and purpose of the product should also play a part. (For instance, a new programmable pocket calculator at £15 would seem directed more at the 'general public' end of the spectrum than the 'hobbyist or rich'. How it could be used and by whom would be as important in deciding the advantages to be promoted and the technical level of the factual data provided as the other criteria listed.) Yet a further point to be considered might be the type of retail outlet in which it is sold. The difference between a mail-order supplier, a general store, and a large specialist outlet with trained salesmen affects the supplementary information the consumer may acquire at the point of purchase.

Should Consumer Information Standards be put into practice, there might well be a two-tier role for advertisements: a joint educational task for the particular product field (comparable with explaining star ratings for freezer cabinets or for petrol) and competitive brand advertisements underlining differences between specific products.

Advertisements as a source of information

Consumer Information Standards would be concerned with the sum total of information needed by consumers. Advertisements are only one of a wide variety of sources through which consumers acquire knowledge upon which buying or other behaviour decisions are based. People may have personal experience of a product, or consult a friend or retailer. They may learn from print or broadcast editorial, general or specialist. They may subscribe to *Which?* or belong to a consumer group—and they have advertisements.

Unlike most other information sources, advertisements are freely available and come looking for consumers. They are known to be biased: to present products, services, or ideas with their best faces forward. And they are always identifiable as advertisements. The variety of purposes for which advertisements are used—commercial, social, and personal— makes it hard to generalize about information content or to isolate advertisement information from other sources, but there are many illustrations of the fact that an element of persuasion is important both in imparting information and translating information into action. Perhaps the closest to a purely informative advertisement is a financial statement which is published for legal reasons only, such as a fully subscribed share prospectus. Its sole function is to place that information, which consists only of objectively ascertainable facts, on record. Were its aim to encourage consumers to absorb or to act upon that information, it would undoubtedly be produced differently. Advertisements which are designed to communicate hard facts must provide an incentive for the facts to be absorbed.

The confines of space affect the content of every kind of advertisement. A television commercial has a median 30 seconds, or about 60 words, to communicate its message, so non-verbal communication is important. It is as easy to inform or misinform through pictures, gestures, sound effects, style, casting, and tone of voice as it is through words. All kinds of information may be given non-verbally, from a demonstration of the intended role or function of the product to showing the kind of people or homes associated with its use. Provided such 'clues' are relevant and accurate, they can be very important. One consumer who claimed to be 'vaguely interested' in double glazing became very immediately interested in a particular brand when she saw a 'before and after' illustration of precisely the leaded windows she had in her house. 'Other manufacturers may have done the same, but this one showed me they actually *welcomed* my kind of problem.'

How much non-verbal information is received and understood depends largely on personal experience. If adult consumers can misinterpret information, how much more likely it is that children, with very little experience, may be misled. The Independent Broadcasting Authority (IBA) Code of Practice takes particular note of children and requires that certain non-verbal information be included:

> Children should normally be able to judge the size of a toy by relation to some known object such as a child's hand. Demonstrations of a toy in use should accurately represent what a normal child would experience in using it. Similarly, shots of toys which are not self-propelled moving of their own account may be shown only if the film also demonstrates clearly how they are propelled in real play. ... Sound effects, say of the toy's real counterpart, should not be used in a way which would wrongly imply that the toy makes similar sounds.*

Clearly, the quality of information is even more important than the quantity.

While Consumer Information Standards would help to define those areas where consumers need quite a lot of detailed fact, there is not necessarily a direct correlation between a high 'importance' rating and a need for high 'information content' in an advertisement. The high-priced, infrequent purchases with which they are concerned are rarely made as a direct response to an advertisement. The advertisement is more likely to be designed to attract initial interest, make some competitive statement, and direct the reader or viewer to a further source of information, such as a leaflet or shop. It is in sales literature that the chief opportunity exists for presenting information as the NFCG, for one, would like to see it: in a way that enables comparisons to be made easily. It is common practice for cars, refrigerators, cookers, and other consumer durables to print a short specification of the product, and this might be extended to other fields.

Perhaps too much basic knowledge is assumed for everyday familiar products. Every year couples set up home for the first time, have their first child, buy their first washing machine or refrigerator, discover new found leisure, or increased pressure on their time. Their needs, habits, and

* ITCA Notes of Guidance No. 4.

attitudes change, and what others have discovered by experience they must find out in other ways. How many tins of baked beans, for instance, give heating instructions?

Advertisements—Assessing the Information Role

The information given in an advertisement tends to be an extension of information on the pack or a demonstration of the product. In practice, the two are rarely seen in conjunction. Most advertisements are read or viewed some way from the shop and only selected impressions are retained in any detail. The predominant requirement of manufacturers' consumer advertising is to communicate the brand name. The supporting evidence for the choice of brand varies enormously, but there are a number of points which may indicate the inclusion of specific information.

Is the advertisement the sole source of information?

Mail-order advertisements are virtually the sole source of information about the products they sell, and need to pack enough information to justify a responsible buying decision into what is usually a small space. Mail order is a valuable service for a number of different groups, including those who do not have easy access to shops, the housebound, and those with special needs. Any Saturday 'Bargain Column' or 'Postal Shopping' section displays a range of products which readers might be hard put to find through normal high street shops, ranging from self-adhesive name and address labels to commode chairs and equipment for the incontinent. The majority of mail-order shoppers use these advertisements with discrimination. Common sense warns them that it is unwise to send for a garment simply described as 'green' if they wish it to match or tone with something they already possess. It should, nevertheless, be recognized that some of the target groups to whom they are addressed may be particularly vulnerable. Anxiety for a bargain may outweigh natural caution in relating price to likely quality. Those shopping for a personal product which they consider embarrassing to buy over the counter may be reluctant to complain if it is unsuitable. Those unused to business transactions often omit such elementary information as their name and address.

Old hands as mail-order customers regard the information that is *not* included as important. 'Of course that folding bike doesn't have a three-speed gear: if it did, they would have said so.' Not all customers, however, have the experience (or perhaps the cynicism) to read between the lines, and disappointment may result.

The more elaborate mail-order advertisement (certain 'limited editions', for instance) may give too much 'information'. The luxury of spreading itself over four pages and appearing to ask and answer every conceivable question may give an impression of comprehensive scope which lulls the reader into a false sense of security and confidence. Again, it is not quantity but quality that counts.

Is the consumer being asked to part with money?

The Mail Order Readers' Protection Scheme goes some way towards reassuring those who are diffident about sending money for goods they have not seen and those concerned by the risk of sending money to a company they do not know. The Advertising Standards Authority found the comparatively high proportion of complaints relating to mail order rarely concerned advertisement claims: most often they related to inefficient administration. This could indicate that consumers use their common sense when buying by post and that advertisers recognize their responsibilities to provide adequate information. It would, nevertheless, be helpful for all postal shopping columns to include such basic reminders as 'Have you kept a note of the advertiser's name and address and have you included your own?'

The Mail Order Publishers' Authority (MOPA) has set a useful lead in its latest Code of Practice*, developed in conjunction with the Office of Fair Trading, for its members who supply books and records by mail:

'3.4 Every advertisement which could result directly in a respondent entering into a contractual commitment to receive goods should include a short, simple statement of the essential points of the offer, clearly displayed, for the recipients to keep. Such statement shall include the full address of the advertiser. Where it is not possible to include these points except on the order form to be returned to the advertiser, the advertiser must supply the respondent with the statement together with the goods.'

This could well be copied by other mail-order suppliers, to the mutual advantage of customers and advertisers.

What is the consumer's experience?

Where consumers are likely to have limited experience, if any, of a particular product or product field, there is clearly a need for more hard fact. The criteria should be whether the information is both relevant and useful. Some hi-fi buffs may flatter themselves that they understand references to '30w output RMS', 'dynamic range of high frequency signals', 'better linearity', 'coreless DC motor', 'built-in DC-DC converter' and the like. Perhaps the average reader of *Radio Times* (where these particular phrases appeared) is more likely to feel blinded by science, because they are outside his or her experience. The response might be: 'This is a highly technical field which I don't understand, but this product seems to have advantages.' There are more likely to be good reasons for technical language in a specialist magazine, but in general it is more helpful to consumers to qualify technical phraseology by what it actually means in practice. Standard arguments about misled consumers buying a product once only simply do not hold water for expensive, one-time purchases.

*See Bibliography p.288—Mail Order Publishers' Authority (1977).

If the product field is itself a new one, considerable care is required in presenting information. Solar heating claims have been particularly criticized (whether made editorially or in advertisements). A particularly good summer in 1976 provided an unrealistic basis on which to quote savings, particularly as consumers had no standards for comparison and evaluation.

Where consumers have wide and regular experience of the product field, it is reasonable for advertisements to concentrate on marginal differences between brands. Advertisements may themselves help to establish the criteria by which people choose to buy, although this often comes from consumers themselves through market research before advertisements are prepared. Long life and reliability are now more important for most consumer durables than qualities such as efficiency or ease of use, which tend to be taken for granted. Compare, too, car advertisements of 1977 with previous years: the emphasis changed to factors like mileage, durability, and protection against corrosion. In more everyday purchasing terms, no toilet soap would bother to say that it gets people clean. Toilet soaps concentrate on marginal differences—such as perfume or colour, or extra benefits—such as deodorizing properties, or the reassurance of mildness—to support value for money:

> Strictly informative advertising (were that possible) could tell the consumer whether or not the advertised product was capable of meeting tangible wants. The consumer, however, also wants help in the purchase situation in deciding which of a range of alternatives will best satisfy his or her other and intangible wants. The advertiser can only help the consumer in this way if he moves away from objective lists of facts and moves towards 'industrial poetry'.*

Is the choice primarily rational?

Where consumer choice is predominantly based upon comparison of objectively ascertainable facts—and there are considerably fewer instances than might be thought—some kind of standardization of information is helpful to consumers. Comparison advertisements, such as those for cars, may be useful starting points, but it must be recognized that they can only provide starting points—by beginning a selection process, or suggesting criteria that may affect choice. Unless, however, they are comparable, their use is limited. Important criteria for refrigerators and freezers are dimensions (will it fit?), capacity (how much will it hold?), and star rating (what will it do?). Currently, dimensions may be quoted without allowing necessary clearance for opening doors or airspace; capacity may be quoted gross or net; three star ratings may be presented in such a way as to suggest four star performance to an inexperienced freezer user.

Is the consumer particularly vulnerable?

Both the Code of Advertising Practice and the Independent Broadcasting Authority's Code recognize that some groups of consumers need special

*See Bibliography p.288—Reekie (1974).

consideration and protection. Both take steps, for example, to ensure that advantage is not taken of children's inexperience. Both list several special categories where people may feel socially or physically inadequate in some way: the balding, the fat, the lonely, for example.

There is plenty of evidence that consumers neither expect nor want advertisements to list the disadvantages of a product. Nevertheless, it may be desirable to include reservations to protect the vulnerable. In many cases, this is difficult. Self-medication with anything from a simple headache remedy to a corn plaster requires a degree of self-diagnosis of which some people may not be capable. It also requires simple directions to be followed carefully. Were the risks of misapplication or misuse to lead to widespread restrictions on such products or on making their existence known, the National Health Service would be unable to cope with the increased demands.

Easiest to define as needing special care are areas where the nature of the product or service defines the target group as particularly vulnerable. Loans without security are one example. Anyone interested in such a loan could be assumed to be ineligible for, or ignorant of, alternative ways of borrowing money, and to have difficulty in making ends come within touching distance. Within this group will be found a proportion of the feckless and bad managers who are within the target simply because they have difficulty in coping. Selective information can make it seem all too easy for them, leading to an additional burden which further complicates their problems.

Does over-selection mislead?

Pressures of time or space require all advertisements to be selective. While it is fairly easy to select 'truths' or 'facts' in such a way as to give a false impression, the Code of Advertising Practice requires advertisements to be honest as well as truthful. The most blatant examples of misleading over-selection are probably political advertisements—exempt from the Code's requirements and outside its remit. The frustration and impotence consumers feel about ways in which they can influence Government are not helped by the 'information' in political advertisements or party political broadcasts upon which they appear to be expected to base their decision to vote.

Have claims been justified?

Both the Independent Broadcasting Authority and the Code of Advertising Practice require justification for any claim to be made immediately available on request. This means that such justification must be held ready, in an instantly accessible form, before publication of the advertisement. This apparently simple requirement can present difficulties: the form in which such justification is presented; differences of interpretation; the fact that the complete confidence in which such justification is treated by IBA, ASA, and CAP conflicts with many consumers' representatives' desire to have claims justified publicly. Public justification of claims could raise problems of industrial security, and can be avoided by prompt and responsible provision of information to the regulatory authorities on request.

Where is further information available?

The information given in advertisements interacts with a wide variety of other information sources. In many cases, the principle sources of information are packs and pack leaflets, or instruction manuals. These can go considerably further than is necessary or practical in an advertisement, with the added advantage of being read in conjunction with the product. In the case of low unit price products—confectionery, for example—the best information may be given, at less than the price of a stamp, by sampling the product. For more serious, considered purchases—with a higher potential Consumer Information Standard rating—booklets may be offered, or advice services available. Certainly advertisements for such products should consider the need to direct readers or viewers to sources of further information.

How much information do consumers want?

While Consumer Information Standards may indicate how much information consumers should have available to them, they by no means express how much information consumers want. Reactions range from 'My mind's made up: don't confuse me with facts' to 'You're telling me more than I wish to know'.

It must be recognized that increased availability of information does not necessarily mean better-informed consumers. Lord Young, when Chairman of the National Consumer Council, said:

> Consumers' information about what is available on the market relative to the great variety of goods and services there are is actually less complete than it was when there were fewer goods and services. We also know that, quite apart from whether the job of being a good consumer becomes more difficult, despite whatever Consumers' Association and similar bodies will be able to do, many people don't actually want to take the time to get the information that would enable them to be a somewhat more adequate consumer. There are great limits set by time and energy on what people are able to do in order to shop around between shops and manufacturers.

This view is perhaps even more marked in the US. Stephen Greyser, executive director of the Marketing Science Institute, was responsible for the Sentry Study, *Consumerism at the Crossroads**. While US and UK experiences differ, the points Stephen Greyser made when introducing the

*See Bibliography p.290—Consumerism at the Crossroads (1977).

study are of interest. He reported that US consumers are highly self-critical. They agree that there is generally enough information available for consumers to make sensible buying decisions, and even more strongly that most consumers do not use the information available about different products in order to buy one of them. They also agree that many of the mistakes consumers make are the result of their own carelessness.

Stephen Greyser commented:

> But what questions these attitudes raise regarding some of the heavily information-oriented policy proposals being offered to help consumers! Even if the information environment were to be improved, the Sentry study data raises doubts in my own mind that people will want significant additional amounts of information, will use additional information if available, and (after the fact) will consider the costs of providing that additional information to have been worth it... Personally, I think that one of the underexploited areas for improving consumer protection is the work that consumers do for themselves in their individual consuming roles. In terms of the study data, it seems to me that the public is asking for a better grade of assistance and protection on the part of both business and government rather than more government *per se*.

Where marketing and the consumer movement could cooperate more closely and more profitably is in this 'better grade of assistance'. Information needs have changed as consumer priorities have changed, and close and continuous monitoring is needed to ensure that the quality and relevance of information in advertisements is appropriate to changing consumer needs. It is even more important that the creative communication skills of the advertising business develop in parallel, so that the information is presented in a way that attracts interest and actively encourages consumers to absorb and act upon it.

18. Advertising: the legal framework

Richard Lawson

Unlike other countries of the world, most notably those of the EEC, the UK has not produced any single code of advertising law. Instead it has developed a two-fold, pragmatic approach: using existing heads of the common law such as contract or tort where these might help to control abuses, and using Acts of Parliament in those areas where the common law is of no avail. It is, in fact, to a survey of the common law that we shall turn first, making due apologies for the apparently random selection of advertising practices examined. The explanation is that only a few practices ever lend themselves to common law control and this is the feature which they all share.

Common Law Controls

Controlling extravagant claims

There are few practitioners in advertising who have never heard of Mrs Carlill's action against the Carbolic Smoke Ball Company.*[1] The latter had advertised their smoke ball to the public as the ultimate guarantee against catching influenza. Anyone, the advertisement insisted, who used their smoke ball yet still succumbed would receive a reward of £100. As a token of the company's good faith, the advertisement went on, £500 had been deposited with the Alliance Bank of Regent Street.

The inevitable happened and Mrs Carlill claimed her £100. The company pleaded in vain that their offer of a reward was a mere puff, not to be taken seriously. It was too specific for that, the Court of Appeal held, paying particular heed to the alleged bank deposit. The advertisement embodied a serious offer which Mrs Carlill accepted when purchasing and using the smoke ball. The £100 was therefore hers.

Nor was this the last such case, although a distinguished writer once spoke of *Carlill* v. *Carbolic Smoke Ball Co.* as being a 'red light' over the desk of the advertising copywriter.[2] The not dissimilar claim which

---

*The numbered references are to law case reports, listed at the end of the chapter.

featured in *Wood* v. *Lektric Combs Ltd.*[3] was that 'within ten days' the Lektric Comb would banish all grey hair. This was coupled with the fateful words '£500 guarantee'. And it was this guarantee which had to be made good, on the principle established in Mrs Carlill's case, when the grey-haired Mr Wood used the comb without success.

The validity of these decisions remains, although—hardly surprisingly—the litigation seems to have come to an end. A person who makes a purchase on the strength of a definite claim in some advertisement can sue for breach of contract when the claim goes unfulfilled. This extends to assertions vividly proclaimed by some businesses that they will make up the difference should less be paid elsewhere for the goods they are selling.

Unauthorized endorsements

The practice of promoting goods and services by obtaining the plaudits of some famous person has mushroomed over the last decade but is not new. This form of sales promotion is entirely lawful. Where it has come up against the law, specifically the law of defamation, is the occasional use of a person's endorsement, and not always a famous person, without that person's prior approval.

Take, for example, the case of *Plumb* v. *Jeyes Sanitary Fluid Co. Ltd.*[4] Some years after he had been photographed on point duty, the picture of PC Plumb was used in an advertisement for Jeyes foot-wash, PC Plumb being shown mopping his brow and saying: 'Phew, I can't wait to get home and wash my feet in Jeyes sanitary fluid.' Since the implication of the advertisement was that the constable's feet were malodorous and that he, a public servant, had been lending his name to commercial advertisement, defamation was alleged and proved. So was it in *Rutherford* v. *Turf Publishers*,[5] where the name of a professional footballer was used to promote a system of pools gambling, when professional footballers were forbidden by their ruling body from betting on football matches. So was it again in the more recent case of *Stockwell* v. *Kellogg Cornflakes Co.*,[6] where a photograph of *Miss* Stockwell was used to promote cornflakes as an ideal meal for pregnant mothers.

None of these really compares with the famous case of *Tolley* v. *J. S. Fry & Sons*,[7] where the House of Lords laid it down as definitive law that defamation could be a suitable weapon against the unauthorized endorsement. Cyril Tolley was a famous amateur golfer. J. S. Fry & Sons, the chocolate manufacturers, began a newspaper promotion in which a cartoon of Cyril Tolley was shown with a block of chocolate sticking prominently from his pocket, accompanied by this caption: 'The caddy to Tolley said: Oh Sir! Good Shot, Sir, the ball see it go, Sir. My word how if flies, Like a cartet of Fry's. They're handy, they're good and priced so low, Sir'.

Cyril Tolley, being an amateur golfer, sued for libel. His argument was that a natural inference would be that he had undertaken a paid commercial proposition and had thereby prostituted his amateur status. He contended that his apparent testimonial would lower him in the estimation of right-minded people. The House of Lords agreed and the action for libel was won.

Viscount Blanesburgh was a lone dissenter: he thought that no-one would really believe that Tolley had lent his name to the promotion. This was a view which found favour, however, in *Blennerhassett* v. *Novelty Toys*.[8] A promotion for yo-yos featured one Blennerhassett of the Stock Exchange so besotted with his toy that he was eventually incarcerated in a lunatic asylum. A Mr Blennerhassett who really did work at the Stock Exchange, being subject to much teasing and banter, brought an action for libel but failed. No-one, the court judged, would believe that the reference really was to the real Mr Blennerhassett.

If an aggrieved party is unable to prove defamation, his chances of success are not good. In *Corelli* v. *Ward*,[9] where a postcard showed imaginary scenes from the plaintiff's life, the judge found that no authority existed for restraining the publication of a person's portrait.[10] So also in *Dockrell* v. *Dougall*,[11] where the name of a well-known doctor was used to promote a medicine, the jury (perversely perhaps) rejected a claim for libel so the plaintiff was left to assert that he had a right of property in his name and that his right had been infringed. But it was ruled that there was 'no such authority for such a proposition . . . it goes too far and is unsound'.

An extension of this proposition, that a person has a right of property in his voice, is similarly uncertain. In *Sim* v. *Heinz*,[12] the actor Alistair Sim claimed that his distinctive tones were being copied in a television advertisement for baked beans. The matter was not resolved, but the judge observed that it would be 'a grave defect' in the law were such conduct held to be lawful.

If defamation is plainly incapable of proof, plaintiffs have occasionally been tempted to prove the offence of passing-off, a tort based on the principle that 'nobody has any right to represent his goods as the goods of somebody else'.[13] In *McCulloch* v. *May*[14] the plaintiff was 'Uncle Mac', a popular favourite with children, who attempted to stop the marketing of 'Uncle Mac's Puffed Wheat'. The judge held that the offence of passing-off had not occurred, because the parties were not business rivals. He was not prepared to extend the action of passing-off where the plaintiff was 'not engaged in any degree in producing or marketing puffed wheat'.

The Australian High Court in *Henderson* v. *RCA*[15] dissociated themselves from this decision, stating that the tort of passing-off arises where *A* states that his business is the same as, or is connected with, the business of *B*. So holding, they found the offence committed where a company distributing a record of dance-music had featured prominently on the sleeve a photograph of the Hendersons, a well-known pair of professional dancers. Of course, there was a common field of activity in this case anyway, which considerably lessens its impact.

It must be recognized that, in the case of public figures, exposure and publicity is the very essence of their profession and hence they cannot be over-zealous in maintaining their privacy. In the Canadian decision in *Krouse* v. *Chrysler Products*,[16] the defendants advertised their products by distributing a football 'spotter' which enabled football fans to identify players. Prominently featured in a photograph was Bobby Krouse, a Canadian footballer. Krouse had not consented to this and sued for damages.

His action failed. There was no case in passing-off, the Supreme Court held, because plaintiff and defendant shared no common field of activity. *Henderson* v. *RCA* was distinguished on the ground previously observed that it did involve a shared field of business activity. The Supreme Court also ruled out any invasion of privacy (an idea which has not yet taken root in England) but without rejecting it as a possible head of action in future case. Why it did not succeed here was because it was not Krouse which was identified with the products of Chrysler, but rather the game of football. Such invasion of privacy as was committed here was of the minor, trivial kind which people in the public eye must learn to accept.[17] But in the more recent Canadian Case of *Athans* v. *Canadian Adventure Camps* (1978)[17] O.R. (2d) 425, the court held that an invasion of privacy *had* occurred where a picture of an athlete was used without consent in certain advertising.

It also appears that where a photograph or picture is suitably appropriate, it may lawfully be attached to the particular goods or services. In *Harrison and Starkey* v. *Polydor Ltd.*[18] a record album was issued of taped interviews given by the Beatles as well as some Beatles music. It was proposed to attach to the album a number of Beatles photographs. The group objected to this since it would indicate their recommendation, approval, licence, or sponsorship, citing *Henderson* v. *RCA* in support.

The judge distinguished the Australian decision on the ground that no relevant connection existed between the record and the Hendersons. In the present case, there was every connection between the Beatles tape and the photographs. He also held that no one would confuse the 'Beatles Tapes' with anything issued by the Beatles or by their own company.

The common law control over unauthorized endorsements has developed in piecemeal fashion. It seems that, unless he can prove defamation or (less easily) passing-off, the aggrieved plaintiff has no remedy, however sorely treated he may have been. A more vigorous recognition of a right of privacy is plainly needed, but is apparently not forthcoming.[19] However, Lord Denning remarked that whenever 'any grievous cases come up we find that the lawyers produce a remedy'.

Comparative advertising

The practice has grown of late whereunder one product is praised while its competitor, expressly named, is damned. This form of advertising, known to its practitioners as 'knocking copy' or more prosaically as 'comparative advertising', has both statutory and common law limitations.

It is possible that the Trade Descriptions Act 1968 exerts some control over comparative advertising. Section 1 of the Act, as we shall later explore in some detail, prohibits the application to goods of false trade descriptions. Section 4(1)(c) states that the use of a trade description in such a way as is likely to be taken as a reference to particular goods constitutes the application of a trade description. It can be argued from this that, read literally, the Act creates an offence out of the false disparagement or description of another's goods. There is no judicial authority for this, however, and it is doubtful if behaviour of such a kind is within the mischief of the legislation.

It is, however, probable that the deliberate disparagement of another's products will constitute an offence under section 15 of the Theft Act 1968. In *R.* v. *Mandry*,[20] it was held to be obtaining by deception for a trader knowingly to make the false claim that goods he was selling were much more expensive elsewhere. Where, therefore, a dealer knowingly makes a false statement as to the quality of another's products, it is likely that that is obtaining property by deception, or at the least attempting so to obtain.

The third, and last, possible example of statutory control derives from the Trade Marks Act 1938, Registration of a mark gives exclusive right to the use of that mark, a right which the Court of Appeal in *Bismag Ltd.* v. *Amblins*[21] held was infringed when a trader compared his goods with those of another. In making the comparison, he referred to his competitor's goods by their registered trade mark.

It must be conceded that many of today's comparative advertisements seem to fall within the *Bismag* principle and hence to be in breach of the Act: perhaps their seeming immunity from action is because that case has attracted considerable criticism and is not regarded as an altogether sound view of the law.

If statute has little control over comparative advertising, it can hardly be said that the common law has a great deal more to offer. Indeed, the avowed policy of the law has been to have as little as possible to do with this form of promotion.

In effect, the courts have ruled that they will intervene only where the comparison has been so extreme as to constitute defamation of goods (or, for that matter, services). In *White* v. *Mellin*,[22] the appellant was a retailer of the respondent's food for infants. On every bottle of Mellin's food sold, he stuck a label recommending the purchase of his own infants' food as being 'far more nutritious and healthful than any other preparation'. An injunction was refused, there having been no false disparagement of the respondent's food. Extravagant praise, it was said, used by a trader in puffing his own goods, will not give rise to a cause of action merely because they impliedly disparage those of others.

Again, it was said in *Evans* v. *Harlow*[23] that the publication of a mere caution against goods by a manufacturer claiming to sell something better is not actionable. To decide otherwise, Lord Denman considered, '...would be to open a very wide door to litigation, and might expose every man who said his goods were better than another's to litigation'. The Court of Appeal have also held that a statement that goods are superior to those of a rival is not actionable even if untrue and the cause of loss: the courts cannot be made the forum for trying the relative merits of goods.[24]

These cases, and the last case in particular, have to be read against the restatement of the law arising from the case of *De Beers Products Ltd.* v. *I EG Co. of New York Ltd.*[25] The plaintiffs manufactured a natural diamond abrasive called 'Debdust'. The defendants marketed a rival product called MBS-70. As part of a sales drive, the defendants had a pamphlet circulated called 'Tech-Data 1' which purported to record laboratory experiments on the two products and which made statements comparing Debdust adversely with MBS-70. As a result, the plaintiffs issued a writ claiming damages for slander of goods. It was held that if a trader chose to denigrate his rival's goods, the test was whether a reasonable man would take the claim as serious or not. Since the interested parties had been presented with what purported to be a proper, scientifically conducted test, it must have been intended to be taken seriously. The report had been so framed that it would not be dismissed as an idle puff. Accordingly, since disparaging statements had been made, the defendants would be liable if further investigation showed that those statements had been made maliciously.

Where defamation is alleged, the plaintiff will often seek an interlocutory injunction before trial of the issue. In *Bestobell Paints Ltd.* v. *Bigg*,[26] a house was decorated with the plaintiff's paint. So unsatisfactory was the paint, and so unsightly the result, that the defendant placed a huge notice on the house declaring: 'This house is painted with CARSON'S paint'. An action was brought for libel; but before the case was heard, an injunction was requested seeking removal of the notice. The judge refused. An injunction, he held, will be granted only where a statement is obviously untruthful and libellous. This, he thought, was not so here.

Statute Law

Statutory control of advertising is every bit as piecemeal as common law control. While it is true that both the Food and Drugs Act 1955 and the Medicines Act 1968, impose general prohibitions on the false and misleading advertising of food, drugs, and medicines, there is no such unified control of the advertising of goods and services generally. Instead, there is a vast range of statutes all imposing restrictions or regulations, but only in areas of strictly limited, though not unimportant, concern. Among these are the Consumer Credit Act, the Betting, Gaming and Lotteries Act, the Town and Country Planning Act, the Cancer Act, and many others. There are, however, two Acts of Parliament which present a more coherent approach to advertising control, and these are the Fair Trading Act and the Trade Descriptions Act.

Fair Trading Act

In the present context, the Fair Trading Act 1973 creates no new law but rather a way of making new law. Where the Director-General of Fair Trading detects a consumer trade practice which is inimical to the consumer interest and has any of the undesirable effects specified in section 17 of the Act, he may make proposals to the Consumer Protection Advisory Committee for a change in the law. If there is a positive response from the Committee, the matter passes to the Secretary of State for Prices and Consumer Protection, who can reject the proposals or lay them before Parliament in the form of a statutory instrument. Approval by each House gives the instrument legal effect.

The first instrument to pass into law was the Consumer Transactions (Restriction on Statements) Order 1976/1813 which, by 1 November 1978, will have achieved the aim of making unlawful the use of exclusion clauses already rendered ineffective by the Supply of Goods (Implied Terms) Act 1973.

The second instrument is the Mail Order (Place of Business) Order 1976/1812. This requires mail-order advertisers to incorporate the address of their place of business into the advertisement.

A third proposal accepted by the Consumer Protection Advisory Committee is that dealers should reveal their trade where the context of the advertisement, such as its placement in the classified columns, suggests a private individual. This was duly implemented by the Business Advertisements (Disclosure) Order 1977/1918.

There is also a fourth proposal, on V A T-exclusive prices, on which the Committee has reported, but on which no Parliamentary action had yet been taken at the time of writing.

Trade Descriptions Act

Enacted in 1968 in the light of the Report of Molony Committee on Consumer Protection (Cmnd 1781), the Trade Descriptions Act has done much to ensure a decent standard of honest and truthful advertising. It contains three main charging provisions, those in sections 1, 11 and 14.

Section 1 creates the offence of applying a false trade description to goods or of supplying or offering to supply goods to which a false trade description is applied. Two things must first be noted. Section 1 only applies to businesses, so that statements made by private individuals are not caught by the Act. The other point is that an offence is committed irrespective of the state of mind of the accused. He can be devoid of intent yet still offend against the Act.

A trade description is defined in section 2. It is an indication, direct or indirect, of any of the following: quantity, size, or gauge; method of manufacture, production, processing, or reconditioning; composition; fitness for purpose, strength, performance, behaviour, or accuracy; any physical characteristics not previously mentioned; testing by any person and the results; approval by any person or conformity with a type approved by any person; place or date of manufacture, production, processing, or reconditioning; person by whom manufactured, produced, processed, or reconditioned; other history, including previous ownership or use.

In *Cadbury* v. *Halliday Ltd.*,[27] the court explained that, to fall within section 2, the description had to be such that it could be adjudged true or false when made. Thus, to flash mark bars of chocolate 'extra value' did not constitute the application of a trade description since the expression was devoid of real meaning. It could not be said to be true or false.

It seems that motor vehicle dealers often fall foul of section 1, either by supplying cars with false odometer readings or by advertising an unroadworthy vehicle in such terms as 'immaculate', 'in excellent condition', or 'in beautiful condition'.[28] However, the British Gas Corporation also committed an offence when it falsely advertised a gas-cooker as being ignited by hand-held battery pack. This, the court held, was a false statement as to the cooker's composition.[29]

The provisions of section 14 of the Act can broadly be said to extend the provisions of section 1 to services. There is, however, this important difference: section 1 applies no matter what the offender's state of mind was. Section 14, on the other hand, only covers statements known to be false or made recklessly.

The definition given to recklessly is that it extends to statements made regardless of whether they are true or false. In *MFI* v. *Nattrass*[30] the original form of an advertisement was for louvre doors carriage free. Subsequently, the advertisement also offered folding door gear to be used with the louvre doors, again carriage free. What the advertisers meant to say was that the goods would be carriage free where both doors and door gear were bought. A customer who bought the door gear alone complained when he was charged for carriage, and the advertisers were duly convicted. The point was that their manager had spent a few minutes considering the offending advertisement but had failed to ask himself whether it had more than one meaning. Since he had not put this question, he had issued the advertisement recklessly—that is to say, regardless of whether it was true or false.

A gap which some regard as being exposed in the Act is that it does not apply to promises. In *Beckett* v. *Cohen*[31] and *R.* v. *Sunair Holidays Limited*,[32] promises were made as to the provision of services, but in neither case were they kept. First the Divisional Court, then the Court of Appeal, held that promises were outside the scope of section 14, which only applies to statements which are true or false when made. Such a diagnosis cannot be made of promises. It was conceded, however, that even a promise can be caught by section 14 if made with no belief that it would be fulfilled. Then it would no longer really be a promise: it would be a simple misstatement of fact, the fact being the present state of a man's mind.

If this is a gap in the Act, it was partially closed by the House of Lords in *British Airways Board* v. *Taylor*.[33] A passenger booked a flight, this later being confirmed in writing. He was turned away when he claimed his seat, however, in consequence of the airline's deliberate policy of overbooking.

The Divisional Court said no offence was committed since the airline had merely failed to honour their promise of a seat. The House of Lords disagreed. Section 14(2)(a), they pointed out, brought within the Act anything 'likely to be taken' for a false statement as to the provision of services. The confirming letter, they held, was likely to be so taken; and since, in view of the overbooking policy, it was false when made, the terms of section 14 had been infringed. The House of Lords never dissented from the basic proposition, however, that promises are outside the scope of section 14.

A danger exposed as inherent in section 14, and section 1 for that matter, is that of multiple prosecutions. In *R. v. Thompson Holidays Ltd.*,[34] a brochure contained statements which were admittedly in breach of section 14. The company pleaded guilty after one set of holidaymakers complained of the statements. But they resisted a further prosecution when a second set of holidaymakers complained, because, they argued, they had already been convicted for that offence. The Court of Appeal disagreed, saying that an offence was committeed every time the false statements were read and someone was misled. Lord Justice Lawton pointed out that a false advertisement broadcast on television was made to every viewer and so numberless separate offences arose. But the Court did not rule out that too many prosecutions might constitute an 'abuse of process'. Just where the line was to be drawn, no-one was prepared to say, and that must remain uncertain.

Section 11 of the Act is concerned with pricing offences, but only in relation to goods. It is an offence under section 11(2) to offer goods for supply at a price below that actually charged. In *Doble v. David Greig Ltd.*,[35] a bottle of blackcurrant juice was marked at a certain price, but carried a label around its neck saying '4d. refundable deposit'. It was not clear whether the price marked took account of the deposit or whether the 4d. was to be added and then refunded. A notice at the cash desk, a few yards away and not visible from the shelf, stated that no deposits were being charged. It was held that this was too late to correct the situation and that an offence was committed at the shelf because of the ambiguous pricing.

Section 11 of the Act also attempts to curb claims that goods are being sold below a recommended price or at a reduced price. If such are not genuine, an offence is committed. Furthermore, section 11(3) invests the phrases 'recommended price' and 'reduced price' with specific meanings. The former must be a price recommended by the manufacturer or producer and be the recommended retail price for the area where the goods are offered. In the case of reduced price offers, section 11(3) requires the higher price to have lasted for not less than 28 days continuously during the preceding six months. The effect of section 11(3), both in regard to recommended and reduced prices, is considerably weakened by the further provision that its terms do not apply where the contrary is expressed.

Even apart from this, the reduced price provisions had been rendered virtually unenforceable by the decision in *House of Holland Ltd.* v. *London Borough of Brent*.[36] Over a period of two months, goods were advertised as being sold at reduced and then further reduced prices even though there was only the initial reduction. The prosecution failed since they had not examined the whole six-month period prior to the offer. Only if they could show that, during that period, there had been no higher price ruling for 28 consecutive days was an offence committed. The burden thus imposed on enforcement authorities, of monitoring the price of an item continuously over a period of six months, has virtually rendered this part of the Act unenforceable.

A further check on section 11 was imposed by *Feiner* v. *Barnes*.[37] Shopkeepers sold posters of the moon at 98p. They had allowed their supplier to include their name as stockists of the posters in an advertisement. The advertisement, which the shopkeepers did not see in advance, indicated a price of 80p. The defendants were acquitted since they did not give the false indication in the advertisement. The mere fact that they agreed to be named as stockists imposed no duty upon them to obtain a copy of the advertisement and check it.

The European Connection

The UK is almost unique in Europe in having no legislation concerned specifically with control of advertising and commercial practices. Sweden's Marketing Practices Act 1976 exerts direct control over advertising, giving a consumer ombudsman power to take emergency action where necessary. Luxembourg legislated in 1974 to control dishonest commercial practices, as did Belgium in 1972 and Denmark, also in 1974. France enacted the *Loi Royer* in 1973 which, in addition to forbidding misleading advertising, empowers the courts to order corrective advertising: and the most notorious example of direct legislative intervention has, justly, always been taken to be the West German law on unfair competition 1909, which prohibits unfair commercial practices. It is also worth pointing out that the Canadian Combines Investigation Act and the Australian Trade Practices Act forbid misleading advertising, while the Consumer Information Act 1978 does the same in the Irish Republic.

A recent White Paper* recommended against a single-clause ban on misleading advertising; but this will not be the end of the affair, since the EEC now has plans to legislate on such matters for the nine member States.

The power to take such action derives from Article 100 of the Treaty of Rome which established the Community. This provision enables the Community to take action to harmonize the laws of member States where the absence of such harmonization has the effect of distorting the market.

*See Bibliography p.289—OFT: Review of the Trade Descriptions Act 1968 (1976).

Where member States have different laws governing advertising, such distortion is inevitable: some promotions are legitimate in some countries, but not in others.

Already, a Cosmetics Directive has been enacted by the E E C, which the U K is required to implement as part of its domestic law. This prohibits misleading advertising with regard to cosmetic products. More important Directives, now in the final stages of planning, cover, first, the advertising, presentation, and labelling of foodstuffs and, second, misleading and unfair advertising. The first mentioned will impose strict control on the methods of advertising both drinks and foodstuffs, while the second seeks to prohibit misleading and unfair advertising generally. Interestingly, comparative advertising will be permitted under those proposals to the extent that it is neither misleading nor unfair. Provision is made for corrective advertising and for interested parties taking civil action to prevent advertising which infringes the law.

Neither the foodstuffs Directive nor the advertising Directive has yet been formally adopted by the E E C, but there is no doubt whatsoever that they will be. If normal procedure is followed, the U K will probably be required to implement the provisions of the E E C legislation by the beginning of the 1980s.

Conclusion

The traditional response in the U K to undesired commercial practices has been to legislate to prohibit the particular practice, never to adopt the universal prohibition favoured in other countries. This has always been the manner in which abuse of income tax laws has been dealt with. Again, in the absence of general legal intervention, the U K has been content to allow the advertising industry to control itself. The rising tide of consumerism and membership of the E E C are now combining to change all this. Whether this will be for the better will remain a moot point for a considerable time.

References to Legal Cases

1. [1893] 1Q.B. 256.
2. Turner, *Shocking History of Advertising* (Penguin).
3. *The Times*, 12 January 1932.
4. *The Times*, 15 April 1937.
5. *The Times*, 29 October 1925.
6. *The Times*, 31 July 1973.
7. [1931] A.C. 331.
8. (1933) 175 LTJ 393.
9. (1906) 22 TLR 532.
10. *Ibid.*, at p.533.
11. (1899) 80 LT 556.
12. [1959] 1 All E.R. 547.

13. [1947] 2 All E.R. 845.
14. (1915) 84 L.J. Ch. 449.
15. (1960) SR (NSW) 576.
16. (1974) 40 DLR (3rd) 15.
17. See *Woodward* v. *Hutchins*,reported in *The Times*, 20 April 1977.
18. [1977] FSR 1.
19. In *Bernstein* v. *Skyviews & General, Ltd.* (*The Times*, 10 February 1977) there was held to be no right to prevent another photographing your property.
20. [1973] 1 WLR 1232.
21. [1940] 2 All E.R. 608.
22. [1895] A.C. 154.
23. (1844) 5 Q.B. 624.
24. *Hubbock & Sons Ltd.* v. *Wilkinson, Heywood & Clark, Ltd.* [1899] 1 Q.B. 86.
25. [1975]2 All E.R. 599.
26. *The Times*, 16 July 1975.
27. [1975] 2 All E.R. 226.
28. See *Robertson* v. *Dicicco* [1972] RTR 431; *Chidwick* v. *Beer* [1974] RTR 415; *Norman* v. *Bennett* [1974] 3 All E.R. 351.
29. *British Gas Corporation* v. *Lubbock* [1974] 1 All E.R. 188.
30. [1973] 1 All E.R. 762.
31. [1973] 1 All E.R. 120.
32. [1973] 2 All E.R. 1233.
33. [1976] 1 All E.R. 65.
34. [1974] 1 All E.R. 823.
35. [1972] 2 All E.R. 195.
36. [1971] 2 All E.R. 296.
37. *The Times*, 13 June 1973.

INTERNATIONAL DEVELOPMENTS

19. Consumerism: an American response

Ester Peterson

When the consumer movement first emerged, the business community was thunderstruck. It reacted to it as something un-American—as a force that was bent on destroying our free enterprise system. Business almost uniformly failed to realize the legitimacy of the consumer movement, or that consumerism could be used effectively as a marketing tool.

Most business people misjudged the depth and commitment of consumer advocates. They were unable to comprehend that, in our complicated and impersonal society, consumers and their spokesmen have much to say that is of value to all elements in our economy. This crucial fact about the relationship between business and the consumer movement became clear to me when I was President Lyndon B. Johnson's special assistant for consumer affairs between 1964 and 1967.

After President Nixon's election, I returned to private life, and soon thereafter I received an offer from the president of a regional retail food chain, Giant Food, to join the company as consumer adviser to the president. This was a revolutionary move. Up to that time, no consumer advocate with a shred of credibility would have thought of joining what was then considered to be the enemy camp—and no company with any interest in its own self-preservation would have considered opening up its corporate secrets to the prying eyes of someone thought to be bent on its destruction. But Joseph Danzansky, president of Giant Food, a Washington-based supermarket chain, had the vision to perceive a changing world and the courage to fly in the face of conventional wisdom of that time. He understood before almost anyone else in business that the best interests of both consumers and business lay in dialogue and in a joint approach to mutual problems. He saw that it is far preferable and more productive for both consumers and business to be advocates rather than adversaries.

My conditions for accepting the job were stringent. I would have to be the consumer's ambassador to the company's top management—not a public relations spokesperson for the company to the consumer. I wanted

209

to make the distinction clear. I insisted on complete freedom to speak my mind both within and outside the company. I said I had to have a hand at the levers of corporate power—to participate in decision making at the highest levels. I asked for a corporate commitment to try to implement the ideas for consumer reform that had been fashioned during my Government service. Somewhat to my surprise, my terms were accepted. My consumer friends promptly accused me of 'selling out', while some of the firm's vice-presidents lamented that I would probably prevent them from selling out of anything.

Three Realities

In assuming my new responsibilities, I recognized the three major consumer realities of the time, which still govern today.

Scepticism

The first is that consumers are sceptical. Merchants have always been the object of a certain amount of scepticism. Perhaps the public view can best be expressed by the fact that the ancient Roman god Mercury was the patron of both merchants and thieves. In America, Watergate and subsequent scandals deepened this scepticism. The average American's belief in his institutions—business as well as Government—has been shaken to an extent that is rare in American history.

Knowledge

The second reality of our environment in the 'seventies is that the average consumer is more knowledgeable and more demanding than at any time in the past. Sixty years ago, Upton Sinclair shocked the American public with his revelations about the meat processing industry and the content of some processed foods. Now, the concern of the average shopper is likely to be focused on different processing considerations. Consumers want to know about nitrites, artificial colours, preservatives, sodium, fat, and cholesterol contents of foods and their possible carcinogenic or vascular effects.

Professionalism

The third consumer reality of the 'seventies is that consumerism is a broad and growing movement. It is organized (but certainly not monolithic), vocal, and ever-present. The consumer movement has followed in the footsteps of all historical reform movements. It began by isolating legitimate consumer grievances and organizing under strong, inspirational leaders such as Ralph Nader. It does have its share of instant experts who are too often short on expertise and long on rhetoric. However, I think the movement is evolving into one characterized by greater professionalism

210

and an increasing degree of consumer statesmanship. Just as the black liberation movement has wisely progressed from violence to economic development, so must the consumer movement ultimately realize that the real gains are to be found in working with Government and business, and particularly within business. Along these lines, it is interesting to note that just within the past two or three years, a new profession has sprung up—the consumer affairs professional within business. In fact, they have their own professional society now, with membership numbering in the hundreds: it is called SOCAP—The Society of Consumer Affairs Professionals. And they are having an impact. And universities are increasingly adding courses in consumer studies.

Giant's programme of dialogue and joint action with consumer advocates, industry and Government has proved to be a significant competitive advantage for the company. It is being emulated.

We learned from experience that the road was not easy. A first essential step in establishing our programme was to win the support and confidence of the company's key vice-presidents, many of whom had been seared by previous confrontations with consumer groups. A Consumer Action Task Force already existed within the company. It was composed of key people whose support and cooperation would be crucial to the success of any consumer programme. It was, in effect, the company's power structure and could implement as well as devise programmes. It included the vice-presidents in charge of store operations, advertising and sales promotion, purchasing, manufacturing, warehousing, and distribution and was chaired by the assistant to the president.

The task force became the medium for a process of mutual education. It took time to build trust, but as the vice-presidents gradually came to understand that consumerism is a constructive force, their suspicion and hostility began to ebb. In turn, I got a priceless inside glimpse into the dynamics of a corporation. If I had had access to this kind of information when I was in the White House, needless conflict could have been avoided. Many issues could have been resolved in the market place rather than in legislative and regulatory chambers.

Objectives

Our next step was to hammer out a series of objectives to serve as the framework for our consumer programme. President Kennedy had given an important impetus to the budding consumer movement in his unprecedented consumer message to Congress. That message contained his Consumer Bill of Rights. Those rights were the right to safety, the right to be informed, the right to be heard, and the right to choose.

Our task force members unanimously agreed to adopt this format, adding the right to redress and the right to service. The difficulty came in spelling out those rights in concrete form. When we started talking about specifics such as open dating, unit pricing, nutrition labelling, chemical additives, unsafe toys, and so on, some members of management got nervous. I was warned that many of the proposed programmes were untested, that we had insufficient information in some cases (about food additives, for example), and that we had no way of knowing whether Giant could deliver.

We agreed that some of the proposals should be further explored before we became committed to them publicly. We also agreed that if, after a reasonable period of time, the programme did not live up to our hopes, we would drop them. The task force members swallowed hard, crossed their fingers, and accepted most of the pledge. The Giant Food 'Consumers' Bill of Rights' was adopted and appeared as a full-page advertisement in local newspapers. Today it hangs on the walls of all our vice-presidents' offices as a constant reminder of our commitment to consumers.

I must describe an essential method that we use in fulfilling these rights. At the time of the establishment of our department, the firm agreed on our establishing *ad hoc* committees to help us devise our programme and to advise us on consumer needs. The committees are composed of experts in the field being considered—they come from the universities, Government, professional societies, consumer organizations, suppliers, and, of course, company officers. Such committees have structured our programmes regarding over-the-counter labelling, nutrition labelling, and safety, among others. In addition, we have general advisory committees composed of local consumer organization representatives and men and women chosen from among our shoppers. These groups provide a strong realistic background against which we can test our ideas and through which we can institute change.

Quality and Hygiene Control

To ensure the right to safety, Giant established a Quality Assurance and Sanitation Department. Its staff develops product specifications, maintains surveillance over food products in its own microbiology and food chemistry laboratories, sets sanitation policies, tests generic drugs, etc., and oversees implementation through its inspection programmes. The chief officer reports to the president of the company. The independence of the department is paramount. Here we test questionable toys and look for potential hazards, such as small parts, sharp edges or points, or poor quality. If they are found to be dangerous or if they do not pass our tests, we do not buy them or they are removed from sale.

Food Additives

Consumers have also been concerned with the safety of chemical additives in foods. Our commitment said we would try to follow the policy of 'When in doubt—leave it out'. But we found that was not easy. We decided that, where possible, we would offer shoppers a choice between products with and without additives. We offered maraschino cherries without red dye and

212

are increasing our product lines that have no preservatives, enhancers, or artificial colourings.

The issue of nitrate and nitrite content in meats illustrates the need to consider the trade-offs that often are implicit in changes that consumers demand. After long experimentation by our suppliers aimed at developing a hot dog without these additives, it was found that such a packaged product could be given a shelf life of only three days. Consumers' habit of keeping these for a long time, rather than freezing or eating them immediately, raised the spectre of spoilage and food poisoning. One of our advisory committees, composed of home economists, reluctantly concluded that the trade-off in perishability was not worth the risk. So we shelved the project temporarily, while awaiting new technology and the results of efforts with our suppliers to reduce the amount of nitrates and nitrites in this product.

The effort was not wasted, however. Experimentation has continued. New products, that may meet the objections raised against the earlier one, are being developed. We have been looking at bacons, for instance. No-one is ready to market them yet, but we are working on it.

Other safety issues involve the environment. As a result of consumer suggestions several years ago, Giant began selling our own line of recycled paper products—towels, toilet paper, and napkins. The industry has increased its usage of recycled paper scraps in these products, so that we no longer market separate recycled products. But we led in responding to public awareness of this issue.

Consumer Information

The right to be informed covers a great many areas. Giant expresses the commitment to the consumer's right to be informed in three ways: first, through improvements in labelling that provide better information at the point of purchase; second, through institutional advertisements in newspapers and on radio and television, tied closely to our consumer programmes; and third, through commentary on issues of the day affecting consumers and food retailers.

Unit pricing

Unit pricing is a key weapon in our consumer information arsenal. We have unit pricing on more than 12 000 items in our stores. Unit pricing has proved to be a superb inventory management tool. It has more than paid for itself by reducing price-marking errors and by improving inventory control and the company's in-stock condition. Before unit pricing, each store was found to have about 300 price-marking errors per inspection. Now pricing errors have been practically eliminated.

Open dating

Processors and retailers have been dating products for years for freshness control—except that the dates have been in code. Consumers have often asked that the dates be in plain English so that they too could determine the freshness of the goods they were buying. Many company officers feared that shoppers would buy only those goods carrying the most recent dates, leaving huge inventories of perfectly good food to spoil. The fears have been groundless: once customers could understand the dating, by and large their confidence in the store increased and they bought the items on top or in front.

At the same time, the knowledge that customers could determine the freshness of an item caused store clerks to sharpen their rotation practices. At Giant, open dating has improved rotation, reduced spoilage, and helped to sell more private label products (we can open date only our own brands). We are now beginning 'care' labelling to help the customer take better care of the commodity after getting it home. The message on the label tells the customer, in effect, 'If you take care of it, here is how long this food will last.'

Nutrition labelling

Taking our cue from a major recommendation of the White House Conference on Food, Nutrition and Health, we determined to work out a scheme of nutrition labelling. We invited people representing all concerned groups to meet and develop a plan on which all of us could agree. Dr Jean Mayer, chairman of the White House Conference, chaired our committee of 13. Some industry members were reluctant at first to sit down with representative consumers, especially any who were close to Ralph Nader, but gradually the group learned how to work together.

While nutrition labelling was being debated across the country and resisted by some national manufacturers, Giant, Government officials, and private label suppliers could see ahead and cooperated fully in developing a plan. The plan became part of the basis of the labelling system eventually developed by the Food and Drug Administration.

We continue to focus on nutritional concerns and have developed advisory committees covering such areas as labelling information, drained weight labelling, percentage ingredient labelling, and nutrition labelling of produce and meats. We hope these committees will make recommendations that will improve our present system of nutrition labelling and help consumers to choose their foods on the basis of information provided at point of purchase.

In the early 'seventies we were approached by a group of idealistic law students who were interested in full disclosure of ingredients on items covered by federal standards of identity. (If recipes for certain foods are listed with the federal Government, listing of the ingredients on the package is not required.) Most consumers were unaware, for example, that caffeine is an ingredient in cola drinks. Working with the students, we began a disclosure programme of listing ingredients in order of predominance on all

214

our private label (own brand) products, though we did not have to do so.

One of the areas first explored by our Nutrition Labelling Advisory Committee was 'percentage of ingredient' labelling. It found that the area posed a host of problems. For example, should the percentage of ingredients be figured before or after cooking? And what about dehydrated ingredients?

A subcommittee eventually dealt with the technical problems of percentage of ingredient labelling. Instead of attempting to provide the percentages of all ingredients, the group decided to do so only on the major claimed ingredients. Labels would show, for example, the amount of pork in pork and beans (less than 1 per cent) and the amount of beef in beef stew (25 per cent).

Now the Food and Drug Administration has proposed such labelling and even more detail on baby foods. They are finding resistance, but we hope we led the way. I only wish we had a private label baby food to work with.

Drug ingredient labelling

Giant decided to disclose the exact quantities of all active ingredients in non-prescription drugs and to make a full disclosure of ingredients in all health and beauty aids bearing the Giant label. This information is particularly important to people with allergies and other health problems.

Giant's most recent consumer programme involves generic prescription drugs. Consumers want to know if generic drugs are as good as brand names and if they cost less. In the Quality Control Laboratory, Giant tests generic prescription drugs to be sure they are consistent in quality, batch to batch. We do this even though the law does not require it. We also require a certificate of analysis for each batch of generic drugs as evidence that the products meet Government standards.

In our newspaper advertisement and consumer booklet, we explain that a drug's generic name is its common, chemical name, not protected by a trademark. Because we stand behind the generic drugs we sell, we encourage consumers to ask their physicians if their prescription can be filled generically. Since brand names generally cost at least twice as much as generics, this can mean big savings for consumers.

We have not hesitated to be very frank with the public in our advertisements. When high meat prices were a cause of great concern to our customers, we spoke out about them. We decided to inform consumers about the reasons for high meat prices and what can be done about them. In what was to become a most controversial advertisement, we did just that. We pointed out that excessive demand drives prices up, and we told the public about good protein substitutes.

We have made mistakes in our consumer programme, but we have not hesitated to admit them in these public messages. Noteworthy was our attempt to label ground beef according to its fat content. We announced a 90-day test and then found that the state of the art would not enable us to obtain measurements of the proportions of fat in each category of ground beef that met our accuracy standards. So we dropped the system and made our failure known. 'The test is a flop', the advertisement read, and so it was. But we have not given up; we are now working on a new technique. We have not been harmed when we have been candid in such a matter. Apparently, people admire those who are not afraid to own up to their errors.

It would seem that the implementation of the right to choose would pose no difficulties for a company that offers shoppers a choice of 12 000 items in its grocery departments alone. Yet there are times when the right to choose must be weighed against other considerations.

For example, as we have seen, the desire of some who want certain potentially harmful or hazardous products removed from the shelves must be balanced against the desire of other people to buy them. Fruit-scented cleaning products, foods containing additives, and chemical laundry products are examples. Often the demand for these products is in response to heavy national advertising.

Complaints

An essential part of our commitment to the consumer's right to be heard is a good system for registering customer complaints and for having them acted on. An effective programme requires prompt attention to customer enquiries and complaints. We have published a guide called 'Help Us Help You'. We could have called it a complaint guide, but we try to be positive when we can. In order to respond effectively to complaints, we need certain facts from consumers. All complaints are individually investigated. We use no form responses. Suggestions from our customers have made an impact on policy.

Giant Food experienced little difficulty in implementing the right to redress. Throughout food retailing, industry policy has been to maintain an unconditional, money-back guarantee on all products. Some customers have abused this right and our policy is not quite as liberal as it once was. For example, our store managers often made refunds on items that were sold by our competitors, not us. The managers were instructed to make refunds without comment in order to avoid embarrassing customers. We still want to avoid embarrassing customers, but in some questionable situations we now ask for proof of purchase. In my opinion, responsibility is a two-way street. Our consumer advisory committees support this principle knowing that losses from these unjustified returns—as well as from pilferage—eventually are reflected in higher retail prices.

Giant Food management has no regrets about launching its programme. What seemed to some people to be a highly risky alliance has turned out to be a breakthrough for consumers as well as a great competitive asset for the company. Furthermore, in these times of shortages of goods and inflation of prices, Giant's forthrightness with the public has earned the company a sympathetic ear for its side of the story.

Universal Product Code

We have weathered one great crisis as we attempted to get people out of their little boxes and into new mechanisms of dialogue and progress. Difficulties arose over the implementation of what the retail food industry regards as the greatest technological breakthrough in the history of the supermarket: the Universal Product Code (known in the U K as Article Numbering) and the computer-assisted checkout.

The Universal Product Code is a system being used by food manufacturers across the country to provide each individual product with its own unique identification number or 'fingerprint'.

It appears as a series of bars, which can be read by laser-based scanning equipment as numbers.

There is no price hidden in this code. The price is fed into a computer.

When the shopper checks out products at the store, the checker passes the package with the Universal Product Code over a scanner which is built into the checkstand. The scanner instantaneously checks the code against the information stored in the computer memory, and flashes the product name and retail price on a visual display unit in front of the shopper.

It simultaneously prints the name of the product and the price on the consumer's receipt tape. For example, instead of reading 'Gr' as a conventional cash register receipt tape would read, the new computer checkout tape reads, 'Giant Honey'. This is a breakthrough for consumers, who today get only the department and the price on their receipt tape. The new tape also tells whether each item is taxable, and provides a record of the total tax, credits and store coupons, the amount tendered, food stamps due and paid, and the change due to the customer. The tape also shows the date, time, store number, and checkout lane for the customer's transaction. Customers thus have a record for use in budgeting, tracking prices from week to week, and from store to store, and many other uses.

We experienced consumer resistance to the introduction of the system because, I believe, consumers were not involved in its initial introduction and did not understand the new system. They were afraid of what they did not understand. The battle came because industry wanted to conduct a test which would take advantage of the equipment's ability to function without stamping prices on every item, although the price was clearly marked on the shelf and on the receipt tape.

Frankly, I disagreed with Giant's decision to open its first test store without prices on each item. I was not against the principle of the test, but I thought it would be wiser to keep prices on until the public was familiar with the new system and perhaps until the steep rate of inflation that was then prevailing had moderated somewhat.

Our Consumer Advisory Committee on the computer-assisted checkout advised Giant not to proceed with the test, and when the recommendation was not followed, some of its members joined in a drive for legislation to prevent such testing.

A lesson can be learned from this experience. The technology of the computer-assisted checkout is a tremendous improvement over the conventional supermarket. But, because consumers fear that they will not know the price of the item they purchase after taking it from the shelf, there has been a push for legislation to require all supermarkets to price mark each product. Such legislation could 'freeze' the supermarkets into a position which would make it difficult, if not impossible, to experiment with other methods of ensuring price knowledge to the consumer.

Two new issues which are emerging in our country are the electronic funds transfer system (EFTS) and the metric system. The experience with the computer-assisted checkout has emphasized the need to involve consumers in decision-making. Consumer participation must be encouraged with EFTS and metrication or I am afraid consumers will not understand these new programmes, and thus will resist their implementation.

Establishing a Consumer Programme

While it is desirable to have an in-house advocate with consumer credentials to bridge the gap between the company and its market, a company of any size can have a successful programme without a 'name' consumer representative. Today, Giant Food is not the only retailer with a popular consumer programme.

In establishing a consumer programme the following points are important to remember.

—Top management must be totally committed to the principles of open dialogue with consumers, maximization of quality, service, and value, and a good corporate citizenship.
—The person given the responsibility for carrying out the consumer programme must have the ear of the chief executive and report directly to him or her. This person must be included when policy is made.
—Establishment of a 'cosmetic' consumer programme will fool no one. A programme designed solely to gain favourable publicity and win public support will fail. It must have substance.
—The Consumer Department should be charged with working to change the market place for the good of consumers, not merely with 'educating' them on how to cope with the market place as it is. The department must be given the power to change the things that can be changed, the right to explain honestly what cannot be changed, and the background to know the difference.

A consumer programme is no substitute for clean stores, good products, and efficient management. Now, however, business is coming to realize that these basic principles of good operation are not enough. Consumers want a voice in the decisions that affect them, and a good consumer programme gives them that voice.

We still have a long way to go. But there has been a breakthrough. Consumers and business are talking to each other, even working with each other in areas of mutual concern. The result can only be a more democratic market place that better serves the American people. The situation is not precisely parallel to that prevailing in the U K, but there may be lessons to learn. A man whom I consider to have been one of the greatest figures of the twentieth century—the Reverend Martin Luther King, Jr.—perhaps said it best, in the completely American vernacular of an old Negro clergyman, whose prayer he once quoted: 'Lord', he said, 'We ain't what we ought to be, and we ain't what we want to be. We ain't what we're gonna be, but thank God, we ain't what we was!'

20. Representing the consumer in business: J. C. Penney—a US case study

David Schoenfeld

I would like to begin by defining two key terms: *consumer* and *market place*. The consumer is the person at the end of the marketing chain, the one who accepts or rejects the offers that come from the market place. There was a time—obviously long, long ago—when the market place with which the consumer had to deal was simply another person who had something to sell. This one-to-one relationship was certainly simple compared with what consumers had been facing for some years.

The market place now consists of layer upon layer of producers and marketers on the one side and the consumer on the other, so that there is no longer any question of a balanced scale. To make the balance even less favourable to the consumer, the Government is now very much in the marketing picture. Many Government regulations and policies have the avowed purpose of protecting the consumer, but their final shape is influenced by many forces representing various interests. So the market place that the lone consumer has to deal with today is a giant machine of incredible complexity.

The consumer movement was born as soon as the odds against the consumer began to be obvious, and there is no denying that it has grown to be an important element in our society. But until very recently, it has stood off to the side, acting as a critic of the market place, a dissenting voice. It has been concerned mainly with remedying situations that already exist and achieving redress for wrongs already committed. The point that the consumer movement has missed for so many years is that acting as a critic after the fact is a finger-in-the-dyke operation.

Consumers as Part of the Market Place

What consumers really need is a voice in the decision-making processes of both business and Government. The fact is that consumers are part of the market place, rather than something outside it. They are shaped by it, but they also help to shape it. Changes in their values and life-styles have a direct impact on the kinds of goods and services that can be sold, which in turn affect the ones that are produced. Also, what consumers decide to do or not do with their discretionary income affects business very directly. What this adds up to is that there are three, not two, partners in the market place—business, Government, *and consumers*.

While this three-way partnership is a fact, many people in business and Government are hesitant about altering traditional styles of operation. Business has been slow to recognize and understand the need for consumer involvement. But the consumer movement is now making its first major attempt to assume its rightful role in the market place. The tool that it is using for this purpose is consumer representation. The decision-making process is incomplete unless the consumer perspective is represented. By incorporating the consumer perspective, the decision maker has *all* the options available for consideration and thus has a much better chance of making the right decision. Furthermore, by involving the consumer before the fact, the decision maker can avoid the kind of adverse reaction after the fact that has been so common in the past.

These first steps toward consumer representation in business are very important to the consumer movement, because it cannot continue to spin on a separate axis. It cannot be the change-agent that it should be if it remains on the outside, satisfied simply to comment on what happens inside. The major obstacle to consumer involvement in decision making has been lack of knowledge about the processes of the market place. This is an obstacle that can be removed by consumer representation, which can provide consumers with a better understanding of how the market place works and how to deal with it effectively. This in turn will result in improvements in the entire structure of the market place and benefits to both business and consumers.

The point of consumer representation is to change the status of the consumer from being the target of the market place to being a co-director of it. This sounds good from the consumer's point of view, but why should business accept it? The answer is very simple—for economic survival. Today's kind of business cannot survive in tomorrow's world unless it meets the changing needs of consumers. Business *must* respond to changes in the life-styles and behaviour of consumers, as well as to the changing structures of society. There is no better way for the business mechanism to achieve positive change than to involve all the players in the action and to create an environment which can accommodate itself to new ingredients.

Representation in Government

The need for consumer representation in Government is just as acute, for all the same reasons. In fact, probably consumer representation could not succeed in the private sector—business—unless it were also in place in the public sector—Government—and vice-versa. The decisions of one sector directly impinge on the decisions of the other. Therefore, consumer representation in each of the sectors should be fairly similar and fully cooperative.

In the U S, the current struggle for representation in Government focuses around two pieces of legislation, the Agency for Consumer Advocacy and Public Participation in Federal Regulatory Agencies Proceedings (S.270). There is no need here to go into the provisions of structure of these legislative efforts. However, these efforts have reached a higher level than ever before, simply because the administration itself has indicated its full commitment to and support of this concept. This is the first time in almost eight years that such a situation has existed. The standard ploy that is used by the opposition elements is that these bills would add another layer of bureaucracy. However, my own view is that this type of legislation is badly needed, to inject the consumer perspective into Government activities and proceedings of all types. These bills are ways of creating the fair balance of interests that a free enterprise system mandates, with as many competing viewpoints present as possible. The net effect should be to strengthen the Government process, rather than to hamper it.

Representation in Business

As for consumer representation in business, so far it has been largely a knee-jerk reaction to the activities of the consumer movement and to the fact that business itself has been the primary target of the consumer movement. Consumers have seen the business community as the major force in shaping the market place, and blamed business for the market place's shortcomings. As a result, business has been forced to make some efforts to come to grips with this social phenomenon, the consumer movement, but has had little understanding of its staying power or its clout.

Some of the efforts toward consumer representation that have been made by particular businesses are window dressing—superficial attempts to placate consumers. Other businesses have seized on the idea as a way of presenting the company to consumers in the best possible light. The result is a combination of public relations and marketing. Still other businesses feel that consumer representation means the handling and satisfactory resolution of complaints, to maintain the loyalty of the customers to the company's products or services. All too few operations have seen that consumer representation is actually not a problem but an opportunity to examine the company's policies, procedures, and directions more effectively and efficiently, in order to establish a more direct relationship with consumers.

It is a relatively new concept for the decision makers in a company to accept and incorporate the philosophy of a different voice on the team, a voice whose mission is to present the consumer to the company and to provide a means whereby the consumer perspective can be brought to the direct attention of those with the key responsibilities for shaping that specific part of the market place. Consideration of the consumer perspective is a difficult step, because traditionally the two main elements in decision making have been legal problems and business considerations, in terms of what consumers will buy. However, by listening more attentively to the consumer voice, the decision makers soon find that more consumers can be converted into customers.

The Consumer Advocate

There is a further step that is in many ways even harder for a business to accept—that is, to place a consumer advocate with a strong pro-consumer bias within the operation. For this to work, this individual must be provided with the freedom to disagree publicly with the company on consumer issues. Clout or not, used or not, this is an important tool. It is needed to affirm the credibility of the consumer advocate, both internally and externally. However, an advocate who raises questions, who discusses issues from a different perspective, one which does not relate directly to short-term profitability, is not viewed with universal pleasure nor received with open arms in every quarter of the organization.

A key measure of the consumer advocate's effectiveness is where his or her commitment lies. My operational theory is that the advocate's commitment to serving the consumer must be the over-riding one. Because the internal advocate has been hired by a specific company, it may be supposed that the element of loyalty to the company would interfere with the advocate's commitment to the consumer. However, if the advocate truly believes that the company must serve the consumer's interests in order to be successful, then there is no dichotomy between the two elements. Consumer advocates must be trained in this large view so that some day they will have a professional status and elements of qualification on a par with accountants, lawyers, and other specialists.

Consumer advocates tread the difficult line of credibility, credibility which is actually composed of two elements. First, there is external credibility. For the advocate to operate effectively, there must be continuous liaison with the outside consumer world. Since it is very difficult to create those contacts after the fact, it is highly desirable to enter the business organization with those credentials in place. But regardless of the starting point, the only way that the consumer advocate can maintain credibility with consumers is to continue to demonstrate commitment to their interests.

Internal credibility is a different matter. The first problem within the organization is to develop understanding of what the function and role of the advocate is. Understandably, the consumer advocate is a new element, one which has not been seen or heard of in the business context before, and which literally does not fit into a neat slot in terms of a specific contribution. In fact, first discussions and impressions seem to dictate that the advocate is working against at least the short-term profit line, if not the long-term line. The realization that the objectives of the consumer interest and the business interest will ultimately overlap and move towards the same point is a difficult concept for middle management, particularly, to accept.

Over and above knowledge of the consumer perspective and the ability to react to particular situations from that perspective, the prime qualification for the consumer advocate within the business structure is patience. Changes do not occur as rapidly, as frequently, or as decisively as we would like. The change may not even be visible to the naked eye at a given time. Sometimes it is simply a matter of a growing awareness within the company that there is an additional factor to be considered. It may not surface at all in any recognizable way, or at least not as feedback to the consumer advocate. The process is an uneven one. Some strides may be made that are identifiable in one situation, but others cannot be segregated from the totality of a particular operation.

Case Study—J. C. Penney Company

J. C. Penney Company is a major United States retailer of clothes, household furnishings, automotive products, drug store merchandise, and insurance. It serves consumers through more than 2100 stores, as well as mail-order catalogues, and also has stores in Belgium. The annual sales exceed US 9^{1}/_{2}$ billion, and the company is one of the largest retailers in the world. I am employed as consumer advocate in the Consumer Affairs Department at the head office in New York City. At J. C. Penney Company, we have a fully fledged Consumer Affairs Department and our director is a vice-president of the company, which means that our point of view is well represented in top management. Our mandate is based on the four rights of the consumer: the right to safety, the right to be informed, the right to choose, and the right to be heard, including redress.

We think we are unique as a Consumer Affairs Department in that our target audience is not the consumer, but rather the company. We believe that consumers will be more responsive to the Penney Company if we do our part in increasing sensitivity to the needs and values of the consumer in every aspect of company operations.

In line with this overall goal of J. C. Penney Company, we are trying to see consumers as they really are. The consumer movement has developed a utopian model for the consumer role, one that is quite alien to the real-life consumer. The consumer movement has typecast the consumer as always being rational, objective, and deliberate, weighing all choices in the market place with great care and watching every penny. However, in actual practice, consumers are quite often irrational, emotional, and impulsive. The direction of each individual consumer is moulded by his or her own peculiar combination of values and attitudes, not someone else's values.

In our Consumer Affairs Department, we are interested in understanding consumers as they really are, not as we would like them to be. To do this, we have established four objectives, along with strategies for achieving them.

224

Facts on consumers for management

The first objective is to provide factual information on the articulated and unarticulated concerns of consumers for consideration and use by all levels of management in the J. C. Penney Company.

To carry out this objective, a comprehensive data base is being developed which will organize all available information from sources inside and outside our company about consumer attitudes and behaviour into one feedback system. We do not plan to duplicate the excellent research that is already being done in other departments of the company, but we are trying to fill in the gaps where information is needed and to analyse patterns of consumer behaviour on a continuing basis. Our purpose is to coordinate all available information to develop the kind of data base that will give the whole company as complete a picture as possible of current consumer thinking.

As one part of this information network, we subscribe to the Yankelovich Research System, which gives us continuing access to its highly respected in-depth analysis of changing consumer attitudes and values and the anticipated impact of these changes on consumer behaviour.

We are also setting up a programme that will allow us to listen to and to have discussions with consumers at the grassroots level. We are calling this our consumer dialogue programme. Our department plans and organizes the outline for an informal 90-minute discussion between an individual Penney store manager and a small group of consumers. The dialogue is held in the store conference room. Our department helps the store manager to find representative consumers, but the manager actually extends the invitation and conducts the dialogue.

The reports that come back to us about these meetings amount to a direct grassroots feedback, as well as an early warning system on emerging consumer issues. This gives us an indication of the climate of the consumer mood in Penney communities which we can compare with the input from other studies. In addition, we feel that we are building credibility for the sincerity of the Penney Company in wanting to listen to the consumer, and it gives direct consumer input to the local Penney store.

The ultimate goal for the data base we are developing is to make it the most respected source of information available on consumer wants, needs, and values, so that all areas of the Penney Company can turn to it with confidence for information about consumers that they may want to use in their decision-making processes.

Consumer education

Our second objective is to continue to maintain and strengthen J. C. Penney's leadership in consumer education.

We already have a nationally recognized consumer education programme with roots dating back more than 50 years. The staff of our

Educational Relations Department have all had experience as educators. They prepare consumer education materials for our stores to give to educators in their communities as a free public service. The materials are non-commercial, dealing with topics that lead the way for new concepts in consumer education. One basic criterion is that they must be materials not avilable from any other source so that they will be really helpful to educators. Besides our publications, we have a staff of five field representatives, who work in our five regions to help J. C. Penney Stores in major metropolitan areas present an annual programme for educators in their communities. Topics vary according to the needs expressed by educators and our Advisory Committees in each community and in no way do they promote merchandise.

Consumer information

Our third objective is to build on our long experience in consumer education to develop a respected consumer information programme wherever J. C. Penney interacts with the consumer.

We have set this objective in direct response to the growing consumer concern for more information. A recent Yankelovich study indicates some interesting figures on what the general public thinks are the reasons for the failure of business to provide more product/service information.

—53 per cent believe that companies want to hide facts which make their product or service less attractive to consumers.
—27 per cent believe that companies feel that most people are not really interested in all that information.

Yet the Yankelovich study shows that consumers feel that companies should be required to give complete information, even if it is too much for the consumers to read. Just knowing that the information is all there gives consumers assurance about the product and the company.

Our strategies for achieving this objective focus on working with various departments in the company to provide consumers with as much information as possible to help them make their own decisions. We do not plan to tell consumers *what* to buy, but to give them the information that they need to help them to know *how* to buy.

One example of what we have already done is in the toy section of our Christmas 1977 catalogue. Working with a panel of child development specialists, and the Merchandise and Catalogue Departments, we developed an editorial page at the beginning of the toy section which gives general information on how toys contribute to the development of children. In addition, there are blocks of copy on the following pages which give more specific information about the different types of toys. We have discovered that a majority (58 per cent) of the J. C. Penney customers who bought toys used this information and we are planning to continue the service in future catalogues.

226

We are also working to develop fully the concept of Consumer Information Centres in our stores, so that we can provide as much information as possible for consumers to use pre-sale, point-of-sale, and post-sale. These centres will be non-commercial and non-promotional.

Consumer Advocacy

Our fourth objective is to heighten my involvement as the department's consumer advocate in the total activities of the J. C. Penney Company to represent the consumer perspective. I am on the staff for a specific reason—because I have a bias, a strong pro-consumer bias. My role as a consumer advocate is to sensitize the Penney Company to the consumer perspective, not to convert them.

I am expected to be active in consumer affairs organizations and receive support to maintain my integrity and credibility as a consumer advocate by having the freedom to disagree publicly with the Penney Company on consumer issues, if for some reason I, as a consumer advocate, am not in agreement with a position taken by the company.

When I see a consumer issue surfacing, I begin working on ways to involve the appropriate departments of the Penney Company. Meetings are set up between the consumer advocates who are interested in a particular issue and J. C. Penney management. By doing this on an *ad hoc* basis rather than through a standing panel, I get viewpoints which are constantly new and relate specifically to the issue.

I am involved in providing the company with the consumer perspective on pending consumer legislation. This input is incorporated in establishing company positions. Recently, we were able to set up communication between consumer groups and the Penney Company on draft legislation on Public Participation in Federal Agency Proceedings. As a result, all parties agreed upon acceptable language which was built into the Bill, and subsequently we testified in support of the legislation. This activity represents an attempt to bring the voice of the consumer into the company, to increase sensitivity of management at all levels to the consumer point of view, and to encourage dialogue between consumer leaders and business management.

Besides the small, relatively informal meetings that I coordinate between consumer advocates and company management, I also help the department once a year to organize a week-long programme focusing on current consumer issues. This programme, which is called the Consumer Affairs Forum, allows professionals from higher education and leaders in business and Government to discuss consumer issues in open forum. In the seven years that we have held these fora, we have repeatedly found that they result in a better understanding of the complexity of the issues and a heightened sensitivity to the other person's point of view.

The last point that I want to make about my role as a consumer advocate for the Penney Company is that there is a distinct difference between my role and that of the director of consumer affairs. My job is to speak for the consumer and consumer interests within the Penney Company with the objective of increasing the level of consumer awareness and understanding, provide the consumer perspectives on issues and legislation, and to serve as a liaison with local and national consumer advocates and other leaders in the consumer movement.

By contrast, the role of the director of consumer affairs is that of a company officer, whose responsibility it is to provide leadership in the development of a coordinated corporate strategy for recognizing the consumer's interests. Bringing a consumer advocate into the company is one part of this strategy.

Structure

In summary, the consumer affairs team consists of the following people:

—The director of consumer affairs.
—A manager of educational relations, with a staff of eight, responsible for the educational publications and programmes our stores provide for educators in the community. This is in direct response to the consumer's right to know.
—A manager of consumer information services. This is a new function which will be responsible for developing consumer information programmes.
—A manager of consumer feedback systems, with a staff of three now and more to be added this coming year as the feedback system begins to take shape. Not only does this respond to the consumer's right to be heard, but it will be one of the pioneering programmes in interpreting consumer behaviour from the consumer perspective.
—My function, as the consumer advocate who brings issues to the surface and creates opportunities to increase sensitivity to consumer concerns.
—An administrative assistant.

Conclusion

The kind of programme we are developing will be a valuable tool for management to use in anticipating consumer wants and needs. Although merchandise innovations are important, today's consumers are sensitive not only to quality and price of merchandise, but to consumer issues and the response of business to them as well. Their increased affluence and education have resulted in higher expectations, both for products and services, and decreased their tolerance of failures. They have become sophisticated in the use of economic power in the market place.

21. The European perspective

William Roberts

I decided to begin this chapter by trying to jot down, in 30 seconds, as many pieces of draft or existing EEC legislation affecting consumers as I could. This is the list.

Advertising, food labelling, hazardous household products, cosmetics, toys, product liability, doorstep selling, electrical safety, energy labelling, trade marks, weights and measures, non-returnable bottles, textile labelling, unit pricing, ceramics, jam, patents, and tyres.

There is more, a lot more. This list, for example, omits the Common Agricultural policy, the Competition Policy, the Environment Policy, the Transport Policy, and the whole series of issues, like Value Added Tax, tied up in economic and monetary union.

It is easy to see from this list that the EEC's policies have important implications for consumers, and thus important implications for marketing. Yet one often has the impression that people in marketing are not as well informed about developments in this area as they might be. Even stronger is the impression that they are rather vague about the way these policies are formed.

This chapter will, I hope, make things at least a little clearer. It begins by setting the policies in context with a description of the aims, instructions and policy-making processes of the EEC. It goes on to discuss the policies themselves, and finishes up by identifying possible future trends. First, though, the basic structure of the Common Market.

Basic Institutions

The Common Market is the collective name given to three European organizations—the European Economic Community (EEC), the European Atomic Energy Community (EURATOM), the European Coal and Steel Community (ECSC). The nine members of the Common Market are: West Germany, France, Italy, the Netherlands, Luxembourg, Belgium, Ireland, Denmark, and the UK. The last three only joined in 1973, when Norway decided not to. Greenland, incidentally, because of its relationship to Denmark, is also a member. The EEC is the most important body from our point of view because it is the Community responsible for the legislation referred to above.

The aims of the EEC are set out in the Treaty of Rome, the Treaty which brought the EEC into being in 1957. Summarizing its purpose rather brutally, the EEC aims to establish a common market, where goods, services, and people can move freely between member States.

Prior to the UK's accession, two main sorts of barriers to trade with the EEC existed—tariffs, and differences in national legislation. For example, a car manufacturer wanting to sell his cars in West Germany would not only have to face a customs tariff but also different construction standards and methods of approval. The EEC has, therefore, tried to make things easier by removing tarrifs on trade within the Community and setting common mandatory standards for a wide variety of products. This latter process is called *harmonization*.

Certain of the EEC's attempts at harmonization have been fraught with difficulty because of the variety of legislation in force in the member States. This has been particularly true of food products, about which feelings sometimes run high. Bread, beer, and ice-cream, for example, have proved impossible to harmonize fully because of the differences in national laws and customs. Accordingly, a different kind of approach has been tried— *optional harmonization*. With optional harmonization, member States do not have to apply the common standard and only the common standard. They are allowed to retain their existing laws but must, as well, permit the free circulation of goods made to the common standard. In other words, two sets of rules operate—national and EEC. The manufacturer thus has a choice. He can either continue making his product as before or he can opt for the common standard. There are, of course, advantages to him in working to the EEC rules because, if he wants to export, he does not have to operate a special production line for that purpose.

The mechanics of harmonization are fairly complex but the main method used to adapt the laws of member States is the *Directive*. Directives are instructions from the EEC to the member States to amend their legislation in accordance with common rules. Member States must, therefore, implement the new rules through their own domestic law.

How Are the Rules Made?

To understand the legislative process in the EEC it is necessary to look first at the Community's institutions. The pinnacle of the power structure is the Council of Ministers. This Council is made up of Ministers of the member States who deal with the particular subject under discussion. The Agriculture Council, for example, will be made up of the nine Ministers of Agriculture plus whoever else the member States feel it appropriate to send. The Chairmanship of the Council rotates (alphabetically) between the member States. In the last six months of 1976, for example, the Dutch held the chair. In the first six months of 1977, it was the UK's turn.

The Council works on proposals from the Commission. This body is, strictly speaking, just the 13 men who act as the heads of the EEC Civil Service. More often, however, the term is applied more widely to the bureaucracy itself. Curiously, it is often imagined that the Commission is enormous. In fact it is not. Its total staff amounts to about 7500 (fewer than the London Borough of Barking) and the number of actual administrators is roughly 2500. Harrods, by comparison, employs about 3500 people. The Commission, in this broader sense, acts as the Community's Civil Service. It drafts, consults, drafts again, and proposes to the Council.

Two more institutions must be mentioned—the Parliament, and the Economic and Social Committee.

The European Parliament operates much as any other assembly— debating and questioning the actions of the executive. Like many other Parliaments, however, it lacks real power in the policy-making process. It is a consultative body and neither the Council nor the Commission are bound by its views. It does, however, have one fearful formal power. It can, acting on a two-thirds majority, dismiss the 13-man Commission. This power has never been used.

The other consultative body, the Economic and Social Committee (ESC), has no obvious counterpart in the UK. It is a committee of 144 people chosen to represent the 'social partners'. It is divided into three groups: employers, employees, and others. Consumers fall into this last group.

Most of the EEC law which affects consumers follows a route from the Commission to the Council and thence to the two bodies described above. From the Parliament and ESC proposals return to the Council, where a final decision is taken.

Besides the formal framework, there exists an informal process of consultation. Most interests have some form of European umbrella organization with an office in Brussels whose task it is to make representations and lobby on their behalf. Consumers have two such organizations: the independent Bureau Européen des Unions de Consommateurs (BEUC), and the Consumers' Consultative Committee (CCC), which is funded by the Commission.

BEUC, founded in 1962, has 12 member organizations, including Consumers' Association (UK) Publishers of *Which?*, Consumentenbond (Holland), Arbeitsgemeinschaft der Verbraucher (West Germany), Association des Consommateurs (Belgium), Union Federale des Consommateurs (France), Forbrugerradet (Denmark), the Union Luxembourgeoise des Consommateurs, and the Consumers' Association of Ireland. More details about BEUC are given in chapter 22.

The CCC has a broader membership. It takes in not only representatives of BEUC but also of trades unions, cooperatives, and family organizations. It is funded by the Commission and is consultative to it, but the Commission is not obliged to act on its advice.

The Common Market and Consumer Affairs

As was said at the outset, the aims of the European Community are, broadly, to establish a common market in goods and services and facilitate trade within the EEC. These aims are spelled out in some detail in the Treaty of Rome. Article 100, for example, deals with the removal of technical barriers to trade and thus the harmonization programme. But there is very little indeed about protecting consumers in the Treaty of Rome. In fact, some aspects of the Treaty could well be used against consumers. Article 100, for example, does not imply levelling up standards. Standards might well be harmonized in order to ensure the free circulation of goods by harmonizing *down*, or even abolishing legislation altogether.

In reality, however, the Community has not generally used its programmes, policies, and legislation to favour trade interests to the detriment of consumers. Although there is no specific commitment to consumer protection in the Treaty of Rome, the Treaty, a little like the American constitution, is so drafted as to permit a wide variety of policy initiatives which depend on the political, social, and economic attitudes prevailing. Throughout Europe, consumer protection has been an area of concern no Government could ignore completely and, although the pace of progress has varied from country to country, few Governments would be likely to support Community initiatives to dismantle their own consumer policies.

In addition, the Community has always been conscious of its slightly negative consumer image as a 'businessman's club' and has sought ways of promoting its 'human face'. Although the view that the Community should exist for all its citizens and not just for traders has long been held, and is enshrined in the Treaty of Rome, it received its most forceful and lucid expression in 1977 in the inaugural speech of Roy Jenkins, incoming President of the Commission. In this speech he laid great stress on the Community's human face, particularly in terms of safeguarding consumer interests. In doing this he was not initiating a new policy. Rather, he was giving a fresh impetus to a watershed decision which had taken place five years earlier.

In October 1972 Community Heads of Government met in Paris. At this summit the need for a greater emphasis on consumer protection was proclaimed and the institutions of the Community were instructed to prepare a programme by January 1974. That programme was prepared and forms the mainstay of initiatives in the field. It is to the programme that we now turn.

Preliminary Programme for a Consumer Protection and Information Policy

The programme's introduction defines its aim as 'a new deal for the consumer' and defines his five basic rights.

—The right to protection of health and safety.
—The right to protection of economic interests.

232

—The right to redress.
—The right to information and education.
—The right of representation (the right to be heard).

This fivefold definition serves as the framework of the programme and provides a convenient way of analysing the impact of the Community on consumer affairs—and hence on marketing.

Health and safety

The principles on which this part of the programme is based are impressive and ambitious: no goods or services should present a health or safety risk under normal or foreseeable conditions of use; quick and simple methods of withdrawing such products from the market should be established; consumers should be informed of any risk involved in using the product; consumers should be protected against the consequences of physical injury caused by defective products and services; foodstuffs, their additives, and packaging should be so controlled as not to harm consumers; electrical and household appliances should be covered by special rules and standards; and certain categories of new products where special risks are involved should be subject to prior authorization before marketing.

Few consumers would object to these principles. They are imaginative, comprehensive, and undoubtedly make good sense from the consumer's point of view. Sometimes less impressive are the efforts which have been made to secure these goals. The programme lists 11 areas of special concern, ranging from foodstuffs to additives in animal feeds. It is worth examining some of these priority areas in a little more detail to see how the principles turn out in practice.

Cosmetics come second on the list. For many years the Commission laboured over the Directive which was finally adopted in 1976. When it comes fully into force, a cosmetics manufacturer will be able to market the same product in all Community countries. How far have consumer interests been served by the Directive? To begin with, the lists of substances included in the Directive are mostly negative. That is, they specify what must *not* be used rather than what *may* be. There is, therefore, no full list of substances for use in cosmetics verified as safe from the consumer point of view. Further, in contrast to U S legislation, there is no requirement upon manufacturers to disclose the ingredients used.

Halfway down the list come 'dangerous substances'. This is a generic name given to a series of Directives regulating the marketing and labelling of a variety of products—paints, solvents, cleaning materials, and bleaches, for example. Common to all these Directives is a system of hazard warning symbols meant to convey to the consumer the risks involved in using the product. Such labels are easy to find in the factory or the laboratory and are supposed to indicate the nature of the risk via a symbol with an intuitively obvious meaning. In other words, the symbol should not have to be learnt—it should be obvious what its message is.

Were any advertising agency to try and get a message across it would test alternatives and measure their effectiveness. Unfortunately, the EEC chose not to do this and it was left to a consumer organization (Consumers' Association of the UK, in association with Aston University's Applied Psychology Department) to run tests. The results of these tests were disturbing. The preliminary research showed quite clearly, for example, that the symbol most likely to appear on household products (that indicating a general hazard) was simply not understood. The symbol, a St Andrew's Cross, was misinterpreted by a majority of people to whom it was shown. A report of this study was published in *Which?* in April 1978. At the time of writing, more work is taking place to produce a better symbol.

Toys, listed as a priority, illustrate another problem faced by consumer organizations. The draft Directive is based upon work carried out in the Comité Européen de Normalisation (CEN), the European standards-making body. But the consumer input to this body, because of its structure, is sadly inadequate. Consequently, consumer organizations are compelled to work on a draft proposed initially without their views being taken into account. This same problem arises with the fourth priority area, cars.

Progress in harmonizing national legislation has been most rapid with cars. At the time of writing, 28 Directives concerned with cars have been agreed. As with toys, however, the pattern has been for the Community to take over existing standards produced by bodies with little or no consumer representation. Tyres offer the worst example of this process.

The draft Directive requires a system of markings on car tyre sidewalls designed to convey several pieces of information, including type of tyre (radial/cross-ply), size, and maximum speed. These codes, which are virtually identical to those currently used in the UK, are far more complicated than, for example, US tyre markings. Whereas the US tyre mark will clearly disclose maximum speed (e.g., max. 70 mph), the European tyre will do this in a code—SR, HR, VR. Nor, under the Directive, will the European tyre have to declare whether it is a cross-ply, although mixing cross-ply and radial tyres incorrectly can be fatal. A radial tyre will have to be marked 'radial' or 'R', and the absence of these marks will indicate cross-ply.

As with hazard warning symbols, no research was undertaken by the EEC Commission to determine whether the codes were understood in countries where they were already in use. Consumers' Association therefore tested the codes with a nationwide sample of fitters in garages and specialized tyre outlets. They were not generally understood. The most disturbing findings related to the distinction between radial and cross-ply tyres. 43 per cent of the fitters interviewed misunderstood the way radial and cross-ply tyre types could be identified by sidewall codes.

Finally, the last priority area, animal feeding-stuffs. This series of Directives illustrates a far more general problem. While a thorough and comprehensive law on animal feeding-stuffs is a necessary condition of consumer protection, it is not a sufficient condition. Laws designed to protect the consumer only fulfil their function if they are observed and enforced.

UK legislation, prior to accession, had already taken a tough line on antibiotic additives in animal feeds. Antibiotics act as growth promoters in animals but their residues in meat, eggs, etc., can have harmful effects on consumers. While not dangerous in themselves, antibiotic residues can lessen the effectiveness of antibiotics used in the treatment of human disease. Consequently, the UK took a firm line on such additives and all but banned them.

Attempts at harmonization of national legislation on additives in animal feeds did not succeed in persuading the French Government to tighten its own law to the same extent. In the event, the French were permitted to continue using antibiotics, including some of the most powerful ones. On the other hand, under a different set of EEC Directives, antibiotic residues themselves are banned. Provided monitoring takes place, consumers in or out of the Community need not have much to fear. But, certainly in the UK, no systematic checks for antibiotic residues appear to take place other than on penicillin in milk. This is, perhaps, understandable, given the cost of monitoring. But if the consumer is to be protected from antibiotic and other residues (hormones, for example) a choice must be made between funding a monitoring scheme and banning certain additives altogether. One leading UK food retailer, for example, has taken its own intitiative by refusing to sell chickens caponized with hormones, even though the practice is still legal under Community rules.

There are, clearly, many ways in which the Community could improve its performance in terms of protecting the consumer's health and safety. The examples cited here show how, for one reason or another, consumer demands have not always been met by the Commission's programme. But firms do not have to wait on the whim of legislators. They are free, if they so wish, to take the initiative themselves and meet consumer demands before they, and their competitors, are compelled to do so by the law. We will return to this theme later in the chapter.

Economic interests

The principles underpinning this section of the programme are again impressive, although perhaps they beg a few questions.

Purchasers should be protected against one-sided contracts, unfair exclusions of their rights, harsh credit conditions, high-pressure selling, and demands for payments for unsolicited goods; the consumer should be protected against the economic consequences to him of defective products; advertisements should not mislead and claims made should be capable of substantiation; information provided in advertisements or labels should be accurate; the consumer should get reliable after-sales service for durables; and the range of goods available should, as far as possible, represent an adequate choice for consumers.

First in the programme's list of priorities comes credit. Leaning heavily on the U K Consumer Credit Act 1974, the draft Directive deals with most common abuses. In this field the main criticisms made by U K consumer organizations have been about the pace of implementation rather than the rules themselves.

The programme's second priority is a frequent target of consumer policies—advertising. The Commission (Directorate General XI rather than the Consumer Protection Service) did, in 1976, issue a preliminary draft Directive. At the time of writing the draft is far from being agreed but it is still useful to look at the general approach chosen.

Unlike the main piece of U K legislation on advertising (the Trade Descriptions Act 1968) the Directive contains a general prohibition of false, misleading, and unfair claims. The U K Act, in contrast, tends to treat different claims in different ways. Claims relating to prices and price reductions are subject to particular rather than general rules; advertisements for services are covered by less onerous rules than advertisements for goods. The Act is dealt with more fully in Chapters 3 and 18.

Second, the draft Directive introduces a new concept: unfair claims. This criterion appears to have been borrowed from the U S. Its most obvious use would seem to be to prohibit advertisements which play on fear. Advertisements which sought to imply, for example, that unless a product was used the consumer would be seen as inferior in some way would, presumably, be caught, as would claims playing on superstition or the particular susceptibilities of the audience to which they were directed—children, for example.

A third innovation, from the U K point of view, is the possibility of *class actions*. In the original draft, member States were required to permit civil actions on the part of consumers as a whole to be brought by, for example, consumer organizations. The thinking behind this was that the economic loss to an individual implied by the purchase of a particular product on the basis of a false, misleading, or unfair claim would probably be insufficient to justify an action for damages on his part alone. On the other hand, if an advertisement deceived a large number of consumers, the total economic loss implied could be quite large. A consumer organization, in bringing an action for damages on behalf of all those misled, could secure redress by taking the risks of litigation upon itself.

It is too soon to say whether this provision will remain in the final Directive. But it is worth noting that France and West Germany already permit class actions, as does, of course, the U S.

The original draft also dealt with misleading technical devices used in advertising. As an example of what might be caught by the Directive we will take a U S television commercial for car window glass. A camera positioned inside a car showed the view through the side window. The first shot was of a competitor's product and gave very bad results. The second shot, for the glass being advertised, was infinitely better. These results were hardly surprising as in the first shot the window was smeared with vaseline and in the second shot the window was wound down completely giving a clear view outside.

Given the widespread use of technical devices, particularly in TV commercials, restrictions could have quite a big impact.

The fact that the draft is still at an early stage makes it impossible to say exactly what its final effect will be, but it is worth emphasizing that one change that has been asked for by consumer organizations relates to ambiguous claims. In 1975, BEUC published a comparative study of advertising in the UK and West Germany, One of its criteria for analysing misleading advertisements was ambiguity. By this it meant that some claims had more than one meaning—one misleading, one not. As an example it took the Stella Artois claim that it was 'EUROPE'S STRONGEST-SELLING LAGER' in the context of an advertisement also proclaiming: 'STELLA'S FOR THE FELLAS WHO TAKE THEIR LAGER STRONG'. It argued that there were two reasonable interpretations of the claim. It could be taken to mean that Stella was the strongest seller (in marketing terms) in Europe, or that it was the strongest lager on sale in Europe, which it was not. The report found many similar ambiguous claims.

Consumer organizations have therefore pressed for a revision to the Directive such that no reasonable interpretation of an advertisement or a claim should be misleading. They have argued that it should not be enough for an advertiser to show that one out of a variety of plausible interpretations is true. Because of the frequency of such claims, it is clear that a provision on these lines would have a major effect.

Finally, the draft Directive deals with comparative advertising. That it does so in some detail and appears to apply stricter rules for comparative than for non-comparative advertisements is hardly surprising, given the legislative restrictions on comparative advertisements in many European countries. Even so, it does seem likely that comparative advertisements will become more and more common in the future if and when the Directive is law. Consumer organizations have welcomed this prospect.

Just as many European countries have restrictions on comparative advertising under their unfair competition laws, so too do they restrict another marketing tool familiar in the UK: premium offers. Although no draft Directive has yet appeared, one is, at the time of writing, in preparation, following a special study of premium offers commissioned by the EEC. One can only guess at its probable content but it seems likely that, following the pattern of West Germany, for example, the Directive will seek either to eliminate or severely restrict the use of premium offers. UK consumer organizations would resist moves in this direction.

One draft Directive which is much further advanced is that on contracts negotiated away from business premises. The draft is usually referred to as the 'doorstep selling' Directive but covers many other practices, including party-plan selling and sales by an agent through a catalogue.

The two main provisions of the draft are a 'cooling-off period' for such transactions and a written contract. Both are subject to a lower money limit to exclude, for example, door-to-door sales of milk and bread. The principles underlying the Directive are, not surprisingly, supported by all consumer organizations.

It is clearly the case that the consumer finds himself at something of a disadvantage when involved in deals like these. Once a salesman has been invited into the house (or invited himself) most people find it harder to break off negotiations than they would in a shop. Often, one suspects, goods are bought at least partly to get rid of the salesman. A cooling-off period gets round this by allowing the consumer, if he wants to, to reconsider the deal away from the pressure of a salesman.

Running parallel with the draft Directive on doorstep selling is the draft Directive on product liability. This piece of Community legislation is arguably the most fundamental of all those mentioned in the programme. By imposing strict liability on manufacturers of defective goods it could be said to do more to shift the balance of advantage between producer and consumer than any of the other Directives referred to above. What, in essence, is proposed is that the consumer who suffers physical and economic damage caused by an unsafe product will have an automatic claim against its producer without having to prove that the producer was negligent.

Certain consumer organizations have pressed for the extension of the principle to defects not leading to physical or economic damage. If the washing machine breaks down, they argue, the consumer should have a definite claim against the manufacturer. He should not be pushed back and forth between retailer and manufacturer.

The legal arguments are complex but it is certainly true that durables go 'phut' more often than they go 'bang' and that all consumers want in such cases is to be able to reach someone who will fix the machine quickly and conveniently.

The safety of consumers has long been an issue of concern to legislators and the arguments for such legislation are irrefutable. Moving into the area of their economic interests the issues become far less clear-cut and, in some cases, less obviously a subject for legislation. The last of the principles laid down in this section of the programme illustrate the point well: 'The range of goods available to consumers should be such that as far as possible consumers are offered an adequate choice'. It is difficult to see how legislation can do more here than provide a competitive environment in which business can operate. At the same time, it is hard to envisage detailed legislation covering after-sales service (the penultimate principle in the list). These are precisely the areas where firms cannot easily be pushed by the law but have to be pulled by the market. Equally, they seem to be areas where scope exists for gaining a competitive edge by serving the consumer better.

Consumer information and education

From the marketing point of view, the more important aspects of the programme are contained in the section on information.

The principles underlying this section are that the consumer should be given sufficient information to enable him to: assess the basic features of the goods and services offered—like nature, quality, and price; make a rational choice between competing products and services; use these products and services safely and to his satisfaction; and claim redress for any injury or damage resulting from the products or services. Among the more specific of the proposals contained in the priorities laid down is that on food labelling. The Directive on food labelling is already well advanced at the time of writing. There are four main changes in UK law implied by the current draft.

First, date-marking will be compulsory. Most manufacturers and retailers already mark their perishable goods with a sell-by date on a voluntary basis. In fact, Marks and Spencer's have emphasized their practice of date-marking as a plus for consumers. Under the Directive, however, many foods will have to be date-marked not with a 'sell-by' date but with a 'best use before' date. This system, technically called minimum durability, already operates in Canada, using the phrase 'best before'.

Second, additives will have to be disclosed both specifically (using an 'E' number) and generically—'colour (E150)', for example. This already happens in France.

Third, a percentage declaration of certain ingredients will have to be made. The law in France requires this already and in the UK some firms do it voluntarily. Birds Eye, for example, disclose the percentage of meat content of their beefburgers, and Plumrose do the same on their canned meat products.

Fourth, foods packed in a liquid medium, like canned peas in brine, will have to bear a label disclosing their 'drained weight'—the weight of the solid food element. Again, drained weight legislation exists in other countries—Denmark, for example.

Last but one in the list of priorities is a proposal on price display, including unit pricing. Since the programme was published, two drafts in this field have been produced. The first, on unit pricing, is still at a very early stage but would require all foodstuffs, unless packed in certain set quantities, to be labelled with their unit price. The second, at an even earlier stage, deals with the display of prices for goods and services. It would control the way prices are displayed (inclusive of Value Added Tax, for example) and the goods and services for which prices must be displayed (like price lists in hotels). Both these proposals go far beyond existing UK legislation.

One further initiative taken by the Commission must be mentioned although it does not appear in the programme—energy labelling. The energy crisis prompted the Community to investigate ways in which domestic energy savings could be made. Accordingly, it proposed a Community system of energy labelling for a range of domestic electrical appliances. Should this scheme come to fruition, washing machines, tumbler driers, freezers, and several other appliances will have to disclose the amount of energy they consume and, possibly, how they rate against their competitors. France has already made such a scheme compulsory.

Conclusion

In the space available it has been impossible to give a comprehensive description of all the Commission's plans in the field of consumer affairs. But, given that reservation, what lessons might we draw for marketing?

The main lesson is that the Community has taken a wide variety of initiatives and given a fresh impetus to consumer protection legislation. The changes implied by the Directives described above will certainly not happen overnight (indeed, the Commission's time-scale has been described as 'geological') and a few may not happen at all. But changes will take place and will impose common rules on all firms.

In the meantime, the firm wishing to act now, in anticipation of new Community rules, has the opportunity to do so. But why should it? Why should it not act as many firms do now and use its energies instead to try to 'pull the teeth' of proposed legislation? The answer is fairly simple. The kinds of changes being put forward are being proposed to meet a demand from consumers and the momentum behind the consumer movement is growing. The firm which acts now will do it before both it and its competitors are forced to.

22. Glossary of organizations active in consumer affairs

Julia Aspinall

CONSUMER ORGANIZATIONS

Consumer Advice Centres

The first Consumer Advice Centre, occupying shop premises in a main street, was opened in 1969. The centre was set up, staffed and financed by Consumers' Association in an attempt to persuade local authorities to establish such centres. In 1972 the first local authority financed centre was opened, and by mid 1977 well over one hundred centres were in operation. There are now also a number of mobile units which operate in rural areas. Advice centres often work in close cooperation with Citizens' Advice Bureaux (CABx) and other advice-giving agencies.

Consumer Advice Centres vary considerably in the services they offer. The most comprehensive are those which offer both pre-purchase advice and information and a post-shopping complaints service dealing with civil and criminal complaints. If complaints arise about faulty goods and services, advice centre staff will try to mediate between the parties concerned. In addition, many centres contribute to the education of the community on consumer affairs by providing a wide range of explanatory leaflets and booklets, arranging lectures for local organizations, and mounting exhibitions. Many centres also provide a weekly monitoring of local food prices.

The Advice Centre Servicing Unit, run by Consumers' Association, provides training programmes, information services, and leaflet material for established advice centres. It also provides a consultancy service for local authorities interested in the possibility of establishing a consumer advisory service in their own area.

In addition to the general advice offered by Consumer Advice Centres, there are specialist centres dealing with housing, money, and legal matters.

Consumer Affairs Group of National Organisations (CAGNO)

The Consumer Affairs Group of National Organisations was formed in 1970 with the aim of providing a meeting place where consumer organizations might discuss common problems, exchange information, attempt co-ordination of views, and take joint action where appropriate.

Membership of the Group is by invitation and is dependent upon the organization's field and scope of activities coming within the interests of consumers (in the widest sense of the term). The Group has no formal constitution and no source of revenue other than the provision, by the National Council of Social Service, of accommodation and its secretariat.

CAGNO, The National Council of Social Service, 26 Bedford Square, London WC1B 3HU

Consumers' Association (CA)

Founded in 1956 as a non-profit-making company, Consumers' Association launched its magazine *Which?* in October 1957. The magazine was published quarterly until 1959, when it changed to a monthly.

CA came into being to help redress the imbalance between the power of the seller and the power of the buyer by providing impartial and technically based guidance on the ever increasing variety of goods and services.

Its methods are to test products and investigate services, and to publish the results in *Which?* or its satellite publications (*Motoring Which?*, *Money Which?*, *Holiday Which?*, and *Handyman Which?*—all published quarterly). The information given in the magazine covers the quality, performance, and value for money of products.

All products tested by CA are purchased anonymously. In addition to being put through stringent technical laboratory tests, user tests and surveys of CA members' experiences are carried out when applicable. Surveys are also used to find out peoples' attitudes, needs, and experiences on such matters as the servicing of consumer goods and private and public services used by consumers.

As important as the service it provides to its members is the campaigning work that is undertaken by CA. When research shows that legislation needs to be strengthened or introduced, or when a product's design or conditions of sale need to be improved, the reports are sent to Government and suppliers. Many products and services have been improved and new legislation introduced as a result of such campaigns.

As the major voluntary consumer organization in the country, CA has played an invaluable part in establishing the importance of the consumer and consumer affairs in general. It was responsible for stimulating awareness on a local level by organizing a conference in 1961 which led to the establishment of local consumer groups. In conjunction with the University of Loughborough, CA set up in 1970 the Institute for Consumer Ergonomics, whose purpose is to find out exactly what goods and services people really want, or need. It successfully campaigned for the establishment of local Consumer Advice Centres after pioneering in this field by setting up the first advice centre in Kentish Town, London, in 1969.

The overall policy of the Association is formulated by an elected Council of consumers. Council members may neither be engaged in business nor paid for their services to the Association. The Council is elected by the Association's Ordinary Members, who are subscribers of three or more years' consecutive standing. Members of the Council retire in rotation, but may be re-elected.

CA is financially independent, being funded by subscriptions from members who take *Which?* and its satellites. CA also receives money from the media and Government on a consultancy contract basis. The Government income is used to ensure that the consumer view is put forward on proposed EEC legislation.

CA does not allow anything it publishes to be used in any form of advertising or sales promotion, and it does not carry advertising in any of its publications.

In addition to *Which?* and the four satellites, CA publishes the *Good Food Guide* to restaurants; a series of publications on subjects of special interest to consumers; the *Drug and Therapeutics Bulletin* for medical subscribers, providing authoritative assessment of drugs; a series of separate publications on projects in depth on such subjects as contraceptives and slimming; and *Whichcraft*, an educational aid for the use of secondary school pupils which is published six times a year and comprises classroom notes and exercises, together with teachers' notes.

Consumers' Association, 14 Buckingham Street, London WC2N 6DS.

Institute for Consumer Ergonomics (ICE)

The Institute was founded in 1970 by Consumers' Association (CA) and the University of Technology, Loughborough. Consumer ergonomics research as carried out in the Institute is concerned with the evaluation and design of goods, services, buildings, and environments that are used and experienced by the public. The results are disseminated to manufacturers, designers, purchasers, planners, and legislators in a form which they can understand. The Institute has undertaken a wide variety of research projects for Government agencies, charities, and other organizations such as CA. These projects range from the design of safe domestic products for the consumer to the design of urban rapid transit systems. In addition, projects have been carried out for industry.

The Institute is governed by its Council, consisting at present of ten members, some of whom reflect the interests of its founder organizations, and others concerned with protecting consumers and attending to their needs. The Council decides on policy issues, and the Directorate, consisting at present of three members of the university's academic staff, is responsible to the Council for the day-to-day running of the Institute.

The Institute is a non-profit-making company, limited by guarantee, and is registered as a charity. It is funded by the sponsors of its research.

In addition to a large number of specially commissioned reports, the

Institute has written articles for numerous publications (including consumer journals at home and abroad) and books.

Institute for Consumer Ergonomics, University of Technology, Loughborough Leicestershire LE11 3TU.

National Federation of Consumer Groups (NFCG)

Local Consumer Groups

Formed in 1963, the National Federation of Consumer Groups is an association of voluntary, independent local consumer groups throughout the UK. The aims of the Federation are to increase the awareness of consumers, to identify and promote the proper interests of consumers and the means of their protection, and to provide a channel for consumer opinion and representation.

The NFCG's main activities are encouraging the formation of new consumer groups, helping existing groups to maintain professional standards, and representing the views of groups to Government and national agencies. In addition, the Federation acts as a clearing house for news and ideas between groups; it organizes national surveys in which all groups may take part; its Legislation Committee considers how new laws will affect the consumer; and, above all, it provides a two-way channel of communication between consumer opinion and Government bodies (like the Office of Fair Trading and the Metrication Board) and trade and industry organizations. The Department of Prices and Consumer Protection consults the NFCG.

The NFCG is an autonomous, non-profit-making, non-party-political, non-sectarian organization. The elected Executive Committee conducts the business of the Federation.

The NFCG is financed by subscriptions from member groups, individual members, and Associates (a statutory, voluntary, or commercial organization which agrees with the aims of the Federation), an annually reviewed grant from Consumers' Association, and occasional help from the Department of Prices and Consumer Protection.

The local groups consist of people of all kinds who have come together on a local basis to press for better goods and better services in their own community. The activities of local groups range from conducting surveys on such issues as grocery prices, bus services, packaging, facilities for the elderly; campaigning on local consumer issues; handling individual consumer complaints; giving talks on its work to all kinds of organizations; becoming involved in consumer education; keeping close touch with local authority departments, chambers of trade and commerce; providing consumer representatives for official bodies such as gas consumer councils; and cooperating with other voluntary groups where the problem is one of common concern.

Most local groups publish their own magazines or news letters which are available on subscription to their members, and often broadcast on local radio.

Addresses of local groups may be obtained from the Secretary of the NFCG.

National Federation of Consumer Groups, Office No. 7, 70/76 Alcester Road South, Birmingham B14 7PT.

Research Institute for Consumer Affairs (RICA)

Established in 1963, the Research Institute for Consumer Affairs provides a research service for investigating how adequately goods and services meet the needs of users. Its findings are directed not only to the consumer, but also to the providers of the goods and services whose actions affect his welfare.

RICA has a special interest in the needs of the underprivileged consumer, especially the physically handicapped. It researches the goods and services provided by central and local government, nationalized industries, grant-aided bodies, the professions, and other bodies. The methods employed include physical testing, observational studies, attitude surveys, and desk research. As occasion warrants, RICA works closely with Consumers' Association.

Research projects are frequently sponsored by bodies such as the Sports Council, the Child Poverty Action Group, the National Fund for Research into Crippling Diseases, as well as Government departments.

As an independent charitable trust, RICA seeks financial assistance from foundations, Government departments and other bodies, either as commissions or covenanted grants. It occasionally receives financial help from Consumers' Association and CA's research facilities are made available to the Institute.

The results of the Institute's findings are published in various journals (including UK and international consumer magazines) and independently. They cover such subjects as 'The consumer's view of building maintenance', 'Children's playgrounds' and 'Invalid tricycles: drivers' experiences'.

Research Institute for Consumer Affairs, 43 Villiers Street, London WC2N 6NE.

WOMEN'S ORGANIZATIONS

Co-operative Women's Guild

The Co-operative Women's Guild was founded in 1883. It has nearly 900 branches in England and Wales and a total membership of about 24 000.

The aims and objects of the Guilds are to promote through the expansion of Co-operation such conditions of life as will ensure for all people equal opportunities for full and free development; to educate women in the principles and practice of Co-operation in order that they shall be loyal members of their societies and play a full part in the control of the Co-operative movement; to encourage and prepare women to take part in

245

local, national, and international affairs; to work for the establishment of world peace, and to provide social, cultural, and recreational activities through which members may live a full and interesting life.

Each Guild plans its own programme, depending on the topics of the day and the interests of its members. About six meetings throughout the year are devoted to a national programme theme on such subjects as 'Consumers on low incomes', 'State education', 'The mass media', etc.

Each Guild elects its own officers and committee, and district sectional and national officials. Policy is decided by an Annual Congress which is attended by one member of each individual Guild who has one vote.

The National Executive Committee which conducts the affairs of the Guild between Congresses is elected by the branches on a sectional basis, one member from each of the ten Sections. The Committee meets five or six times a year.

The Co-operative Women's Guild has strong ties with women in many countries. Through Guild activities, women are encouraged and help to play a full part in Co-operative and community affairs. Many serve on Co-operative Committees, as councillors, magistrates, on Consumer Councils, and a great variety of local committees such as Home Safety, Road Safety, Old People's Welfare, etc.

Individual Guilds are mainly financed by contributions from their members. Generally, local Co-operative Societies provide meeting rooms free or at a nominal rent. The national organization receives a grant from the Co-operative Wholesale Society and the Co-operative Union. All other income comes from members, either directly through affiliation fees or indirectly through sales, appeals, money-raising events, etc.

Co-operative Women's Guild, 342 Hoe Street, London E17 9PX.

National Council of Women of Great Britain

The National Council of Women of Great Britain is a voluntary pressure group which was founded in 1895 to promote human rights and conditions of life to assure opportunities for full and free development of all the people of the U K. It exerts pressure, either through Parliamentary channels and local authorities, through work done in its branches (which are grouped into regions) and at national level through widely representative special committees covering such topics as consumer affairs, education, the media, housing, health, and social welfare.

The Council is non-party-political and non-sectarian. Membership is open to any woman or affiliated society who wants to help put the Council's aims and objectives into effect. The Council's work is carried out by its Committee of Management, to which individuals, branches, and affiliated societies elect members.

In addition to its direct membership, it provides representation and coordinating machinery for, and draws on the expertise of, some 90 affiliated societies of widely ranging interests. Its policies are formulated and implemented by Conference resolutions and its governing body—the Committee of Management—which includes representatives from every level of the Council, and from its affiliated societies.

Many members serve on consumer consultative and advisory bodies. The Council is represented on the UK EEC Consumers' Co-ordinating Group and cooperates with other consumer organizations. It is also a member of the Women's National Commission.

It is totally financed from voluntary subscriptions. Reports of working parties and memoranda to Government are published and are available to outside bodies. The Council also publishes a bi-monthly newsletter, *Council.*

The Council is affiliated to the International Council of Women and is one of the 17 countries which makes up the European Centre of that organization.

National Council of Women, 36 Lower Sloane Street, London SW1W 8BP.

National Federation of Women's Institutes (NFWI)

The first Women's Institute was opened in 1915 and two years later the National Federation was formed. The main purpose of the Federation is to provide a democratically controlled educational and social organization for countrywomen, and to give them the opportunity of working and learning together to improve the quality of rural life and to enable them to develop their own skills and talents. The Federation is a non-sectarian and non-political organization and membership is open to all women and girls. Local WIs are completely independent, each being affiliated to a County or Island Federation as well as to the National Federation. At present there are 63 County Federations covering England, Wales, the Isle of Man, and the Channel Islands, each of which is also affiliated to the NFWI.

The NFWI runs its own independent adult education college near Oxford which arranges about 200 short-stay courses for 4000 members each year. It also organizes Co-operative Markets in villages and small towns where home-grown and home-made produce is sold direct to the general public. Markets are generally open once or twice a week and the producers, who need not be WI members, are both men and women. Almost all the revenue is returned to the producers, a small percentage of the gross turnover being paid to the NFWI in return for advice and administrative help.

The National Federation itself is run by an executive committee elected biennially by secret ballot. At each level the aims and objects of the movement are carried out through a series of subcommittees, each covering a different aspect of the work.

Representatives of Government and local authority departments sit on relevant National Federation and County Federation committees. On occasion, public bodies such as the BBC, IBA, and the Sports Council also nominate representative members.

Income is derived from a number of sources including an annual subscription, investments, and small grants from two Government departments. Various bodies make grants for specific projects. Federations get help from local education authorities as funds permit and also organize fund-raising events to supplement subscription and other income.

The NFWI publishes a number of books and leaflets, together with several service items, on subjects associated with its work. These can cover topics as varied as wine-making, drug abuse, international affairs and drama. The movement's magazine *Home and Country* is published monthly.

National Federation of Women's Institutes, 39 Eccleston Street, London SW1W 9NT.

National Housewives Association Ltd (NHA)

The National Housewives Association started in the autumn of 1973 as small protest groups of housewives spread over the country, coming together at a time when rising prices cut living standards.

The aims and objectives of the Association are to enable housewives to make their voices heard and attended to when their interests are at stake. The Association is concerned with both local and national issues. On a local level, activities range from campaigning to ensure that the cottage hospital remains open to bringing unfair trading practices to the notice of trading standards officers. On the national level, the NHA is especially concerned with conservation and reclamation, the economic state of the country, food prices, and topical consumer problems, including EEC matters.

The Association is non-party-political, non-profit-making, and non-sectarian. Its governing body is drawn from women from various parts of the country who have shown an interest in and knowledge of the affairs of their neighbourhood and the country as a whole. This national executive meets quarterly to discuss progress and future tactics.

The NHA operates on a small budget which consists of annual subscriptions from members and a charitable trust.

Branch chairmen and the national headquarters produce and disseminate newsletters to members.

National Housewives Association, 20 Headlands Close, Great Missenden, Buckinghamshire.

National Union of Townswomen's Guilds (NUTG)

Founded in 1928, the National Union of Townswomen's Guilds brings together some 2500 Guilds and over 100 Federations. The objects of the Guilds are to advance the education of women irrespective of race, creed, and party, so as to enable them to make the best contribution towards the common good; to educate such women in the principles of good citizenship; and to provide or assist in the provision of facilities for recreation or other leisure time occupation for such women with a view to improving their conditions of life.

Townswomen's Guilds attain these objects by serving as a centre for arousing interest in any subject concerning the life and well-being of the individual and the family in the home and of the community—local, national, and international; encouraging members to equip themselves as individuals for service to the community, by the study of any subject and, in so doing, develop their powers of discrimination and their ability to make decisions on questions affecting the common good; encouraging members to develop their creative faculties and to cultivate an informed and critical sense of appreciation.

Each Guild holds regular monthly meetings to enable all members to play a full part in the Guild activities. In addition, every Guild supplies lectures, demonstrations, and classes in any subject for which there is sufficient interest, frequently with the assistance of local education authorities. Guilds also provide recreational and social opportunities for their members.

Officers and committee members are elected by the members at the Guild Annual General Meeting. Guild representatives are appointed to act as delegates to the Federation Council and the National Council.

The Guilds are financed by members' subscriptions. Most of them initiate their own fund-raising activities. Money raised may be spent only in accordance with the objects of the movement as a whole. The National Union is supported by a grant-in-aid from the Department of Education and Science towards the cost of developing the movement and its facilities.

To bring together the views and work of members of all Guilds, the NUTG publishes a monthly magazine, *The Townswoman,* which seeks to combine a record of local, regional, and national activities with advice on a wide range of educational and recreational work.

National Union of Townswomen's Guilds, 2 Cromwell Place, London SW7 2JG.

NATIONALIZED INDUSTRY CONSUMER COUNCILS

Airport Consultative Committees

The British Airports Authority owns and manages seven airports in the UK: Heathrow, Gatwick, and Stansted in the South-East, and Glasgow, Edinburgh, Prestwick, and Aberdeen in Scotland.

The Airports Authority Act 1965 (since replaced by the Airports Authority Act 1975) which constituted the British Airports Authority, required it to establish facilities for consultation for users of each of its airports, for local authorities in the vicinity, and for other organizations representing the interests of persons concerned with the locality.

The Authority has accordingly set up Consultative Committees at each of its airports, in some cases taking over committees which had existed at the airport before it was owned by the Authority. The date of foundation of each Committee varies considerably, the oldest—at Heathrow—having had their first meeting in 1948.

The main objectives of each Committee are to advise the British Airports Authority on any matters which are referred to them by the Authority; to consider any questions concerning the airport as it affects the users, organizations, and committees represented; to make suggestions to the airport management on any administrative matters which can further the interests of the communities represented; and to stimulate local interest in the achievements of the airport. Each Committee has a sub-committee known as the Passenger Services Committee, which reflects the interests of passengers at the airport. Although the British Airports Authority suggests organizations from which members of the Committees may be chosen, individual members are appointed by each Committee. Committees meet quarterly, but Heathrow's meets monthly (except August). Meetings are open to the public, and are attended by the press.

The British Airports Authority finances the cost of meetings, printing and stationery costs, and the cost of each Committee's Annual Report.

Airline Users Committee

The Airline Users Committee was set up by the British Civil Aviation Authority in July 1973 to assist it in safeguarding the interests of airline users and to investigate individual complaints against airlines, when a complainant has been unable to obtain satisfaction from the airline concerned.

The members of the Committee are appointed by the Civil Aviation Authority. They have diverse interests and are representative of a wide range of airline users—business travellers, holidaymakers, consignors of freight—from different regions of the U K. They review the trade practices of publicly and privately owned airlines as they affect the users, as well as the ways in which individual airlines deal with consumer matters.

The Airline Users Committee advises the Civil Aviation Authority on all matters of interest to airline users. It has made recommendations on a variety of airline facilities for passengers at airports and on board aircraft, overbooking on scheduled services, improvements to regional services, and tariffs. It also advises on the interests of special groups of passengers, such as the handicapped.

The Committee does not have any power to deal with hotel or holiday standards. Nor does it have the power to arbitrate on claims for refund or compensation, which have to be negotiated by the parties concerned and may in some cases, where agreement is not reached, become a matter for the courts.

The Airline Users Committee is financed by the Civil Aviation Authority.

The Committee sometimes publishes its recommendations. It also publishes general information leaflets, which are made available to the public, and an Annual Report.

Airline Users Committee, Space House, 43-59 Kingsway, London WC2B 6TE.

Central Transport Consultative Committee (CTCC)

Transport Users Consultative Committees (TUCCs)

The Central Transport Consultative Committee was first established on 19 December 1947, was reconstituted under the Transport Act 1962, and had its functions amended by the Transport Act 1968. In addition to an independent chairman, the Committee now consists of the chairman of the eleven Area Transport Users Consultative Committees and not more than six other members appointed by the Secretary of State for Prices in consultation with the Secretary of State for Transport.

The CTCC may consider any matter (except charges) affecting the services and facilities provided by the British Railways Board and the National Freight Corporation and their subsidiaries. In particular, the Committee must consider such matters which arise from representations by users of those services, or which are referred to it by the Secretary of State for Transport or the Secretary of State for Prices and Consumer Protection, the British Railways Board, or the National Freight Corporation. Recommendations of the Central Committee are notified to the Board, the Corporation, and the Secretaries of State, who may give directions to the Board or the Corporation on matters dealt with in such recommendations. The CTCC is not required to consider railway closures, which are specifically delegated to the TUCCs.

The CTCC is constituted for the whole of the UK and is sponsored by the Department of Prices and Consumer Protection. It produces an Annual Report, which is published by HMSO as a House of Commons Paper.

In March 1978, the Government said it intended to extend the powers of the CTCC and rename it as the National Transport Consumers' Council.

The eleven TUCCs were also established under the Transport Act 1947, were reconstituted under the Transport Act 1962, and had their functions amended by the Transport Act 1968. They are independent and each has similar terms of reference to the CTCC, with the added requirement to consider railway closures. In addition to an independent chairman, each TUCC consists of about 20 members appointed by the Secretary of State for Prices and Consumer Protection in consultation with the Secretary of State for Transport. These are nominated from such bodies as local authorities, trades unions, industry and commerce, tourist boards, women's organizations, and organizations for pensioners and the disabled.

Central Transport Consultative Committee, 3-4 Great Marlborough Street, London W1V 2EA.

Domestic Coal Consumers' Council (DCCC)

The Domestic Coal Consumers' Council was set up under Section 4 of the Coal Industry Nationalisation Act 1946. It comprises a chairman, deputy chairman and around 20 members who are appointed by the Secretary of State for Prices and Consumer Protection from among nominations provided by such bodies as local authority organizations, women's organizations, coal merchants' associations, trades unions, etc. The Secretary of State may also appoint individuals not attached to any particular organization. Members represent domestic consumers of coal and solid smokeless fuels, the merchant suppliers, and the principal manufacturers of solid smokeless fuels. Two senior representatives of the National Coal Board attend meetings at the invitation of the Council.

The terms of reference of the Council are to consider any representation on the sale or supply of solid fuel for domestic purposes made to them by consumers, or any matter which appears to the Council to be one to which consideration ought to be given. The principal matters with which the Council concerns itself are broad issues of adequacy of supplies and service, prices, and the maintenance of quality.

The National Coal Board explains to the Council its plans for changes in prices, services, and supplies offered to merchants and the public and gives serious consideration to the Council's views.

The Council is required by statute to make an Annual Report to the Secretary of State which is laid before Parliament, and it disseminates leaflets and posters to the public relating to the Council's complaints procedure. The Department of Prices and Consumer Protection finances the Council.

At the instigation of the DCCC, the Approved Coal Merchants Scheme was set up in 1962 to raise the standard of service to the public in the sale of solid fuel. The Scheme is administered by a National Panel and 12 Regional Panels. The chairman of the DCCC sits as an Assessor on the National Panel and consumer members of the Council sit on the Regional Panels for the parts of the country in which they live. The Regional Panels interview those intending to set themselves up as coal merchants and satisfy themselves as to their suitability and knowledge. The rules of the Scheme provide that if there are subsequent shortcomings in the organization or conduct of the member's business, his membership may be terminated.

Domestic Coal Consumers' Council, Dean Bradley House, 52 Horseferry Road, London SW1P 2AG.

Electricity Consumers' Council

Electricity Consultative Councils

Electricity Consultative Councils are independent bodies set up by Parliament in 1948 to represent and safeguard the interests of existing and prospective electricity consumers in the areas covered by the Area Electricity Boards—twelve in England and Wales and two in Scotland. Each Council has its own staff and office.

A Council's functions are to consider any matters affecting the distribution of electricity in its area, including the variation of tariffs and the provision of new or improved services or facilities. Councils also consider representations received from customers who are not satisfied with the action taken by an Electricity Board in connection with their original enquiry or complaint. They will also investigate complaints about the servicing of appliances bought from the showrooms operated by the Boards. The duty is also laid upon Councils to consider any matter affecting the variation of the Bulk Supply Tariff of the Central Electricity Generating Board for distribution in each area.

Council members are appointed by the Secretary of State for Prices and Consumer Protection, with the advice of the National Consumer Council or its appropriate national Council and after consultation with the Minister responsible for the industry. At least two-fifths, but no more than three-fifths, of the members appointed to the Councils are nominated by local authority associations and the remainder are persons representing agriculture, industry, labour, and general interests of consumers. All members serve voluntarily and only receive out-of-pocket expenses for work undertaken. Finance for the Councils' work is provided by central Government. Each Council normally issues an Annual Report.

Until mid 1977, the Electricity Consultative Councils had no national body. Each Council, in rotation, acted as the convening Council. However, in July 1977, the Secretary of State for Prices and Consumer Protection announced that an Electricity Consumers' Council would be set up for England and Wales, initially on a non-statutory basis. This decision was implemented in November 1977. The Council has a paid chairman and full secretarial staff and includes among its membership the chairmen of the area Electricity Consultative Councils.

Electricity Consumers' Council, Fifth Floor, 119 Marylebone Road, London NW1 5PY.

National Gas Consumers' Council

Regional Gas Consumers' Councils

The Gas Act 1948 led to the establishment of consultative councils for the gas industry in Great Britain. When the industry's structure was adapted under the Gas Act 1972, the 12 Area Councils were renamed Regional Gas Consumers' Councils. The Act also established a National Gas Consumers' Council of which the 12 chairmen of the Regional Councils are members. Additional members are appointed by the Secretary of State for Prices and Consumer Protection for their particular expertise, background, and experience in the consumer world. The Secretary of State appoints the chairman and deputy chairman.

Councils consist of up to 31 members who are nominated by local authorities, local women's organizations, trades unions, industry, and commerce. Local committees represent the interests of districts within the region so that attention can be paid to differing local conditions and individual consumer problems.

The functions of the Regional Councils are to take up representations on behalf of the gas consumer if a first approach to the British Gas region does not resolve the issue. If appropriate, they can make representations on the consumer's behalf to industry and the Secretary of State via the National Council.

The National Gas Consumers' Council deals directly with the British Gas Corporation, Government, or other appropriate organizations, on policies concerning the supply of gas, tariffs, gas fittings and appliances, servicing, etc. It make take action on its own initiative or following representations from any of the Regional Councils.

Members of the Regional Councils meet regularly and, through the local committees, monitor progress on the many issues of concern to gas consumers. As a result of their findings, they make representations to British Gas Regional Offices or to the National Gas Consumers' Council on issues which are to be taken up at a national level, or which may affect other regions. Council meetings are open to the press.

Responsibility for the Councils rests with the Secretary of State for Prices and Consumer Protection. The Department of Energy is the sponsoring department for the gas industry, but on issues relating to the interests of gas consumers and to the work of the Councils, there is joint consideration by both departments.

The National Council and the Regional Councils produce and disseminate leaflets giving general advice to consumers, and each Council produces an Annual Report.

National Gas Consumers' Council, Fifth Floor, Estate House, 130 Jermyn Street, London SW1Y 4UJ.

Post Office Users' National Council (POUNC)

Machinery for representing users existed in various forms for many years, but POUNC was established as an independent statutory body in the Post Office Act 1969, which made the Post Office a separate national Corporation.

The prime endeavour of POUNC is to safeguard and represent the interests of Post Office users, both large and small. The Post Office has the duty of consulting it about major changes in main services, but in practice there are regular contacts with them at many levels about tariffs and the provision, quality, and conditions of service. While POUNC strives to influence policy at the formative stage, it also pursues individual failures of service where the Post Office response to a complaint appears to be unsatisfactory.

In addition to the National Council, with a membership of up to 32, there are similar and associated councils for Northern Ireland, Scotland, and Wales. Members are drawn from various backgrounds and areas to represent a broad cross-section of users. They are appointed by the Secretary of State for Prices and Consumer Protection and are supported by a full-time staff.

The expenditure of the Council, including staff costs and the travelling expenses of members, is financed by the Department of Prices and Consumer Protection.

Annual Reports are laid before Parliament. A number of reports on tariff references have been published, in addition to reports on major *ad hoc* enquiries.

Post Office Users' National Council, Waterloo Bridge House, Waterloo Road, London SE1 8UA.

PROFESSIONAL, TRADE, AND INDUSTRY ORGANIZATIONS

Advertising Standards Authority Limited (ASA)

The ASA is an independent body and was set up in 1962 by the trade association for the industry, the Advertising Association. Its function is to promote and enforce the highest standards of advertising in the interests of the public, in particular through the British Code of Advertising Practice. The Authority regulates and controls advertising in the press, on posters, in the cinema, and by direct mail. The broadcasting of advertisements during independent television transmissions is regulated by the Independent Broadcasting Authority.

The advertising industry operates a self-regulatory system of advertising control, the rules of which are laid down in the British Code of Advertising Practice. Broadly speaking, the aims of the Code are to ensure that advertisements are legal, decent, honest, and truthful; that they are prepared with a sense of honesty to the consumer; that they conform to the principles of fair competition as generally accepted in business; and that no advertisement should bring advertising into disrepute or reduce confidence in advertising as a service to industry and to the public.

The ASA supervises the running of the whole control system, ensuring the Code is properly and fairly applied; that the Code of Advertising Practice Committee (the body that actually administers the Code) functions smoothly; that the Code is kept up-to-date; that all cases are properly investigated and that the public interest is fully served. Complaints about advertisements are received from the public and are investigated by ASA staff or through the CAP Committee.

ASA maintains close liaison with the Department of Prices and Consumer Protection and other Government departments, the Office of Fair Trading, consumer bodies, trading standards departments, trade associations, social organizations, and many other bodies.

The Authority publishes details of the outcome of its investigations, naming those advertisers who have offended against the Code. In addition the Authority may recommend to media that they withhold advertising space or time from advertisers; such recommendations are always accepted. Media themselves may also withdraw trading privileges from advertising agencies.

The ASA is a company limited by guarantee and is totally financed by the advertising business, through the Advertising Standards Board of Finance. The chairman is independent, is paid a salary, and is responsible for appointing the other members of the Authority. At least half and not more than two-thirds of the Authority's Council must be entirely unconnected with advertising, and those who are sit as individuals and not as representatives of any sectional interest. The Authority has its own premises.

Advertising Standards Authority Ltd, 15/17 Ridgmount Street, London WC1E 7AW.

Environmental Health Officers Association

The Environmental Health Officers Association was founded as an unincorporated body in London in 1883 and in 1891 was registered as an incorporated company limited by guarantee.

The Association is both a professional and educational body which is dedicated to the promotion of environmental health. It is concerned primarily with ensuring that the training of environmental health officers is maintained at a proper standard, encouraging the highest possible standard of efficiency in the work of environmental health officers, and giving information and advice to members to assist them in carrying out their duties.

The Association performs a valuable function by its ability to speak collectively for environmental health officers. It draws on the knowledge and experience of its members. It is regularly consulted by Government departments and makes representations to such departments whenever this appears necessary. The Association also scrutinizes Parliamentary Bills and other proposals for legislation relating to the duties of environmental health officers, and efforts are made to secure necessary amendments.

The Association appoints eight representatives to serve on the Environmental Health Officers' Education Board, the body which regulates the training and qualification of environmental health officers. Meetings of the Association, which are organized by Centres and Branches, are held throughout the year. Members gather together to discuss subjects of common interest and to advance their knowledge. Courses of lectures and weekend seminars are also arranged. Various scholarships and educational awards are available to members.

The Association has approximately 6000 members, most of whom are employed by local authorities in England, Wales, and Northern Ireland. The Scottish officers have their own organization, the Scottish Institute of

Environmental Health. Full membership is granted only to those people who are qualified for appointment as environmental health officers in the UK. There is a small number of elected Fellows.

For administrative purposes, England and Wales are divided into 14 Centres. Northern Ireland forms a separate Centre of its own. The affairs of each Centre are conducted by a Centre Council. The Centres are sub-divided into Branches whose affairs are managed by a Branch Committee.

The Association's General Council is responsible for the management and direction of its affairs and consists of representatives elected annually by the Centre. The General Council appoints four standing committees to deal with detailed business: legal and technical, public relations and congress, education and policy, and resources.

The Association holds an Annual Environmental Health Congress and from time to time one-day conferences on subjects of special interest are held. The Association's principal source of finance is its members' subscriptions.

The official journal of the Association, published monthly, is *Environmental Health,* which contains authoritative articles on subjects within the sphere of the environmental health officers. An annual report of the environmental health of the country is published before the annual Congress.

The Environmental Health Officers Association, 19 Grosvenor Place, London SW1X 7HU.

Institute of Consumer Advisers

The Institute of Consumer Advisers was founded in April 1974. Its main aims include the improvement of standards of consumer services, the protection of the professional status of consumer advisers, and the provision of an authoritative voice for their aims and opinions.

Its main activities are commenting on draft legislation and consultative documents emanating from Government departments and bodies. The Institute works closely with other trade associations, particularly the Institute of Trading Standards Administration. It liaises with ITSA over the Diploma in Consumer Affairs. Members sit on BSI and other relevant Committees.

The small governing body is elected by secret ballot, and the Institute holds an Annual General Meeting and Conference. There are branches throughout the country.

The Institute is financed by subscriptions from members and publishes a bi-monthly newsletter, *Help and Advice.*

Institute of Consumer Advisers, 27 Chesterwood Road, Kings Heath, Birmingham B13 0QG.

Institute of Trading Standards Administration (ITSA)

The Institute of Trading Standards Administration is the professional organization of trading standards and consumer protection officers in local authorities. Its members are responsible for the administration and enforcement of consumer protection statutes, notably the Weights and Measures, Trade Descriptions, Consumer Protection, and Consumer Credit Acts (see the entry for Trading Standards/Consumer Protection Departments). In many authorities they are involved in running consumer advisory services, often from shop-front advice centres (see the entry for Consumer Advice Centres).

The desire to influence weights and measures legislation and to promote uniformity in its administration led to the formation in 1894 of the Incorporated Society of Inspectors of Weights and Measures. The name was changed to its present title in 1972.

Generally, the Institute is responsible for professional training and qualification, for standards of conduct, and for liaison with central Government and other organizations on all aspects of trading standards and consumer affairs. Such aims are achieved through national and local courses at universities, colleges, etc., seminars, conferences, and meetings.

The Institute's legal and technical publications, regular papers, and circulars, together with the official journal, *Monthly Review*, form an important source of information, keeping members aware of and advised on new or proposed legislation which affects the activities or responsibilities of the Trading Standards Administration and Advisory Services.

In addition to maintaining high professional standards, ITSA makes representations to local and national government, and trade associations.

Institute of Trading Standards Administration, Estate House, 319D London Road, Hadleigh, Benfleet, Essex SS7 2BN.

The Retail Trading-Standards Association (RTSA)

The Retail Trading-Standards Association was founded in 1935 and was the only pre-war organization of any significance working on behalf of consumers. It differs fundamentally from other trade organizations in that its activities are concerned with the maintenance of high trading standards in the advertising and selling of goods and services to the public, and in the development of standards of quality and safety of goods, particularly textiles.

The Association is supported by retailers, manufacturers, and other trade associations. It is unique as a trade association in admitting to membership Citizens' Advice Bureaux, trading standards authorities, and consumer organizations.

The aim of RTSA is to demonstrate that honest traders share with the public a dislike of unfair and deceptive trading practices. It acts as a watchdog for the trade and speaks out against trading practices which are judged to be misleading or unfair. The Association and its members work with standards-making organizations and other associations towards recognition of agreed standards of retail practice which give sensible rules for advertising, for the presentation of descriptions of goods, and for selling methods.

The Association receives information from its members, other organizations, and the public about activities considered to be deceptive or unfair. After investigation, the RTSA may issue a warning or, in exceptional cases, institute criminal proceedings. The Association also advises its members about legislation relating to the description and selling of goods as well as technical matters relating to quality and performance standards. The RTSA acts as a pressure group and campaigning body and ensures that the implications for trade and the consumer are properly explained and understood when legislation or other action is proposed.

The affairs of the Association are run by a Board of Management appointed by the Council of Management which is, in turn, appointed by members of the Association.

The RTSA is financed by its subscription income—one-third from retailers, one-third from manufacturers, and one-third from other subscriptions—the sale of its services, and investment income.

The Association keeps its members informed by publishing a Bulletin and specialist publications. The RTSA's Technical Advice and Information Service is available to all members.

Retail Trading-Standards Association, 360-366 Oxford Street, London W1N 0BT.

Trading Standards/Consumer Protection Departments

Previously known as Weights and Measures Departments, local authority Trading Standards Departments are responsible for enforcing legislation protecting the consumer. In particular, they are responsible for the enforcement implications of the Trade Descriptions Act, the Unsolicited Goods and Services Act, the Prices Act, the Weights and Measures Act, the Food and Drugs Act, and the Consumer Credit Act. While it may be well known how such departments contribute to the economic well-being of the community, through enforcement of the above fair trading legislation, what is perhaps not so well known is the contribution such departments make to consumer safety and safety of the community. Controls cover safety in the home through the Consumer Protection Act, safety on the highway through the Road Traffic Act, and safety in industry through the Petroleum Acts and the Health and Safety at Work Act. In addition, many Trading Standards Departments are involved in providing consumer advice—they run most of the Consumer Advice Centres in existence.

The service offered by Trading Standards Departments has grown considerably in recent years with the introduction of new consumer protection laws. All officers working in the departments are fully trained and qualified—those undertaking enforcement work are required to have the newly designated Diploma in Trading Standards or, if qualified before 1976, a Certification of Qualification to act as inspectors of weights and measures.

GOVERNMENT DEPARTMENTS AND OTHER PUBLIC BODIES

Consumer Protection Advisory Committee (CPAC)

The Consumer Protection Advisory Committee was established by section 3 of the Fair Trading Act 1973. Its members are appointed by the Secretary of State for Prices and Consumer Protection. It consists of not less than 10 and not more than 15 members. In appointing members, the Secretary of State must ensure that the committee includes one or more persons who have knowledge or experience (a) in the production or supply of goods, (b) in the enforcement of consumer protection legislation, and (c) of organizations established, or activities carried on, for the protection of consumers. The Secretariat is provided by the Fair Trading Division of the Department of Prices and Consumer Protection.

The functions of the CPAC are set out in Part II of the Fair Trading Act and can only be triggered off by a reference by the Secretary of State, or any other Minister, or the Director-General of Fair Trading. The consumer practices which can be referred to the CPAC are defined as those which relate to the terms or conditions (including price) subject to which goods and services are supplied; the way in which consumers are informed of the terms and conditions; advertising, labelling, or making of goods and other forms of promotion of goods or services; methods of salesmanship; packaging of goods; and methods of demanding or securing payment for goods or services supplied. A reference by the Director-General may also include proposals to control the consumer trade practice.

The Committee is required to pronounce upon whether the consumer trade practice referred adversely affects the economic interest of consumers in the UK. The CPAC must take account of representations made to them by interested parties and can hear oral evidence.

The CPAC reports to the Secretary of State and, where the Director-General has proposed controls over the consumer trade practice, may suggest modifications to those proposals.

The Committee has made a number of reports which have been published as House of Commons papers.

Consumer Protection Advisory Committee, Millbank Tower, Millbank, London SW1P 4QU.

Department of Prices and Consumer Protection (DPCP)

The Department of Prices and Consumer Protection was set up in March 1974, under a Secretary of State, and took over responsibility from the former Department of Trade and Industry for policy on prices and con-

260

sumer affairs, and from the Ministry of Agriculture, Fisheries and Food for the policy on food prices.

The Department is the focal point for measures to deal with the generality of prices questions. It sponsors the Price Commission and has the principal responsibility for policy over the whole range of retail prices (including food prices), except those for the nationalized industries. It has overall responsibility for policy on food subsidies, although other departments undertake the detailed administration.

The Department deals with consumer affairs generally and is responsible for policy on fair trading, trading standards, weights and measures (including metrication), monopolies, mergers and restrictive trade practices, consumer credit, and consumer safety.

Under the general heading of fair trading, the DPCP is concerned with all aspects of competition policy (including the EEC competition rules), consumer advice and protection, and the safety of consumer goods. The DPCP is responsible for implementing legislation on consumer credit.

The organizations which fall within the sphere of its responsibility are the Price Commission, the Monopolies and Mergers Commission, the Metrication Board, the British Hallmarking Council, the Hearing Aid Council, the National Consumer Council, the Consumer Protection Advisory Committee, and the nationalized industry consumer councils.

In addition to the Department's affairs being covered in the weekly journal *Trade and Industry*, the Department publishes its own monthly *Consumer Information Bulletin,* which is circulated to news media and consumer organizations to supplement the Government's programme of leaflets and advertising. It includes news of interest to consumers, contributed by various Government departments and consumer organizations, and helps to explain new legislation.

Department of Prices and Consumer Protection, Millbank Tower, Millbank, London SW1P 4QU.

National Consumer Council (NCC)

The National Consumer Council was set up by the Government in early 1975 and the first meeting of the Council took place in May of that year. Associated Consumer Councils linked to the NCC were established in Scotland, Wales, and Northern Ireland.

The NCC's main aim is to promote action for furthering and safeguarding the interests of consumers, and to ensure that those who take decisions which will affect the consumer can have a balanced and authoritative view of the interests of the consumers before them. Although the NCC speaks for all consumers, it has, as it was invited to do by the Government, attached particular concern to the problems of the disadvantaged and inarticulate.

The Council makes representations of the consumer view to central and local government, to Government agencies, to industry (including the nationalized industries), and to any other quarter where the consumer voice should be heeded—including making representations on the existing law and proposed legislation. The NCC also represents the consumer on appropriate Government and other bodies and international organizations, including those which exist within the framework of the European Community. It is charged with promoting consumer representation in the nationalized industries, and making representations where necessary upon the adequacy and availability of consumer advice services and upon the needs of such services for supporting facilities. It advises Ministers on the exercise of their powers of appointment in the consumer field, and considers and reports on the consumer interest in matters referred to it by the Secretary of State for Prices and Consumer Protection.

The NCC is concerned with matters of general policy and the adequacy and availability of assistance for consumers with individual problems. It is not able to handle individual complaints, which are the responsibility of agencies such as Citizens' Advice Bureaux, Consumer Advice Centres, Trading Standards Departments, nationalized industry consumer councils, and others.

The NCC is a non-statutory body, financed by a grant-in-aid from the Government, but is otherwise wholly independent of it. The Chairman and members are appointed by the Secretary of State for Prices and Consumer Protection. Five members are chosen from the lists of nominees submitted by the main consumer and women's organizations; others are invited to serve in an individual capacity.

The NCC publishes reports of its research, some of which is referred to it by the Department of Prices and Consumer Protection. These reports include *Consumers and the Nationalised Industries* and *Paying for Fuel*. It has also published a number of discussion papers and policy pamphlets, including those on tenancy agreements, industrial democracy, means-tested benefits, and a review of local advice services.

National Consumer Council, 18 Queen Anne's Gate, London SW1H 9AA.

The Northern Ireland Consumer Council

The Northern Ireland Consumer Council was established in May 1975, on an extra-statutory basis, by the Minister of State within the responsibility of the Department of Commerce for Northern Ireland. The Council is not able to deal with individual complaints, but refers enquirers to the appropriate body. Its terms of reference are to provide a central body of opinion on Northern Ireland consumer affairs; to advise the Department of Commerce on consumer protection matters; to establish appropriate links with the Office of Fair Trading in order to assist the OFT in carrying out its functions in relation to Northern Ireland; and to work in close harmony with the National Consumer Council.

The Council directs its attention towards matters of special concern to consumers in Northern Ireland and primarily makes its presence and views felt by bringing pressure to bear on the Minister of State. The Minister also consults the Council on various issues.

The Council is appointed by the Minister of State and consists of up to 18 members, including the chairman. Members are appointed for a two-year term, are unpaid, and are drawn from various organizations reflecting the consumer interest. The Council is funded by the Department of Commerce.

Northern Ireland Consumer Council, 176 Newtownbreda Road, Belfast BT8 4QS.

Office of Fair Trading (OFT)

The Office of Fair Trading is a Government agency and was created by the Fair Trading Act 1973. The Director-General of Fair Trading is appointed by the Secretary of State for Prices and Consumer Protection.

The Director-General's statutory powers are concerned with consumer affairs, consumer credit, monopolies, mergers and restrictive practices.

The aim of the OFT is to encourage competition which is both fair between one business and another and fair to the consumer. The Director-General keeps under review trade practices that relate to goods or services which appear likely to injure consumers' economic interests, or their health or safety. Information relating to the supply of these goods and services comes from sources such as Citizens' Advice Bureaux, Consumer Advice Centres, consumer organizations, local authority Trading Standards Departments, trade organizations, the media, and through the OFT's own information-gathering activities. If a trading practice is identified which may be operating to the economic disadvantage of consumers, the Director-General may make a reference to the Consumer Protection Advisory Committee. He may also propose new laws to safeguard consumers from unfair practices in trading.

Under the Act, the Director-General is allowed to take action against individual traders or companies who persistently break the civil or criminal law in a manner which is detrimental to consumers. The Director-General may encourage trade organizations to institute or revise and disseminate voluntary codes of practice for their members which will safeguard and promote the interests of consumers.

Under the Resale Prices Act 1976, the OFT looks into reports of attempts to re-impose minimum resale price maintenance. Parties adversely affected or the Crown may take civil proceedings.

Under the Consumer Credit Act 1974, the Director-General is responsible for issuing licences to all businesses offering credit or hiring goods to individuals, where the credit or rental is £5000 or less. The OFT has established a public register of licences granted, a copy of which is held at Edinburgh, Belfast, and Cardiff. Before granting a licence, the Director-General must ensure that the applicant is a 'fit person' to carry on a credit business. The general working and enforcement of the Act are kept under review by the Director-General. He may advise the Secretary of State for Prices and Consumer Protection where, for example, a change in the law seems appropriate. He is also responsible for issuing certain exclusions from the provisions of the Act and is the final arbiter in disputes between a consumer and a credit reference agency about the correctness of information held by the agency on the consumer. The Office has the duty of disseminating information about the Act to both traders and consumers.

Under the Fair Trading Act, the OFT is responsible for identifying situations which deserve investigation and referring them to the Monopolies and Mergers Commission. The Director-General maintains an economic information system to help him identify possible monopoly situations.

The Director-General's main responsibilities on mergers are outlined below.

—He advises the Secretary of State whether or not a reference should be made to the Monopolies and Mergers Commission, where any merger or proposed merger appears to fall within the scope of the Fair Trading Act.
—He advises on what action should be taken in the light of the Commission's report, following a reference.
—He seeks appropriate undertakings from the parties concerned, if requested by the Secretary of State, on the basis of the Commission's findings.
—He monitors the fulfilment of those undertakings and advises on any necessary changes.

Restrictive trade agreements concerned with goods and services are considered by the OFT and, if registrable, placed on the Register of Restrictive Agreements. The Director-General has a duty to refer a registered agreement to the Restrictive Practices Court unless he is able to make representations to the Secretary of State that restrictions do not merit such proceedings and the Secretary of State directs him accordingly. The Director-General also follows up information or complaints which suggest that restrictive agreements are being operated without particulars being furnished for registration.

The Director-General is empowered to publish information and advice to consumers. The Office produces a wide variety of booklets, leaflets, and posters, which are distributed through Citizens' Advice Bureaux, Consumer Advice Centres, libraries, and other local authority outlets.

Office of Fair Trading, Field House, Bream's Buildings, London EC4A 1PR.

Price Commission

The Price Commission was set up in 1973 under the Counter-Inflation Act which provided power to control price increases and profits through a Price Code.

The Commission's primary responsibility was originally to administer the successive Price Codes. The Price Commission Act 1977 provided for a new Code, dealing only with the limitation of profit margins, with a life of only 12 months. The power to include detailed provisions in the Code about the justification of price increases by reference costs was abolished.

Under the new control, larger companies must, as in the past, notify proposed price increases to the Commission before implementing them. The Commission scrutinize them in the light of the factors specified in Section 2 of the Act, not for conformity to a detailed Price Code. The Commission are empowered to conduct a three-month investigation into a price increase (or a price, in cases where prenotification is not required). During this period prices may be frozen. The Commission are also empowered to investigate the margin of a distributor. The Commission report their findings to the Secretary of State for Prices and Consumer Protection and make reasoned recommendations. The Commission are not permitted, however, to recommend any restriction which has the effect of reducing a firm's profit below a minimum laid down in regulations. Under the 1977 Price Commission Act, the Secretary of State has powers to give effect to the Commission's recommendations.

The Commission will continue to carry out examinations of particular sectors upon the direction of the Secretary of State, who is now empowered by the Act to enforce their recommendations.

If the Secretary of State so desires, the Commission may be given responsibility for supervising certain orders and undertakings under the Fair Trading Act 1973.

The Commission's regional offices carry out inspections of the smaller local firms to ensure that they are complying with the Price Code. They also collect prices for the Commission and attend to enquiries and complaints about prices from the public.

Price Commission, Neville House, Page Street, London SW1P 4LS.

Scottish Consumer Council (SCC)

The Scottish Consumer Council was established by the Government in September 1975. It is associated with the National Consumer Council and complements the work of the N C C in matters which are of general concern to Scottish consumers. Its main function is to make representations of the consumer view to central and local government, to the Director-General of Fair Trading, to industry, and to any other quarter where the voice of the consumer should be heard.

The Council is concerned with matters of general policy and does not deal directly with individual consumers' complaints, which are the responsibility of other advice-giving agencies.

The SCC operates with a small staff and therefore tries to concentrate its main attention on those areas which no other consumer body is actively pursuing, especially in the areas of consumer law in Scotland and local advice services. It has defined as its main objectives:

Creating in Scotland a more general acceptance of the right of consumers to be heard wherever their interests are involved; ensuring that protection under the law for Scottish consumers shall be at least equal to that of their UK counterparts; building up a widespread network of advice and support for consumers in Scotland; encouraging self-help and self-reliance among Scottish consumers.

In addition to initiating research and action, the SCC responds to consultation documents issued by Government departments and agencies on proposed changes in existing legislation and in information provision to consumers.

The SCC receives a proportion of the grant-in-aid paid to the National Consumer Council by the Government. Although financed by the Government, it is otherwise independent of it. The Council is a non-statutory partisan body. Members of the Scottish Consumer Council are appointed by the Secretary of State for Prices and Consumer Protection in consultation with the Secretary of State for Scotland, and represent a wide spectrum of consumer and community interests.

The SCC publishes reports of its work as well as contributing evidence to reports published by the National Consumer Council.

Scottish Consumer Council, 4 Somerset Place, Glasgow G3.

Welsh Consumer Council (WCC)

The Welsh Consumer Council was set up in July 1975. It has the same aims and objectives as the National Consumer Council, but is specifically charged with identifying and representing the interests of consumers in Wales. Most of its staff time and resources are devoted to projects and research which highlight the particular needs of people there. It works closely with the National Consumer Council on matters of importance to the UK as a whole and its chairman sits on the Council of the national body. The Council cooperates and works with groups concerned with the plight of the needy, the old, the disabled, and the young, and has concentrated its efforts primarily on the quality and cost of services rather than goods. It has especially concerned itself with council house allocation, transport in rural areas, the simplification of benefit forms, planning, and education.

In addition to initiating research and action and giving its opinion on matters of concern to the consumer, the WCC also responds to requests from the Government to submit evidence.

The WCC is governed by the same articles and memorandum as the National Consumer Council and receives a proportion of the grant-in-aid paid by the Government to the NCC. It is independent both of the NCC and the Government. Its Council members are appointed by the Secretary of State for Prices and Consumer Protection in consultation with the Secretary of State for Wales. Members represent a wide spectrum of consumer and community interests.

The WCC publishes reports of its work, as well as contributing evidence to reports published by the National Consumer Council.

Welsh Consumer Council, 8 St Andrews Place, Cardiff CF1 3BE.

OTHER RELEVANT ORGANIZATIONS

British Standards Institution—Consumer Standards Advisory Committee (CSAC)

The forerunner of the Consumer Standards Advisory Committee, the Women's Advisory Committee, was founded in 1951. Its purpose is to advise the Executive Board of the British Standards Institution on all matters affecting the interests of consumers and, in particular, to represent the consumer interest in the preparation of standards and certification schemes for consumer products and services.

Through the CSAC and its representatives on technical committees, BSI has regular contact with lay consumers and is able to involve them closely at all stages in the development of a wide range of national and international standards in the consumer field. The work of the Committee is limited by the number of consumer representatives available to sit on technical committees, and recently its membership was extended. The restructured Committee is supported by four Consumer Co-ordination Committees which have the main task of providing consumer representatives to serve on technical and certification committees.

In addition to representation on nearly 200 technical committees, the CSAC has an important consultative role to play. It comments on Government consultative documents, proposed codes of practice and EEC draft Directives, as well as making known to the relevant bodies its views on wider issues of consumer concern, such as consumer safety, metrication, etc.

As an advisory Committee, the CSAC reports to the Executive Board which, subject to the overall sanction of its subscribing members, is responsible for BSI policy. The Committee brings together representatives from a wide range of consumer organizations throughout the country; it has 19 members on its main Committee and 52 on its Consumer Coordination Committees.

The Committee, as part of the BSI, is totally financed by the Institution, whose income is made up of sales, a Government grant-in-aid, and subscriptions from organizations (firms, trade associations, local authorities, professional institutions) interested in its work.

The British Standards Institution itself, through its Kitemark and Safety Mark Schemes, looks after the consumer interest by checking that products claiming to comply with British Standards in fact do so.

Consumer Standards Advisory Committee of the BSI, 2 Park Street, London W1A 2BS.

Centre for Consumer Education and Research in Scotland (CERES)

The Centre for Consumer Education and Research in Scotland was established in 1976. Based at Queen Margaret College, its main aims are to undertake studies and research on consumer education and behaviour, and to bring the expertise of the College to bear on the solution of problems in the consumer interest. The main activities of the Centre are outlined below.

—It initiates research and investigation relevant to consumer behaviour and education. The expertise of departments within the College (such as Home Economics and Communication Arts) is utilized on research projects.
—It liaises with institutions and persons involved in consumer affairs in Scotland, and in consumer studies and research relevant to Scotland.
—It disseminates information on matters relating to consumer education and affairs.
—It provides a resource and statistics bank for work in consumer studies.
—It supports academic staff engaged in research and investigation in the consumer field.

CERES is instituted within Queen Margaret College, Edinburgh. The College was founded in 1875, is a Scottish Central Institution, and allocates the Centre's budget from general funds made available by the Scottish Education Department.

CERES has no publications of its own, although members of its staff contribute to academic journals in its field.

Centre for Consumer Education and Research in Scotland, Clerwood Terrace, Edinburgh EH12 8TS.

Citizens' Advice Bureaux (CABx)

National Association of Citizens' Advice Bureaux (NACABx)

Citizens' Advice Bureaux arose out of the wartime need to give an emergency help, information, and advice service to the public. The Citizens' Advice Bureaux service aims to alleviate personal distress and confusion by providing free, confidential, impartial, and independent advice or information on any subject to anyone who asks. It will also approach organizations on behalf of an enquirer and mediate between them. It aims to exert a responsible influence on the content of social policy by pointing out the practical difficulties or omissions in current legislation, and it aims to remedy problems causing local or national anxiety by alerting and chanelling Government and public concern.

The CABx service deals with practical personal problems of all kinds and makes available to the individual accurate information and skilled advice on health, housing, legal, and social matters. The bureaux give advice on legislation and encourage people to benefit from the services provided by the State. Details of enquiries specifically related to consumer matters are passed on by the bureaux to the Office of Fair Trading to help identify areas where there are difficulties.

In addition to this role of providing basic information, many bureaux have adopted a more dynamic approach, by providing active support for clients. This kind of support ranges from negotiating with shops and landlords and visiting invalids who need advice, to representing individuals at industrial and social security tribunals.

Each CAB is a self-governing unit, is mainly financed by the local authority, and works closely with other local advice agencies. Many CAB workers are voluntary but, whether paid or unpaid, they receive specialist training in consumer legislation and advice.

Every bureau is a member of the National Association of Citizens' Advice Bureaux and is represented through area committees on its Council. The service began in 1939. The NACABx, constituted in 1973, is responsible for the policy of the movement. It provides a comprehensive and regularly updated information service to bureaux, gives full information on new legislation and services, and provides guidance on the day-to-day servicing of the bureaux.

The National Council is the main policy-making body of the CABx. Although it meets only four times a year it has a number of committees which deal with policy on a month-to-month basis.

Financial support to the national office is provided in the main by central Government, supplemented by voluntary funds and subscriptions from bureaux, sales, and a contribution from the National Council of Social Service voluntary funds.

National Association of Citizens' Advice Bureaux, 110 Drury Lane London WC2B 5SW.

Co-operative Union Ltd

The Co-operative Union was formed in 1869 and originally was set up to organize Co-operative societies and diffuse knowledge of the principles of Co-operation. Now that the movement is well established, the Union has turned its energies to coordinating and advising Britain's Co-operative retail societies, and acting as their national spokesman. With the exception of agricultural Co-operation, the Union represents all branches and organizations of Co-operative activity. Its pronouncements are generally made after detailed discussion and debate within the Union, and are regarded as the opinion of the Co-operative movement as a whole. The Union propagates consumer interests through economic, political, and educational channels.

The Union is not a trading organization (except for the sale of its publications) and does not conduct an auditing service. Societies are automatically advised on general Co-operative issues through the Union's Information Bulletin, and individual societies are able to consult the Union on their own specific problems.

The political arm of the movement is the Co-operative Party, which ultimately is responsible to the central executive and the Co-operative Congress—the annual meeting of the member societies of the Union. Established in 1917, the Co-operative Party is represented in the Commons and Lords and, under the terms of a national agreement with the Labour Party, the Party is enabled to put forward up to 30 candidates sponsored and endorsed by the movement.

Immediate matters of policy are decided by the central executive, which consists of 19 members. These members are representatives of retail societies (9 members elected by regional sections), the Co-operative Wholesale Society (8 appointed members), and the Scottish Sectional Board (2 appointed members). There are various subcommittees, (the main one being the General Purposes Committee), some of which may be appointed to deal with specific questions.

The Union is financed totally by contributions from affiliated societies, their payments for the main part being related to turnover.

The main publications of the Co-operative Union are *British Co-operation, The Co-operative Directory,* and *Co-operative Statistics.*

Co-operative Union Ltd., Holyoake House, Hanover Street, Manchester M60 0AS.

Good Housekeeping Institute

The Good Housekeeping Institute was started in 1924 as an offshoot of *Good Housekeeping* magazine, with the object of testing food, household products, and appliances, and giving informed advice to consumers on household and consumer matters through *Good Housekeeping* magazine, with particular emphasis on the buying and use of labour-saving appliances, food, cookery, and consumer rights.

The Institute's activities have expanded to take commissioned work from manufacturers who may want independent testing on appliances or household products. In 1967 it started 'The Better Way' section of *Good Housekeeping* magazine, which deals with consumer affairs and reports on comparative tests on food and household appliances. It also runs a reader advisory service for the purpose of answering queries on household matters and cooking, and advising on value-for-money household buys.

The Institute is represented on various BSI committees and contributes to groups working on behalf of consumers in Europe. It is asked to give evidence on various consumer matters by the Department of Prices and Consumer Protection, the Office of Fair Trading, and other Government bodies.

The Good Housekeeping Institute is owned by the National Magazine Company, which finances it. It is a non-profit-making organization but gets revenue from the sale of books and bulletins, and from work commissioned by manufacturers and public-relations agencies.

It provides material for books on cookery, home management, freezing, etc., which are published under the imprint of the Ebury Press.

Good Housekeeping Institute, Chestergate House, Vauxhall Bridge Road, London SW1V 1HF.

National Council of Social Service (NCSS)

The National Council of Social Service is an independent voluntary body which was founded in 1919. Financed by Government grants and donations, the Council comprises some 450 representatives of national voluntary organizations, local coordinating bodies in counties, towns and neighbourhoods, Citizens' Advice Bureaux, professional associations, and public bodies.

The Council aims to contribute to the strength of the voluntary social sector by providing it with a national focus, and by speaking on its behalf, particularly in response to the activities, policies, and proposals of central and local government.

It aims also to develop the effectiveness of the work of defined voluntary organizations, groups, and individuals in the field of social action, and to ensure that newly identified social needs are met by the most appropriate means, including the formation of new groups.

The identification of a particular need sometimes leads to the establishment of a new organization which becomes independent when circumstances make it possible. Bodies set up by the NCSS include the Youth Hostels Association, Age Concern, the National Children's Bureau, and the Charities Aid Foundation. A recent departure has been the National Association of Women's Clubs, and the National Association of Citizens' Advice Bureaux became independent at the end of 1977.

The NCSS has four main sections. The National/International section pursues topics of concern to voluntary organisations, such as taxation, charity law and fund raising, holds meetings of interest groups and organizes working parties and conferences. It looks outward from Britain, monitoring developments in international social policy, especially in the EEC, and organizes programmes for overseas social work professionals. The Community Organizations Group provides information, advisory and headquarters services for groups of local bodies. Development Services to the Voluntary Sector recognizes new work for the Council and seeks to develop it. Such initiatives come from both NCSS staff and its outside members. Projects have a fixed term and involve national and local networks of member bodies of the Council. The section for Administration and Central Services covers information, training and development, legal services, publications and advice to members, non-members and the general public.

In many of its activities, the NCSS works closely with Councils of Social Service in Scotland, Wales, and Northern Ireland, formulating with them policies for the whole of the UK.

National Council of Social Service, 26 Bedford Square, London WC1B 3HU.

Public Interest Research Centre Ltd (PIRC)

Social Audit Ltd

The Public Interest Research Centre Ltd is a registered charity and was founded in 1971. It conducts research into corporate activities. Social Audit Ltd is a non-profit-making body which is independent of PIRC but acts as its publishing arm. The purpose of 'social audits' is to investigate the impact of major companies, or Governments, or corporations on employees, consumers, the local community, and the physical environment. Reports researching areas where the consumer's interest is prejudiced by faulty Governmental or business organization, or dissecting the power structure of important firms manufacturing consumer goods, have been published with the aim of improving Government and corporate responsiveness to the public generally.

The two organizations are funded mainly by grants and donations, and through the sale of publications. Their work has been supported by the Joseph Rowntree Social Service and Charitable Trusts. Support for individual projects has been received from bodies such as the Social Science Research Council and the Ford Foundation.

Social Audit publications are produced on a one-off basis.

Social Audit Ltd, 9 Poland Street, London W1V 3DG.

ORGANIZATIONS OVERSEAS

Bureau Européen des Unions de Consommateurs (BEUC)

BEUC was founded in February 1962 and since May 1973 has had a permanent office in Brussels. BEUC comprises 12 organizations belonging to the Common Market countries. All the organizations affiliated to BEUC are non-profit-making and are completely independent of commerce and industry.

BEUC's role is to represent and defend European consumer interests to the Common Market institutions, especially to the Commission. It does so in the following ways.

—It plays a decisive role in the Commission's Consumer Consultative Committee, so that the defence of specific consumer interests can be independently guaranteed.
—It undertakes research projects for the Commission's Environment and Consumer Protection Service on such subjects as misleading advertising, doorstep selling, consumer education, after-sales service, and transport.
—It supplies information and research to the Commission itself in order to counterbalance the influence of industry and commerce. BEUC also discusses agricultural products in each of the Agricultural Consultative Committees.

—It makes known to the European Parliament and the Economic and Social Committee the positions that B E U C has taken up with the Commission. It attends hearings, and maintains contacts with political groups.
—It exerts pressure at the level of the Council of Ministers, to bring about decisions in the direction desired by consumers.

B E U C holds an Annual General Meeting to which Ordinary and Associate Member organizations are admitted. This meeting controls B E U C: it lays down the programme of work for the future year, appoints the Council, and approves the Council's progress report. The Council consists of Ordinary and Associate Members who are elected for a three-year period.

B E U C is financed by its members' subscriptions. It publishes the results of studies undertaken for the Commission's Environment and Consumer Protection Service.

Bureau Européen des Unions de Consommateurs, boite 3, 29 rue Royale, Brussels 1000.

Consumers' Consultative Committee (CCC)

The Consumers' Consultative Committee was set up in 1973 and is attached to the Environment and Consumer Protection Service of the European Commission. Its overall aim is to make the voice of European consumers heard on all Community affairs affecting them. The C C C can give its opinion on a subject either at the request of the Commission, on its own initiative, or by participating in the numerous specialist committees working within the Commission.

Within the framework of a Community policy for consumer protection and information, the C C C has expressed the consumer's point of view on many proposals drawn up by the European Commission concerning such topics as door-to-door selling, product liability, and consumer credit. In response to a request from the Commission, the C C C has also given its opinion on proposed agricultural prices.

There are 25 members of the Committee, 15 of whom represent consumer organizations, co-operatives, trades unions, and family organizations. The remaining 10 seats are set aside for the C C C's experts—'persons particularly qualified in consumer affairs'. Members are appointed by the European Commission on a three-yearly, renewable basis.

The Secretariat is provided by the European Commission's Environment and Consumer Protection Service and meetings take place at least four times a year in European Commission premises. A Bureau—consisting of the chairman, representatives from the four sections represented on the Committee, and the independent experts—undertakes preparatory work between meetings and provides some continuity in dossiers. Working groups of several CCC members and *ad hoc* experts are frequently set up to examine a document or a certain topic of interest.

By asserting the presence of consumer organizations in the Commission, the CCC encourages an exchange of views with numerous other institutions and professional bodies organized at Community level. Industrial and commercial organizations are increasingly in contact with the Committee.

Consumers' Consultative Committee, rue de la Loi 200, B-1040, Brussels.

International Organization of Consumers' Unions (IOCU)

IOCU was founded on 1 April 1960 and its aims are listed below.

—To authenticate, assist, and actively promote genuine efforts throughout the world in consumer self-organization as well as Government efforts to further the interests of the consumer.
—To promote international cooperation in the comparative testing of consumer goods and services, and to facilitate the exchange of test methods and plans.
—To promote international cooperation in all other aspects of consumer information, education, and protection, and to collect and disseminate information relating to consumer laws and practices throughout the world.
—To provide a forum in which national bodies working exclusively for the interests of the consumer may discuss consumer problems and possible solutions to them.
—To act as a clearing house for the publications of such bodies and to regulate (subject to any regulations promulgated by or applicable to the bodies themselves) the use of such published material.
—To publish information on subjects connected with the interests of the consumer.
—To maintain effective links with the United Nations and its agencies and other international bodies, with a view to representing the interests of the consumer at the international level.
—To give all practical aid and encouragement to the development of consumer educational and protective programmes in the developing countries, through the United Nations and its agencies and in other suitable ways.
—In general, to take such action as may further these objects.

Its main activities are the representation of national consumer organizations at international level, the study and development of technical aspects of consumer affairs, the fostering of consumer education, and the provision of facilities for discussion of consumer problems and objectives.

Every two years IOCU holds a General Assembly which is attended by delegates from Associate member organizations. The Council of fifteen, including the president, is elected at the General Assembly. The president and five other council members form an executive committee.

The Organization has 101 member organizations from 45 countries. It is financed by membership fees and the sale of its publications. It publishes *International Consumer* annually and, for its own members only, a quarterly *Consumer Review* and the *IOCU Newsletter*.

International Organization of Consumers' Unions, 9 Emmastraat, The Hague, Netherlands.

23. Bibliography

compiled by Susan Samuel

Apart from the general section at the beginning, the references in the bibliography are listed under the chapter headings to which they principally relate. However, some references are relevant to more than one chapter.

Consumer Protection: General

Bibliographies

DAVID, N. (1975). *Reference Guide for Consumers*. Bowker. 327 pp. Book attempts to gather together the varied sources of US consumer information, evaluate the multi-media material, and present the whole in ready reference form.

OLANDER, F. AND LINDHOFF, H. (1973). *A Bibliography of Recent Consumerism Literature: Preliminary Version*. International Institute of Management, Berlin. 39 leaves.

OLANDER, F. AND LINDHOFF, H. (1974). *Consumer Action Research: A Review of the Consumerism Literature and Suggestions for New Directions in Theoretical and Empirical Research*. International Institute of Management, Berlin. 54 pp. Contains a useful bibliography of consumerism and marketing literature, pp. 53-64.

SAMUEL, S. (1977). *Consumer Bibliography*. Second edn. Office of Fair Trading. 69 pp. Publication date of most items is since 1970. Sections on consumer protection, consumer credit, advertising, consumerism and marketing, consumer education, etc. Annotated entries. Author index.

THOMAS, P. (1977). *Consumer Action and Consumer Protection*. Library Association Public Libraries Group (Readers' Guide no. 10). 46 pp. Includes books, pamphlets, and periodical articles from the U K and overseas, many of historical interest. Entries are annotated.

Books and articles

FULOP, C. (1977). *The Consumer Movement and the Consumer*. Advertising Association. 115 pp. Examination of the *raison d'être* of the consumer movement, especially as it affects the economic interests of consumers. Argues that legal protection of the consumer should be enacted as a last resort and that voluntary codes and better consumer education may be more successful in providing protection.

HADDEN, T. (1975). 'Guidance for consumers'. *New Society*, 18 September 1975, pp. 638-9. Comments on the work of different types of organization, i.e., O F T, National Consumer Council, Consumer Advice Centres, small claims courts, etc. Chart on the functions of the different agencies and how they interrelate.

MARTIN, J. AND SMITH, G. W. (1968). *The Consumer Interest*. Pall Mall Press. 280 pp. Now out of print but should be obtainable in public libraries. Descriptive and analytical examination of the economic and social changes of recent decades that have led to the creation of organized consumer activity, and an evaluation of the consumer movement.

MITCHELL, J. (1976). 'Management and the consumer movement'. *Journal of General Management, 3*, no. 4, 1976, pp. 46-54. General survey of the consumer movement, development of Government departments (particularly OFT) and independent consumer organizations.

ROBERTS, E. (1966). *Consumers*. Watts. 220 pp. Covers development of the consumer movement in the US, Europe and the UK. Reading list.

TRADE, BOARD OF (1962). *Committee on Consumer Protection*. (Chairman: J. T. Molony) Final report. Cmnd 1781. HMSO. 331 pp.

Journals

Consumer Affairs. Consumer Relations Bureau, JWT Group (J. Walter Thompson Co. Ltd). 6 issues p.a. Provides advance information on developments in consumer protection and comment on their likely implications and the response from business.

Consumer Information Bulletin. Department of Prices and Consumer Protection. Monthly. Official Government newsletter on subjects of consumer interest. Indexed.

Consumer Review. International Organization of Consumers' Unions, The Hague. The journal consists of a collection of indexes to: standards, consumer legislation, test methods, new publications, and bibliographies, new accessions, and translations held in IOCU library.

Consumerism. Commerce Clearing House, Chicago. Weekly. Covers 'new developments for business', all aspects of consumer protection in the US, from federal to local county matters. References are given to new Bills, items in the Federal Register, new publications. Items are listed under general subject headings. Quarterly index.

Journal of Consumer Affairs. American Council on Consumer Interests. 2 issues p.a. Official journal of the ACCI. Scholarly articles, survey results, book reviews, and communications.

Journal of Consumer Policy/Zeitschrift for Verbraucherpolitik. Luchterhand verlag, Neuwied 1, West Germany. Quarterly. First published in March 1977 with articles in English and German. Describes itself as an 'organ for the scientific analysis of the consumer situation and ... attempts to define the consumer interest'. It will publish empirical research on consumer and producer conduct, will examine public policy in the consumer sphere and its social and economic consequences. Current consumer affairs and legislation will be covered in a reports section.

Journal of Consumer Studies and Home Economics. Blackwell Scientific Publications, Oxford. Quarterly. This new journal aims to meet the demand for a periodical in which significant developments and ideas can be brought to the attention of people in consumer studies and home economics. Includes research papers, review articles, communications, news and comment, and book reviews.

Consumer Protection Reporting Service (ed. D. P. Rothschild and D. W. Carroll). 2 vols. Anderson Publishing Co., Cincinatti. Looseleaf, updated by supplements every six months. Source of information on the legal and para-legal aspects of the US consumer movement on four levels—federal, state, local, and private.

Social Audit. Public Interest Research Centre. This quarterly journal (now discontinued) produced detailed reports on the work of Government, corporate, and other bodies, and was concerned with improving Government and corporate responsiveness to the public. The centre hopes to produce occasional reports in this field on a one-off basis in future.

Statistical sources

CHARTERED INSTITUTE OF PUBLIC FINANCE AND ACCOUNTANCY, SOCIETY OF COUNTY CONSUMER SERVICES OFFICERS, AND SOCIETY OF COUNTY TREASURERS. *Consumer Protection Statistics*. Actuals 1975-6 and estimates 1976-7. 38 pp. Statistics cover England and Wales only.

INSTITUTE OF TRADING STANDARDS ADMINISTRATION (1976). *The Trading Standards and Consumer Protection Service. Statistical Report 1974-75*. 12 pp. Statistics compiled from figures supplied by 75 local authorities in England and Wales.

METHVEN, M. J. (1976). 'The Office of Fair Trading—our vital statistics'. Manchester Statistical Society, Stockport. 11 pp. This paper was read to the Society on 2 December 1975 and covers consumer complaint statistics and economic indicators to identify monopoly and uncompetitive situations.

MITCHELL, J. (1977). 'A systematic approach to analysing consumer complaints'. *Journal of Consumer Studies and Home Economics,* **1,** no. 1, March 1977, pp. 3-20. Discusses the OFT system for recording and classifying consumer complaints.

MORRIS, D. and REESON, D. I. (1977). 'The economics of Consumer Advice Centres and consumer complaints'. *Monthly Review,* **85,** no. 6, June 1977, pp. 125-128. Statistical data examined from the figures recorded by OFT, local authorities, and county treasurers. Authors hope to extend their work to an examination of the costs and benefits of complaining.

OFFICE OF FAIR TRADING. *Annual Report of the Director-General of Fair Trading.* House of Commons Paper published each spring, HMSO. Each report contains a 'classification of consumer complaints' culled from a series of quarterly data on complaints collected since 1974 in cooperation with local authorities and Citizens' Advice Bureaux. Complaints are classified by type of goods or services, by criminal legislation, and by trading practice.

1.   Some Lessons for Marketing

BARKSDALE, H. C., DARDEN, W. R., AND PERREAULT, W. D. (1976). 'Changes in consumer attitudes toward marketing, consumerism and government regulation: 1971-1975'. *Journal of Consumer Affairs,* **10,** no. 2, Winter 1976, pp. 117-39. Findings of three national surveys indicate that the level of consumer discontent did not change substantially between 1971 and 1975, despite expanding efforts to advance the interests of the consumer.

BEST, A. AND ANDREASEN, A. R. (1976). *Talking Back to Business: Voiced and Unvoiced Consumer Complaints.* Center for Study of Responsive Law, Washington DC, 117 pp. Reports reactions of urban households to purchases made in 34 common consumption categories. Report recommends education programmes to help consumers reassess their complaining practices, and training of consumer advisers.

DIAMOND, S. L. *et al.* (1976). 'Consumer problems and consumerism: analysis of calls to a consumer hot line'. *Journal of Marketing,* **40,** January 1976, pp. 58-62. Analyses the kinds of problems consumers have and the type of people who use a consumer hot line, identifies the particular business sectors complained about most, and examines the interactions of consumers with the particular companies/businesses involved in complaints.

GAZDA, C. M. AND GOURLEY, D. R. (1975). 'Attitudes of businessmen, consumers and consumerists toward consumerism'. *Journal of Consumer Affairs,* **9,** Winter 1975, pp. 176-86. Study assesses attitudes of the above towards several important issues. Concludes that consumer groups should try harder to elicit and then represent the views of consumers; that more effective self-regulation by industry may help reduce consumer complaints and avoid further Government controls; that consumers want more and better product information and are in favour of corrective advertising.

KANGUN, N. *et al.* (1975). 'Consumerism and marketing management'. *Journal of Marketing,* April 1975, pp. 3-10. Survey on how consumers perceive consumerism and the implications of these perceptions for marketing managers.

2.   Consumers' Association and *Which?*

(See chapter 22, and also references listed under 'Books and Articles' in the General section of this Bibliography.)

CENTRAL OFFICE OF INFORMATION (1976). *Fair Trading and Consumer Protection in Britain.* Reference pamphlet 44, HMSO. 59 pp. Describes the various forms of consumer protection provided by legislative action, and considers the work of Government-sponsored and independent consumer organizations. Reading list.

COFFIN, C. (1976). 'The new consumer institutions: an interim report'. *Consumer Affairs,* no. 21, June/July 1976, pp. 1-5. Survey of developments in consumer organizations and institutions since 1972, and a discussion on consumer legislation passed 1972-74.

JENNINGS, M. (1974). 'The consumer achievement'. *Marketing*, September 1974, pp. 32-3, 35. Growth of consumer organizations and their influence.

MACINTYRE, C. (1974). 'The pressure groups'. *Marketing*, September 1974, pp. 51-5. Guide to official and voluntary bodies, and how they work.

WRAITH, R. (1976). 'The consumer cause: a short account of its organisation, power and importance'. Royal Institute of Public Administration, 1976, 80 pp. Brief study of the framework, mainly in England and Wales, within which the consumer movement is developing, and a description of consumer protection services in central and local government, nationalized industries, and the EEC.

3. The Legal Framework of Consumer Protection

England and Wales

ACKROYD, E. (1973). 'Fair trading: an operational guide' in *Management Decision*, **11**, no. 6, pp. 335-67. MCB Management Decision Ltd, Bradford. This monograph identifies five essential elements for an effective policy to promote consumer interest; protection, information, advice, education, and representation, and assesses the extent to which the Fair Trading Act will contribute towards them.

BORRIE, G. AND DIAMOND, A. L. (1973). *The Consumer, Society and the Law*. Third edn. Penguin. 352 pp. Bibliography, table of statutes. Surveys whole field of consumer law as it stood in 1973, and possible future developments. Covers sellers and producers, hire purchase, banking, travel, etc.

CHALMERS, M. D. (1975). *Sale of Goods Act 1893*. Seventeenth edn, revised by Michael Mark. Butterworth. 407 pp. Standard work. Law as at 1 August 1975.

COLLEGE OF LAW (1974). *Fair Trading and Consumer Protection*. 96 pp. 1973 lectures on implied terms, exemption clauses, civil remedies and their enforcement, Trade Descriptions Acts, Fair Trading Act, UK competition law.

CONFEDERATION OF BRITISH INDUSTRY (1976). *Fair Trading—Guidance for Industry and Commerce*. August 1976. 27 pp. Outline for those engaged on manufacturing or providing basic services on the provisions of the Fair Trading Act 1973.

CUNNINGHAM, J. P. (1974). *The Fair Trading Act 1973: Consumer Protection and Competition Law*. Sweet & Maxwell. 675 pp. Table of statutes, table of cases, list of Monopolies Commission reports. Book 1: consumer protection; Book 2: competition law. Law as at 1 June 1974.

DOBSON, A. P. (1975). *Sale of Goods and Consumer Credit*. Sweet & Maxwell. 264 pp. Student textbook on sale of goods, hire purchase, and consumer credit law as at February 1975.

HERMANN, A. H. AND JONES, C. (1977). *Fair Trading in Europe*. Kluwer-Harrap. 443 pp. Provides practical guidance to the law and practice in 15 countries on anti-trust and consumer protection. Describes the institutions that implement fair trading policy and their current practice, as well as the laws themselves. Main work gives the law as at May 1976, and a section on the latest developments brings the work up to December 1976.

HOLT, R. (1976). 'How to use the Office of Fair Trading' *Legal Action Group Bulletin*, June 1976, pp. 127-8. Useful article on the powers and duties of the Office of Fair Trading.

LAW COMMISSION (1969). *Exemption Clauses in Contracts, First Report: Amendments to the Sale of Goods Act 1893*. Law Commission and Scottish Law Commission, HMSO. 69 pp. (Sess. 1968-69, HC 403; Law Com. no. 24; Scot. Law Com. no. 12)

LAW COMMISSION (1973). *Provisional Proposals relating to the Exclusion of Liability for Negligence in the Sale of Goods and Exemption Clauses in Contracts*. Working paper no. 39, Scottish Law Commission memorandum no. 15, HMSO. 103 pp.

LAW COMMISSION (1975). *Exemption Clauses: Second Report*. Law Commission and Scottish Law Commission, HMSO. 209 pp. (Sess. 1974-75, HC 605; Law Com. no. 69; Scot. Law Com. no. 39.)

LAW COMMISSION (1977). *Law of Contract: Implied Terms in Contracts for the Supply of Goods*. Working paper no. 71, HMSO. 60 pp.

NATIONAL CHAMBER OF TRADE (1977). *Retailers and the Sale of Goods*. Henley-on-Thames. 20 pp. Explains the responsibility of retailers in the field of consumer law and gives a suggested code of practice for the service trades.

Office of Fair Trading (1975). *Fair Deal across the Counter.* Prepared by OFT in consultation with the National Federation of Consumer Groups, National Chamber of Trade, Retail Trading-Standards Association, and the Institute of Trading Standards Administration. Leaflet.

Office of Fair Trading (1976). *Review of the Trade Descriptions Act 1968: A Report by the Director-General of Fair Trading.* Cmnd 6628, HMSO. 99 pp. Detailed study of the working of the Act and recommendations on how it should be strengthened.

O'Keefe, J. A. (1971). *Law relating to Trade Descriptions.* Butterworth. 1971. Looseleaf, with supplement service. Standard work.

O'Keefe, J. A. (1977). *The Law of Weights and Measures.* Second edn. Butterworth. Looseleaf, with supplement service. Standard work.

Retail Trading-Standards Association (1973). *Consumer protection and . . . the Fair Trading Act 1973.* RTSA. 14 pp. A brief guide for retailers and manufacturers on the legal implications of the new consumer protection law that will affect them.

Product liability

Bennigson, L. A. and Bennigson, A. I. (1974). 'Product liability: manufacturers beware!' *Harvard Business Review*, May/June 1974, pp. 122-132. Analyses the experience of several companies, and common manufacturing errors. Itemizes the most effective ways of dealing with the current US liability laws.

Gray, I. (1975). *Product Liability: A Management Response.* AMACOM, New York. 239 pp. US product liability laws, litigation process, role of insurance, and prevention of errors are all discussed.

Law Commission (1975). *Liability for Defective Products.* Working paper no. 64, Scottish Law Commission memorandum no. 20, HMSO. 172 pp. Considers the existing law and possible changes.

Law Commission and Scottish Law Commission (1977). *Liability for Defective Products: Report on a Reference under Section 3(1)(e) of the Law Commissions Act 1965.* Cmnd 6831, HMSO. 96 pp. Report recommends that producers of defective products causing death or personal injury should be made strictly liable at law to pay damages. States that remedies under present law provide insufficient protection and redress.

Miller, C. J. and Lovell, P. A. (1977). *Product Liability.* Butterworth. 386 pp. Legal text, table of statutes, case list, appendices on EEC draft Directive and European convention on product liability.

Product Liability in Europe (1975). A collection of reports prepared for the conference on product liability in Europe held in Amsterdam on 25 and 26 September 1975. Kluwer-Harrap. 155 pp. Survey of Europe and the US including appendices on the draft conventions and draft EEC Directive.

Small Claims Courts

Birks, M. (1975). *Small Claims in the County Court: How to Sue and Defend Actions without a Solicitor.* Revised edn. HMSO. 74 pp. Booklet issued by the Lord Chancellor's Office gives full details of how to sue, how to act as defendant, specimen particulars of claim, etc.

Consumer Council (1970). *Justice Out of Reach: A Case for Small Claims Courts.* HMSO. 34 pp. Research project to discover to what extent the English legal system of the day was helpful to consumers in civil actions.

Consumers' Association (1973a). *How to Sue in the County Court.* CA. 248 pp. Takes the reader step by step through what is involved in bringing a case and enables him to sue in the County Court in a consumer case without the help of a solicitor.

Consumers' Association (1973b). 'Small claims and the consumer'. *Which?*, October 1973, pp. 292-5. Surveys US small claims courts, county court system, Scottish sheriff courts.

Dodd, C. (1974). 'Small claims courts'. *Distributor*, September 1974, pp. 105-6. Article on 'superfluous, unsatisfactory' new small claims courts.

Harper, T. (1975). 'Settling small claims' *New Society*, 23 January 1975, p. 98. Surveys the new local 'arbitration court' and the weaknesses of a voluntary arbitration scheme and its future. Also looks at the official small claims arbitration service in the county courts.

280

NATIONAL INSTITUTE FOR CONSUMER JUSTICE (1974). *Redress of Consumer Grievances.* NICJ, Washington DC. 56 pp. Reports on four ways of resolving consumer disputes in the US: business-sponsored mechanisms, arbitration, small claims courts, class actions.

SHERWIN, M. (1975). 'The Westminster small claims court'. *LAG Bulletin*, March 1975, pp. 65-6. Details of types of case handled, procedures, costs, statistics. etc.

Consumer credit

BENNION, F. (ED.) (1976). *Consumer Credit Control.* Oyez. Looseleaf binder with supplement service to update the work. Contains a detailed examination of the complex consumer credit legislation and gives full annotations and cross references.

GOODE, R. M. (1974). *Introduction to the Consumer Credit Act 1974.* Butterworth. 500 pp. Introductory guide to a very complex piece of legislation. Though reasonably detailed, it does not purport to be an exhaustive analysis of the Act, but attempts to provide an insight into its structure and the impact of its various provisions on specific types of transaction.

GRIEG, C. MCNEIL (1974). *Short Guide to the Consumer Credit Act 1974.* Hire Purchase Trade Association. 80 pp. Not a legal textbook, but aims to enable the reader to find his way through this long and complex statute and to explain the principal matters dealt with in the Act, and its requirements.

GUEST, A. G. AND LLOYD, M. G. (EDS.) (1975). *Encyclopedia of Consumer Credit Law.* Sweet & Maxwell. Looseleaf binder with supplement service. Information, explanation, and advice on new law and practice, with reproduction of the Act, SIs, general notices, etc.

JOHNSON, H. (1976). *The Consumer Credit Act 1974.* MCB, Bradford. 48 pp. Commentary on the Act amplified by reference to draft regulations issued by DPCP.

TRADE AND INDUSTRY, DEPARTMENT OF (1971). *Consumer Credit: Report of the Committee.* Committee on Consumer Credit (Chairman: Lord Crowther), Cmnd 4596, HMSO. 2 vols. The Crowther Committee examined the law as it then was, and many of its recommendations were incorporated into the Consumer Credit Act 1974.

TRADE AND INDUSTRY, DEPARTMENT OF (1973). *Reform of the Law on Consumer Credit.* Cmnd 5427, HMSO 59pp. Outlines measures under which the consumer will have comprehensive protection. Many of these were incorporated in the Consumer Credit Act 1974.

Scotland

CLARKE, M. (1976). *Consumer Law in Scotland: A Discussion Document.* Scottish Consumer Council, Glasgow. 20 pp. Paper attempts to analyse where the divergencies between English and Scots law have led to unequal rights both in the law itself and in the legal system by which those rights must be enforced. The Scottish Consumer Council is to make further enquiries with a view to recommending action.

MARTIN, A (1977). 'Consumer legislation: grasping the thistle'. *Campaign*, 14 January 1977, p. 21. Examines differences between English and Scottish consumer legislation.

SCOTTISH LAW COMMISSION (1977). *The Legal System of Scotland.* Second edn. HMSO, Edinburgh. 48 pp. Prepared by the legal staff of the Scottish Law Commission and of the Office of the Solicitor to the Secretary of State for Scotland. Covers civil and criminal law, legal aid, administrative tribunals, etc.

4. Consumer Protection in Local Government

CORFIELD, J. J. (1976). 'The trading standards/consumer protection service in the UK'. *Consumer Affairs*, No. 23, October/November 1976, pp. 1-5. Definitive review of the work of trading standards officers.

INSTITUTE OF TRADING STANDARDS ADMINISTRATION (1976). *ITSA: The Trading Standards/Consumer Protection Service in 1976.* Leaflet produced by ITSA on the service and its functions.

PAINTER, A. A. (1973). *The Councillor and Consumer Protection*. Published and distributed for *Local Government Review* by Barry Rose Publishers. 11 pp. Covers the development of legislation, responsibilities of local government, how services are provided, and the relationship between members and officers.

PHILLIPS, A. D. (1977). 'Consumer advice'. *Monthly Review*, **85**, no. 7, July 1977, pp. 149-51. Describes services that should be readily available to the public, such as CACs, mobile units, freephone/freepost contact procedures, publicity, etc. There is great potential for development.

5. Local Advice for Consumers

BELL, P. (1976). 'Downtown advice—High Street information service'. *Assistant Librarian*, June 1976, pp. 106-7. Survey of the work of Consumer Advice Centres and their co-operation with local libraries.

BISHOP, G. H. (1977). Three articles on Consumer Advice Centres—how they help traders, and their liaison with trading standards officers. *Monthly Review*, **85**, nos. 1, 2, and 3, January, February, and March 1977. Major objective of CACs is to bring about a fair solution where consumers have a justifiable complaint. Necessity for referral to enforcement officers where the complaint comes under criminal law.

CLEGG, G. (1976). 'Information service for Consumer Advice Centres'. *Assistant Librarian*, June 1976, pp. 104-5. Examines the development of CACs and the information they provide.

GRAY, C. (1975). 'How to make the most of your High Street guerillas'. *Value Today* (no longer published), no. 6, April 1975, pp. 2-8. Describes functions of different types of advice centre, including CABx, CACs, Law Centres, etc.

JENNINGS, M. (1976). 'Consumer Advice Centres—the new shop in the High Street'. *Consumer Affairs*, no. 21, June/July 1976, pp. 6-11. Three case studies on CACs and their work. The Centres are now totally accepted as part of the local authority information network.

MCROBERT, R. (1974). 'Consumer advice service'. *Trade and Industry*, 12 September 1974, pp. 523-4. General article on the provision of consumer advice services.

NATIONAL CONSUMER COUNCIL (1977). *The Fourth Right of Citizenship—a Review of Local Advice Services*. NCC. 80 pp. A comprehensive review of the role of advice services, with recommendations on how the system could be improved.

SCOTTISH CONSUMER COUNCIL (1977). *Let the People Know: Local Advice Services in Scotland: Discussion Document*. Scottish Consumer Council, Glasgow. 70 pp. Covers the present advice network in Scotland, including CABx, housing advice and legal advice centres, etc., as well as CACs.

TILLEARD, M. AND CLEGG, G. (1976). 'Consumer advisory services'. *Aslib Proceedings*, **28**, no. 2, February 1976, pp. 56-68. Covers the history of the consumer movement and the development of consumer bodies as sources of consumer information at the local level, and Consumer Advice Centres.

6. Nationalized Industry Consumer Councils

CONACHER, G. (1975). 'A nationalised industry's view'. *Consumer Affairs*, issue 15, May/June 1975, pp. 5-8. Deals with the electricity industry and the consumer.

CONSUMER COUNCIL (1968). *Consumer Consultative Machinery in the Nationalised Industries*. HMSO. 118 pp. Now superseded by the National Consumer Council report on the same subject (see below), but covered consumer consultative machinery in the electricity, gas, solid fuel, and public transport industries, and its conclusions are still of interest. Field study was carried out on consumers' knowledge of and experience of the consultative machinery, and detailed statistical findings are set out in Appendix V.

GUMMER, J. (1975). 'How to deal with big brother'. *Value Today* (no longer published), no. 5, March 1975, pp. 26-31. Guidelines on how to resolve problems with big business and nationalized industry. Gives details of reference books that will help in dealing with commercial companies, and key men to complain to by name.

JUSTICE (1976). *The Citizen and the Public Agencies: Remedying Grievances*. Justice. 106 pp. Report considers adequacy or otherwise of the present formal machinery for redressing citizens' grievances against the nationalized industries. Concludes that the system needs strengthening, especially to improve public confidence in the arrangements for redress, and that a Nationalized Industries and Agencies Commissioner should be established.

NATIONAL CONSUMER COUNCIL (1976). *Consumers and the Nationalised Industries*. National Consumer Council Report no. 1, HMSO. 225 pp. Covers arrangements for consumer representation in those industries having domestic consumers as their paying customers. Includes results of a detailed questionnaire on the composition and operation of the consumer councils, and makes proposals for change.

REEVES, P. (1975). *Electricity and Gas Consumers' Guide*. Centre for Protective Law Studies, Oxford. 23 pp. Summarizes the practice of supply authorities and the law applicable to domestic gas and electricity consumers.

TISDALL, P. (1975). 'Do consumer councils really give power to the people?' *The Times*, 13 March 1975, p. 15.

TOZER, N. (1974). 'The deal for consumers in state industries'. *Consumer Affairs*, issue 11, July/August 1974. pp. 3-4.

7. A Marketing View of the Consumer
and
12. Future Developments in Marketing

AAKER, D. A. AND DAY, G. S. (EDS.) (1974). *Consumerism: Search for the Consumer Interest*. Second edn. Collier Macmillan, Free Press. 460 pp. Collection of readings on many aspects of consumerism from historical and current perspectives to the pre-purchase, purchase, and post-purchase phases. For the businessman and student. Three new topics have been added for the second edition—ecology, social issues in advertising, and anti-trust policy and enforcement.

ALLVINE, F. C. (ED.) (1973). *Public Policy and Marketing Practices: Proceedings of a Workshop*. American Marketing Association, Chicago. 409 pp. Conference focused on the question of public policy and only touched on the topic of consumerism. 26 papers.

BLOOM, P. N. AND SILVER, M. J. (1976). 'Consumer education: marketers take heed'. *Harvard Business Review*, January/February 1976, pp. 32-6, 40-2, 149. Covers, among other things, the consumer education programmes of individual US companies.

'Borrie prefers it voluntary'. *Campaign*, 13 May 1977, p. 2.

'Business and consumer-commercial vitality'. *Commerce America*, 8 November 1976, pp. 4-7. Establishment of a Consumer Affairs Division within the US Department of Commerce and its policy as an 'in-house consumer advocate . . . to bring the views of the consumer into balance with those of business in policy and program decisions of the Department'.

'Consumerism: a marketing special'. *Marketing*, September 1974 (whole issue). Articles on the Director-General of Fair Trading; the consumer achievement; checklist on the effectiveness of a company's customer relations; how to handle complaints; guide to pressure groups.

DAY, R. L. (1976). 'Prescription for the market-place—everyone listen better'. *Business Horizons*, December 1976, pp. 57-64. Factors which have led to increased criticism of the marketing system are documented, and programmes to counter consumer unrest suggested.

DRUCKER, P. (1969a). 'Consumerism in marketing'. Address to the National Association of Manufacturers, New York, April 1969.

DRUCKER, P. (1969b). *The Practice of Management*. Heinemann. 399 pp.

GAEDEKE, R. M. AND ETCHESON, W. W. (EDS.) (1972). *Consumerism: Viewpoints from Business, Government and the Public Interest*. Canfield Press, San Francisco. 401 pp. Covers history of the consumer movement, consumer regulation, the consumer challenge to business, international consumerism, and possible future developments. Appendices give: I. list of significant consumer legislation enacted at the federal level during the past century; II. lists of selected bills introduced in the Ninety-second Congress; III. review of major Government-financed or Government-sponsored consumer protection activities in 10 foreign countries. The book is designed for consumer economics and business students and as a supplement to an introductory text on marketing.

GREYSER, S. A. AND DIAMOND, S. L. (1974). 'Business is adapting to consumerism'. *Harvard Business Review*, September/October 1974, pp. 38-40, 44-8, 52-8. Comprehensive report interprets opinions of *Harvard Business Review* readers. Broad recognition and growing acceptance characterize management's attitude to consumerism—seen by a growing number of executives as an opportunity rather than a threat.

GREYSER, S. A. (1974). 'The response to consumerism'. *Advertising Quarterly*, Autumn 1974, pp. 26-9. Poses series of consumerism issues and questions to help marketers to appraise their programmes in the light of the changed consumer-affected environment. Many opportunities for marketers lie in viewing consumerism as an opportunity, not as anti-business.

INSTITUTE OF MARKETING AND OFFICE OF FAIR TRADING (1975-6). 'Marketing and the consumer'. Six special supplements appeared bi-monthly in the journal *Marketing*, from October 1975. Jointly produced by the Institute of Marketing and the OFT. Only factor that the contributors had in common was an interest in marketing and also in the consumer. The series was intended to promote discussion and a two-way exchange of ideas between buyers and sellers that might lead to action.

JENNINGS, M. (1976). 'Consumerism... industry's response'. *Consumer Affairs*, issue 19, January/February 1976. pp. 1-10. Examines the response of industry to the threat and opportunity presented by consumerism, using prominent organizations as examples of current action, and reviewing official reaction to the initiatives of industry.

JONES, MARY GARDINER AND GARDNER, DAVID M. (EDS.) (1976). *Consumerism: A New Force in Society*. D. C. Heath, Lexington (Mass.). 187 pp. Proceedings of a conference sponsored in October 1974 by the College of Commerce and Business Administration of the University of Illinois and the James S. Kemper Foundation of Chicago, for the exchange of ideas between the business community, the non-profit sector, consumer organizations, Government, and academics on the role and likely future of the US consumer movement.

KOTLER, P. (1966). 'Diagnosing the Marketing Take Over'. *Journal of the Institute of Marketing*, August 1966. Haymarket Publishing, London.

LEVITT, T. (1970). *The Marketing Mode: Pathways to Corporate Growth*. McGraw Hill, New York.

LEVITT, T. (1972). 'Marketing: making the concept real?' *Marketing* May 1972, pp. 36-9, 41, 57.

LUTHANS, F. AND HODGETTS, R. M. (1976). *Social Issues in Business: A Text with Current Readings and Cases*. Macmillan. 596 pp. Useful section on 'the consumerism issue', and readings, pp. 350-471. Covers product liability, consumer protection legislation, business response to consumerism, safety, and complaints handling.

MCGUIRE, E. P. (1973). *The Consumer Affairs Department: Organization and Functions*. The Conference Board, New York. 114 pp. Select bibliography on consumerism and consumer relations. Describes rationale, organization, and responsibilities for company units established to manage consumer affairs programmes as a positive response to the same forces giving rise to the consumerism movement. Report is based primarily on the experiences of 149 companies with formal consumer affairs units and is in two parts: the first focuses on the organization and operations of all the units studied; the second looks at the particular operations of 16 companies having consumer affairs organizations.

MURRAY, BARBARA (ED.) (1973). *Consumerism: The Eternal Triangle: Business, Government and Consumers*. Goodyear, Pacific Palisades, California. 469 pp. Readings on the social, economic and marketing aspects of consumerism as they relate to US Government, legislation, institutions, business and its marketing and advertising functions, and to the low income consumer.

RINES, M. (1974). 'An interview with John Methven'. *Marketing*, September 1974, pp. 28-30, 65.

RODGER, L. W. (ED) (1973) *Marketing Concepts and Strategies in the Next Decade*. Associated Business Programmes Ltd., Chapter 1.

RODGER, L. (1976). 'Marketing—the light that failed?' *Woolward Royds Review*, No. 1, August 1976. 8 pp. Marketing concept can be developed... to serve the best interests of society and (to provide) a means of earning a socially responsible reward for a company.

ROSENBERG, L. J. (1975). 'Retailers' responses to consumerism'. *Business Horizons*, October 1975, pp. 37-44. Progress report on consumerism in retailing, based on views of major retail organizations.

284

WEDDERBURN, D. L. (1972). 'Consumerism—a positive approach'. *Journal of the Society of Cosmetic Chemists*, no. 7, November 1972, pp. 1-7. Paper discusses origins of some misunderstandings between manufacturer and consumer, and suggests techniques to ensure that products are appropriate for their purpose and live up to claims made for them.

8. Market Research and Consumer Attitudes

BARKSDALE, H. C. AND DARDEN, W. R. (1972). 'Consumer attitudes towards marketing and consumerism'. *Journal of Marketing*, **36**, October 1972, pp. 28-35. Exploratory study on reactions of a national sample of consumers to business policies and practices, the consumerism movement and protective Government legislation.

BRITISH MARKET RESEARCH BUREAU (1976). *Public Attitudes to Advertising: 1976 Survey*. Advertising Association. 47 leaves. Survey commissioned by the Advertising Association as part of BMRB's omnibus survey on British life, with a section on consumerism.

BUSKIRK, R. H. AND ROTHE, J. T. (1970). 'Consumerism—an interpretation'. *Journal of Marketing*, **34**, October 1970, pp. 61-5. Forces underlying the present upsurge in consumer activity are analysed and some dangers of the remedies proposed by some consumer advocates are considered. Implications of the consumer movement for corporate policy are discussed and recommendations made for corporate action.

CORLETT, T. (1977). *Advertising and the European Consumer: Public Attitudes to Advertising in the UK, USA and EEC*. Advertising Association. 26 pp.

GAEDEKE, R. M. (1970). 'What business, government, consumer spokesmen think about consumerism'. *Journal of Consumer Affairs*, **4**, no. 1, Summer 1970, pp. 7-18. Survey was assembled from a large number of frequently stated assertions about consumerism, and the article records the different perceptions held and concludes that consumerism is a fluid and hard-to-define phenomenon.

KOTLER, P. (1972). 'What consumerism means for marketers'. *Harvard Business Review*, May/June 1972, pp. 48-57. Consumerism is here to stay and will be 'ultimately profitable' for those companies that can see it as an opportunity. A consumer orientation can lead to needed new products and increased customer satisfaction and goodwill.

NELSON, E. (1973). 'Consumerism, its nature and significance to market planning'. In *ESOMAR/WAPOR Congress*, Budapest 1973, pp. 441-62.

NOP MARKET RESEARCH LTD (1975). *Consumerism*. Survey of adults over 16 years, fieldwork carried out in April 1975. Overall picture emerging from the survey with regard to quality, reliability, and after-sales service is the low esteem with which most consumers view the products available today. However, it is easy to obtain product information. NOP found widespread ignorance of any consumerist movement or organization.

RESEARCH SURVEYS OF GREAT BRITAIN LTD (1977). RSGB omnibus syndicated survey on consumer protection: fieldwork—December 1976. JN-6612. 36 leaves. Survey based on a representative sample of housewives. Concentrated on awareness and experience of the following bodies: DPCP, OFT, and Consumer Advice Centres.

J. WALTER THOMPSON CO. LTD (1976). *Consumer Change in the mid-70s*. 32 pp. Articles on the new freedom; a summary of the social and psychological developments of the 'sixties and early 'seventies: consumer frustrations in a changing world, slumpflation, and the new order.

J. WALTER THOMPSON CO. LTD (1973). *Living in Britain*.

WIGHT, R. (1972). *The Day the Pigs Refused to be Driven to Market: Advertising and the Consumer Revolution*. Hart-Davis, MacGibbon. 256 pp. Deals with the growth of consumer power, its activities, and its relationship with business, with particular reference to advertising.

9. Handling Consumer Complaints

CHAMBERS, P. (1974). 'Coping with consumer militancy'. *International Management*, November 1974, pp. 34-5, 38-9. Development of company programmes to react quickly and positively to forestall and answer customer complaints. Case studies of worldwide corporations' programmes included.

CONFEDERATION OF BRITISH INDUSTRY (1974). *Industry and the Consumer: The Final Report of the Study Group on Consumer Complaints and Consumer Counselling*. CBI. 23 pp. Group was set up to consider the appropriate local and national framework for dealing with consumer complaints and counselling against the background of current legislation, and legislation in prospect. Recommendations included: complaints should be treated with respect and regarded as sources of potentially useful information; manufacturers and suppliers should have a proper system for receiving, investigating and acting on complaints; and consumer education should be developed.

'Consumer affairs—threat or opportunity?' *Consumer Affairs*, no. 25, January/February 1977, pp. 1-24. Report of major speeches made at Forbes Publications Conference in London on 3 March 1977, co-sponsored by OFT, Institute of Marketing, CBI, Retail Trading-Standards Association, and US Embassy. Details of their consumer affairs programmes were given by representatives of Giant Food, J. C. Penney, Currys, Lever Bros., and Timpson.

MOORE, C. (1975). *How to Handle Customer Complaints: A Company Guide to Customer Relations and Consumer Rights*. Gower Press. 116 pp. Covers development of consumer protection and company responsibility to the consumer, types of complaints and how to handle them, organization of customer relations departments, company policy, and the customer, company and the law.

10. The Retailer's Response to the Consumer Movement

MONTGOMERY, J. D. (1975). 'Consumerism . . . a company lawyer's view'. *Consumer Affairs*, issue 14, March/April 1975, pp. 6-8. Suggests that the flow of consumer legislation has added only a little to the responsibilities of the company lawyer. Time has come for the consumer movement to move on from 'consumer protection' to 'fair trading' i.e., a balance between buyer and seller.

RETAIL TRADING-STANDARDS ASSOCIATION (1975). *Honest, Fair and Legal: The Retailer, the Law and the Customer*. RTSA. 24 pp. Simple outline of the major provisions of the law as it affects the retailer and contributes to fair trading, plus some general points on assistance to customers.

RETAIL TRADING-STANDARDS ASSOCIATION (1972). *Questions You Ask . . . the Trade Descriptions Acts 1968 and 1972*. RTSA. 28 pp. Short guide for the distributive industry.

11. Standards and Marketing

BRITISH STANDARDS INSTITUTION (1974). *A Standard for Standards*. BSI. 4 vols. Contents: 1. Introduction to standardization; 2. Drafting of British standards; 3. BSI committee organization and procedures; 4. Guide to BSI editorial practice.

BRITISH STANDARDS INSTITUTION (1976). 'The changing role and priorities of BSI'. *Consumer Affairs*, no. 22, August/September 1976, pp. 1-4. BSI reviews its role in its seventy-fifth year and outlines envisaged changes and their implications.

Consumer Report. British Standards Institution. Irregular. Replaces the quarterly newsletter of the same name previously published by the Consumer Standards Advisory Committee of the BSI.

HEMENWAY, D. (1975). *Industry Wide Voluntary Product Standards*. Ballinger, Cambridge, Massachusetts. 141 pp. Survey of US standardization, specifically industry-wide voluntary product standards; does not cover internal company standards, mandatory standards, or service standards.

WOODWARD, C. D. (1972). *BSI: The Story of Standards*. BSI. 101 pp. History of BSI to 'seventies. Chapter 11, pp. 69-77, is about standards for the consumer.

13-15. Codes of Practice

ADVICE CENTRE ON THE ORGANIZATION OF INDUSTRIAL AND COMMERCIAL REPRESENTATION (1977). *The Sectoral Representation of British Industry and Commerce: A Guide to Employers' Organizations and Trade Associations in the UK and Links between them.* Third edn. ACOICR. Comprehensive guide to the numerous organizations representing the different sectors of industry and commerce, arranged by the Standard Industrial Classification, and showing the links between them.

ALLEN, A. P. (1977). 'Codes of practice: not worth the paper they are written on!' *Monthly Review*, **85**, no. 3, March 1977, pp. 55-7. Despite the title, the article examines some of the most successful aspects of the codes so far produced in consultation with the OFT. Feels that in the dialogue leading up to and in the implementation of codes, trading standards officers have been provided with a ready-made and self regulating 'enforcement tool'.

CLARKE, J. (1977). 'Trade Associations: are there too many?' *Trade and Industry*, 7 January 1977, pp. 14-5. Discusses Devlin Committee recommendation in 1972 that a more rational system of associations should be developed and that the CBI and Association of British Chambers of Commerce should jointly sponsor but not control 'a centre of advice serving as a clearing house of current information on developments in the whole field ...'

CONSUMERS' ASSOCIATION (1976). 'Reliability and servicing'. *Which?*, January 1976, pp. 13-6. Examines standards of reliability and servicing for domestic appliances since 1971 and concludes that there has been little change in reliability, while the standard of servicing has gone down despite the introduction of AMDEA's voluntary code.

CONSUMERS' ASSOCIATION (1977). 'Reliability and servicing of domestic appliances'. *Which?*, February 1977, pp. 61-5. Standard of servicing has now improved slightly, although still not all that good.

CO-OPERATIVE UNION (1976). *Consumer Protection Committee. Consumer Code.* Co-op Union. 14 pp. Code of practice on standards of retailing behaviour.

ELECTRICITY COUNCIL (1975). *Domestic Electrical Appliance Servicing by Electricity Boards: Conciliation Procedure; Arbitration Scheme.* Electricity Council. 21 pp.

GIORDAN, M. (1974). 'Trade associations, codes of practice and the rising tide of consumer action'. *Consumer Affairs*, Issue 9, March/April 1974, pp. 6-8. Discusses suggestion by the Director-General of Fair Trading that a code of practice might be introduced in the domestic appliance industry, and various other codes with some consumer content.

INSTITUTE OF TRADING STANDARDS ADMINISTRATION (1975). 'A consideration of voluntary codes of practice'. *Monthly Review*, **83**, no. 10, October 1975, pp. 217-24. Panel discussion on codes of practice issued by AMDEA, ABTA, Electricity Council and the Association of Mail Order Publishers. ITSA's views.

MARSH, S. E. (1977). 'Voluntary codes of practice'. *New Law Journal*, 28 April 1977, pp. 419-20. Surveys working of codes already in being. Major advantage of many codes is that they clarify what protection is offered to the consumer or what the industry perceives its obligations to be. Effectiveness of codes will depend largely on the publicity they are given and on the willingness of the association members to accept the codes and modify their practices.

MARTIN, A. (1976). 'How to follow the trading code'. *Campaign*, 3 September 1976, p. 16. Examines the complex area of trade codes, explains their legal status, and discusses how they should be strengthened.

MITCHELL, J. (1977). *'Business and the Consumer' The Director's Handbook.* Second edn. McGraw-Hill. Deals with the obligations firms may take on to consumers over and above their legal responsibilities.

OFT-approved codes of practice

ASSOCIATION OF BRITISH LAUNDERERS AND CLEANERS LTD (1976). *Code of Practice for Domestic Laundry and Cleaning Services.* 16 pp. *See also:* OFFICE OF FAIR TRADING (1976). *Launderers and drycleaners.* Leaflet in the 'For your protection' series.

ASSOCIATION OF BRITISH TRAVEL AGENTS (Amended 1975/6). *Codes of Conduct governing the Conduct between ABTA Tour Operators and ABTA Retail Agents and Members of the Public.* ABTA. 7 pp. *See also:* OFFICE OF FAIR TRADING (1976). *Package holidays abroad.* Leaflet in the 'For your protection' series.

ASSOCIATION OF MANUFACTURERS OF DOMESTIC ELECTRICAL APPLIANCES (1974). *Principles for Domestic Electrical Appliance Servicing.* AMDEA. 16 pp. *See also:* OFFICE OF FAIR TRADING (1975). *Electrical servicing.* Leaflet in the 'For your protection' series.

FOOTWEAR DISTRIBUTORS FEDERATION (1976). *Voluntary Code of Practice for Footwear.* FDF. 8 pp. *See also:* OFFICE OF FAIR TRADING (1976). *Shoes.* Leaflet in the 'For your protection' series.

MAIL ORDER PUBLISHERS' AUTHORITY (1977). *Code of Practice*. MOPA.
MOTOR AGENTS ASSOCIATION (1976). *Motor Industry Code of Practice*. MAA.
NATIONAL ASSOCIATION OF SHOE REPAIR FACTORIES AND ST CRISPINS BOOT TRADES ASSOCIATION LTD (1976). *A Guide to the Code of Practice for Shoe Repairs*. 16 pp. *See also:* OFFICE OF FAIR TRADING (1976). *Shoes*. Leaflet in the 'For your protection' series.
RADIO, ELECTRICAL AND TELEVISION RETAILERS ASSOCIATION LTD (1976). *RETRA Code of Practice for the Selling and Servicing of Electrical and Electronic Appliances*. RETRA. 12 pp.
SCOTTISH MOTOR TRADE ASSOCIATION (1976). *SMTA Used Car Code*. 6 pp. *See also:* OFFICE OF FAIR TRADING (1976). *Cars*. Leaflet in the 'For your protection' series.
VEHICLE BUILDERS AND REPAIRERS ASSOCIATION (1975). *Code of Practice for Vehicle Body Repair (Motor Car and Caravan Sector)*. VBRA. 8 pp. *See also:* OFFICE OF FAIR TRADING (1976). *Cars*. Leaflet in the 'For your protection' series.

16. Advertising: What the Consumer Wants

ADVERTISING ASSOCIATION (1975). *Advertising in Perspective in Industry and Society*. AA. 64 pp. Papers delivered at a symposium in December 1974, specially prepared as the basis for discussion between the AA, DPCP, and OFT.
ADVERTISING ASSOCIATION (1976). *Public Attitudes to Advertising*. AA.
DIVITA, S. F. (ED.) (1974). *Advertising and the Public Interest*. American Marketing Association, Chicago, Illinois. 264 pp. Selected papers from a conference held in May 1973 on the role and function of advertising in society. Advertising and consumerism and advertising regulation are among the subjects covered.
HODGES, L. AND MEDAWAR, C. (1974). 'Advertising—the art of the permissible'. *Social Audit* (no longer regularly published), 2, no. 1, Summer 1974, pp. 17-40. Examines the history of advertising's voluntary control system and suggests improvements.
MEDAWAR, C. AND HODGES, L. (1973). 'The social cost of advertising'. *Social Audit* (no longer regularly published), 1, no. 1, Summer 1973, pp. 28-52. Report 'tentatively develops the theme that information lends power which is open to use or abuse at the discretion of those who have the information—and at the expense, often, of those who do not'. Sections on the primary service of advertising, the kind of information supplied, safeguards over means by which advertisements are produced, and controls.
NATIONAL CONSUMER COUNCIL (1977). *Advertising–Legislate or Persuade?* NCC. 20 pp. A review of statutory controls, voluntary controls and misleading advertising, with discussion and recommendations.

17. Advertising as Information for Consumers

ADVERTISING ASSOCIATION (1974). *Action for Advertising*. AA. 11 pp. Work and aims of the Advertising Association.
ADVERTISING ASSOCIATION (1976). *The Self-Disciplinary Control System for Advertising. Major Developments from the 1974 AA Conference*. AA. 4 pp.
ADVERTISING STANDARDS AUTHORITY (No date). *What Can It Do for You?* ASA. Leaflet on the work of ASA and how to complain about misleading advertisements.
The Case for Advertising. J. Walter Thompson Co. Ltd, 1975-6. Seven papers, each dealing with a different aspect of the subject. Two further papers, one on facts and figures, one on advertising and the nationalized industries, were published later, in June 1976.
CENTRAL OFFICE OF INFORMATION (1976). *Advertising and Public Relations in Britain*. Reference pamphlet no. 146, HMSO. 30 pp. First section describes the organization of the advertising industry, including Government publicity and controls imposed on advertising by statute and by self-regulation; the second surveys the public relations business and the use made of it by central and local government.
GOODMAN, E. (1976). 'Rules of conduct'. In *Financial Times* survey 'Advertising and Marketing', 4 October 1976, p. 16. The Advertising Standards Authority's new code of conduct—voluntary action to produce this has helped delay threatened legislation.
KING, S. (1973). *Developing New Brands*. Pitman.
REEKIE, W. D. (1974). *Advertising: Its Place in Political and Managerial Economics*. Macmillan.

288

18. Advertising: The Legal Framework

CARPENTIER, M. (1976) 'Persuade or legislate? the debate continued: 1'. *Advertising Quarterly*, Autumn 1976, pp. 11-3. Article based on contribution by the Director, Environment and Consumer Protection Service, European Commission, during a debate at the Advertising Association conference in July 1976. Question is not 'Why legislation?' but 'How much?' The law is there to set and maintain a balance of interests.

LAWSON, R. (1975). *Advertising and Labelling Laws in the Common Market*. Jordan. Looseleaf. Updated by supplement service. Guide to laws, regulations and self-disciplinary codes of practice.

LAWSON, R. (1976). 'Legal control begins at Calais. But will it stop there?' *Campaign*, 30 July 1976, p. 18. Survey of statutory controls on advertising in Europe.

OFFICE OF FAIR TRADING (1976). *Review of the Trade Descriptions Act 1968: a Report by the Director-General of Fair Trading*. Cmnd 6628, H M S O. 99 pp.

ROBERTS, E. (1976). 'Persuade or legislate? the debate continued: 2'. *Advertising Quarterly*, Autumn 1976, pp. 14-6. Argues that self-regulation and codes of practice are not sufficient; small public body, Government-financed, should be set up to look after the public interest in advertising.

TURNER, E. S. (1952). *Shocking History of Advertising*. Michael Joseph. 303 pp.

WOOLLEY, D. (1976). *Advertising Law Handbook*. Second edn. Business Books. 106 pp. Guide to the main regulations, restrictions, and the more important voluntary codes affecting business.

19. Consumerism: An American Response
and
20. Representing the Consumer in Business: J. C. Penney—a US Case Study

BLUM, M. L., STEWART, J. B. AND WHEATLEY, E. W. (1974). 'Consumer affairs: viability of the corporate response'. *Journal of Marketing*, April 1974, pp. 13-9. Study on new consumer affairs departments set up in some corporations. Suggests improvements for their operation and topics for future research.

CHAMBER OF COMMERCE OF THE UNITED STATES, WASHINGTON DC. The Chamber has produced several booklets giving advice to business on creating good consumer relations in its own interests as well as those of consumers. Guidelines are given on informing and educating the public and, on complaint handling, and local chambers of commerce are encouraged to establish business–consumer relations committees.

CLUTTERBUCK, D. (1975). 'RCA cuts consumer complaints'. *International Management*, March 1975, pp. 20-2. Deals with the R C A Corporation's consumer affairs vice-president and the way his department functions.

CRON, R. (1975). *Assuring Customer Satisfaction: A Guide for Business and Industry*. Van Nostrand Reinhold. 364 pp. Business and industry have been slow to recognize the potential of the consumerism movement. This book provides signposts for the organization, manpower, structure, and procedural systems and approaches needed to cope with consumerism.

DAKIN, T. (1975). 'US businesses get consumers on their side'. *Marketing*, February 1975, pp. 34-5, 66. British businessmen could learn from the highly profitable way in which some U S companies have used consumerism as a marketing tool. Examples of some companies' actions are given.

'Disgruntled customers finally get a hearing'. *Business Week*, 21 April 1975, pp. 138-41. Many companies are hiring consumer affairs managers to cope with complaints.

GOODMAN, E. (1976). 'A new job title to meet a craze'. *Financial Times*, 29 October 1976, p. 19. Consumer affairs departments in U S companies, and the exploitation of the trend towards more consumer protection are discussed.

HASKINS, J. S. (1975). *The Consumer Movement*. Franklin Watts, New York. 122 pp. Historical survey of the U S consumer movement, with chapters on consumer protection in several industries, and consumerism attitudes of big business.

PETERSON, E. (1974). 'Consumerism as a retailer's asset'. *Harvard Business Review*, May/June 1974, pp. 91-101. Giant Food's approach to consumerism in 1970; the then novel idea of treating consumers' demands with respect.

SENTRY INSURANCE (1977). *Consumerism at the Crossroads*. Sentry Insurance, US. A National Opinion Research Survey of public, activist, business and regular attitudes towards the consumer movement.

21.   The European Perspective

BUREAU EUROPÉEN DES UNIONS DE CONSOMMATEURS (1974a). *An Examination of Doorstep Selling in Europe*. Prepared for the Environment and Consumer Protection Service of the EEC. BEUC, Brussels. 69 pp. Report covers 'everything that is not sold at a shop or other premises of a seller, with the exception of household deliveries such as groceries and milk'. Sources contributing information were the consumer associations and consumers themselves.

BUREAU EUROPÉEN DES UNIONS DE CONSOMMATEURS (1974b). *A Study of Advertising in the UK and the Federal Republic of Germany*. BEUC, Brussels and Consumers' Association. 263 pp. Study was made to collect information to enable the EEC Commission to formulate a policy on advertising on a community-wide basis.

BUREAU EUROPÉEN DES UNIONS DE CONSOMMATEURS (1975). *After-Sales Service in Nine EEC Countries*. Prepared for the Environment and Consumer Protection Service of the Commission of the EEC. BEUC, Brussels. Reprinted by Graham, Trotman and Dudley, 1976, 273 pp. Covers: legislation governing after-sales service and consumer product warranties in the EEC countries; advanced legislation in Sweden and the US; voluntary codes of practice and industry initiatives; select examples of after-sales service and warranty provisions; survey of consumer experiences with after-sales service and guarantees; recommendations to the Commission.

COUNCIL OF EUROPE (1972). *Committee of Ministers. Working Party on Misleading Advertising*. Consumer protection report. Council of Europe, Strasbourg. 99 pp. Twelve member states participated in this survey.

COUNCIL OF EUROPE (1973). *Subcommittee on Legal Protection of Consumers. Door-to-door sales: exchange of information on legislation and legislative activity in the field of door-to-door selling and house canvassing*. Council of Europe, Strasbourg. 23 pp.

MERCIER, P. A., SCARDIGLI, V. AND LE TARNEC, J. (1976). *Division Analyse Sociale. Ministère de la Justice. Service de Coordination de la Recherche. La Protection juridique et judiciaire des consommateurs (première note sur la phase exploratoire)*. CREDOC. No. 4 513, Juin 1976. 52 pp.

EUROPEAN COMMUNITIES COMMISSION. *European Consumers: Their Interests, Aspirations and Knowledge on Consumer Affairs: Results and Analyses of a Sample Survey Carried Out in the Nine Countries of the EEC*. Brussels. 175 pp. Survey covers attitudes to prices, advertising, consumer organizations, product testing, public authorities, political parties, the Common Market, and behaviour of dissatisfied consumers.

SUMNER, J. (1977). 'The EEC and the development of consumer protection policy', *Consumer Affairs*, no. 26, March/April 1977. pp. 1-7. Progress of EEC proposals through various stages and an outline of the principal draft Directives under discussion at the time of writing.

Index

ABLC (Association of British Launderers
    and Cleaners) Code of Practice:
  requirements of, 164
  launch of, 164
  undertakings, 164–167
  investigation of complaints, 165
  compensation under, 165
  complaints conciliation, 166–167
  as condition of membership, 167
  achievements, 167–168
Additives:
  Giant Food Inc. and, 212–213
  in animal feeds, 235
  disclosure of, 239
Advertisements, advertising:
  public's attitudes to, 95–96
  as misleading, 96
  direct-response, 171–181
  what the consumer wants from, 171–181
  expectations and needs from, 171–176
  information from, 172–176
  complaints about, 176–180
  compensation for misleading, 178–179
  the right to 'puff' in, 179–181
  possible ways forward, 180–181
  as information for consumers,
    182–194
  announcement, 183
  source of, 183–184
  as justification for buying decision, 184
  use of testimonials in, 184, 196–198
  where advertisements appear, 184–185
  presentation, 185
  distortion of information in, 185
  responses to content, 185–186
  pre-testing of, 185–186
  information needs, 186–189
  effect of confines of space on, 187–188
  assessment of information role, 189–194
  mail order, 189–190
  technical language in, 190
  standardization of information in, 191
  vulnerability of consumers and, 191–192
  justification for claims in, 192–193
  the legal framework of, 195–206

common law controls in, 195–200
extravagant claims in, 195–196
unauthorized endorsements in, 196–198
comparative, 198–200
controls in Europe for, 204–205
EEC draft Directives on, 236–237
Advertising Association, 173
  review of public attitudes to advertising,
    173–174
Advertising draft EEC Directive, 236–237
  unfair claims, 236
  class actions, 236
  misleading technical devices, 236–237
  comparative advertising, 237
Advertising Standards Authority Ltd, 7, 143,
    173, 176, 190, 193, 255–256
  Bulletin, 176
  British Code of Advertising Practice, 177
  and the right to 'puff', 179–180
  complaints about mail order, 190
Advice, consumer, 52–53, 61–71
  need for, 62–63
  future developments in, 69–71
  NCC report on, 70
Advice Centres, Consumer (see Consumer
    Advice Centres)
Advice Centre Servicing Unit, 241
Agency for Consumer Advocacy (USA),
    222
Airline Users Committee, 250–251
Airport Consultative Committees, 249–250
America, United States of, 7
  consumerism and Giant Food Inc., 209–
    219
  representing the consumer in business in,
    220–227
Animal feeding-stuffs, draft EEC Directive
    on, 234–235
Arbitration, 43, 146, 157–158
Article Numbering (Universal Product
    Code), 217–218
Association of British Launderers and
    Cleaners, 160–168
  code of practice (see also ABLC), 163–
    168

Minimum Standards of Service for Domestic Laundry and Drycleaning Work, 162–163
  Good Laundering Guarantee, 163
  regional sections, 163–164
  Customer Advisory Service, 166–167
  annual report of, 167
Association of British Travel Agents, 149, 150
Association of Manufacturers of Domestic Electrical Appliances, 147
  code of practice, 147
Attitudes to consumerism, 22–23

Bailment, 38
Bargain price offers, 148
Barriers to trade, 230
Behaviour, consumer, 90–92
Brands, own-label, 90–91
  attitudes to, 91
Breakages, liability for, 35
British Code of Advertising Practice, 7, 177, 191–193
  and the right to 'puff', 179
  justification for claims made, 192–193
British Standard Code for Care Labelling, 114
British Standards:
  and marketing, 120–128
  by the First World War, 121
  postwar developments, 121–123
  safety and performance, 123–124
  implementation, 124–125
  production time, 125–126
  consumer representatives for committees, 126
  obvious principles, 127
  consumer requirements, 127–128
  certification schemes, 127
  codes of practice in accordance with, 151
British Standards Institution, 59, 120
  Royal Charter of 1929, 121
  Kitemark, 122–123
  Schemes of Supervision and Control, 122
  safety mark, 122–123
  Test House and Inspectorate, 123
  budget, 124
  Consumer Standards Advisory Committee, 267
Bureau Européen des Unions de Consommateurs, 21, 272–273
  report on advertising, 172, 237
  members of, 231
Business:
  consumer programmes in, 209–219
  representing the consumer in, 220–228
Business Advertisements (Disclosure) Order 1977, 201

Care labelling, 113–114
  British Standard Code for, 113–114

Central Transport Consultative Committee, 79, 251
Centre for Consumer Education and Research in Scotland, 268
Citizen's Advice Bureaux, 6, 63–64, 268–269
  consumer complaints function, 6, 70
  grants to, 63
  disadvantages of, 64
  handling complaints, 146
  monitoring complaints, 150
Class actions in advertising, 236
Classified advertisements, 171, 174, 175
Code of Advertising Practice, 7, 177, 191–193
  and the right to 'puff', 179
  justification for claims made, 192–193
Codes of Practice, 7, 136–137, 143–153
  advantages of, 136–137, 144–145
  difficulties with, 144
  enforcement of, 144–145, 149
  aims and objectives of, 145–146
  features of, 146–149
  sanctions under, 149
  breaches of, 149
  monitoring of, 149–151
  encouraging results of, 150
  disappointments about, 150–151
  limitations of, 151–153
  or legislation? 152
  Motor Industry Code of Practice, 154–159
  for laundries and drycleaners, 163–168
  Independent Broadcasting Authority's, 188, 191–193
  Mail Order Publishers' Authority's, 190
  Code of Advertising Practice, 177, 191–193
Comité Européen de Normalisation, 234
Commercial advertising, 171–181
Commission of the EEC, 231
Commissioner for Local Government, 55
Comparative advertising, 198–200, 237
Comparative testing:
  reasons for, 12–13
  influence on goods and services, 14–15
  European Testing Group, 21–22
Compensation:
  under ABLC Code of Practice, 165
  for misleading advertisements, 178–179, 180–181
Complaints, consumer:
  firms' response to, 8
  using as a source of management information, 8, 136
  number made in 1976, 56
  handling, 97–107, 136
  as basis for codes of practice, 145
  handling within code of practice, 146–147
  within Motor Industry Code of Practice, 157–158

within A B L C Code of Practice, 165–167
about advertising, 176–180
about mail order, 189–190
Giant Food Inc. and, 216–217
Conciliation under A B L C Code of Practice, 166–167
Conditional sale agreements, 39–40
'Conditions', 29
Confederation of British Industry: comments on complaints handling, 136
'Consume by' date, 92
Consumer advice, 52–53, 61–71
    need for, 62–63
    future developments in, 69–71
    N C C report on, 70
Consumer Advice Centres, 20, 62–63, 64–71, 241, 242
    the first, 64
    services offered, 65–68
    involvement with manufacturers, 68–69
    liaison with retailers, 69
    future developments for, 69–71
    closures, 70
    handling complaints, 146
    monitoring complaints, 150
Consumer advocates: (see also Consumer Affairs, Director of; Consumer directors)
    function and role, 223–224
    in J C Penney Company, 224–228
    involvement in company activities, 227–228
Consumer Affairs Department:
    of J C Penney Company, 224–228
    objectives for, 224–228
Consumer Affairs, Director of, 138–139
    (See also Consumer directors and Consumer advocates)
Consumer Affairs Group of National Organizations, 241–242
Consumer attitudes and market research, 88–96, 225
Consumer behaviour, 90–92
Consumer Bill of Rights, 211–212
Consumer Council, 50
    report on nationalized industry consumer councils, 74, 76
Consumer councils for nationalized industries (see Nationalized Industry Consumer Councils)
Consumer Credit Act 1974, 27, 40–42, 236
    licensing under, 40
    claims under, 41
    repayment under, 41
    'rule of 78', 41
    extortionate credit bargain, 41
    truth in lending, 42
Consumer Credit Bill, 40
Consumer, definition of, 220
Consumer directors, 87, 137–139 (see also Consumer affairs, Director of; Con-

sumer advocates)
    in Giant Food Inc. 209–219
Consumer groups, local, 21
    (see also National Federation of Consumer Groups)
Consumer Information Standards in advertising, 186–188, 193
Consumerism:
    attitudes to, 22–23
    nature of, 88–89
    growth of, 97
    business fears of, 97–98
    and marketing men, 116–117
    an American response to, 209–219
Consumerists: who are they? 89–90
'Consumer law', 49
Consumer organizations:
    constituency for, 19–20
    awareness of, 94
    demands of, 112
    consultations with O F T, 145
    glossary of, 241–245
Consumer Protection Act 1961, 44–45, 50, 123
Consumer Protection Advisory Committee, 260
    references to, 46–47
    orders stemming from reports by, 201
'Consumer protection codes' (see Codes of practice)
Consumer Protection Departments, 50, 53, 259–260
Consumer Protection in the E E C, 232–240
    preliminary programme for, 232–240
Consumer Protection and Information Policy Programme (E E C), 126, 232–240
    aim of, 232
    consumer's rights in, 232–233
    health and safety within, 233–235
    economic interests within, 235–238
Consumer protection in local government, 6, 50–60
    in county councils, 52, 54
    in district councils, 52, 54
    in London boroughs, 52
    typical functions of, 53–54
    control of, 54–55
    objectives of, 55
    enforcement, 55–58
    criminal convictions, 56
    collaboration with traders, 58–60
Consumer protection legislation, 24–49, 145, 148–149
    in Scotland, 47–49
    consumer perspective on, 227
Consumer Reports (U S A), 9
Consumers' Association, 4, 9–23, 61, 64, 74, 86, 122, 125, 183, 242–243
    (see also Which?)
    early history, 10–11

membership, 11
Ordinary Members, 11
laboratory, 14
campaigning, 17–19
deprived consumers, 20
international work, 21–22
advice centre, 64, 242
testing hazard symbols, 234
testing tyre codes, 234
Consumers' Consultative Committee of the
    EEC, 231–232, 273–274
membership of, 231–232
Consumer Standards Advisory Committee,
    126, 267
Consumers Union (USA), 9–10
Consumer Transactions (Restriction on
    Statements) Order 1976, 201
Contracts (see Sales contracts)
Convention on Product Liability (Council
    of Europe), 33–35
Co-operative Union Ltd, 269–270
Co-operative Women's Guild, 245–246
Cosmetics Directive (EEC), 205, 233
Council of Ministers of the EEC, 230–231
chairmanship of, 230–231
Credit, consumer, 39–42
    Crowther Committee on, 40
    White Paper on, 40
    within the EEC Consumer Protection
        Programme, 236
Credit notes, 32–33
Credit reference agencies, 42
Credit sale agreement, 40
Criminal law, 43–44
    consumer protection and, 55–58
Crowther Committee, 40
Customer Relations Department, 99–106
    (see also Customer relations officer and
        Consumer affairs department)
    routing complaints to, 101–102
    complaints procedures, 102
    investigation of complaint by, 102–103
    follow up by, 103–104
    information feedback from, 104
    direct access to consumer, 106–107

Customer relations officer, 100–106
    (see also Customer relations department;
        Consumer affairs department)
    qualifications of, 100
    reporting line to, 100–101

Dangerous substances:
    directives on, 233–234
Date stamping, open, 92
    Giant Good and, 213–214
    within Food Labelling Directive, 239
Defamation:
    of character in advertising, 196–198
    of goods in advertising, 199–200
Default notice, 41

Defective goods:
    injuries caused by, 33–35
    liability for (see Product liability)
Department of Prices & Consumer Protec-
    tion, 69, 260–261
    and the NICCs, 74, 79
Directives (EEC), 230–240
    cosmetics, 205, 233
    draft on toys, 234
    draft on tyres, 234
    on animal feeding-stuffs, 234–235
    draft on credit, 236
    draft on advertising, 236–237
    draft on doorstep selling, 237–238
    draft on product liability, 238
    on food labelling, 239
Director of Consumer Affairs, 138–139
    (see also Consumer Advocates and Con-
        sumer Directors)
Direct-response advertising, 171–181
Domestic Coal Consumers' Council, 73, 79,
    252
Doorstep selling:
    cash loans, 42
    draft (EEC) Directive on, 237–238
Drugs, ingredient labelling, 215–216
Drycleaning, 160–168
    Code of Practice for, 163–168
Durability of products:
    consumer expectations, 147–148
    minimum (food), 239
Dunpark Committee, 48–49

Economic and Social Committee of the
    EEC, 231
Education, consumer, 68, 126–127, 165
    and J C Penney Company, 225–226
    within EEC Programme for a Consumer
        Protection and Information Policy,
        238–240
Electricity Consultative Councils, 79, 252–
    253
Electricity Consumers' Council, 252–253
Energy labelling, 239–240
Engineering Standards Committee, 120
Environment, attitudes towards damage to,
    91–92
Environmental health, 51–52
Environmental Health Departments, 67
Environmental Health Officers Association,
    256–257
Environment and Consumer Protection
    Service, 139
Estimates, 39
Europe (see European Economic Com-
    munity)
European Economic Community, 229–240
    and advertising, 204–205
    Cosmetics Directive, 205
    formal framework of, 229–231
    members of, 229–230

aims of 230, 232
informal process of consultation of, 231
and consumer protection, 232–240
Preliminary Programme for a Consumer Protection and Information Policy, 232–240
European Parliament, 231
European Testing Group, 21–22
Exclusion Clauses, 30, 37, 38–39, 148
in the laundry industry, 161–162, 164

Fair trading, 46–47
Fair Trading Act 1973, 46–47, 123, 143, 163
section 124, 143
Part II, 152
orders under, 200–201
Food and Drugs Act 1955, 51
review of, 51
misleading advertising, 200
Food labelling, 51, 60, 93
new products, 57–58
of canned fruit and vegetables, 143
and nutrition, 214–215
of drug ingredient, 215–216
directive on, 239
and declaration of ingredients, 239
Food Standards Committee, 59, 92

Gas Act 1972, 74
Gas Consumers' Councils, 79, 253–254
General Purposes Committees in local government, 54
Giant Food Inc. (USA), 209–219
mistakes in consumer programme, 215–216
principles for a consumer programme, 218–219
Good Laundering Guarantee, 163
Good Housekeeping Institute, 270–271
Goods, carriage of:
damage during, 29
contract for, 29
Goods, maintenance of, 39
Goods, ownership of, 28–29
sale or return, 29
on approval, 29
Goods, payment for, 27–28
deposits, 27–28
by cheque, 28
Goods, replacement of, 33
Goods, return of, 32–33
Government departments, glossary of, 260–267
Guarantees, 35–36, 148

Handyman Which? 11
Harmonization:
within EEC, 230
optional, 230
Health, environmental, 51–52
Hire Purchase Acts, 25, 40

Hire Purchase agreements, 39–40
termination of, 42
Hodgson Committee, 50
Holiday Which? 11
Home Launderers' Consultative Council, 113–114
House of Commons Select Committee on Nationalized Industries, 76
Hygiene control, in Giant Food Inc., 212

Implied terms, 29–30
Independent Broadcasting Authority: Code of Practice, 188, 191–193
Information:
consumer, 4–5, 112–114, 147–148
from advertising, 172–176, 182–194
Giant Food Inc. and, 213–216
J C Penney Company and, 226–227
centres in stores, 227
within EEC Programme for a Consumer Protection and Information Policy, 238–240
Injuries:
caused by defective goods, 33–35
on shop premises, 35
liability for, 33–35
Institute for Consumer Ergonomics, 17, 243–244
Institute of Arbitrators, 146, 157–158
Institute of Consumer Advisers, 257
Institute of Marketing, 83, 86
Institute of Trading Standards Administration, 53, 59, 258
Institute of Weights & Measures Administration, 53
Institution of Civil Engineers, 120
International Organization of Consumers' Unions, 21, 274–275

Kitemark (BSI), 122–123
'Knocking copy', 198–200

Labelling:
(*see also* Labelling of food)
of dangerous substances, 233–234
energy, 239–240
Labelling of food, 51, 57–58, 60, 93
of new products, 57–58
of canned fruit and vegetables, 143
and nutrition, 214–215
of drug ingredient, 215–216
EEC Directive on, 239
and declaration of ingredients, 239
Laundry industry, 160–168
Code of Practice for, 163–168
Legal codes:
civil, 24
criminal, 24
Liability for breakages in shops, 35
Liability for defective products (*see* Product liability)

Licensing:
  under Consumer Credit Act, 40
  requirement of Code of practice, 152
Local advice (*see* Consumer advice)
Local Advice Centres (*see* Consumer Advice
    Centres)
Local consumer groups, 21, 244–245
  (*see also* National Federation of Con-
    sumer Groups)
Local Government Acts:
  1972, 51
  1948, 63
Local government, consumer protection in,
    6, 50–60
  Trading Standards (Consumer Pro-
    tection) Departments, 50, 53, 64, 67
  Environmental Health Officers/Depart-
    ments, 51, 67
  in county councils, 52, 54
  in district councils, 52, 54
  in London boroughs, 52
  typical functions of, 53–54
  control of, 54–55
  objectives of, 55
  enforcement of, 55–58
  criminal convictions, 56
  collaboration with traders, 58–60
Local government reorganization, 51–52, 65

Mail order advertising, 189–190
  complaints about, 190
Mail order (Place of Business) Order 1976,
    201
Mail Order Publishers' Authority, 190
  Code of Practice, 190
Mail Order Readers' Protection Scheme, 190
Maintenance of goods, 39
Management, facts on consumers for, 225
Marketing:
  some lessons for, 3–8
  view of the consumer, 83–87
  reasons for failure in, 83–84
  at point of sale, 84–85
  and the consumer lobby, 85–86
  and consumer affairs conferences,
    86–87
  and consumer directors, 87
  and consumerism, 116–117
  and British Standards, 120–128
  future developments in, 129–140
  principles and practice, 129–131
  purpose of, 132
  commitment to consumer, 132–133
  and the EEC perspective, 139
  affects of EEC legislation on, 229–240
Marketing and the Consumer, 87
Marketing concept, 130–135
  philosophical and practical weaknesses,
    131
  making it work, 131–135
  implementation of, 133

internationalization of, 134–135
  future possibilities for, 135–139
Marketing directors, appointment to boards,
    137
Market place:
  definition of, 220
  consumers as part of, 220–221
Market research:
  and consumer attitudes, 88–96
  limitations of, 94–96
  interpretation of results, 95–96
Media:
  comments on goods and services, 5
  as complaints investigators, 98
  as crusaders, 145
  and advertising, 171–181
Medicines Act 1968, and misleading adver-
    tising, 200
Minimum Standards of Service for Domestic
    Laundry and Drycleaning Work,
    162–163
  adoption of, 163
Molony Committee/Report on Consumer
    Protection 1962, 5, 20, 50, 63, 122,
    133, 165, 201
Money Which? 11
Monitoring Codes of Practice, 149–151
Monitor surveys, 88–93
Motor Agents Association, 147, 148, 150
  and the Motor Industry Code of Practice,
    154–159
  membership, code of practice as con-
    dition of, 156
  Annual Report, 156
  logo, 157
Motor Industry Code of Practice, 154–159
  objects of and reasons for, 154–155
  reaction to, 155–156
  publicising, 156–157
  as condition of membership, 156
  advertising campaign for, 157
  procedure under, 157–158
  enforcement of, 158–159
  influence of, 158
  breaches of, 158–159
  updating, 159
  consumer's role, 159
  making it work, 159
  distribution of, 159
Motoring Which? 11

National Association of Citizens' Advice
    Bureaux, 63, 268–269
National Consumer Council, 6, 19, 86, 93,
    136, 261–262
  report on local advice, 70
  report on the nationalized industry con-
    sumer councils, 74, 75, 76, 139
National Council of Social Service, 271
National Council of Women of Great Britain,
    246–247

National electricity Council (*see* Electricity Consumers' Council)
National Federation of Consumer Groups, 5, 10, 19, 86, 244–245
(*see also* Local consumer groups)
  formation of, 21
  monitoring codes of practice, 150
  Consumer Information Standards of, 186–188
National Federation of Women's Institutes, 247–248
National Gas Consumers' Council, 79, 253–254
National Housewives Association Ltd, 248
National Industrial Conference Board of US: survey on consumer affairs departments, 138
National Transport Consumers' Council, 251
National Union of Townswomen's Guilds, 248–249
Nationalized industry consumer councils, 72–79, 139
  origins of, 72–73
  composition of, 73–74
  N C C report on, 74, 75, 76, 139
  handling complaints, 74–76
  communication with, 75–76
  and impact on policy, 76
  limitations of, 76–77
  complaints records of, 77–78
  future development of, 78
  glossary of, 249–255
Northern Ireland Consumer Council, 262–263
Nutrition labelling:
  Giant Food Inc. and, 214–215

Office of Fair Trading, 6, 46–47, 86, 126, 263–264
  enforcement of Consumer Credit Act, 40–42
  review of the Trade Descriptions Act, 45
  returns on consumer complaints, 56
  Codes of Practice, 143–153
  Motor Industry Code of Practice, 154, 159
  A B L C Code of Practice, 163
  Mail Order Publishers' Authority Code of Practice, 190
Ombudsman (local government), 55
Organizations, overseas, glossary of, 272–275
Organizations, professional, trade and industry, glossary of, 255–260
Own label brands, 90–91
  attitudes to, 91

Parliament, European, 231
Penney Company, J C, 224–228
  Consumer Affairs Department, 224–228
  Consumer Affairs Forum, 227

Post Office Advisory Committees, 79
Post Office Users' National Council, 72, 77, 79, 254–255
Post-shopping complaints, 67–68
Premium offers: preparation of draft E E C Directive, 237
Pre-shopping advice, 66–67
Price Commission, 264–265
Price information, 68
  (*see also* Unit Pricing)
  in advertising, 175
  display, 239
Price reductions:
  R T S A's voluntary code for advertising, 114–116
  marking down goods, 114
  comparison with prices elsewhere, 115
  comparison with recommended prices, 115
  special purchases and clearance lines, 116
  seconds, imperfect, and substandard, 116
  under Trade Descriptions Act, 203–204
Prices, recommended: under Trade Descriptions Act, 203–204
Private labels (*see* Own brands)
Product liability, 33–35
  Council of Europe Convention on, 33
  Royal Commission, 34
  draft E E C Directive, 34–35, 124, 238
  report of Law Commissions for England & Wales and for Scotland, 34–35
Public Interest Research Centre, 22, 272
Public Participation in US Federal Regulatory Agencies Proceedings, 222
Public Protection Committee in local government, 54

Quality control:
  in Giant Food Inc., 212
Quotations, 39, 159

Recommended prices:
  under Trade Descriptions Act, 203–204
Reorganization of local government, 51–52, 65
Repairs to cars, 159
Representation, consumer:
  in business, 221, 222–228
  in government, 221–222
Research Institute for Consumer Affairs, 245
Restrictive Practices Court, 144
Retailing and the consumer movement, 108–119
  retailers' resistance to, 109
  customers' needs, 110–112
  basic needs of, 110–111
  optional/luxury needs of, 111–112
Retail practice:
  standards of, 114
  rules concerning, 117–119

Retail Trading-Standards Association, 108, 258–259
  and standards of retail practice, 108
Royal Commission on Civil Liability and Compensation for Personal Injury, 34

Safety mark, BSI's, 122–123
Safety standards, 123–124
Sale of Goods Act 1893, 26, 45, 148
  implied terms, 29–30
  warranties, 31
  in Scotland, 48
  complaints within, 67
Sales of goods, 24–36
  (see also Sales contract)
  offer and acceptance, 25–27
Sale, after the, 31–32
Sales contract:
  in writing, 25–26
  word of mouth, 26
  conduct over, 26
  terms and conditions of, 26
  in breach of, 26
  implied terms of, 29–30
  right to sell, 29
  description of goods in, 29–30
  and merchantable quality of goods, 30
  fit for the purpose, 30
  consumer sale, 30
  exclusion clauses in, 30
  trader's rights and, 31–32
  consumer's obligations and, 32
Sales promotions:
  relevance of, 92
  practices for, 143
  use of endorsements in, 196–198
Schemes of Supervision and Control, 122
Scotland, consumer protection in, 47–49
Scottish Consumer Council, 70, 265–266
Scottish Motor Trade Association, 154, 157, 158
Select Committee on the Nationalized Industries, 76
Service contracts, 36–37
  maintenance of goods and, 39
Services, supplies of, 24, 36–39
Shoppers' Guide, 10, 122
Shopping:
  advice before purchasing, 66–67
  complaints after purchasing, 67–68
Small claims in the County Courts, 42–43, 146
  deficiences in system, 43
Small print conditions, 161–162
Social Audit Ltd, 272
Society of Consumer Affairs Professionals (USA), 211
Society of Motor Manufacturers and Traders, 154, 158
Standards (see British Standards)
Strasbourg Convention (Council of Europe)

on product liability, 33–35
Summary cause process, 48, 146
Sunday trading, 25
Supplies of services, 24, 36–39
Supply of Goods (Implied Terms) Act 1973, 26–27, 148

Tariffs, 230
Teaching kits, 126
Testimonials in advertising, 184, 196–198
Theft Act 1968, advertising and the, 199
Toys, draft EEC Directive, 234
Trade descriptions, 45–46, 201–202
Trade Descriptions Act 1968, 45–46, 50, 60, 165, 236
  review of, 45
  section 28, 54
  offences against, 67
  section 11, 114
  breach of, 177
  and advertising, 198–199, 201–204
  gaps in, 202–203
  multiple prosecutions under, 203
  pricing offences under, 203–204
Trade Marks Act 1938, advertising and the, 199
Trading practices, unfair, 144
Trading Standard Departments/Officers, 50, 53, 64, 67, 259–260
  enforcement of criminal law, 67
  handling complaints, 146
  monitoring complaints, 150
Transport Users' Consultative Committees, 79, 251
Treaty of Rome, 204, 230, 232
Tyres:
  draft EEC Directive on, 234
  codes for marking, 234

Unfair Contract Terms Act 1977, 36–39, 148, 152, 168
  in Scotland, 48
Unfair trading practices, 144
Unit pricing:
  Giant Food Inc. and, 213
  within EEC Food Labelling Directive, 239
United States of America:
  consumerism and Giant Food Inc., 209–219
  representing the consumer in business in, 220–227
Utility schemes, 122
Universal Product Code (Article Numbering), 217–218
  consumer resistance to, 217

Value Added Tax, 147
  exclusive prices, 152, 201, 239
Vehicle Builders' and Repairers' Association, 151–152

Warning symbols, 233–234
Warranties, 31, 147
Weight, drained, 239
Weights and measures, 44
Weights and Measures Acts 1878 and 1963, 44, 50
Weights and Measures Departments, 50, 53
Welsh Consumer Council, 266–267
Which? 4, 9–23, 61, 64, 86, 122, 183, 242–243

(see also Consumers' Association)
choice of projects, 11–12
scope of reports, 11–12
reports on hazard warning symbols, 234
Women's Advisory Committee (BSI), 122
Women's organizations, glossary of, 245–249

Yankelovich Research System, 225–226